Foundations *of*
Semantic
Web
Technologies

CHAPMAN & HALL/CRC
TEXTBOOKS IN COMPUTING

Series Editors

John Impagliazzo

ICT Endowed Chair
Computer Science and Engineering
Qatar University

Professor Emeritus, Hofstra University

Andrew McGettrick

Department of Computer
and Information Sciences
University of Strathclyde

Aims and Scope

This series covers traditional areas of computing, as well as related technical areas, such as software engineering, artificial intelligence, computer engineering, information systems, and information technology. The series will accommodate textbooks for undergraduate and graduate students, generally adhering to worldwide curriculum standards from professional societies. The editors wish to encourage new and imaginative ideas and proposals, and are keen to help and encourage new authors. The editors welcome proposals that: provide groundbreaking and imaginative perspectives on aspects of computing; present topics in a new and exciting context; open up opportunities for emerging areas, such as multi-media, security, and mobile systems; capture new developments and applications in emerging fields of computing; and address topics that provide support for computing, such as mathematics, statistics, life and physical sciences, and business.

Published Titles

Pascal Hitzler, Markus Krötzsch, and Sebastian Rudolph,
Foundations of Semantic Web Technologies

Forthcoming Titles

Uvais Qidwai and C.H. Chen, Digital Image Processing: An Algorithmic Approach with MATLAB®

CHAPMAN & HALL/CRC
TEXTBOOKS IN COMPUTING

Foundations *of*
Semantic
Web
Technologies

Pascal Hitzler
Markus Krötzsch
Sebastian Rudolph

CRC Press
Taylor & Francis Group
Boca Raton   London   New York

CRC Press is an imprint of the
Taylor & Francis Group an **informa** business

A CHAPMAN & HALL BOOK

Chapman & Hall/CRC
Taylor & Francis Group
6000 Broken Sound Parkway NW, Suite 300
Boca Raton, FL 33487-2742

© 2010 by Taylor and Francis Group, LLC
Chapman & Hall/CRC is an imprint of Taylor & Francis Group, an Informa business

No claim to original U.S. Government works

Printed in the United States of America on acid-free paper
10 9 8 7 6 5 4 3 2 1

International Standard Book Number: 978-1-4200-9050-5 (Hardback)

Library of Congress Cataloging-in-Publication Data

Hitzler, Pascal.
    Foundations of Semantic Web technologies / Pascal Hitzler, Sebastian Rudolph, Markus Krötzsch.
        p. cm. -- (Chapman & Hall/CRC textbooks in computing)
    Includes bibliographical references and index.
    ISBN 978-1-4200-9050-5 (hardcover : alk. paper)
    1. Semantic Web. I. Rudolph, Sebastian, Dr. II. Krötzsch, Markus. III. Title.

TK5105.88815.H57 2009
025.042'7--dc22   2009024576

Visit the Taylor & Francis Web site at
http://www.taylorandfrancis.com

and the CRC Press Web site at
http://www.crcpress.com

To Anja, Anne, and Conny

... and to Merula

About the Authors

The authors of this book currently work at AIFB, University of Karlsruhe, Germany. They are acknowledged researchers in the area of semantic technologies and related fields, witnessed by notable publication records as well as program committee and editorial board memberships of international conferences, journals, and book series. Their comprehensive teaching activities include university lectures, summer school courses, and tutorials at high-level conferences. All three authors contributed to the OWL 2 standard as participants of the OWL working group of the World Wide Web Consortium.

PD Dr. Pascal Hitzler is currently assistant professor at AIFB and will join the Kno.e.sis Center at Wright State University, Dayton, Ohio, in September 2009 as faculty member. He obtained his PhD in mathematics from the National University of Ireland, University College Cork, in 2001. From 2001 to 2004 he was a postdoctoral researcher at the Artificial Intelligence Institute of Dresden University of Technology, Germany. In 2003, he spent three months as research associate at Case Western Reserve University, Cleveland, Ohio. His diverse research interests span Semantic Web, knowledge representation and reasoning, neural-symbolic integration and formal foundations of computer science. He is editor-in-chief of the IOS Press book series Studies on the Semantic Web. For more information, see http://www.pascal-hitzler.de/.

M.Sc. Markus Krötzsch is a researcher at AIFB where he is also working on his PhD thesis. He received his Master of Science at the International Center for Computational Logic at Dresden University of Technology in 2005. His research is focused on knowledge representation on the Semantic Web, its practical applications, and its algorithmic and logical foundations. He is the lead developer of the highly successful Semantic Web application platform *Semantic MediaWiki*, and maintainer of the *semanticweb.org* community portal. Before his work on OWL 2, he participated in the W3C Rule Interchange Format (RIF) working group. For more information, see http://korrekt.org/.

Dr. Sebastian Rudolph is assistant professor at AIFB. He obtained his PhD in mathematics at the Institute for Algebra at Dresden University of Technology in 2006. His active research interests include algebra, complexity theory, logic, machine learning, optimization, database theory, and computational linguistics. In 2009, he stayed as visiting researcher at the Oxford University Computing Laboratory where he collaborated with the Information Systems group. Besides his academic work, he is a semiprofessional classical singer. For more information, see http://sebastian-rudolph.de/.

Foreword

Metadata and semantics for information search, integration and analysis has been practiced for three decades. Conceptual modeling and knowledge representation that enable rich description of information, and when needed associated reasoning, have been with us for a while too. But as the Web brought much larger variety (heterogeneity) and size with it, coming together of the semantics, the Web technologies and all the data that goes with it, was inevitable. Nearly a decade after Tim Berners-Lee coined the term Semantic Web, it has transformed into a growing, important, and well recognized interdisciplinary area of Computer Science. W3C's effort has led to widely adopted language standards, which has contributed to the development of Semantic Technologies for the Web of data, and a host of new and established companies are innovating tools, applications, products and services based on these standards and technologies at a rapid pace. With three key conferences focused on this topic, including the flagship International Semantic Web Conference, as well as at least 20 other conferences offering Semantic Web as a significant subarea of interest, the Semantic Web is a topic that is here to stay.

I started teaching a graduate course on Semantic Web in 2001 and have continued to offer it annually since. All these times, I used a series of papers and presentations as my course material. An important reason was that the field was rapidly growing and evolving, and what I taught just last year seemed outdated the next time around. There have been a number of books with Semantic Web in the title but most of them have been a collection of articles or papers with limited attention to what one might call the discipline core. A couple of other books offered as textbooks have largely focused on languages and syntax, rather than foundations. As Semantic Web is rapidly entering curricula at universities and other educational institutions worldwide, there is an increasing need for excellent textbooks which can be used as a basis for courses and self-study. I am pleased to introduce this book – *Foundations of Semantic Web Technologies* – to address this need. It might just fit my own need to cover the fundamental and core part of my course which I might complement with more applied and interdisciplinary aspects such as those requiring use of NLP, learning, statistics and database technologies.

This book is unique in several respects. It contains an in-depth treatment of all the major foundational languages for the Semantic Web and in particular provides a full treatment of the underlying formal semantics, which is central to the Semantic Web effort. It is also the very first textbook which addresses the forthcoming W3C recommended standards OWL 2 and RIF. Furthermore, the covered topics and underlying concepts are easily accessible for the reader due to a clear separation of syntax and semantics, i.e. of the basic required knowledge and advanced material despite the fact that some of the topics covered do represent a moderate to high level of difficulty. The authors of *Foundations of Semantic Web Technologies* are well-regarded researchers and teachers on the topic of the book and members of the prominent Semantic Web research group at AIFB, University of Karlsruhe, in Germany. Their didactic skills combined with their deep understanding of the material make it accessible for students at foundational or advanced levels, for researchers in adjacent areas, and for interested practitioners in application domains. I am confident this book will be well received and play an important role in training a larger number of students who will seek to become proficient in this growing discipline.

Amit Sheth
Kno.e.sis Center (knoesis.org), Wright State University
Dayton, OH USA

Introduction

The goal of this book is to introduce the foundations of Semantic Web technologies to a level of detail and depth which is not found in any other textbook currently available. It is a book written for university courses as well as for self-teaching, and suitable for researchers and practitioners alike. It is based on five years of experience of the authors in teaching this subject.

In these five years a lot of things have happened. Semantic Web went from a hyped research subject to one almost pronounced dead to one being invested in by major IT companies. It turns out that it is not only alive and kicking – it is actually growing rapidly, supported by substantial funding from research organizations and industry. IT and venture capital companies are investing. Numerous large-scale applications have been established, and more are being developed.

At the same time, Semantic Web technologies are still rapidly evolving. No textbook is able to keep up with the speed of the most recent developments, and indeed those which try are bound to be already outdated when they appear. We take a different approach for this book. We focus on the established foundations which have already become relatively stable over time, and we make an effort to convey these very thoroughly. Our presentation thus includes not only basic introductions and intuitions, but also technical details and formal foundations. Especially the advanced aspects are in our opinion not sufficiently treated in any of the currently available English-language textbooks.[1] We are confident that the reader will benefit from the increased depth of this book, even when relying on our intuitive explanations without studying the advanced material in detail.

So in this book, we convey foundations. But what are these foundations? The basic idea of the Semantic Web is to describe the meaning (i.e. the *semantics*) of Web content in a way that can be interpreted by computers. Programs can then exploit (more) human knowledge to execute tasks, enabling powerful applications not only on the Web. The first step for this is to cast knowledge into a machine-processable form. The resulting descriptions are often called *ontologies*, and the machine-readable formalisms that they are based on are called *ontology languages*. So a major goal of this book is to convey ontology languages in detail and depth – and with an obvious focus on languages stan-

---

[1] It is certainly peculiar that many Semantic Web textbooks try to treat semantic technologies without explaining their *semantics* in detail – thereby neglecting the actual core of the subject area.

dardized by the World Wide Web Consortium for this purpose. On this basis, we can consider methods for evaluating, querying, and further enriching ontological information. This already includes some advanced topics that are not quite as stable yet. Finally, we also consider some topics that are clearly beyond foundations, namely tools, applications, and engineering aspects. Our overview of these quickly evolving areas cannot be definite, but it provides many pointers that are useful for employing Semantic Web technologies in practice.

Quick Guide to Reading the Book

For better accessibility, we have carefully separated basic material from advanced content in our presentation of Semantic Web technologies. Chapters and sections with basic content provide a thorough first introduction to a given technology, including intuitive explanations and an amount of technical detail that suffices for many practical applications. Advanced parts provide a detailed view on more sophisticated aspects that are necessary to gain an in-depth understanding of the subject. Readers who are new to Semantic Web technologies can easily skip advanced material on a first reading. The following diagram provides an overview of the parts of this book, and sketches the rough dependencies between them:

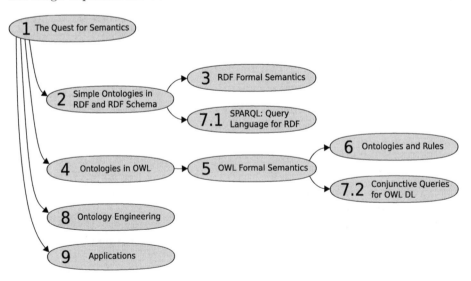

Basic material is found in Chapters 1, 2, 4, and in Section 7.1. More advanced content is then provided in Chapters 3, 5, 6, and in Section 7.2.

Chapters 8 and 9 focus on applied topics that are mostly independent from the descriptions of concrete technologies. An overview of the content of each chapter and more detailed suggestions for reading are given below.

Each chapter closes with references to further in-depth reading and to original publications. The technical chapters each also provide a set of exercises on the material, meant for coursework or to aid the self-studying reader to rehearse the contents. Solutions to all exercises are provided in Appendix D. Some further appendices provide essential background information for some of the technologies that this book builds on. Again, a detailed overview is given below.

A comprehensive index at the end of the book can be used to look up definitions quickly. It includes all relevant notions and all syntactic identifiers and keywords that are used throughout the book.

Chapter Overview

We give a brief overview of the contents and significance of each chapter.

Chapter 1 introduces the essential motivations and ideas behind Semantic Web technologies. It illustrates how various developments in science and technology have influenced the semantic technologies of today. It also briefly explains a number of important notions – including "ontology" and "Semantic Web" – that appear in all later chapters.

Chapter 2 introduces the syntax and underlying intuition of the *Resource Description Framework* RDF and of its extension *RDF Schema*. Both are fundamental technologies for representing (meta)data on the Semantic Web.

Chapter 3 details the formal underpinnings of RDF and RDF Schema by explaining in depth their formal semantics. This also includes an introduction to the idea and motivation of formal semantics in general. This advanced material can be skipped on a first reading, since the intuitive explanations provided in Chapter 2 are sufficient for a basic understanding of RDF(S).

Chapter 4 introduces the syntax and underlying intuition of the *Web Ontology Language* OWL, including the forthcoming revision called *OWL 2*. OWL provides advanced concepts for representing knowledge for the Semantic Web.

Chapter 5 covers the formal underpinnings of OWL by explaining in depth its relation to *first-order predicate logic* and to *description logics*. It also contains a detailed treatment of algorithms for automated reasoning with OWL. This chapter contains some of the most advanced material in the book and may be skipped at the first reading.

Chapter 6 treats rules and rule languages, especially those that can be used in combination with the Semantic Web technologies discussed in previous chapters. This advanced material is not covered by any standard yet – the forthcoming *Rule Interchange Format* RIF is expected to fill this gap. This book is, to the best of our knowledge, the first to provide a textbook introduction to RIF.

Chapter 7 deals with query languages for the Semantic Web. In particular, it contains an in-depth treatment of the *SPARQL Protocol and RDF Query Language*. It also contains an introduction of *conjunctive queries* for OWL, which can possibly be skipped at first reading.

Chapter 8 deals with aspects of ontology engineering – an important area that is still evolving rapidly today. This chapter gives an overview of ontology engineering approaches, and presents modeling guidelines, methods of quality assurance, and selected tools to support ontology development.

Chapter 9 gives an overview of a number of prominent applications of Semantic Web technologies that can be found today. We refrain from writing yet another compilation of possible application areas and scenarios, and focus instead on a variety of application examples which have been realized to date.

In the appendix we provide brief accounts on background knowledge which is needed or helpful for understanding the contents of the book. We suggest that these parts are only consulted when needed, e.g. for a brief introduction to XML or to first-order logic. Appendix A covers *XML* and *XML Schema*, Appendix B lists basic notions from set theory, Appendix C recalls the basics of first-order predicate logic, and Appendix D provides solutions to all exercises from the book chapters.

The Book for Self-Study

The diagram on page xii provides a basic overview of the dependencies between chapters in this book. This is a rough guideline: single sections may still require knowledge about other earlier parts – e.g. Section 6.4.5 also requires Chapter 3 – but such dependencies will be clear from the text, and corresponding sections can be skipped in this case.

Readers with prior knowledge can skip basic chapters: if specific notions or terms are unclear, the index at the end of the book provides an easy way to find more information. We have made an effort to keep the chapters of the book as independent as possible. While Chapter 4, for example, formally uses RDF as introduced in Chapter 2, it can essentially be read without going through the RDF chapter in detail.

Below are some typical reader perspectives with suggestions for reading:

For a comprehensive introduction to the field, one can of course read from end to end. To take it a bit easier, the advanced Chapters 3, 5, and 6 can be skipped on a first reading to return to them later to acquire a deeper understanding.

To learn about RDF, readers should study Chapters 2 and (optionally) 3, as well as Section 7.1. Rules can be an interesting addition: Sections 6.1 and 6.2, and the RDF-related parts of Section 6.4 provide a good introduction.

To learn about OWL, readers should study Chapters 4 and 5, as well as Section 7.2. Moreover, many OWL-related engineering hints are given in Chapter 8. Rules can be an interesting addition: most of Chapter 6 is relevant to OWL.

Readers with prior knowledge of semantic technologies should freely choose chapters and sections to deepen their understanding. Advanced material is especially found in Chapters 3, 5, and 6, including some recent developments that have not been presented in a coherent textbook treatment elsewhere.

A quick reference on semantic technologies is provided through the index, which contains almost every syntactic element and keyword that occurs in any of the discussed technologies. This is particularly useful for practitioners who need quick access to core definitions.

The Book for Teaching

There are various ways to use this book as a basis for teaching Semantic Web technologies. Our selection and organization of content was in fact strongly influenced by our own experiences in teaching this subject. In general, the dependencies and guidelines for self-study are also valid when planning university courses. Below are some typical choices:

The Comprehensive Overview of Semantic Technologies For an all-inclusive course on semantic technologies, it makes sense to treat all basic and applied chapters in their order, together with selected aspects of the advanced Chapters 3, 5, and 6 as deemed suitable. It is often a good idea to include a session on XML (Appendix A), and, if formal semantics are included, a brief recap of first-order logic (Appendix C). Further related topics can easily be included at the discretion of the teacher, e.g. to provide more details on XML, or to include a digression to rule languages and logic programming.

We have gathered excellent experiences when applying this scheme to a one-semester course for graduates and advanced undergraduates (15 sessions of 90 min each, accompanied by biweekly tutorials). The syllabus in this case was: introduction (Chapter 1); basics of XML (Appendix A); RDF and

RDF Schema (two sessions, Chapter 2); recap of formal semantics and first-order logic (Appendix C); RDF(S) semantics (Chapter 3); OWL (two sessions, Chapter 4); OWL semantics (Chapter 5); SPARQL and its semantics (two sessions, Section 7.1); querying OWL (Section 7.2); OWL and Rules (two sessions, Chapter 6); application overview (Chapter 9). This is a dense syllabus that could easily be stretched over more sessions, especially when including further material.

An Applied Course on the Semantic Web   To give an overview of basic semantic technologies and their use, one can focus on Chapters 2 (RDF), 4 (OWL), 7 (SPARQL), 8 (engineering), and 9 (applications). If possible, this can be combined with hands-on exercises using, e.g., some freely available ontology editor like Protégé (see Section 8.5.1). This approach is also well-suited for a one-week tutorial. Another viable option is to teach this material as part of a lecture that already covers XML or Web technologies in greater detail.

Knowledge Representation and Reasoning on the Web   If the target audience is already familiar with foundational aspects of knowledge representation and reasoning, it makes sense to present semantic technologies as a modern application of these topics. In this case, one may want to skip some of the technical and syntactic details in Chapters 2 and 4, and focus instead on the semantic and proof-theoretic content of Chapters 3 (RDFS semantics, optional), 5 (description logics), 6 (rules), and 7 (SPARQL could be omitted). This syllabus can be extended with advanced material from logic programming, deductive databases, or modal logic, depending on preference.

Seminar Work with this Book   Students can use this book in self-study to prepare seminar presentations. Since individual chapters are relatively independent it is easy to perform preparations in parallel without relying too much on prior material or on the quality of the presentations of fellow students. The dependency graph and the above suggestion for dividing the content into individual sessions are a good guideline for selecting topics.

The above covers some typical approaches for teaching based on this book. In addition, selected single topics can be covered in courses on related material, e.g. when discussing Web technologies, mark-up or modeling languages, or knowledge representation. We also have used some of the material in courses that focus on further applications and research topics related to the Semantic Web. Besides detailed treatment of ontological modeling and quality assurance (Chapter 8) and reasoning algorithms for OWL (Chapter 5), these courses also included material on semantic search, (semantic) Web Services, usage and user interface aspects for semantic technologies, and advanced topics related to OWL reasoning and its combination with rules. Pointers to suitable literature can be found at the end of each chapter. For further topics in this interesting field of research, please see [SS09] and the proceedings of the annual *International Semantic Web Conference*, of the Semantic Web track of the annual *World Wide Web Conference*, and other central dissemination events for Semantic Web research.

In all of the above cases, the material in Chapter 1 is a good basis for introducing and motivating the field of semantic technologies, where emphasis can be placed on the aspects most relevant to the audience at hand.

Additional Online Resources

This book is accompanied by the website

`http://www.semantic-web-book.org/`

where we provide updates, errata, slides for teaching, and links to further resources. Feedback, questions, or suggestions for improvement are always welcome – they can be sent via email to `authors@semantic-web-book.org`.

Karlsruhe, Germany

Pascal Hitzler
Markus Krötzsch
Sebastian Rudolph

Acknowledgments

It is quite impossible to acknowledge all those who made the emergence of this book possible. The fact that *Semantic Web* is a success in research, teaching and practice has to be attributed to the ongoing efforts of the growing number of researchers and practitioners in the field, many of whom we know personally and meet frequently at international conferences. Their excellent work is the foundation of this book.

We thank Randi Cohen of Taylor & Francis for her support in bringing this book into existence.

We thank the students of the lectures this book is based on for their constructive feedback.

We thank our colleagues at AIFB[2] and KSRI,[3] University of Karlsruhe, at the FZI Forschungszentrum Informatik in Karlsruhe[4] and at ontoprise GmbH for the extremely enjoyable and productive cooperations while researching and shaping the foundations for the *Semantic Web*. At the heart of these cooperations is Rudi Studer, who – as always – provided us with an ideal environment for our efforts.

We are very grateful for a very thorough review of an early draft of this book provided by Ian Horrocks, which helped us to improve the presentation and to get rid of some bugs. We thank Michael Kifer, Ora Lassila, Uli Sattler, Steffen Staab, Johanna Völker, and Denny Vrandečić for discussions and insights on particular topics covered in the book.

We thank the participants of the W3C OWL Working Group – the lively discussions in and around the work in the group helped us to deepen our understanding of the language.

We thank Gerhard Brewka, Frithjof Dau, Matthias Knorr, and Stefan Schlobach for detailed feedback on our German book on the topic.[5] We are also grateful for the many reports on bugs and typos which we have received from the following people: Martin Becker, Philipp Cimiano, Fabian David Leuchtner, Margrita Kascha-Bader, Alexander Kirk, Martin Knechtel, Thomas Krekeler, Serge Linckels, Stefan Wiegreffe, Andreas Wülfing.

We thank all those we should also have mentioned here but forgot to include in the list. We accept responsibility for all remaining mistakes.

---

[2] http://www.aifb.uni-karlsruhe.de/Forschungsgruppen/WBS/english/
[3] http://www.ksri.uni-karlsruhe.de/
[4] http://www.fzi.de/ipe/
[5] http://www.semantic-web-grundlagen.de/

Contents

List of Figures

Chapter 1

The Quest for Semantics

In this chapter, we explain the basic motivations and ideas underlying Semantic Web technologies as presented in this book, along with some of the history of these ideas. This gentle introduction prepares the stage for the more technical parts that are covered in subsequent chapters.

From its very beginnings, the development of Semantic Web technologies has been closely related to the World Wide Web. This is is not surprising, given that the inventor of the WWW – Sir Tim Berners-Lee – has originally coined the term "Semantic Web" and has inspired much research in this area. Important goals of the approaches that are described in this book are indeed very similar to the goals of the Web in general: to make knowledge widely accessible and to increase the utility of this knowledge by enabling advanced applications for searching, browsing, and evaluation. And, similar to the traditional Web, the foundation of Semantic Web technologies are data formats that can be used to encode knowledge for processing (relevant aspects of it) in computer systems, although the focus is on different forms of knowledge.

However, viewing the WWW as the only origin and inspiration for the technologies that are described in this book would not do justice to their true history. More importantly, it would also hide some of the main motivations that have led to the technologies in their present form. To avoid such a narrow perspective in this chapter, two further strands of closely related endeavors are explained here. One is the general approach of *building abstract models* that capture the complexities of the world in terms of simpler ideas. Modeling in this sense pervades human history – a comprehensive historic account is beyond the scope of this book – but underlying methods and motivations are highly relevant for the semantic technologies that are available for us today.

A second, more recent approach is the idea of *computing with knowledge*. The vision of representing knowledge in a way that allows machines to automatically come to reasonable conclusions, maybe even to "think," has been a driving force for decades of research and development, long before the WWW was imagined. Again, a brief look at this line of development helps us to understand some of the motivations and ideas behind the technologies presented in this book. Thus we arrive at the following three main topics that provide conceptual underpinnings for the Semantic Web:

- Building models: the quest for describing the world in abstract terms to allow for an easier understanding of a complex reality.

- Computing with knowledge: the endeavor of constructing reasoning machines that can draw meaningful conclusions from encoded knowledge.

- Exchanging information: the transmission of complex information resources among computers that allows us to distribute, interlink, and reconcile knowledge on a global scale.

Within this introductory chapter, we briefly outline the ideas underlying each of these topic areas within Sections 1.1, 1.2, and 1.3. Thereafter, in Section 1.4, we explain how these ideas come together in what is often described as *Semantic Web technologies* today. As in every chapter, we conclude with a brief guide to useful references for further reading that is given in Section 1.5.

1.1   Building Models

Generally speaking, a model is a simplified description of certain aspects of reality, used for understanding, structuring, or predicting parts of the real world. In a most general sense, forming models of the world is part of our very ability to reason and to communicate. In this section, we are interested in *scientific modeling*, and especially in those developments that influence today's semantic technologies. Numerical models, such as those described by physical formulae, are less relevant for our considerations and will not be discussed in detail.

Beginnings of scientific modeling can be traced back to ancient philosophy. The Greek philosopher Plato (429–347 BC) proposed answers to some of the most fundamental questions that arise during modeling: What is reality? Which things can be said to "exist"? What is the true nature of things? This marks the first major contribution to a philosophical field now known as *ontology* – the study of existence and being *as such*, and of the fundamental classes and relationships of existing things. Interestingly, the term "ontology" has become very important in today's semantic technologies, but with a rather different meaning: in computer science, an ontology is a description of knowledge about a domain of interest, the core of which is a machine-processable specification with a formally defined meaning.[1]

Ontology in the philosophical sense was further advanced by Plato's student Aristotle (384–322 BC). In contrast to his teacher, Aristotle held the view that models are not given as universal ideas that are merely reflected by reality, but rather that they should be *derived* from careful observations of reality – a view that had great influence on the development of science

---

[1] Ontology is not the first field of study to experience such terminological (ab)use, as is apparent when speaking of "Alaska's impressive geography" or "the biology of Dragonflies."

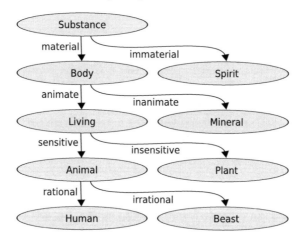

FIGURE 1.1: The *Tree of Porphyry*, an early tree structure in knowledge modeling; diagram based on a translation in [Sow00]

in centuries to come. Applying this approach, Aristotle developed ten categories to classify all things that may exist, and he described subcategories to further specify each of them. For example, Aristotle's category of animals is composed of rational ones (humans) and irrational ones (beasts). Typical for traditional classifications, subcategories in Aristotle's model are exhaustive, i.e. each thing in a category belongs to one of its subcategories, and mutually exclusive, i.e. each thing in a category can belong only to one of its subcategories.

These early approaches toward scientific classification also introduce the use of *structure* in modeling. The philosopher Porphyry (circa 234–305) developed the Tree of Porphyry, a small tree-shaped model that captures the hierarchical relationships of some of Aristotle's categories in a graphical form (see Fig. 1.1). Tree structures, concept hierarchies, and inheritance of properties are notions that are essential for numerous modeling tasks, and that are still found in many applications today.

Numerous influential scientific models have been developed in later centuries, often building upon the basic idea of classification that is found in the works of Aristotle. Carolus Linnaeus (1707–1778) laid the basis for modern biological classification by introducing *Linnaean taxonomy* as a means to classify all life forms. The term *taxonomy* – composed of the Greek words *taxis* (order) and *nomos* (law, science) – has since become the name of the science of classification, but it is also used to refer to individual hierarchical classification schemes. Other important classifications include the WHO's International Classification of Diseases (ICD), the Köppen classification of climates, and the spectral classification of stars in astronomy,[2] all of which have their origins in the 19th century.

As in ancient philosophy, a major goal of modern classification still is to order natural objects to establish a better understanding of their true nature. Carefully chosen categories are often the basis for obtaining further new insights. For studying a new species of animals, for example, it is necessary to first classify that species to distinguish it from others. Another important purpose of classification is communication, as is illustrated by the aforementioned ICD which was introduced to exchange mortality and morbidity statistics internationally.

But classification is not only relevant when dealing with natural objects and phenomena. The same methods are similarly useful for organizing human-made objects, for example, for ordering books in a library. One of the first modern classifications for books was presented by Melvil Dewey (1851–1931) with the Dewey Decimal Classification (DDC), but earlier approaches for organizing libraries can be traced back to ancient Asian and European libraries. An interesting aspect of these approaches is that their purpose is not so much to understand the structure of existing literature but rather to simplify the search for actual books. This predates today's use of semantic technologies for information search and retrieval, and it shows that the construction of models may also be an engineering task that is driven by practical applications rather than by purely scientific considerations.

The abundance of taxonomic classifications suggests that hierarchical structures are a basic and, possibly, the most relevant structure in modeling. In many cases, however, mere hierarchies are not sufficient for describing a domain of interest, and some scientific models are even based on non-hierarchical structures altogether. The celebrated periodic table of chemical elements is a classical example of a model of the latter kind.[3] In other cases, hierarchical and non-hierarchical information are combined. A modern *thesaurus*, for instance, is an ontology that describes relationships between words of a human language. Words are ordered hierarchically based on how general their meanings are[4] whereas relationships such as *synonymy* (having the same meaning) and *antonymy* (having opposite meanings) are not hierarchical.

As opposed to classical taxonomies, many modern modeling approaches allow objects to belong to more than a single most specific category. Dewey's classification of books still follows the traditional approach: for example, a book might belong to category 636.8 if its main subject is cats, and this classification determines its position in a shelf about "Animal husbandry" (636).

---

[2]As opposed to the other examples, the spectral classification is not hierarchical.

[3]In 1870, this tabular structure had been proposed because it was found to be most suitable for capturing known properties of chemical elements. It was revealed only later that this arrangement could be explained by the underlying atomic structures.

[4]This is called *hyponymy*, e.g., "happiness" is a hyponym of "emotion."

Assigning a unique position to a book is useful in a library, but not so much in a computerized catalog. Consequently, modern library classification systems often allow multiple topics to be assigned to a book. A related approach is to classify objects based on multiple independent aspects, so-called *facets*, such that they may be described by a combination of criteria rather than by a unique category. Browsing and searching books in today's book databases, for example, is often based on facets such as title, author, and publisher.

In summary, the history of scientific modeling exposes a steep increase not only in the number of models that have been created, but also in the structural complexity and diversity of these models. This development has been supported by the development of modeling languages that can be used to specify (the structure of) models without ambiguity. A typical example from computer science is the Unified Modeling Language UML that is used in software engineering. Many further languages have been devised in the field of artificial intelligence that plays a prominent role in the next section.

1.2 Calculating with Knowledge

In the preceding section, we outlined the efforts taken to store and structure knowledge for the sake of ultimately being accessed and processed by human beings. Note that following this line of thought, the active use of knowledge in the sense of drawing conclusions from known facts was a task to be carried out by human beings.

However, Aristotle had pointed out that the process of logical deduction, mostly semiconsciously performed by humans, can itself be formalized and externalized by casting it into a set of rules to be used in a way very reminiscent of arithmetics, e.g. as follows, where the third line indicates the conclusion from the previous two lines.

$$\frac{\text{All A are B.}\quad\text{All B are C.}}{\text{All A are C.}}$$

Those rules (which he named *syllogisms*) were domain-independent in the sense that they provided template-like ways for inferring knowledge in which the placeholders could be substituted by domain concepts, e.g.:

$$\frac{\text{All men are mortal.}\quad\text{All Greeks are men.}}{\text{All Greeks are mortal.}}$$

Aristotle thus hinted at the fact that logical thinking in a way has its own existence, independent from opinions and attitudes of individual persons. The idea of externalizing and standardizing human reasoning showed up sporadically in the subsequent centuries. In his work "Ars generalis ultima," Ramon Llull (1232–1315) designed a system of logic and even semi-mechanical devices in order to create new knowledge out of a set of a priori facts. These mechanisms were meant to support interreligious discourse by deriving Christian doctrines from initial statements the monotheistic religions agreed upon. In the same line of thought, Gottfried Leibniz (1646–1716) formulated the desire to resolve conflicts in scientific or philosophical discourse by just calculating[5] the correct answer:

> "If controversies were to arise, there would be no more need of disputation between two philosophers than between two accountants. For it would suffice to take their pencils in their hands, to sit down to their slates, and to say to each other...: Let us calculate." (Gottfried Leibniz, Dissertio de Arte Combinatoria, 1666.)

However, only from the 19th century on, the endeavor of capturing logical thinking in a calculus was continuously pursued. It started with George Boole (1815–1864) and his seminal book "An Investigation of the Laws of Thought" where he introduced propositional (or what it is alternatively called: Boolean) logic.

Gottlob Frege (1848–1925) was the first to invent the principle of quantification (his "Begriffsschrift" appeared in 1879). He laid the foundations of first- and second-order predicate logic, although mainly unnoticed by his contemporaries. His idiosyncratic style of notation might have been one reason for this. So it was Charles Sanders Peirce (1839–1914) who made this development popular, introducing a better notation for quantification which in essence is still being used today (he just wrote Σ and Π as quantifier symbols instead of $\exists$ and $\forall$).

The advent of expressive logical formalisms was accompanied by a common attitude called *logicism*. More and more experts were convinced that – opposed to logic being just a sub-discipline of mathematics – all rational thought and hence all mathematics could be based on logic. More precisely, it was held that every mathematical truth could be deduced from a few *axioms*, i.e. postulates the truth of which is immediately clear. The "Principia Mathematica," published in 1910–1913 by Alfred N. Whitehead (1861–1947) and Bertrand Russell (1872–1970), constitutes the peak of this movement. In three volumes, the authors develop set theory and arithmetics in a strictly formal deductive way. Clearly, these achievements encouraged David Hilbert (1862–1943) to set up his program to base mathematics on a few axioms and

---

[5] As one of the inventors of differential and integral calculus he was well aware that much more than everyday arithmetics can be captured in an algorithmic, mathematically rigorous way.

deduction principles, such that the truth of any mathematical statement can be decided by an algorithm. Note that accomplishing this mission would have fulfilled Leibniz' dream.

The enthusiasm was turned down in the early 1930s, when Kurt Gödel (1906–1978) showed that such an algorithm cannot exist. Instead, every system of axioms and deduction rules that is capable of describing arithmetics is *incomplete*, i.e. there must exist statements which can be neither proven nor refuted. A rather similar argument was used by Alan Turing (1912–1954) for showing that there is no generic way to tell whether a computer program will terminate or not. Gödel and Turing provided valuable insights about the limits of formal logic. They established central notions like *decidability* and *computability* which allowed us to categorize logical problems and gave a more clarified view on what can be done with automated means.

Despite these discouraging findings, a new "common sense logicism" arose rather soon. In summer 1956, John McCarthy organized a 2-month brainstorming get-together of leading researchers which was held at Dartmouth College. Inspired by the accessibility of digital computers, they explored the possibility of employing those devices to simulate or generate intelligent behavior. In the course of this event, the term *artificial intelligence* (AI) was coined. The task of deducing knowledge from known facts was felt to be one of the central issues to achieve that goal. Among the different approaches to artificial intelligence, a prevalent one was that of implementing logical deduction via symbol manipulation, based on the principle of the *Physical Symbol System Hypothesis*:

> "A physical symbol system has the necessary and sufficient means for general intelligent action." (Newell, Allen; Simon, H. A. (1976), "Computer Science as Empirical Inquiry: Symbols and Search," Communications of the ACM, 19)

Once again, experts were confident that the problem of capturing human thinking was about to be solved. In the mid-1960s it was commonly conjectured by AI protagonists that the goal of building a machine exhibiting human intelligence would be accomplished within a single decade.

It turned out that scientists had underestimated the aspired goal in at least two ways: First, the amount of knowledge that would have to be specified for even modest AI applications turned out to be overwhelming. This rendered the process of transforming human knowledge into a machine-processable form a costly and tedious task. This problem is commonly referred to as the *knowledge acquisition bottleneck*. Second, the applied inference techniques worked well for small examples with limited knowledge involved but turned unacceptably slow for medium- or large-scale tasks. Moreover, findings in complexity theory revealed that in many cases this slowdown is unavoidable in principle. This showed that the encountered difficulties were caused by the intrinsic hardness of the given tasks that could not be overcome by faster hardware or clever engineering. In a way, this was the first time the issue of *scalability* emerged, which has been one of the central requirements in Semantic Web technologies from the beginning.

As a consequence of this, research focused on goals that were more modest. For restricted domains of expertise, symbolic approaches implementing moderately expressive but computationally performant formalisms still worked out very well. So-called *expert systems*, mostly rule-based, were built for highly structured areas like medicine and biology. In these domains they were capable of competing with (or even outperforming) human experts.[6] As the first broadly adopted AI technology, expert systems had established a solid position on the market by the mid-1980s.

Encouraged by the availability of both appropriate funding as well as faster computers with larger memories, there have been serious attempts to tackle the knowledge acquisition bottleneck and to work toward general-purpose knowledge-based systems: the artificial intelligence project Cyc,[7] founded in 1984 by Douglas Lenat, aims at building an everyday common sense ontology including an inference engine. The current Cyc ontology comprises several millions of logical statements.

1.3 Exchanging Information

While computation was certainly the main motivation for constructing early computers, the aspect of *communication* between these machines soon became an important problem as well. Already in the late 1950s, computers were available at various sites throughout the U.S., and joint projects required data to be transmitted between them. Telecommunication as such had been established for some time, telephones being a commodity, and this existing infrastructure was used to build the first long-distance connections between computers. However, many decades of development were required to arrive at the ubiquitous global communication networks that we use today, with the World Wide Web as the most prominent medium that was built on top of this infrastructure.

Work on computer networking progressed significantly in the 1960s. The American computer scientist J.C.R. Licklider (1915–1990) was the first to envision computer networks in a modern sense in a series of memos in 1962. An invention that has been crucial for realizing this idea was *packet switching* –

---

[6]MYCIN, an early expert system for diagnosing bacterial infections and suggesting medical treatment, was shown to provide an acceptable therapy in more cases than human experts did.

[7]http://www.cyc.com/

the notion of splitting transmissions into small "packets" that are transmitted individually – which is attributed to the independent works of Paul Baran, Donald Davies, and Leonard Kleinrock. Packet switching separated the concerns of physical transmission (which line to use) from the concerns of digital communication (which data to exchange).

Various communication protocols that were developed during and after the 1960s allowed more computer networks to be established. In 1969, the first packet-switching network went online: ARPANET was a network of four computers that was run by the Advanced Research Projects Agency of the U.S. Department of Defense. Other local networks soon followed, and the problem of *inter-network* communication became relevant. In 1974, the Internet Protocol Suite (TCP/IP) was published as a way to overcome the diversity of computer networking protocols. With more and more networks connecting, the global communication infrastructure that is now called the Internet emerged. Significant world-wide growth and commercialization of the Internet started in the 1980s.

Applications such as email and Usenet (online discussion boards) were the most popular uses of the Internet in its first decades. Only in 1989, the Englishman Tim Berners-Lee, working for CERN in Switzerland at that time, made a proposal to overcome communication problems of physicists collaborating around the world: what he conceived is a common medium that enables the exchange of interlinked hypertext documents between diverse computer systems. He dubbed his invention the World Wide Web. By the end of 1990, he provided first versions of the Hypertext Transfer Protocol HTTP, the Hypertext Markup Language HTML, the first Web browser and HTML editor, and the first Web server software. The ideas upon which these components are based are not entirely new, but the new combination of technologies enables a hitherto unknown global exchange of information.

In 1991, the first Web server outside of Europe is established, and Tim Berners-Lee announced the Web in a public newsgroup post:

> "The WorldWideWeb (WWW) project aims to allow links to be made to any information anywhere. ... The WWW project was started to allow high energy physicists to share data, news, and documentation. We are very interested in spreading the web to other areas, and having gateway servers for other data. Collaborators welcome!" (Tim Berners-Lee, alt.hypertext, 1991)

During the 1990s, the World Wide Web emerged as the most popular medium of the Internet. It gained commercial relevance starting from the middle of the decade, without being stopped by the "dot-com bust" at the end of the millennium. Yet, like the WWW itself, innovative Web applications such as wikis and blogs continue to be introduced for personal and public community use long before they are adopted by industry.

Today, the Web – just like the Internet – is used not only for consuming information passively, but also for creating and publishing new content, distinguishing it from traditional media. This was reinforced by popular websites that simplify user contributions: Wikipedia, Flickr, YouTube, and numerous social networking sites are typical examples. Increasing amounts of knowledge are created by individuals, leading to a phenomenon that Lawrence Lessig – law professor and creator of the Creative Commons licenses[8] – has described as *read-write culture*, as opposed to "read-only culture":

> "Passive recipients of culture produced elsewhere. Couch potatoes. Consumers. This is the world of media from the twentieth century. The twenty-first century could be different. This is the crucial point: It could be both read and write." (Lawrence Lessig, Free Culture, 2004)

This has significant technological consequences, too. The Web remains a distributed information space that provides a plethora of heterogeneous knowledge sources in many formats. Information exchange on the Web is only possible by agreeing on standard data formats, and by exploiting the hyperlinks that turn distributed resources into a Web-like structure. The latter is used not only by human readers for browsing, but also by search engines for gathering and ranking Web pages. The key feature of HTML is that links are denoted using dedicated mark-up that enables machines to "understand" them without human assistance.

But classical search engines, in spite of their success, have turned out to be insufficient for managing the ever increasing amounts of Web content. Instead of relying on text-based search only, Web applications have introduced further paradigms for organizing and searching information. A popular example is *tagging*, which typically is used to provide statistical search and browsing functionalities based on simple keywords ("tags") that users assign to resources. This approach has been particularly successful for structuring content that is not primarily text-based – pictures, videos, but also products in online shops. Both the approach of social tagging in general and the resulting tag structures have been called *folksonomy*, which is a merger of "folk" and "taxonomy" even though folksonomies are not classifications in the traditional sense. *User ratings* are another example of user-contributed information that is used to improve search. Many other search features are based on structured knowledge that is associated with the subject of interest: shop items have a price, company products have technical specifications, blog entries have a date. This development is further supported by the availability of specialized software for managing content that is not just arbitrary hypertext. Weblogging tools and Web shop applications are typical examples.

---

[8]http://creativecommons.org/

Summing up, there has been an obvious trend toward adding more "structure" to Web resources. Many of the above examples are, however, not based on any common standard and it is thus difficult to exploit this data other than by using a website's particular search interface. Comparatively few sites provide structured data for download, even though this is already common for some application areas. For example, virtually all news sites today export data in RSS or ATOM feeds to which readers can subscribe. These standard formats encode data about news items in a way that allows them to be displayed and searched in a wide range of news reader applications. Another recent approach to improve data exchange on the Web is *Web Services*. In this case, data is transmitted to a Web server which computes and returns a result based on this input. A very basic example is the Google Maps service: coordinates of landmarks are sent to the server; an HTML-embedded map that displays those locations is returned. The formats for input and output in this case largely depend on the given Web Service, but approaches exist for providing Web Service interface descriptions in standardized formats that can be transferred over the Web.

These recent developments – the growth of active user contributions and the increased exploitation of structured data – coincide with a general improvement in usability and interactivity of Web user interfaces. The term "Web 2.0" has often been associated with these developments, although this terminology wrongly suggests that there was a clear-cut change in the underlying Web technology or in its use. Tim O'Reilly, who coined the term, expressed the view that "Web 2.0" rather describes a change in the attitude towards using and exploiting the Web. However, in the light of the continuous change of the Web and its usage, the approach of versioning the WWW is hardly adequate to describe the complexity of current and future developments.

1.4 Semantic Web Technologies

The Semantic Web has been conceived as an extension of the World Wide Web that allows computers to intelligently search, combine, and process Web content based on the meaning that this content has to humans. In the absence of human-level artificial intelligence, this can only be accomplished if the intended meaning (i.e. the *semantics*) of Web resources is explicitly specified in a format that is processable by computers. For this it is not enough to store data in a machine-processable syntax – every HTML page on the Web is machine-processable in a sense – but it is also required that this data is endowed with a formal *semantics* that clearly specifies which conclusions should be drawn from the collected information.[9] Clearly, this would be an impossible endeavor when aiming at all human knowledge found on the Web, given that it is often hard enough for humans to even agree on the contents of a certain document, not to mention formalizing it in a way that is meaningful to computers. In reality, of course, the purpose of the Semantic Web is rather to enable machines to access *more* information that hitherto required human time and attention to be used. While this is a reasonable goal from a practical viewpoint, it also means that "Semantic Web" does not refer to a concrete extension of the World Wide Web, but rather to an ideal toward which the Web evolves over time. At the same time, any progress in this field can similarly be useful in applications that are not closely related to the Web. This book thus focuses on the underlying *Semantic Web technologies*, chiefly *semantic technologies*, that are available today.

Realizing the above mentioned goals makes it necessary to address a number of difficult challenges that are not addressed by classical Web technologies. This is where the topics discussed in Sections 1.1 and 1.2 come to the fore. Expressing human knowledge in a formally specified language is a classical modeling task. The rich experiences gathered within this domain throughout history are an important guide in identifying relevant modeling structures up to the present day. The most recently developed Semantic Web language *OWL 2* (see Section 4.3), for instance, has been influenced by feature requests from modeling use cases in life sciences. Moreover, semantic technologies can draw from modeling methodologies, software applications, and corresponding user-interface paradigms that have been developed for supporting humans in the task of constructing models.

How knowledge is to be modeled also depends, of course, on the intended usage of the constructed model. On the Semantic Web, one would like computer programs to draw conclusions from given information, so that aspects of formal knowledge representation and reasoning come into play. In the first place, the insights gathered in this field help us to understand the fundamental difficulties and limits that one has to be aware of when constructing "reasoning machines" as discussed in Section 1.2. On the practical side, semantic technologies can build on algorithms and tools that were developed for solving relevant inferencing problems.

The above discussion views the development of the Semantic Web as an approach of incorporating knowledge modeling and automatic deduction into the Web. Conversely, it is also true that semantic technologies introduce aspects and features of Web applications into the domain of formal modeling and knowledge representation. Most basically, the Web introduces a notion

---

[9]Note that, indeed, the term "semantics" occurs with two distinct interpretations in the previous two sentences. In the first sense, it refers to the meaning that texts in a human language have: this is the usage common in linguistics. In the second sense, it refers to the formal interpretation of a computer language: this is the usage common in computer science. Both notions of the term are found in discussions of the Semantic Web.

of distributed, heterogeneous, yet inter-linked information that is novel to the other disciplines. Whereas Web data is indeed independently published and maintained in many sources, it is still universally accessible based on global addressing schemes and standardized protocols. More specifically, the Web emphasizes the importance of clearly specified, standardized languages that can be used to exchange data across software boundaries. Although there are some examples of earlier standardization activities around knowledge representation formalisms,[10] the Semantic Web clearly has increased the practical importance of standardization in this area. Most of the relevant standardization efforts, including all technology standards covered in this book, have been conducted under the lead of the *World Wide Web Consortium* (W3C). These activities have also facilitated tool interoperability and information exchange in application areas beyond the Web.

The remainder of this section gives a short overview of what has *actually* been done in the pursuit of the goals of the Semantic Web, eventually leading up to the technologies discussed in this book. The idea of adding "semantics" to the World Wide Web has been around since its very beginning, although the concrete approaches toward achieving this goal have changed over time. Semantics (in the sense common in computer science) had long been studied for mark-up languages, including hypertext languages like the ones that inspired HTML. In the latter case, the semantics of language constructs typically determines how programs should present parts of a document to users – a usage that is still most common when discussing HTML today. However, also the notion of encoding higher-level knowledge into hypertext had been around early on, for instance, in the form of "typed links" that, besides defining a hyperlink to another document, also provide some clue regarding the intended meaning of that link. Tim Berners-Lee himself already pursued the idea of a more semantic Web during the 1990s.

These ideas, however, gained major public attention only when Berners-Lee and others published a seminal article entitled "The Semantic Web" in *Scientific American* in 2001. Envisioned within this paper is a ubiquitous Web within which complex knowledge is exchanged and processed by intelligent agents to assist humans in their daily routines – the described scenario would require not just a Semantic Web but also significant advances in AI and natural language processing, as well as ubiquitous computing and intelligent environments. Accordingly, the work has created high expectations that fueled research and development, but it has also repelled some communities on account of being so far from reality. Yet, there has been a significant increase of Semantic Web activities since the beginning of the new millennium, though usually with goals which are somewhat more modest and therefore achievable within a reasonable time-span.

---

[10]The most prominent example is the logic programming language *Prolog* that is covered by the ISO/IEC 13211 standard, cf. [DEDC96].

In subsequent years, the W3C published a number of standards for Semantic Web formats that facilitate the exchange of semantically rich information. These include the basic *Resource Description Framework* RDF (Chapters 2 and 3) and the more expressive *Web Ontology Language* OWL (Chapters 4 and 5) in 2004,[11] and the *SPARQL Protocol and RDF Query Language* (Chapter 7) in 2008. An update and extension of the Web Ontology Language, known as *OWL 2*, is to be completed in 2009 (Section 4.3), and the specification of rule-based Semantic Web languages is the ongoing quest of the *Rule Interchange Format* (RIF) standardization activity (Chapter 6).

At the same time, many developments have increased the availability of machine-processable data on the Web. Some applications, such as the RDF Site Summary (RSS 1.0), are based on the new standards, while others have provided *ad hoc* solutions for the increasingly relevant problem of exchanging semantic information. Indeed, the Semantic Web initiative was sometimes criticized among Web developers for being overly ambitious and not really suited to serve some of the immediate needs of current applications. Solutions have been proposed to directly address particular problems in specific application domains, e.g., for the purpose of encoding personal contact data. A notable effort in this direction is so-called *microformats* which use attribute values in HTML documents for embedding small chunks of semantic data into Web pages. The major advantage of microformats over other general-purpose technologies is simplicity[12] which comes at the price of more limited application areas and extensibility. The term *"lowercase* semantic web" is sometimes used to contrast these simpler approaches with the grand Semantic Web endeavor as envisioned in 2001.

Even today, some people still perceive "uppercase" and "lowercase" approaches toward the Semantic Web to be in competition rather than to be complementary approaches toward the same goal. What actually happened, though, is that there have been a number of advances in reconciling both developments. The W3C has developed the *RDFa* standard for embedding RDF-based semantic data into HTML pages, thus addressing similar use cases as current microformats. Moreover, the W3C's *GRDDL* specification provides a framework for extracting RDF data from HTML and XML formats, so that XML-based information can be combined with other Semantic Web data more easily. Likewise, the amount of semantic data that is available on the Web has grown considerably in recent years, and data sources have become increasingly inter-linked. This is possible since the identifiers used in Semantic Web languages follow the same construction principles as URLs on the classical Web: the name of any object can thus also be interpreted as a Web address. This leads to the notion of *linked data*, referring to semantic data all identifiers

---

[11]Strictly speaking, an early version of RDF was published in 1999, but the 2004 standard is a major revision.

[12]This regards usage and writing; *extracting* microformat data from HTML is not simple.

of which are pointers to Web addresses where further information about the according objects can be found.

In the light of these recent developments, the term "web of data" was introduced to describe the Semantic Web as an effort that focuses primarily on data exchange. This reflects the fact that basic semantic data formats have more easily found their way into applications on the Web than more expressive knowledge representation paradigms. The latter, however, have been adopted in areas outside the Web, where it is often easier to manage complex knowledge structures. An overview of some noteworthy example applications is provided in Chapter 9. The increased practical use of semantic technologies is witness to the fact that important base technologies are well-developed – their strengths and weaknesses understood much better than in the early years of the Semantic Web activity – and that they are useful for solving the problems encountered in practice. And indeed, recently we have seen major IT and venture capital companies investing in the segment, while the trend in research projects and funding drifts rather heavily from foundations to applications. New technologies continue to be developed, and it can be expected that they will lead to the solutions that will enable innovative applications with high impact in the next few years.

The purpose of this book is to provide an introduction to this promising field which covers the main body of reasonably stable and well-established core technologies, and also related extensions that are currently being developed and which can be expected to be available soon.

1.5 Further Reading

It is impossible to provide a comprehensive list of references for the broad topics that have been discussed in this chapter, so we mostly confine ourselves to suitable overview publications that provide pointers to further literature.

Some of the early history of formal modeling, especially related to philosophical developments, is described in [Sow00]. An account of the more recent history of knowledge representation and reasoning can be found in [Sow84]. A useful reference for a more general overview of the area of artificial intelligence is [RN03]. The *Cyc* project has been described in [LG90]. Some seminal historic publications should be mentioned: Whitehead's and Russel's *Principia Mathematica* [WR13], Gödel's original incompleteness theorems [Göd31], and Turing's account of the Halting problem [Tur37].

The history and development of the World Wide Web are described by Tim Berners-Lee in [BL00]. Lawrence Lessig's discussion of related cultural phenomena is [Les05]. There is currently little printed material regarding the term "Web 2.0" and there is certainly no single authoritative view on the topic, although Tim O'Reilly registered the term as a trademark and published various characterizations at `http://oreilly.com/`.

The seminal 2001 article about the Semantic Web is [BLHL01], and an update is [SBLH06]. The central website on the W3C Semantic Web activity is `http://www.w3.org/2001/sw/` and includes many pointers to further online resources. A research-oriented account of recent semantic technologies is given in [SS09]. For reading up on the most recent results concerning Semantic Web research and practice, we recommend the following sources.

- the Elsevier Journal of Web Semantics: Science, Services and Agents on the World Wide Web,[13]

- the IGI Global International Journal on Semantic Web and Information Systems,[14]

- the proceedings of the annual International Semantic Web Conferences (ISWC),[15]

- the proceedings of the annual International World Wide Web Conferences,[16]

- the proceedings of the annual Semantic Technology Conferences.[17]

Specific references to the mentioned Semantic Web standards are given in the respective chapters. This excludes two standards that have been mentioned but are not treated within this book: GRDDL ("Gleaning Resource Descriptions from Dialects of Languages") which is specified in [Con07], and RDFa (embedding RDF into XHTML) which is specified in [ABMP08]. Documentation about microformats can be found at `http://microformats.org/`.

---

[13]http://www.websemanticsjournal.org/

[14]http://www.ijswis.org/

[15]http://iswc.semanticweb.org/

[16]http://www.iw3c2.org/.

[17]http://www.semantic-conference.com/

Part I

Resource Description Language RDF

Chapter 2

Simple Ontologies in RDF and RDF Schema

The *Resource Description Framework* RDF is a formal language for describing structured information. The goal of RDF is to enable applications to exchange data on the Web while still preserving their original meaning. As opposed to HTML and XML, the main intention now is not to display documents correctly, but rather to allow for further processing and re-combination of the information contained in them. RDF consequently is often viewed as the basic representation format for developing the Semantic Web.

The development of RDF began in the 1990s, and various predecessor languages have influenced the creation process of RDF. A first official specification was published in 1999 by the W3C, though the emphasis at this time still was clearly on the representation of *metadata* about Web resources. The term metadata generally refers to data providing information about given data sets or documents. In 1999, the latter were mainly expected to be Web pages, for which RDF could help to state information on authorship or copyright. Later the vision of the Semantic Web was extended to the representation of semantic information in general, reaching beyond simple RDF data as well as Web documents as primary subjects of such descriptions. This was the motivation for publishing a reworked and extended RDF specification in 2004.

As of today, numerous practical tools are available for dealing with RDF. Virtually every programming language offers libraries for reading and writing RDF documents. Various RDF stores – also called *triple stores* for reasons that shall become clear soon – are available for keeping and processing large amounts of RDF data, and even commercial database vendors are already providing suitable extensions for their products. RDF is also used to exchange (meta) data in specific application areas. The most prominent example of this kind of usage is likely to be RSS 1.0 for syndicating news on the Web.[1] But also metadata belonging to files of desktop applications are sometimes encoded using RDF, such as in the case of Adobe's RDF format XMP for embedding information in PDF files, or as annotations in the XML-based vector graphics format SVG. We will say more about such applications in Chapter 9.

---

[1] RSS 1.0 and 2.0 are different formats, which pursue the same goal but which, confusingly, are not based on each other. RSS 1.0 stands for *RDF Site Summary*, whereas RSS 2.0 is usually interpreted as *Really Simple Syndication*. See also Section 9.1.2.

FIGURE 2.1: A simple RDF graph describing the relationship between this book and the publisher, CRC Press

This chapter introduces the basics of RDF. Initially, the representation of simple data is our main concern. In the subsequent sections, we have a closer look at the various syntactic formats available for exchanging RDF, and we address some further questions regarding the usage of RDF. Thereafter we consider some specific expressive features that go beyond the description of simple data. RDF is extended to the language *RDF Schema* (RDFS) for this purpose, allowing us to express also general information about a data set. The official formal semantics as used for properly interpreting RDF and RDFS in computer programs is explained in detail in Chapter 3.

2.1   Introduction to RDF

We begin by giving a very basic introduction to the RDF format that also highlights major differences to XML. As we shall see, RDF is based on a very simple graph-oriented data schema.

2.1.1   Graphs Instead of Trees

An RDF document describes a *directed graph*, i.e. a set of *nodes* that are linked by *directed edges* ("arrows"). Both nodes and edges are labeled with identifiers to distinguish them. Figure 2.1 shows a simple example of a graph of two nodes and one edge. In contrast, as recalled in Appendix A, information in XML is encoded in tree structures. Trees are perfectly suited for organizing information in electronic documents, where we are often confronted with strictly hierarchical structures. In addition, information in trees can often be fetched directly and be processed rather efficiently. Why then is RDF relying on graphs?

An important reason is that RDF was not conceived for the task of structuring documents, but rather for describing general relationships between objects of interest (in RDF one usually speaks of "resources"). The graph in Fig. 2.1, e.g., might be used to express that the book "Foundations of Semantic Web Technologies" was published by "CRC Press" if we interpret the given labels to refer to those objects. The relationship between book and publishing house in this case is information which does not in any obvious sense belong hierarchically below either of the resources. RDF therefore considers such relations as basic building blocks of information. Many such relationships together naturally form graphs, not hierarchical tree structures.

Another reason for choosing graphs is the fact that RDF was intended to serve as a description language for data on the WWW and other electronic networks. Information in these environments is typically stored and managed in decentralized ways, and indeed it is very easy to combine RDF data from multiple sources. For example, the RDF graphs from the website of this book could simply be joined with graphs from `http://semanticweb.org` – this would merely lead to a bigger graph that may or may not provide interesting new information. Note that we generally allow for graphs to consist of multiple unconnected components, i.e. of sub-graphs without any edges between them. Now it is easy to see why such a straightforward approach would not be feasible for combining multiple XML documents. An immediate problem is that the simple union of two tree structures is not a tree anymore, so that additional choices must be made to even obtain a well-formed XML document when combining multiple inputs. Moreover, related information items in trees might be separated by the strict structure: even if two XML files refer to the same resources, related information is likely to be found in very different locations in each tree. Graphs in RDF are therefore better suited for the composition of distributed information sources.

Note that these observations refer to the *semantic* way in which RDF structures information, not to the question of how to encode RDF data *syntactically*. We will see below that XML is still very useful for the latter purpose.

2.1.2 Names in RDF: URIs

We have claimed above that RDF graphs enable the simple composition of distributed data. This statement so far refers only to the graph structure in general, but not necessarily to the intended information in the composed graphs. An essential problem is that resources, just like in XML, may not have uniform identifiers within different RDF documents. Even when two documents contain information on related topics, the identifiers they use might be completely unrelated. On the one hand, it may happen that the same resource is labeled with different identifiers, for instance, since there is no globally agreed identifier for the book "Foundations of Semantic Web Technologies." On the other hand, it may occur that the same identifiers are used for different resources, e.g., "CRC" could refer to the publishing house as well as to the official currency of Puerto Rico. Such ambiguity would obviously be a major problem when trying to process and compose information automatically.

To solve the latter problem, RDF uses so-called *Uniform Resource Identifiers (URIs)* as names to clearly distinguish resources from each other. URIs are a generalization of URLs (Uniform Resource Locators), i.e. of Web addresses as they are used for accessing online documents. Every URL is also a valid URI, and URLs can indeed be used as identifiers in RDF documents that talk about Web resources. In numerous other applications, however, the goal is not to exchange information about Web pages but about many different kinds of objects. In general this might be any object that has a clear identity in the context of the given application: books, places, people, publishing houses, events, relationships among such things, all kinds of abstract concepts, and many more. Such resources can obviously not be retrieved online and hence their URIs are used exclusively for unique identification. URIs that are not URLs are sometimes also called *Uniform Resource Names* (URNs).

Even if URIs can refer to resources that are not located on the Web, they are still based on a similar construction scheme as common Web addresses. Figure 2.2 gives an overview of the construction of URIs, and explains their relevant parts. The main characteristic of any URI is its initial scheme part. While schemes like `http` are typically associated with a protocol for transmitting information, we also find such schemes in many URIs that do not refer to an actual Web location. The details of the protocol are obviously not relevant when using a URI only as a name. The book "Foundations of Semantic Web Technologies" could, e.g., use the URI `http://semantic-web-book.org/uri` and it would not matter whether or not a document can be retrieved at the corresponding location, and whether this document is relevant in the given context. As we shall see later on, RDF makes use of various mechanisms of XML to abbreviate URIs when convenient.

As shown in Fig. 2.1, nodes and edges in RDF graphs both are labeled with URIs to distinguish them from other resources. This rule has two possible exceptions: RDF allows for the encoding of data values which are not URIs, and it features so-called *blank nodes* which do not carry any name. We will take a closer look at both cases next. Later we will also return to the question of finding good URIs in practice, in a way that ensures maximal utility and reliability in semantic applications. For now we are satisfied with the insight that URIs, if they are well-chosen, provide us with a robust mechanism for distinguishing different entities, thus avoiding confusion when combining RDF data from distributed sources.

2.1.3   Data Values in RDF: Literals

URIs allow us to name abstract resources, even those that cannot be represented or processed directly by a computer. URIs in this case are merely references to the intended objects (people, books, publishers, ...). While URIs can always be treated as names, the actual "intended" interpretation of particular URIs is not given in any formal way, and specific tools may have their own way of interpreting certain URIs. A certain Web Service, e.g., may recognize URIs that refer to books and treat them in a special way by displaying purchasing options or current prices. This degree of freedom is useful and in fact unavoidable when dealing with arbitrary resources. The situation is different when dealing with concrete data values such as numbers, times,

The general construction scheme of URIs is summarized below, where parts in brackets are optional:

$$scheme : [//authority] path [?query] [\#fragment]$$

The meaning of the various URI parts is as follows:

scheme The name of a URI scheme that classifies the type of URI. Schemes may also provide additional information on how to handle URIs in applications. Examples: `http`, `ftp`, `mailto`, `file`, `irc`

authority URIs of some URI schemes refer to "authorities" for structuring the available identifiers further. On the Web, this is typically a domain name, possibly with additional user and port details. The authority part of a URI is optional and can be recognized by the preceding `//`. Examples: `semantic-web-book.org`, `john@example.com`, `example.org:8080`

path The path is the main part of many URIs, though it is possible to use empty paths, e.g., in email addresses. Paths can be organized hierarchically using / as separator. Examples: `/etc/passwd`, `this/path/with/-:_~/is/../okay` (paths without initial / are only allowed if no authority is given)

query The query is an optional part of the URI that provides additional non-hierarchical information. It can be recognized by its preceding ?. In URLs, queries are typically used for providing parameters, e.g., to a Web Service. Example: `q=Semantic+Web+book`

fragment The optional fragment part provides a second level of identifying resources, and its presence is recognized by the preceding #. In URLs, fragments are often used to address a sub-part of a retrieved resource, such as a section in an HTML file. URIs with different fragments are still different names for the purpose of RDF, even if they may lead to the same document being retrieved in a browser. Example: `section1`

Not all characters are allowed in all positions of a URI, and illegal symbols are sometimes encoded by specific means. For the purpose of this book it suffices to know that basic Latin letters and numbers are allowed in almost any position. Moreover, the use of non-Latin characters that abound in many languages is widely allowed in all current Semantic Web formats as well. URIs that are extended in this way are known as *International Resource Identifiers* (IRIs), and they can be used in any place where URIs are considered in this book.

FIGURE 2.2:   The basic construction scheme for URIs

FIGURE 2.3:   An RDF graph with literals for describing data values

or truth values: in these cases, we would expect every application to have a minimal understanding of the concrete meaning of such values. The number 42, e.g., has the same numeric interpretation in any context.

Data values in RDF are represented by so-called *literals*. These are reserved names for RDF resources of a certain datatype. The value of every literal is generally described by a sequence of characters, such as the string consisting of the symbols "4" and "2" in the above example. The interpretation of such sequences is then determined based on a given *datatype*. Knowing the datatype is crucial for understanding the intended meaning: the character sequences "42" and "042", e.g., refer to the same natural number but to different text strings.

For the time being, we will consider only literals for which no datatype has been given. Such *untyped* literals are always interpreted as text strings. The slightly more complex form of literals that contains an additional datatype identifier will be explained later on.

As can be seen in Fig. 2.3, rectangular boxes are used to distinguish literals from URIs when drawing RDF graphs. Another special trait of literals is that they may never be the origin of edges in an RDF graph. In practice, this means that we cannot make direct statements about literals.[2] This constraint needs to be taken into account when modeling data in RDF. Moreover, it is not allowed to use literals as labels for edges in RDF graphs – a minor restriction since it is hard to see what could be intended with such a labeling. Note that it is still allowed to use the same URI for labeling both nodes and edges in a graph, so at least in RDF there is no principle separation between resources used for either purpose.

---

[2]The reason for this restriction is in fact historic, and an official resolution of the RDF-Core working group notes that it could be waived in future Semantic Web languages; see http://www.w3.org/2000/03/rdf-tracking/#rdfms-literalsubjects.

2.2 Syntax for RDF

Up to this point, we have described RDF graphs by means of drawing diagrams. This way of representing RDF is easy to read and still precise, yet it is clearly not suitable for processing RDF in computer systems. Even for humans, understanding visual graphs works without much effort only if the graphs are very small – practically relevant data sets with thousands or millions of nodes do obviously not lend themselves to being stored and communicated in pictures. This section thus introduces ways of representing RDF by means of character strings that can easily be kept in electronic documents. This requires us to split the original graph into smaller parts that can be stored one by one. Such a transformation of complex data structures into linear strings is called *serialization*.

2.2.1 From Graphs to Triples

Computer science has various common ways of representing graphs as character strings, e.g., by using an adjacency matrix. RDF graphs, however, are typically very sparse graphs within which the vast majority of possible relationships do not hold. In such a case it makes sense to represent the graph as the set of edges that are actually given, and to store each edge on its own. In the example of Fig. 2.1 this is exactly one edge, uniquely determined by its start http://semantic-web-book.org/uri, label http://example.org/publishedBy, and endpoint http://crcpress.com/uri. Those three distinguished parts are called *subject*, *predicate*, and *object*, respectively.

It is easy to see that every RDF graph can, in essence, be completely described by its edges. There are of course many ways for drawing such graphs, but the details of the visual layout clearly have no effect on the information the graph conveys. Now every such edge corresponds to an *RDF triple* "subject-predicate-object." As we have seen above, each part of a triple can be a URI, though the object might also be a literal. Another special case is *blank nodes* that we will consider later.

2.2.2 Simple Triple Syntax: N3, N-Triples and Turtle

Our earlier observations suggest that one denotes RDF graphs simply as a collection of all their triples, given in arbitrary order. This basic idea has indeed been taken up in various concrete proposals for serializing RDF. A realization that dates back to 1998 is Tim Berners-Lee's *Notation 3* (N3), which also includes some more complex expressions such as paths and rules. The RDF recommendation of 2004 therefore proposed a less complicated part of N3 under the name *N-Triples* as a possible syntax for RDF. N-triples in turn was further extended to incorporate various convenient abbreviations, leading to the RDF syntax *Turtle* which is hitherto not described in an official standardization document. Both N-Triple and Turtle are essentially parts of N3, restricted to covering only valid RDF graphs. Here we consider the more modern Turtle syntax.

The graph of Fig. 2.3 is written in Turtle as follows:

```
<http://semantic-web-book.org/uri>
    <http://example.org/publishedBy>  <http://crcpress.com/uri> .
<http://semantic-web-book.org/uri>
    <http://example.org/title>
        "Foundations of Semantic Web Technologies" .
<http://crcpress.com/uri>
    <http://example.org/name>        "CRC Press" .
```

URIs are thus written in angular brackets, literals are written in quotation marks, and every statement is terminated by a full stop. Besides those specific characteristics, however, the syntax is a direct translation of the RDF graph into triples. Spaces and line breaks are only relevant if used within URIs or literals, and are ignored otherwise. Our lengthy names force us to spread single triples over multiple lines. Due to the hierarchical structure of URIs, the identifiers in RDF documents typically use similar prefixes. Turtle offers a mechanism for abbreviating such URIs using so-called *namespaces*. The previous example can be written as follows:

```
@prefix book: <http://semantic-web-book.org/> .
@prefix ex: <http://example.org/> .
@prefix crc: <http://crcpress.com/> .

book:uri   ex:publishedBy   crc:uri .
book:uri   ex:title         "Foundations of Semantic Web Technologies" .
crc:uri    ex:name          "CRC Press" .
```

URIs are now abbreviated using prefixes of the form "prefix:" and are no longer enclosed in angular brackets. Without the latter modification it would be possible to confuse the abbreviated forms with full URIs, e.g., since it is allowable to use a prefix "http:" in namespace declarations. The prefix text that is used for abbreviating a particular URI part can be chosen freely, but it is recommended to select abbreviations that are easy to read and that refer the human reader to what they abbreviate. Identifiers of the form "prefix:name" are also known as *QNames* (for *qualified names*).

It frequently happens that RDF descriptions contain many triples with the same subject, or even with the same subject and predicate. For those common cases, Turtle provides further shortcuts as shown in the following example:

```
@prefix book: <http://semantic-web-book.org/> .
@prefix ex: <http://example.org/> .
@prefix crc: <http://crcpress.com/> .

book:uri   ex:publishedBy   crc:uri ;
           ex:title         "Foundations of Semantic Web Technologies" .
crc:uri    ex:name          "CRC Press", "CRC" .
```

The semicolon after the first line terminates the triple, and at the same time fixes the subject `book:uri` for the next triple. This allows us to write many triples for one subject without repeating the name of the subject. The comma in the last line similarly finishes the triple, but this time both subject and predicate are re-used for the next triple. Hence the final line in fact specifies two triples providing two different names. The overall RDF graph therefore consists of four edges and four nodes. It is possible to combine semicolon and comma, as shown in the next example with four triples:

```
@prefix book: <http://semantic-web-book.org/> .
@prefix ex: <http://example.org/> .

book:uri   ex:author book:Hitzler, book:Krötzsch, book:Rudolph ;
           ex:title "Foundations of Semantic Web Technologies" .
```

The above abbreviations are not contained in the official (normative) W3C syntax N-Triples which allows neither namespaces, nor comma or semicolon. Yet, Turtle's syntactic shortcuts are frequently encountered in practice, and they have influenced the triple syntax of W3C's more recent SPARQL specification, introduced in Chapter 7.

2.2.3 The XML Serialization of RDF

The Turtle representation of RDF can easily be processed by machines but is still accessible for humans with relatively little effort. Yet, triple representations like Turtle are by far not the most commonly used RDF syntax in practice. One reason for this might be that many programming languages do not offer standard libraries for processing Turtle syntax, thus requiring developers to write their own tools for reading and writing to files. In contrast, essentially every programming language offers libraries for processing XML files, so that application developers can build on existing solutions for storage and pre-processing. As of today, the main syntax for RDF therefore is the XML-based serialization RDF/XML that is introduced in this section. This syntax also offers a number of additional features and abbreviations that can be convenient to represent advanced features which we will encounter later on, but at the same time it imposes some additional technical restrictions. Readers who are not familiar with the basics of XML may wish to consult Appendix A for a quick introduction.

The differences of the data models of XML (trees) and RDF (graphs) are no obstacle, since XML only provides the syntactic structure used for organizing an RDF document. Since XML requires hierarchic structures, the encoding of triples now must as well be hierarchical. The space efficient Turtle descriptions of the previous section have illustrated that it is often useful to assign multiple predicate-object pairs to a single subject. Accordingly, triples in RDF/XML are grouped by their subjects. The following example encodes the RDF graph from Fig. 2.1:

```xml
<?xml version="1.0" encoding="utf-8"?>
<rdf:RDF xmlns:rdf="http://www.w3.org/1999/02/22-rdf-syntax-ns#"
         xmlns:ex ="http://example.org/">

  <rdf:Description rdf:about="http://semantic-web-book.org/uri">
    <ex:publishedBy>
      <rdf:Description rdf:about="http://crcpress.com/uri">
      </rdf:Description>
    </ex:publishedBy>
  </rdf:Description>

</rdf:RDF>
```

After an optional specification of XML version and encoding, the document starts with a first node of type rdf:RDF. This element is generally used as the root of any RDF/XML document. At this place, we also declare the global (XML-)namespaces for ex: and rdf:. Just as in Turtle, namespaces allow us to abbreviate URIs with QNames, this time building upon the existing XML namespace mechanism. While abbreviations for namespaces are still mostly arbitrary, it is a convention to use the prefix rdf: for the RDF namespace as given in the above example. In the following, elements that have a special meaning in the RDF serialization are recognized by that prefix.

Nested within the element rdf:RDF, we find the encoding of the sole triple of the above example. Subject and object are described by elements of the type rdf:Description, where the XML attribute rdf:about defines the identifier of the resource. The predicate of the encoded triple is represented directly as the element ex:publishedBy.

Multiple triples can be encoded by representing each of them by a separate element of type rdf:Description, which may lead to multiple such elements referring to the same subject. Likewise, the order of the triples is of course not important. However, it is also possible to nest elements of type rdf:Description, possibly leading to a more concise serialization. The following example encodes the graph from Fig. 2.3:[3]

```
<rdf:Description rdf:about="http://semantic-web-book.org/uri">
  <ex:title>Foundations of Semantic Web Technologies</ex:title>
  <ex:publishedBy>
    <rdf:Description rdf:about="http://crcpress.com/uri">
      <ex:name>CRC Press</ex:name>
    </rdf:Description>
  </ex:publishedBy>
</rdf:Description>
```

Here we can see how literals are represented simply as the contents of a predicate-element. The name "CRC Press" is given directly by nesting XML elements instead of creating a second top-level subject element for describing `http://crcpress.com/uri`. Some further abbreviations are allowed:

```
<rdf:Description rdf:about="http://semantic-web-book/uri"
              ex:title= "Foundations of Semantic Web Technologies">
  <ex:publishedBy rdf:resource="http://crcpress.com/uri" />
</rdf:Description>
<rdf:Description rdf:about="http://crcpress.com/uri"
                                  ex:Name="CRC Press" />
```

This syntax requires some explanation. First of all, all predicates with literal objects have been encoded as XML attributes. This abbreviation is admissible only for literals – objects referred to by URIs cannot be encoded in this way, since they would then be misinterpreted as literal strings.

Moreover, the element `ex:publishedBy` makes use of the special attribute `rdf:resource`. This directly specifies the object of the triple, such that no further nested element of type `rdf:Description` is necessary. This is the reason why `ex:publishedBy` has no content so that it can be written as an empty-element tag, as opposed to giving separate start and end tags. This shortcut notation is only allowed for URIs, i.e., every value of `rdf:resource` is considered as a URI.

Since we thus avoid a nested description of `http://crcpress.com/uri`, another description appears at the outer level. The predicate `ex:Name` is again encoded as an XML attribute and the otherwise empty description can be closed immediately.

---

[3]In many cases, we show only the interesting parts of an RDF/XML document in examples. The declaration of `rdf:RDF` can always be assumed to be the same as in the initial example on page 28.

We see that RDF/XML provides a multitude of different options for representing RDF. Some of those options stem from the underlying XML syntax. As an example, it is not relevant whether or not an element without contents is encoded by an empty-element tag instead of giving both start and end tags. A larger amount of freedom, however, is provided by RDF since the same triples can be encoded in many different ways. Our previous two examples certainly do not describe the same XML tree, yet they encode the same RDF graph.

W3C Validator The *W3C Validator* is a Web Service that can be employed to check the validity of RDF/XML documents with respect to the official specification. A simple online form is provided to upload XML-encoded RDF which is then validated. Valid documents are processed to extract individual triples and a visualization of the corresponding graph, whereas invalid documents lead to error messages that simplify the diagnosis of problems. This Web Service can also be used to investigate RDF/XML examples given within this book, though it should not be forgotten that many examples are only partial and must be augmented with a suitable `rdf:RDF` declaration to become valid.
The W3C Validator is found at `http://www.w3.org/RDF/Validator/`

2.2.4 RDF in XML: URIs and Other Problems

Namespaces in RDF/XML have been introduced above as a way of abbreviating URIs in the RDF/XML serialization. The truth, however, is that namespaces in RDF/XML are an indispensable part of the encoding rather than an optional convenience. The reason is that RDF/XML requires us to use resource identifiers as names of XML elements and attributes. But all URIs necessarily contain a colon – a symbol that is not allowed in XML names! Using namespaces, we can "hide" a URI's own colon within the declared prefix.

On the other hand, namespaces can only be used for abbreviating XML tags and attributes, but are not allowed within attribute values and plain text contents between XML tags. This is the reason why we used the complete URI `http://semantic-web-book/uri` in all previous examples, instead of employing a QName `book:uri` as in our earlier Turtle examples. An attribute assignment of the form `rdf:about="book:uri"` is not correct, and `book` in this case would be interpreted as the scheme part of a URI but not as an XML namespace prefix.

Thus we are in the unfortunate situation of having to write the same URI differently in different positions of an RDF/XML document. The next section introduces a method that still allows us to at least abbreviate URIs in cases where namespaces cannot be used. XML has a number of further syntactic restrictions that may complicate the encoding of arbitrary RDF graphs. It is, e.g., not allowed to use a hyphen directly after a colon in XML tags, even though hyphens might occur within URIs. It may thus become necessary to declare auxiliary namespaces merely for the purpose of exporting single elements in a valid way.

Another practical problem is that the percent sign % occurs frequently within URLs since it is used to escape forbidden characters. The string %20, e.g., encodes the space character. Just like colon, the percent sign is not allowed in XML tags, and it can happen that existing URLs cannot be used as URIs in RDF. Fortunately, many problems of this kind are already addressed by existing RDF programming libraries, so that application developers do not need to focus on such serialization issues. Yet they should be aware that there are valid URIs that cannot be encoded at all in XML.

2.2.5   Shorter URIs: XML Entities and Relative URIs

In the above examples, we have always used absolute URIs as values of the attributes `rdf:about` and `rdf:resource`, as the use of namespaces would not be admissible in this context. This section discusses two methods for abbreviating such values as well. While these abbreviations are of course optional additions to the basic syntax, they are very widely used and thus indispensable for understanding most of today's RDF documents.

A simple method to abbreviate values in XML is the use of so-called *XML entities*. An entity in XML is a kind of shortcut that can be declared at the beginning of a document, and referred to later in the document instead of giving its complete value. The following is a concrete example of an XML document using this feature:

```
<?xml version="1.0" encoding="utf-8"?> <!DOCTYPE rdf:RDF[
    <!ENTITY book 'http://semantic-web-book.org/'>
]>

<rdf:RDF xmlns:rdf="http://www.w3.org/1999/02/22-rdf-syntax-ns#"
     xmlns:ex ="http://example.org/">

  <rdf:Description rdf:about="&book;uri">
    <ex:title>Foundations of Semantic Web Technologies</ex:title>
  </rdf:Description>

</rdf:RDF>
```

An obvious novelty in this example is the initial entity declaration enclosed in `<!DOCTYPE rdf:RDF[` and `]>`. This part of the XML document constitutes its *document type declaration* which might provide a so-called *Document Type Definition* (DTD). A DTD can be used to declare entities as above, but also to define a number of further restrictions on the contents of the XML document. All document type declarations used in this book, however, are plain entity definitions, so that we can content ourselves with knowing that entities in RDF/XML are defined as above. In our example, the entity defined is called `book` and its value is `http://semantic-web-book.org/`. Further entities could easily be defined by providing additional lines of the form `<!ENTITY name 'value'>`.

We may now refer to our newly defined entity by writing `&book;` as in the value of `rdf:about` above, and the XML document is interpreted just as if we had written the declared value of the entity at this position. Such entity references are allowed in XML attribute values and within plain text data contained in an element, such as the texts used for serializing data literals in Section 2.2.3. Entities cannot be used within names of XML elements and attributes – there we have to stick to the use of namespaces. In our current example, defining a new entity does not actually shorten the document, but usually entities for common URI prefixes lead to much more concise serializations and may also increase readability. XML also provides a small number of pre-defined entities that are useful for encoding certain symbols that would otherwise be confused with parts of the XML syntax. These entities are `&lt;` (<), `&gt;` (>), `&amp;` (&), `&apos;` ('), and `&quot;` (").

There is another common case in which URIs might be abbreviated: in many RDF documents, URIs primarily stem from a common *base namespace*. A website that exports data in RDF, e.g., is likely to use many URIs that begin with the site's domain name. XML has the concept of a *base URI* that can be set for elements in a document using the attribute `xml:base`. Other attributes in the XML document then may, instead of full URIs, use so-called *relative references*. Such entries refer to a full URIs which are obtained by preceding the entries with the given base URI, as illustrated by the following example:

```
<rdf:RDF xmlns:rdf="http://www.w3.org/1999/02/22-rdf-syntax-ns#"
         xmlns:ex ="http://example.org/"
         xml:base ="http://semantic-web-book.org/" >

  <rdf:Description rdf:about="uri">
    <ex:publishedBy rdf:resource="http://crcpress.com/uri" />
  </rdf:Description>

</rdf:RDF>
```

The relative reference `rdf:about="uri"` is thus interpreted as the URI `http://semantic-web-book/uri`. Values of `rdf:resource` or `rdf:datatype` (explained later) can be abbreviated in the same fashion. Relative references are distinguished from full URIs by lacking a scheme part; see Fig. 2.2. It is possible to use relative references even without declaring the intended base URI beforehand: in this case, the base URI of the document – based on the URL it was retrieved from – is used. This mechanism is less robust since locations of documents may change; hence it is suggested to provide explicit base URIs whenever needed.

A second common use of `xml:base` for abbreviating URIs relates to the attribute `rdf:ID`. This attribute can be used just like `rdf:about`, but it always expects a single fragment identifier as its value, whereas complete URIs are not allowed. The full URI is then constructed by using the given value as a fragment for the base URI (which thus should not contain any fragment), i.e. we can obtain the URI by extending the base URI with the symbol # followed by the value of `rdf:ID`.

Thus we find that `rdf:ID="name"` has essentially the same meaning as `rdf:about="#name"`. The most relevant difference of both ways of writing URIs is that every value of `rdf:ID` must be used only once for a given base URI. An RDF/XML document may thus contain one element with a given ID, but it may still contain further elements that refer to the same URI by means of `rdf:about` and `rdf:resource`.

The Turtle syntax for RDF provides a similar support for relative references, which are resolved by using the base URI (URL) of the document. Setting the base URI explicitly is not encompassed by the current specification, even though the syntax `@base` was proposed for this purpose. Overall, relative references in Turtle are of only minor importance since namespace declarations can be used without the restrictions of the XML syntax.

Figure 2.4 provides an overview of the various forms of abbreviation mechanisms that we have introduced for RDF/XML. Note that a principal difference between XML entities and (base) namespaces is that the former can be declared only once for the whole document, whereas the latter may be declared in arbitrary XML start tags or empty-element tags. The namespaces then apply to the element within which they were declared, and to all subelements thereof. Moreover, entities can be used not only for abbreviating URIs but provide shortcuts for arbitrary text content, even within literal values.

2.2.6 Where Do URIs Come From? What Do They Mean?

Does the use of URIs, which is strictly required throughout RDF, allow for a semantically unambiguous interpretation of all RDF-encoded information? The answer is clearly no. It is still possible to use different URIs for the same resource, just as it is still possible to use the same URI for different things. A possible solution for this problem is the use of well-defined *vocabularies*. As in XML, the term vocabulary in RDF is most commonly used to refer to collections of identifiers with a clearly defined meaning. A typical example is provided by RDF itself: the URI

```
http://www.w3.org/1999/02/22-rdf-syntax-ns#Description,
```

Namespace declaration	Usage: `namespace:name` in XML element names
	Declaration: `xml:namespace="`*<uri>*`"` in XML start tags or empty-element tags; declarations affect XML subtree; multiple declarations possible
Entity declaration	Usage: `&entity;` in XML attribute values or character content (RDF literal values) of elements
	Declaration: `<!ENTITY entity '`*text*`'>` in initial `DOCTYPE` declaration; declaration affects whole document; only one declaration possible
Predefined entities	Usage: `&lt;`, `&gt;`, `&amp;`, `&apos;`, or `&quot;` in XML attribute values or character content (RDF literal values) of elements
	Declaration: predefined in XML, no declaration
Base namespace	Usage: non-URI `name` as value for `rdf:about`, `rdf:resource`, `rdf:ID`, or `rdf:datatype`
	Declaration: `xml:base="`*<uri>*`"` in XML start tags or empty-element tags; declarations affect XML subtree; multiple declarations possible

FIGURE 2.4: Summary of abbreviation mechanisms in RDF/XML

e.g., has a generally accepted well-defined meaning which applications may take into account.

But vocabularies are not just used to define the RDF/XML syntax as such; they are also commonly used to describe information. An example of a particularly popular vocabulary is *FOAF* (*Friend Of A Friend*), which defines URIs to describe people and their relationships (see Section 9.1.2 for details). Even though FOAF is not specified by an official standardization authority, its URIs are sufficiently well known to avoid confusion. Both FOAF and RDF itself illustrate that the intended use and meaning of vocabularies are typically not encoded in a machine-readable way.

One of the major misconceptions regarding the Semantic Web is the belief that semantic technologies enable computers to truly *understand* complex concepts such as "person." The unambiguous assignment of URIs indeed allows us to refer to such concepts, and to use them in a multitude of semantic relationships – actually comprehending the contents of the encoded statements, however, is still the task of the human user. This should be obvious based on our daily experiences of the capabilities and limitations of today's computers, but new technologies often are accompanied by a certain amount of inflated expectations. It is still possible to describe a certain amount of complex relationships that may refer to a certain vocabulary in a way that is readable by machines: this is the main aim of the *ontology languages* RDF Schema and OWL that we consider later on.

In many cases, a vocabulary for a certain topic area is not readily available, and it is clearly never possible to assign URIs to all conceivable resources. Therefore it is required to introduce new URIs on demand, and various proposals and guidelines have been developed for coining new URIs on the Semantic Web. It also makes sense to take the relationship between URLs and URIs into account in this context.

In some situations, very concrete guidelines are available for creating suitable URIs. There is, e.g., an official policy for turning phone numbers into URIs using the scheme `tel`. Similar proposals exist for deriving URIs for books and journals from the ISSN or ISBN numbers.

In numerous other cases, however, it is required to coin completely new URIs. A first objective in this case must be to ensure that the chosen URI is not used elsewhere, possibly with a different intended meaning. This is often surprisingly easy to do by taking advantage of the existing hierarchic mechanisms for managing URLs. By choosing URIs that – when viewed as URLs – refer to locations on the Web over which one has complete control, one can usually avoid clashes with existing URIs. Moreover, it is then possible to make a document available at the corresponding location, providing an authoritative explanation of the intended meaning. The information about the proper usage of a URI thus becomes accessible worldwide.

An important related aspect is the distinction between Web pages and other (abstract) resources. The URL `http://en.wikipedia.org/wiki/Othello`, e.g., at first appears to be a suitable URI for Shakespeare's drama, since it contains an unambiguous description of this resource. If an RDF document assigns an author to this URI, however, it is not clear whether this refers to the existing HTML page or to the drama. One thus could be led to believe that Shakespeare has edited pages on Wikipedia, or that Othello was written collaboratively by authors such as "*User:The_ Drama_ Llama*"! It is thus obvious why URLs of existing documents are not well-suited as URIs for abstract concepts.

On the other hand, we would still like to construct URIs that point to existing Web documents. For users of RDF, it would certainly be useful if URIs could be used to learn more about their intended usage – like an inherent user documentation closely tied to any RDF document. But how can this be accomplished without using existing URLs? One option is the use of fragment identifiers. By writing, e.g., `http://en.wikipedia.org/wiki/Othello#uri` one does not use the URL of an existing Web document (since the fragment "uri" is not defined on the page retrieved at the base URL). Yet, when resolving this URI in a browser, one obtains the same explanatory document as before. This solution is also suggested by the possibility of using relative references together with the attribute `rdf:ID` explained earlier.

An alternative option is the use of redirects: even if no document is found at a given URL, a Web server may redirect users to an alternative page. This is a core functionality of the HTTP protocol. Since the user-side application notices any such HTTP redirect, the retrieved page can still be distinguished from the resource that the original URI referred to. The automatic redirect also has the advantage that a single URI may redirect either to a human-readable HTML description, or to a machine-readable RDF document – the server may select which of those is appropriate based on information that the client provides when requesting the data. This method is known as *content negotiation*. An example is the URI `http://semanticweb.org/id/Markus`: when viewed in a browser, it provides details on the encoded resource; when accessed by an RDF-processing tool such as Tabulator,[4] it returns RDF-based metadata.

The above technical tricks allow us to create unambiguous URIs that link to their own documentation, and this explains to some extent why many URIs still refer to common URL schemes such as `http`.

---

[4]An RDF browsing tool; see `http://www.w3.org/2005/ajar/tab`.

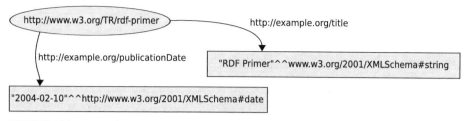

FIGURE 2.5: An RDF graph with typed literals

2.3 Advanced Features

We already have learned about all the basic features of RDF. There are, however, a number of additional and derived expressive means, which are highly important in applications. This section introduces a number of these advanced features in detail. In each case, we consider presentations using RDF graphs, Turtle syntax, and RDF/XML.

2.3.1 Datatypes in RDF

We have already seen in Section 2.1.3 that RDF allows us to describe data values by means of literals. So far, however, all literals we considered have been nothing more than mere character strings. Practical applications of course require many further datatypes, e.g., to denote numbers or points in time. Datatypes usually have a major effect on the interpretation of a given value. A typical example is the task of sorting data values: The natural order of the values "10", "02", "2" is completely different depending on whether we interpret them as numbers or as strings. The latter are usually sorted alphabetically, yielding "02" < "10" < "2", while the former would be sorted numerically to obtain "2" = "02" < "10".

RDF therefore allows literals to carry an explicit datatype. Staying true to our established principles, each datatype is uniquely identified by a URI, and might be chosen rather arbitrarily. In practice, however, it is certainly most useful to refer to datatype URIs that are widely known and supported by many software tools. For this reason, RDF suggests the use of XML Schema. Figure 2.5 illustrates how additional datatype information might be added to an RDF graph. The subject of this example is the RDF Primer document, identified by its actual URL, for which a title text and publication date are provided. These data values are specified by a literal string in quotation marks, followed by ^^ and the URI of some datatype. As datatypes, we have used "string" for simple character sequences, and "date" for calendar days.

It can be seen from the graphical representation that typed literals in RDF are considered as single elements. Any such literal therefore essentially be-

haves just like a single untyped literal. From this we can readily derive the
Turtle syntax for the RDF document in Fig. 2.5:

```
@prefix xsd: <http://www.w3.org/2001/XMLSchema#> .
<http://www.w3.org/TR/rdf-primer>
        <http://example.org/title>  "RDF Primer"^^xsd:string ;
        <http://example.org/publicationDate> "2004-02-10"^^xsd:date .
```

As the example shows, datatype URIs in Turtle can be abbreviated using namespaces. If they were written as complete URIs, they would need
to be enclosed in angular brackets just as any other URI. The representation in RDF/XML is slightly different, using an additional XML attribute
rdf:datatype:

```
<rdf:Description rdf:about="http://www.w3.org/TR/rdf-primer">
  <ex:title rdf:datatype="http://www.w3.org/2001/XMLSchema#string">
    RDF Primer
  </ex:title>
  <ex:publicationDate
            rdf:datatype="http://www.w3.org/2001/XMLSchema#date">
    2004-02-10
  </ex:publicationDate>
</rdf:Description>
```

The general restrictions on the use of namespaces in XML also apply to the
previous example. Since datatype URIs are specified as XML attribute values,
they cannot be abbreviated by namespaces. We may, however, introduce XML
entities for arriving at a more concise serialization.

To obtain a better understanding of RDF's datatype mechanism, it makes
sense to have a closer look at the meaning of datatypes. Intuitively, we would
expect any datatype to describe a certain *value space*, such as, e.g., the natural
numbers. This fixes the set of possible values that literals of a datatype denote.
A second important component is the set of all admissible literal strings. This
so-called *lexical space* of a datatype enables implementations to recognize
whether or not a given literal syntactically belongs to the specified datatype.
The third and final component of each datatype then is a well-defined mapping
from the lexical space to the value space, assigning a concrete value to every
admissible literal string.

As an example, we consider the datatype *decimal* that is defined in XML
Schema. The value space of this datatype is the set of all rational numbers that
can be written as finite decimal numbers. We thus exclude irrational numbers
like π, and rational numbers like $1/3$ that would require infinitely many digits

in decimal notation. Accordingly, the lexical space consists of all character strings that contain only numerals 0 to 9, at most one occurrence of ., and an optional initial symbol + or -. The mapping between lexical space and value space is the well-known interpretation of decimal numbers as rationals. The literal strings 3.14, +03.14, and 3.14000, e.g., are multiple possible ways to refer to the rational number 3.14. It is common in many datatypes that a single value can be denoted in multiple different ways. Applications that support a datatype thus recognize syntactically different RDF literals as being semantically equal.

Most of the common XML datatypes allow for a meaningful interpretation in RDF, yet the RDF specification leaves it to individual implementations to decide which datatypes are supported. In particular, a software tool can conform to the RDF specification without recognizing any additional XML datatypes.

The sole exception to this general principle is RDF's only built-in datatype rdf:XMLLiteral. This datatype allows the embedding of well-formed XML snippets as literal values in RDF. As such, the datatype specifically addresses a possible use case of RDF/XML where it might be convenient to use well-formed XML directly in the place of literal values.

The datatype rdf:XMLLiteral is most commonly used together with an additional function for pre-processing and normalizing XML data. This is achieved by means of the attribute rdf:parseType, which we shall also encounter in various other contexts later on:

```
<rdf:Description rdf:about="http://semantic-web-book/uri">
   <ex:title rdf:parseType="Literal">
      Foundations of
      <br />
      <b>Semantic Web Technologies</b>
   </ex:title>
</rdf:Description>
```

In this example, we have embedded text that uses HTML mark-up into an RDF document. Due to the setting rdf:parseType="Literal", the given XML fragment is normalized internally, and transformed into a literal of type rdf:XMLLiteral. Even though XML snippets that are used in this way need not be complete XML documents, it is required that their opening and closing tags are balanced. If this cannot be guaranteed in an application, it is also common to embed XML fragments into RDF/XML as string literals, using pre-defined entities like & and < to replace XML syntax that would otherwise be confused with the remainder of the RDF document.

At this point we should also make sure that we have not allowed ourselves to be confused by some rather similar terms which have been introduced: RDF literals generally are syntactic identifiers for data values in RDF, whereas the value `Literal` of the attribute `rdf:parseType` merely leads to the creation of one particular kind of literals belonging to the datatype `rdf:XMLLiteral`.

2.3.2   Language Settings and Datatypes

Now that we are more familiar with the comprehensive datatype system of RDF and XML Schema, it is in order to take another look at data values in RDF. The first obvious question is which datatype literals without any type assignment actually have. In fact, such *untyped literals* simply have no type at all, even though they behave very similarly to typed literals of type `xsd:string` for most practical purposes.

An important difference between typed and untyped literals is revealed when introducing language information into RDF. XML in general supports the specification of language information that tells applications whether part of an XML document's content is written in a particular (natural) language. This is achieved by means of the attribute `xml:lang`. A typical example is the language setting in (X)HTML documents as found on the Web, which often contain attribute assignments such as `xml:lang="en"` or `xml:lang="de-ch"` in their initial `html` tag. Not surprisingly, such language information in XML is managed in a hierarchical way, i.e. all child elements of an element with a language setting inherit this setting, unless they supply another value for `xml:lang`.

Language information can also be provided in RDF/XML, but this is semantically relevant only for untyped literals. For instance, one could write the following:

```
<rdf:Description rdf:about="http://www.w3.org/TR/rdf-primer">
   <ex:title xml:lang="fr">Initiation à RDF</ex:title>
   <ex:title xml:lang="en">RDF Primer</ex:title>
</rdf:Description>
```

In serializations of RDF other than RDF/XML, language information is supplied by means of the symbols @. In Turtle this might look as follows:

```
<http://www.w3.org/TR/rdf-primer> <http://example.org/title>
   "Initiation à RDF"@fr, "RDF Primer"@en .
```

This syntax again shows that language settings are really part of the data value in RDF. The above example thus describes a graph of two triples with the same subject and predicate. Likewise, in the graphical representation of RDF, the labels of literal nodes are simply extended to include language settings just as in Turtle.

Similar yet distinct

Both language settings and datatypes in RDF are considered to be part of literals, and their absence or presence thus leads to different literals. This might sometimes lead to confusion in the users of RDF, and it may also impose some challenges when merging datasets. Consider, e.g., the following RDF description in Turtle:

```
@prefix xsd: <http://www.w3.org/2001/XMLSchema#> .
<http://crcpress.com/uri>  <http://example.org/Name>  "CRC Press" ,
                                      "CRC Press"@en ,
                                 "CRC Press"^^xsd:string .
```

This example does indeed encode three different triples. Literals with language settings always constitute a pair of a literal value and a language code, and thus can never be the same as any literal without language setting. The untyped literal `"CRC Press"`, according to the RDF specification, represents "itself", i.e. there is no distinction between lexical space and value space. Whether or not the untyped value `"CRC Press"` is part of the value space of `xsd:string` of course is not addressed in the RDF specification, since XML Schema datatypes are not part of this standard.

In practice, however, many applications expect the two literals without language settings to be equal, which probably agrees with the intuition of many users.

As mentioned above, language settings are only allowed for untyped literals. The justification for this design of the current RDF standard was that the semantics of typed data values is not dependent on any language. The number 23, e.g., should have the same (mathematical) meaning in any language. This view was also extended to strings: values of type `xsd:string` therefore are indeed assumed to encode a sequence of characters, not a text of a concrete language. Another possibly unexpected consequence of this decision is that values of type `rdf:XMLLiteral` do not inherit language settings from their parent elements, even though this would be assumed if the RDF/XML document was considered as XML. RDF thus introduces an exception to the otherwise strictly hierarchical scope of `xml:lang` in XML.

2.3.3 Many-Valued Relationships

So far, we have represented only very simple binary relationships between resources, thus essentially describing a directed graph. But does such a simple graph structure also allow for the representation of more complex data structures? In this section, we will see how relationships between more than two resources can indeed be encoded in RDF.

Let us first consider an example. The following excerpt from an RDF

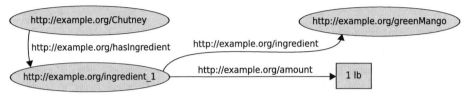

FIGURE 2.6:   Representing many-valued relationships in RDF

description formalizes ingredients of a cooking recipe:

```
@prefix ex: <http://example.org/> .
ex:Chutney  ex:hasIngredient   "1lb green mango",
                               "1tsp. Cayenne pepper" .
```

This encoding, however, is not really satisfying, since ingredients and their amounts are modeled as plain strings of text. Thus it is, e.g., not possible to query for all recipes that contain green mango, unless the whole text including the specified amount is queried. It would therefore be more useful to describe ingredients and their amounts in separate resources. Let us attempt the following modeling:

```
@prefix ex: <http://example.org/> .
ex:Chutney  ex:ingredient   ex:greenMango;    ex:amount    "1lb" ;
            ex:ingredient   ex:CayennePepper; ex:amount    "1tsp." .
```

It is not hard to see that this encoding is even less suitable than our initial approach. While ingredients and amounts are described separately, there is no relationship at all between the individual triples. We could therefore as well be dealing with 1 tsp. of green mango and 1 lb of Cayenne pepper – a rather dangerous ambiguity! An alternative approach could be to model amounts via triples that use ingredients as their subjects. This would obviously clarify the association of amounts and ingredients, e.g., when writing ex:greenMango ex:amount "1lb". Yet this attempt would again yield undesired results (can you see why?[5]).

We are thus dealing with a true three-valued relationship between a recipe, an ingredient, and an amount – one also speaks of ternary (and generally *n-ary*) relations. RDF obviously cannot represent relationships with three or more values directly, but they can be described by introducing so-called *auxiliary nodes* into the graph. Consider the graph in Fig. 2.6. The node

---

[5]Hint: Try to encode multiple recipes that require the same ingredient but in different amounts.

ex:Ingredient1 in this example plays the role of an explicit connection between recipe, ingredient, and amount. Further nodes could be introduced for all additional ingredients to link the respective components to each other.

As can be readily seen, this method can generally be used to connect an arbitrary number of objects to a subject. This, however, requires the introduction of several additional URIs. On the one hand, the auxiliary node itself needs an identifier; on the other hand, additional triples with new predicate names are created. Consequently, our example now contains two predicates ex:hasIngredient and ex:ingredient. Our choice of names in this case reflects the fact that the object of ex:ingredient plays a particularly prominent role among the many values in our example relationship. RDF offers a reserved predicate rdf:value that may be used to highlight a particular object of a many-valued relation as a "main" value. Instead of the graph of Fig. 2.6, we may thus choose to write:

```
@prefix ex:   <http://example.org/> .
@prefix rdf:  <http://www.w3.org/1999/02/22-rdf-syntax-ns#> .
ex:Chutney        ex:hasIngredient  ex:ingredient1 .
ex:ingredient1    rdf:value         ex:greenMango;
                  ex:amount         "1lb" .
```

The predicate rdf:value does not have a particular formal semantics. It is merely a hint to applications that a particular value of a many-valued relationship could be considered as its primary value. Most of today's applications, however, do not heed this additional information. Since, moreover, rdf:value does not play well with the ontology language OWL DL that we introduce in Chapter 4, it is often the best choice to use application-specific predicate names instead.

2.3.4   Blank Nodes

As shown in the previous section, modeling many-valued relationships may require the introduction of auxiliary nodes. Such nodes typically do not refer to resources that were meant to be described explicitly in the first place, and rather introduce helper resources with a merely structural function. It is therefore rarely useful to refer to such resources globally by means of a specific URI. In such cases, RDF allows us to introduce nodes without any URI, called *blank nodes* or simply *bnodes*.

An example for an RDF graph with a blank node is given in Fig. 2.7. This graph essentially describes the same structure as the graph in Fig. 2.6. The second RDF document, however, merely states that there is some resource taking the place of the blank node, but without providing a URI for referring to this resource. As the name "blank node" suggests, this feature is only

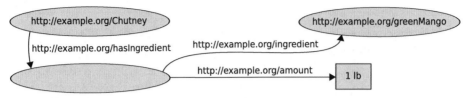

FIGURE 2.7:   Representing auxiliary resources by blank nodes

available for subject and objects of RDF triples. Predicates (i.e. edges) must alway be specified by URIs.

Blank nodes cannot be addressed globally by means of URIs, and they do not carry any additional information within RDF graphs. Yet, the syntactic serialization of RDF necessitates referring to particular blank nodes at least in the context of the given document. The reason is that a single blank node may appear as a subject or object in arbitrarily many triples. Therefore, there must be a way for multiple triples to refer to the same blank node. To this end, blank nodes in a document may be denoted by means of (node) IDs. In RDF/XML this is done by using the attribute `rdf:nodeID` instead of `rdf:about`, `rdf:ID` or `rdf:resource`. The RDF/XML serialization for the graph in Fig. 2.7 could thus be as follows:

```
<rdf:Description rdf:about="http://example.org/Chutney">
   <ex:hasIngredient rdf:nodeID="id1" />
</rdf:Description>
<rdf:Description rdf:nodeID="id1">
   <ex:ingredient rdf:resource="http://example.org/greenMango" />
   <ex:amount>1lb</ex:amount>
</rdf:Description>
```

The label `id1` in this example is only relevant for the given document. Within other documents, in contrast, the same id might well refer to different resources. In particular, the semantics of an RDF document is not changed if all occurrences of a given node id are replaced by another id, as long as the latter was not used yet within this document. This reflects the fact that node IDs are only a syntactic tool to serialize blank nodes. If the given usage of a blank node does not actually require the use of this node in multiple positions, it is also allowed to omit the attribute `rdf:nodeID` entirely. This can be particularly useful when nesting descriptions in RDF/XML. The following example shows yet another possibility of introducing blank nodes without providing an id:

```
<rdf:Description rdf:about="http://example.org/Chutney">
   <ex:hasIngredient rdf:parseType="Resource">
     <ex:ingredient rdf:resource="http://example.org/greenMango" />
     <ex:amount>1lb</ex:amount>
   </ex:hasIngredient>
</rdf:Description>
```

The value `Resource` of the attribute `rdf:parseType` in this case leads to the automatic creation of a new blank node which does not have a node id within the given document. We already encountered `rdf:parseType` earlier with the value `Literal`, where a literal node of type `XMLLiteral` was newly created. In general, `rdf:parseType` modifies the way in which parts of the XML document are interpreted, usually leading to the generation of additional triples that have not been specified directly. All uses of `rdf:parseType` – including those discussed further below – can be avoided by serializing the encoded triples directly. Yet, such "syntactic sugar" is often rather useful for enhancing a document's readability.

In Turtle and similar triple-based serializations, blank nodes are encoded by using an underscore instead of a namespace prefix:

```
@prefix ex:   <http://example.org/> .
ex:Chutney    ex:hasIngredient  _:id1 .
_:id1         ex:ingredient  ex:greenMango;   ex:amount   "1lb" .
```

The given node id again is relevant only for the current document. Turtle allows us to abbreviate nested blank nodes in a way that is structurally similar to RDF/XML:

```
@prefix ex:   <http://example.org/> .
ex:Chutney    ex:hasIngredient
              [ ex:ingredient  ex:greenMango;   ex:amount   "1lb" ] .
```

The predicates and objects within square brackets refer to an implicit blank node without an id. The previous Turtle document thus corresponds to the same RDF graph structure as in the earlier examples. As a special case, it is also possible to write [] for a blank node that does not have an explicit id.

2.4   Simple Ontologies in RDF Schema

In the previous sections, we explained how propositions about single resources can be made in RDF. Essentially, three basic kinds of descriptive elements were used for this: we specified *individuals* (e.g., the authors of this textbook, a publisher or a cooking recipe), that in one way or the other were put into *relation* to each other. More casually, we learned that it is possible to assign *types* to literals and resources, thereby stating that they belong to a class of entities sharing certain characteristics (like natural numbers or ordered lists).

When describing new domains of interest, one would usually introduce new terms not only for individuals (like "Sebastian Rudolph" or "Karlsruhe Institute of Technology") and their relations (such as "employed by") but also for types or classes (e.g., "person", "university", "institution"). As pointed out in Section 2.2.6, a repertoire of such terms referring to individuals, relations and classes is usually called a vocabulary.

When introducing and employing such a vocabulary, the user will naturally have a concrete idea about the used terms' meanings. For example, it is intuitively clear that every university has to be an institution or that only persons can be employed by an institution.

From the "perspective" of a computer system, however, all the terms introduced by the user are merely character strings without any prior fixed meaning. Thus, the aforementioned semantic interrelations have to be explicitly communicated to the system in some format in order to enable it to draw conclusions that rely on this kind of human background knowledge.

By virtue of RDF Schema (short RDFS), a further part of the W3C RDF recommendation which we will deal with in the following sections, this kind of background information – so-called *terminological knowledge* or alternatively *schema knowledge* – about the terms used in the vocabulary can be specified.

In the first place, RDFS is nothing but another particular RDF vocabulary. Consequently, every RDFS document is a well-formed RDF document. This ensures that it can be read and processed by all tools that support just RDF, whereby, however, a part of the meaning specifically defined for RDFS (the RDFS semantics) is lost.

RDFS – whose name space `http://www.w3.org/2000/01/rdf-schema#` is usually abbreviated by `rdfs:` – does not introduce a topic-specific vocabulary for particular application domains like, e.g., FOAF does. Rather, the intention of RDFS is to provide generic language constructs by means of which a user-defined vocabulary can be semantically characterized. Moreover, this characterization is done *inside* the document, allowing an RDFS document to – roughly speaking – carry its own semantics. This allows for defining a new vocabulary and (at least partially) specifying its "meaning" in the document without necessitating a modification of the processing software's program logic. Indeed, any software with RDFS support automatically treats any RDFS-defined vocabulary in a semantically correct way.

The capability of specifying this kind of schema knowledge renders RDFS a knowledge representation language or *ontology language* as it provides means for describing a considerable part of the semantic interdependencies which hold in a domain of interest.

Let us dwell for a moment on the term *ontology language*. In Section 1.1 we have already discussed the notion *ontology* and its philosophical origin. On page 2 we said that in computer science, an ontology is a description of knowledge about a domain of interest, the core of which is a machine-processable specification with a formally defined meaning. It is in exactly this sense that RDFS is an ontology language: An RDFS document is a machine-processable specification which describes knowledge about some domain of interest. Furthermore, RDFS documents have a formally defined meaning, given by the formal semantics of RDFS. This formal semantics will be explained in Chapter 3, although the most important aspects of it will become intuitively clear in the following, when we introduce RDFS.

Let us remark that RDFS, despite its usefulness as an ontology language, also has its limitations, and we will explicate this in Section 3.4. Hence, RDFS is sometimes categorized as a representation language for so-called *lightweight* ontologies. Therefore, more sophisticated applications require more expressive representation languages such as OWL which will be discussed in Chapters 4 and 5, yet usually the higher expressivity comes at the expense of speed: the runtime of algorithms for automated inference tends to increase drastically when more expressive formalisms are used.

Hence the question which formalism to use should always be considered depending on the requirements of the addressed task; in many cases an RDFS representation might be sufficient for the intended purposes.[6]

2.4.1 Classes and Instances

Certainly, one basic functionality that any reasonable knowledge specification formalism should provide is the possibility to "type" resources, i.e. to mark them as elements of a certain aggregation. In RDF, this can be done via the predicate `rdf:type`. Generally, the predefined URI `rdf:type` is used to mark resources as *instances* of a *class* (i.e. belonging to that class). In order to clearly separate semantics and syntax, we always use the term "class" to denote a set of resources (being entities of the real world), whereas URIs which represent or refer to a class are called *class names*.

---

[6]This fact has been put into the common phrase "A little semantics goes a long way" coined by James Hendler.

As an example, it would be straightforward to describe this book as a textbook (which means: a member of the class of all textbooks):

```
book:uri    rdf:type    ex:Textbook .
```

This example also illustrates that it is possible (and, depending on the application domain, very reasonable) to introduce new, user-defined class names.

Obviously, there is no syntactic way of distinguishing URIs representing individuals (like `book:uri`) and class names (such as `ex:Textbook`). Hence, a single URI does not provide direct information whether it refers to a single object or a class. In fact, such a clear distinction is not always possible, even for some real world terms. Even with human background knowledge, it might be hard to decide whether the URI `http://www.un.org/#URI` denotes an individual single organization or the class of all its member states.

Nevertheless, it might be desirable to enforce some clarification by making a definite modeling decision in the context of an RDFS document. Therefore, RDFS provides the possibility to indicate class names by explicitly "typing" them as classes. In other words: it can be specified that, e.g., the class `ex:Textbook` belongs to the class of all classes. This "meta-class" is predefined in the RDFS vocabulary and denoted by the URI `rdfs:Class`. As we already know, class membership is expressed via `rdf:type`, hence the following triple characterizes the URI `ex:Textbook` as class name:

```
ex:Textbook    rdf:type    rdfs:Class .
```

On the other hand, the fact that `ex:Textbook` denotes a class is also an implicit but straightforward consequence of using it as object of a typing statement, hence, the preceding triple also follows from the triple

```
book:uri    rdf:type    ex:Textbook .
```

As an additional remark of little practical relevance, note that the class of all classes is obviously itself a class and hence contained in itself as an element. Therefore the proposition encoded by the following triple is always valid:

```
rdfs:Class    rdf:type    rdfs:Class .
```

Besides `rdfs:Class`, there are a few further class names predefined in the RDF and RDFS vocabularies and carrying a fixed meaning:

- `rdfs:Resource` denotes the class of all resources (i.e. for all elements of the considered domain of interest).

- `rdf:Property` refers to the class of all properties, and therefore to all resources that stand for relations.

- `rdf:XMLLiteral` has already been introduced as the only predefined datatype in RDF(S). At the same time, this name denotes the class of all values of this datatype.

- `rdfs:Literal` represents the class of all literal values, which implies that it comprises all datatypes as subclasses.

- The class denoted by `rdfs:Datatype` contains all datatypes as elements, for example, the class of XML literals. Note that this is another example of a class of classes (and hence a subclass of the `rdfs:Class` class).

- The class names `rdf:Bag`, `rdf:Alt`, `rdf:Seq` and `rdfs:Container` are used to declare lists and will be treated in more detail in Section 2.5.1.

- `rdfs:ContainerMembershipProperty`, denoting the class of contained-ness properties, will be dealt with in Section 2.5.1 as well.

- The class name `rdf:List` is used to indicate the class of all collections. In particular, the empty collection denoted by `rdf:nil` is an element of this class.

- `rdf:Statement` refers to the class of reified triples and will be dealt with in Section 2.5.2.

All those class names also exhibit a common notational convention: URIs representing classes are usually capitalized, whereas names for instances and properties are written in lower case. Note also that the choice for class names is not limited to nouns; it might be reasonable to introduce classes for qualities (expressed by adjectives) as well, e.g., `ex:Organic` for all organic compounds or `ex:Red` for all red things.

Finally, it is important to be aware that class membership is not exclusive: naturally, a resource can belong to several different classes, as illustrated by the following two triples:

```
book:uri    rdf:type    ex:Textbook .
book:uri    rdf:type    ex:WorthReading .
```

2.4.2 Subclasses and Class Hierarchies

Suppose an RDFS document contains one single triple referring to this textbook:

```
book:uri    rdf:type    ex:Textbook .
```

If we now searched for instances of the class of books denoted by ex:Book, the URI book:uri denoting "Foundations of Semantic Web Technologies" would not be among the results. Of course, human background knowledge entails that every textbook is a book and consequently every instance of the ex:Textbook class is also an instance of the ex:Book class. Yet, an automatic system not equipped with this kind of linguistic background knowledge is not able to come up with this conclusion. So what to do?

There would be the option to simply add the following triple to the document, explicitly stating an additional class membership:

```
book:uri    rdf:type    ex:Book .
```

In this case, however, the same problem would occur again and again for any further resource typed as textbook which might be added to the RDFS document. Consequently, for *any* triple occurring in the document and having the form

```
u    rdf:type    ex:Textbook .
```

the according triple

```
u    rdf:type    ex:Book .
```

would have to be explicitly added. Moreover, those steps would have to be repeated for any new information entered into the document. Besides the workload caused by this, it would also lead to an undesirable and unnecessary verbosity of the specification.

Clearly, a much more reasonable and less laborious way would be to just specify (one may think of it as a kind of "macro") that *every* textbook is also a book. This obviously means that the class of all textbooks is comprised by the class of all books, which is alternatively expressed by calling textbook a *subclass* of book or equivalently, calling book a *superclass* of textbook. Indeed, the RDFS vocabulary provides a predefined way to explicitly declare this subclass relationship between two classes, namely, via the predicate `rdfs:subClassOf`. The fact that any textbook is also a book can hence be succinctly stated by the following triple:

```
ex:Textbook    rdfs:subClassOf    ex:Book .
```

This enables any software that supports the RDFS semantics (see Chapter 3) to identify the individual denoted by `book:uri` as a book even without it being explicitly typed as such.

It is common and expedient to use subclass statements not only for sporadically declaring such interdependencies, but to model whole *class hierarchies* by exhaustively specifying the generalization-specification order of all classes in the domain of interest. For instance, the classification started in the example above could be extended by stating that book is a subclass of print media and the latter a superclass of journal:

```
ex:Book       rdfs:subClassOf    ex:PrintMedia .
ex:Journal    rdfs:subClassOf    ex:PrintMedia .
```

In accordance with the intuition, the RDFS semantics also implements transitivity of the subclass relationships, i.e. roughly speaking: subclasses of subclasses are subclasses. Therefore, from the triples written down in this section, the following triple – though not explicitly stated – can be deduced:

```
ex:Textbook    rdfs:subClassOf    ex:PrintMedia .
```

Moreover, the subclass relationship is defined to be reflexive, meaning that every class is its own subclass (clearly, the class of all books comprises the class of all books). Thus, once it is known that `ex:Book` refers to a class, the following triple can be concluded:

```
ex:Book    rdfs:subClassOf    ex:Book .
```

This fact also enables us to model the proposition that two classes contain the same individuals (in other words: they are extensionally equivalent) by establishing a mutual subclass relationship:

```
ex:MorningStar    rdfs:subClassOf    ex:EveningStar .
ex:EveningStar    rdfs:subClassOf    ex:MorningStar .
```

The most popular and elaborated class hierarchies can certainly be found in the area of biology, where – following the classical systematics – living beings are grouped into kingdoms, phyla, classes (as a biological term), orders, families, genus and species. From the RDFS document from Fig. 2.8, we can deduce that the individual Sebastian Rudolph is not only a human but also a mammal. Likewise, by the deducible membership in the class of primates, he logically makes a monkey of himself.

Documents containing only class hierarchies are usually referred to as *taxonomies* and subclass-superclass dependencies are often called taxonomic relations. Certainly, one reason why this kind of knowledge modeling is so intuitive is its closeness to human conceptual thinking. In most cases, a class hierarchy with sub- and superclasses can be conceived as a conceptual hierarchy with subordinate and superordinate concepts or, using common linguistic terminology: hyponyms and hypernyms.

2.4.3 Properties

A special role is played by those URIs used in triples in the place of the predicate. Examples from previous sections include ex:hasIngredient, ex:publishedBy and rdf:type. Although those terms are represented by URIs and hence denote resources, it remains a bit unclear how to concretely interpret them. A (or *the*) "publishedBy" can hardly be physically encountered in everyday life; therefore it seems inappropriate to consider it as class or individual. In the end, these "predicate URIs" describe relations between "proper" resources or individuals (referenced by subject and object in an RDF triple). As the technical term for such relations, we will use *property*.

In mathematics, a relation is commonly represented as the set of the pairs interlinked by that relation. According to that, the meaning of the URI ex:isMarriedTo would be just the set of all married couples. In this respect, properties resemble classes more than single individuals.

For expressing that a URI refers to a property (or relation), the RDF vocabulary provides the class name rdf:Property which by definition denotes the class of all properties. The fact that ex:publishedBy refers to a property can now again be stated by assigning the corresponding type:

```
ex:publishedBy   rdf:type   rdf:Property .
```

Note that rdf:Property itself denotes a class and not a property. It just contains properties as instances. Finally, in addition to explicitly being typed as such, a URI can also be identified as property name by its occurrence as predicate of a triple. Therefore, the RDFS semantics ensures that the above triple is also a consequence of any triple like

```
<?xml version="1.0" encoding="utf-8"?> <!DOCTYPE rdf:RDF[
        <!ENTITY ex 'http://example.org/'>
]>

<rdf:RDF
  xmlns:rdf="http://www.w3.org/1999/02/22-rdf-syntax-ns#"
  xmlns:rdfs="http://www.w3.org/2000/01/rdf-schema#"
  xmlns:ex="http://www.semanticweb-grundlagen.de/Beispiele#">

  <rdfs:Class rdf:about="&ex;Animalia">
      <rdfs:label xml:lang="en">animals</rdfs:label>
  </rdfs:Class>

  <rdfs:Class rdf:about="&ex;Chordata">
      <rdfs:label xml:lang="en">chordates</rdfs:label>
      <rdfs:subClassOf rdfs:resource="&ex;Animalia" />
  </rdfs:Class>

  <rdfs:Class rdf:about="&ex;Mammalia">
      <rdfs:label xml:lang="en">mammals</rdfs:label>
      <rdfs:subClassOf rdfs:resource="&ex;Chordata" />
  </rdfs:Class>

  <rdfs:Class rdf:about="&ex;Primates">
      <rdfs:label xml:lang="en">primates</rdfs:label>
      <rdfs:subClassOf rdfs:resource="&ex;Mammalia" />
  </rdfs:Class>

  <rdfs:Class rdf:about="&ex;Hominidae">
      <rdfs:label xml:lang="en">great apes</rdfs:label>
      <rdfs:subClassOf rdfs:resource="&ex;Primates" />
  </rdfs:Class>

  <rdfs:Class rdf:about="&ex;Homo">
      <rdfs:label xml:lang="en">humans</rdfs:label>
      <rdfs:subClassOf rdfs:resource="&ex;Hominidae" />
  </rdfs:Class>

  <rdfs:Class rdf:about="&ex;HomoSapiens">
      <rdfs:label xml:lang="en">modern humans</rdfs:label>
      <rdfs:subClassOf rdfs:resource="&ex;Homo" />
  </rdfs:Class>

  <ex:HomoSapiens rdf:about="&ex;SebastianRudolph" />
</rdf:RDF>
```

FIGURE 2.8:   Example for class hierarchies in RDFS

```
book:uri  ex:publishedBy  crc:uri .
```

2.4.4   Subproperties and Property Hierarchies

In the previous section, we argued that properties can be conceived as sets of individual pairs and hence exhibit some similarity to classes. Thus, one might wonder whether modeling constructs in analogy to subclass relationships would also make sense for properties. This is indeed the case: RDFS allows for the specification of *subproperties*. For example, the property denoted by the URI ex:isHappilyMarriedTo is certainly a subproperty of the one ex:isMarriedTo refers to, as the happily married couples form a (most probably even proper) subset of all married couples. This connection can be declared as follows:

```
ex:isHappilyMarriedTo  rdf:subPropertyOf ex:isMarriedTo.
```

Again, situations where this kind of information is of advantage are easy to imagine. For example by virtue of the above mentioned triple, the RDFS semantics allows us to deduce from the triple

```
ex:markus   ex:isHappilyMarriedTo   ex:anja .
```

that also the following triple must be valid:

```
ex:markus   ex:isMarriedTo   ex:anja .
```

Consequently, one single subproperty statement suffices to enable an RDFS-compliant information system to automatically recognize all pairs recorded as "happily married" additionally as "married". Note that this way, also properties can be arranged in complex hierarchies, although this is not as commonly done as for classes.

2.4.5   Property Restrictions

Frequently, the information that two entities are interconnected by a certain property allows us to draw further conclusions about the entities themselves. In particular, one might infer class memberships. For instance, the statement that one entity is married to another implies that both involved entities are persons.

Now it is not hard to see that the predicate's implicit additional information on subject and object can be expressed via class memberships: Whenever a triple of the form

```
a    ex:isMarriedTo   b .
```

occurs, one wants to assert, for example, that both following triples are valid as well:

```
a    rdf:type    ex:Person .
b    rdf:type    ex:Person .
```

As in the previously discussed cases, explicitly adding all those class membership statements to the RDF document would be rather cumbersome and would require us to repeat the process whenever new information is added to the document. Again, it seems desirable to have a "macro" or "template"-like mechanism which is entered just once and ensures the class memberships imposed by the predicates.

Fortunately the RDFS vocabulary provides means to do exactly this: one may provide information about a property's domain via `rdfs:domain` and its range via `rdfs:range`. The first kind of expression allows us to classify subjects, the second one to type objects that co-occur with a certain predicate in an RDF triple. The above mentioned class memberships imposed by the predicate `ex:isMarriedTo` can now be encoded by the following triples:

```
ex:isMarriedTo    rdfs:domain    ex:Person .
ex:isMarriedTo    rdfs:range     ex:Person .
```

In the same vein, literal values in the place of the object can be characterized by stipulating datatypes (e.g., in order to specify that a person's age should be a nonnegative number):

```
ex:hasAge    rdfs:range    xsd:nonNegativeInteger .
```

Obviously, domain and range restrictions constitute the "semantic link" between classes and properties because they provide the only way of describing the desired terminological interdependencies between those distinct kinds of ontology elements.

We would also like to address a frequent potential misconception. Suppose an RDFS document contains the triples:

```
ex:authorOf   rdfs:range   ex:Textbook .
ex:authorOf   rdfs:range   ex:Storybook .
```

According to the RDFS semantics, this expresses that every resource in the range of an authorship relation is *both* a textbook *and* a storybook; it does not mean that somebody may be author of a textbook *or* a storybook. The same holds for `rdfs:range` statements. So, every declared property restriction globally affects all occurrences of this property; hence one should be careful when restricting properties and make sure that always a sufficiently general class (i.e. one containing all possible resources that might occur in the subject resp. object position) is used.

Some further consideration is needed to prevent a confusion arising rather frequently. Consider the following RDF knowledge base:

```
ex:isMarriedTo     rdfs:domain   ex:Person .
ex:isMarriedTo     rdfs:range    ex:Person .
ex:instituteAIFB   rdf:type      ex:Institution .
```

Now assume the following triple was to be added to it:

```
ex:pascal          ex:isMarriedTo   ex:instituteAIFB .
```

Omitting deeper contemplations on a possible metaphorical truth of this statement, this example reveals a potential modeling flaw. A certain similarity to the "type mismatch" problem in programming shows up here. One might now expect that this kind of statement is automatically rejected by a system containing the above range statement (as a database system might reject changes if certain conditions are violated). However, RDF range and domain statements do not carry this kind of constraint semantics. The only indicator that something might be wrong is that by adding that triple to the knowledge base, counterintuitively, `ex:instituteAIFB` is additionally typed as a person, i.e. the triple

```
ex:instituteAIFB   rdf:type      ex:Person .
```

is a consequence of the above triples.

2.4.6   Additional Information in RDFS

In many cases it is desirable to endow an RDFS document with additional information which has no semantic impact but increases the understandability for human users. One might argue that – at least when using XML syntax – XML-style comments could just be used for this purpose. However, this would mean relinquishing the basic RDF(S) rationale to represent all knowledge as a graph, including all additional, comment-like information. Therefore, RDFS provides the possibility to embed additional information into the graph, thereby making it "semantically accessible." To this end, RDFS provides a predefined set of property names by means of which additional information can be encoded without relinquishing the basic idea to represent all knowledge as a graph. Thereby, all supplementary descriptions can be read and represented by any RDF-compliant software. We tacitly used `rdfs:label` in Section 2.4.2. Generally, this property-URI serves the purpose of accompanying a resource (which might be an individual but also a class or a property) with a name which is more handy than its URI. This sort of information can be used by tools visualizing the RDF document as a graph, where verbose URIs might impede readability. The object in a triple containing `rdfs:label` as predicate has to be a literal, a syntactic restriction which can be expressed within RDFS by the following triple:

```
rdfs:label    rdfs:range    rdfs:Literal .
```

`rdfs:comment` is used for assigning comprehensive human-readable comments to resources. Especially if new class or property terms are introduced, it is reasonable to write down their intended meaning in natural language. This facilitates the correct and consistent usage of the new terms by other users who might have a look at the documentation if in doubt. `rdfs:comment` also requires a literal as object.

By means of the expressions `rdfs:seeAlso` and `rdfs:isDefinedBy`, it is possible to link to resources that provide further information about the subject resource. This might be URLs of websites or URIs referring to print media. In particular, `rdfs:isDefinedBy` is used to state that the subject resource is (in some not further specified way) defined by the object resource. According to the RDFS semantics `rdfs:isDefinedBy` is stipulated to be a subproperty of `rdfs:seeAlso`.

As an example of the constructs introduced in this section consider the extended passage, given in Fig. 2.9, of the RDFS document from Fig. 2.8.

2.5 Encoding of Special Datastructures

You now know all the central ideas and notions of RDF(S) and the modeling features used most frequently. From here you might proceed directly to Chapter 3 to see how the semantics of RDF(S) – that we tried to intuitively convey

```
  :
xmlns:wikipedia="http://en.wikipedia.org/wiki/"
  :
<rdfs:Class rdf:about="&ex;Primates">
  <rdfs:label xml:lang="en">primates</rdfs:label>
  <rdfs:comment>
    Order of mammals. Primates are characterized by an
    advanced brain. They mostly populate the tropical
    earth regions. The term 'Primates' was coined by
    Carl von Linné.
  </rdfs:comment>
  <rdfs:seeAlso rdf:resource="&wikipedia;Primates" />
  <rdfs:subClassOf rdfs:resource="&ex;Mammalia" />
</rdfs:Class>
```

FIGURE 2.9:   Additional information in RDFS documents

in this chapter – is defined formally and how automated RDF(S) inferencing
can be realized. Or you might go on reading if interested in what additional
possibilities RDF(S) has in stock for modeling more complex datastructures:
lists and nested propositions.

2.5.1   Lists in RDF

Many-valued relationships, as introduced in Section 2.3.3, are used for obtaining a more structured representation of a single object, separating its
single components (ingredient and amount) in distinct triples. The structure
of the triples referring to the auxiliary node thus was specific to the example at hand. In many other cases, in contrast, one simply wants to relate a
subject to a set of objects that play similar roles, e.g., when describing the relationship of a book to the set of its authors. To address such use cases, RDF
offers a number of specific constructs that can be used to describe structures
that resemble lists. This can be achieved in two fundamentally different ways:
with *containers* (open lists) or with *collections* (closed lists).

It is important to note that all of the following additional expressive features
are only abbreviations for RDF graphs that could as well be encoded by
specifying individual triples. As in the case of rdf:value above, lists in RDF
do not have a specific formal semantics that distinguishes such structures from
other RDF graphs.

2.5.1.1   RDF Container

RDF containers allow us to encode RDF graphs that resemble the one in
Fig. 2.7 in a unified way. We have already seen that the introduction of

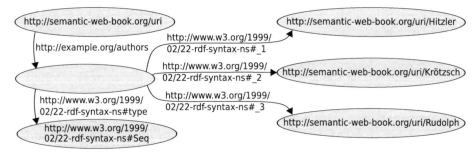

FIGURE 2.10:   A list of type rdf:Seq in RDF

blank nodes can be abbreviated in various serializations of RDF. Containers introduce two additional changes:

- The triples of a list are denoted by standard identifiers instead of using specific URIs such as ex:amount in Fig. 2.7.

- It is possible to assign a *class* to a list, hinting at the desired (informal) interpretation.

An example of a corresponding list is the following specification of this book's authors:

```
<rdf:Description rdf:about="http://semantic-web-book/uri">
 <ex:authors>
  <rdf:Seq>
   <rdf:li rdf:resource="http://semantic-web-book.org/uri/Hitzler" />
   <rdf:li rdf:resource="http://semantic-web-book.org/uri/Krötzsch" />
   <rdf:li rdf:resource="http://semantic-web-book.org/uri/Rudolph" />
  </rdf:Seq>
 </ex:authors>
</rdf:Description>
```

We would normally expect an element of type rdf:Description instead of rdf:Seq in this XML serialization. As explained in Section 2.3.4, this syntax would then also conveniently introduce a blank node. Something quite similar happens in the above case, as can be seen when considering the resulting RDF graph in Fig. 2.10. This graph, however, displays some additional features that require further explanation.

First, we notice that Fig. 2.10 contains one more node than we may have expected. While book, authors, and the required blank auxiliary node are present, we see that, additionally, the blank node is typed as an instance of the class rdf:Seq. This typing mechanism is used to specify the intended usage of a given list. RDF provides the following types of lists:

- `rdf:Seq`: The container is intended to represent an ordered list, i.e. the order of objects is relevant.

- `rdf:Bag`: The container is intended to represent an unordered set, i.e. the order of objects is not relevant, even though it is inherently available in the RDF encoding.

- `rdf:Alt`: The container is intended to represent a set of alternatives. Even though the RDF document specifies multiple objects, only one of them is usually required in a particular application.

Those class names can be used instead of `rdf:Seq` in the above example, but they do not otherwise affect the encoded RDF graph structure. Only when displaying or interpreting a list in a given application, this additional informal information may be taken into account.

A second aspect that can be noted in Fig. 2.10 is that the predicates of the individual list triples are not labeled like the corresponding elements in XML. Indeed, the RDF/XML serialization uses elements of type `rdf:li` for all elements. The graphical representation, in contrast, uses numbered predicates `rdf:_1` to `rdf:_3`. The XML syntax in this case is merely a syntactic simplification for encoding an RDF graph that uses predicates of the form `rdf:_n`. This encoding also applies if the list is of type `rdf:Bag` or `rdf:Alt`, even though the exact order may not be practically important in these cases. This method can be used to encode arbitrarily long lists – the RDF specification defines predicates of the form `rdf:_n` for any natural number n.

As explained above, the RDF/XML syntax for containers is merely a syntactic abbreviation that can also be avoided by serializing the corresponding RDF graph directly. Since blank nodes can be abbreviated in a simple way, Turtle does not provide a specific syntax for RDF containers. One simply specifies the according triples individually when denoting containers in Turtle.

2.5.1.2   Containers in RDFS

By introducing new predefined names, RDFS further extends the options for modeling lists described in the previous section. The URI `rdfs:Container` denotes the superclass of the three RDF container classes `rdf:Bag`, `rdf:Seq` and `rdf:Alt`, allowing us to mark a resource as list without specifying the precise type.

The URI `rdfs:ContainerMembershipProperty` is used in order to characterize properties, i.e. it refers to a class the instances of which are not individuals in the strict sense (as a person or a website), but themselves properties. The only class having properties as members that we have dealt with so far is the class of *all* properties denoted by `rdf:Property`. Consequently the following triple holds:

```
rdfs:ContainerMembershipProperty   rdfs:subClassOf   rdf:Property .
```

Now, what is the characteristic commonality of the properties contained in the class denoted by `rdfs:ContainerMembershipProperty`? All these properties encode the containedness of one resource in the other. Examples of such properties are those expressing containedness in a list: `rdf:_1`, `rdf:_2`, etc. Although this new class might seem somewhat abstract and of disputable use, there are possible application scenarios. For instance, a user might want to define a new type of list or container (as for cooking recipes) together with a specific containedness property (say, `ex:hasIngredient`). By typing this property with `rdfs:ContainerMembershipProperty`, the user makes this intended meaning explicit:

```
ex:hasIngredient   rdf:type   rdfs:ContainerMembershipProperty .
```

When using just RDF, finding out whether the resource `ex:shakespeare` is contained in the list `book:uri/Authors` would require asking for the validity of infinitely many triples:

```
book:uri/Authors   rdf:_1   ex:shakespeare .
book:uri/Authors   rdf:_2   ex:shakespeare .
book:uri/Authors   rdf:_3   ex:shakespeare .
...
```

RDFS provides the property name `rdfs:member` that denotes a property which is a superproperty of all the distinct containedness properties. As a practical consequence, the above mentioned problem can now be solved by querying for the validity of just one triple:

```
book:uri/Authors   rdfs:member   ex:shakespeare .
```

Yet, there is even more to it: according to the RDFS semantics, every instance of the `rdfs:ContainerMembershipProperty` class is a subproperty of the `rdfs:member` property. Now, let's come back to the aforementioned case of the self-defined container type. Even if the user now states

```
ex:cookie   ex:hasIngredient   ex:peanut .
```

using his proprietary property, the characterization of `ex:hasIngredient` as a containedness property enables us to deduce the validity of the following triple:

```
ex:cookie   rdfs:member   ex:peanut .
```

2.5.1.3   RDF Collections

The representation of lists as RDF containers is based on auxiliary predicates `rdf:_1`, `rdf:_2`, `rdf:_3`, etc. The resulting sequences of objects thus can always be extended by adding further triples, but it is not possible to express that a given list is complete and closed. RDF thus introduces so-called *collections* as a means for representing closed lists.

Like containers, collections are not introducing expressivity beyond what can already be stated by RDF triples, but they can allow for more concise RDF serializations. Let us first consider the following RDF/XML fragment:

```
<rdf:Description rdf:about="http://semantic-web-book/uri">
  <ex:authors rdf:parseType="Collection">
    <rdf:Description
         rdf:about="http://semantic-web-book.org/uri/Hitzler" />
    <rdf:Description
         rdf:about="http://semantic-web-book.org/uri/Krötzsch" />
    <rdf:Description
         rdf:about="http://semantic-web-book.org/uri/Rudolph" />
  </ex:authors>
</rdf:Description>
```

This syntactic description of a collection strongly resembles the explicit representation of a single triple, but it contains three objects instead of the usually unique `rdf:Description`. Furthermore, we encounter once more the attribute `rdf:parseType`, this time with the value `Collection`.

The corresponding RDF graph is the *linked list* that is shown in Fig. 2.11. We immediately see that the graph structure differs significantly from the containers introduced in the previous section. The underlying principle of this representation is that any non-empty list can be split into two components: a list head (the first element of the list) and a list rest. The rest of the list can again be decomposed in this way, or it is the empty list without further elements.

We can thus uniquely describe the closed list by specifying its head and rest. As can be seen in Fig. 2.11, the RDF predicates used for this purpose are `rdf:first` and `rdf:rest`. Since any list can be completely described in this way, the URIs of the individual list nodes are not significant. Consequently,

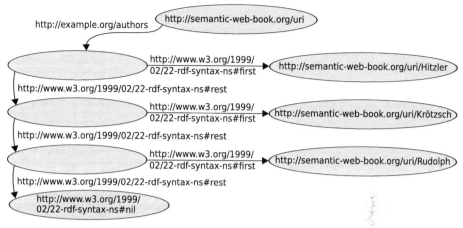

FIGURE 2.11: A collection in RDF

all non-empty (partial) lists in Fig. 2.11 are represented by blank nodes. The only exception is the empty list, which cannot be decomposed further. It is represented in RDF by the URI `rdf:nil`.

The empty list concludes the linked list, and indicates that no further elements follow. We may thus indeed speak of a closed list: By adding additional triples, one could merely produce RDF graphs that are not proper encodings of a collection, but one cannot add additional elements to the list.

Although collections could again be encoded in individual triples, Turtle also provides a more convenient notation for such lists using parentheses. A corresponding Turtle serialization of the above example could be as follows:

```
@prefix book:  <http://semantic-web-book.org/> .
book:uri   <http://example.org/authors>
     ( book:uri/Hitzler  book:uri/Krötzsch  book:uri/Rudolph ) .
```

2.5.2 Propositions About Propositions: Reification

Much more frequently than we are aware of, we make propositions referring to other propositions. As an example, consider the sentence: "The detective supposes that the butler killed the gardener." One naive attempt to model this situation might yield:

```
ex:detective   ex:supposes   "The butler killed the gardener." .
```

One of the problems arising from this way of modeling would be that the proposition in question – expressed by a literal – cannot be arbitrarily referenced in other triples (due to the fact that literals are only allowed to occur as triple objects). Hence it seems more sensible to use a URI for the proposition leading to something like:

```
ex:detective   ex:supposes   ex:theButlerKilledTheGardener .
```

Yet, this approach leaves us with the problem that the subordinate clause of our sentence is compressed into one URI and hence lacks structural transparency. Of course it is easy to model just the second part of the sentence as a separate triple:

```
ex:butler   ex:killed   ex:gardener .
```

Actually, a kind of "nested" representation, where the object of a triple is a triple on its own, would arguably best fit our needs. However, this would require a substantial extension of the RDF syntax.

One alternative option, called *reification*, draws its basic idea from the representation of many-valued relations as discussed in Section 2.3.3: an auxiliary node is introduced for the triple about which a proposition is to be made. This node is used as a "handle" to refer to the whole statement. Access to the inner structure of the represented triple is enabled by connecting the auxiliary node via the property-URIs `rdf:subject`, `rdf:predicate` and `rdf:object` with the respective triple constituents. The corresponding triple is then called *reified* ("thing-made", from lat. *res* thing and *facere* to make). Using this method, our above sentence could be described by the following four triples:

```
ex:detective   ex:supposes    ex:theory .
ex:theory      rdf:subject     ex:butler .
ex:theory      rdf:predicate   ex:hasKilled .
ex:theory      rdf:object      ex:gardener .
```

It is important to be aware that writing down a reified triple does not mean asserting its actual validity. In particular the previous specification does not allow us to conclude the triple:

```
ex:butler   ex:hasKilled   ex:gardener .
```

Note that this makes sense, as the detective's theory might turn out to be false.

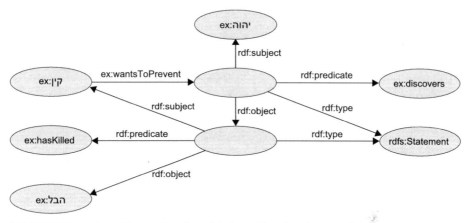

FIGURE 2.12: Example of multiple reification in graph representation

In addition to the reification properties already provided by the RDF vocabulary, RDFS contains the class name `rdf:Statement` that can be used to mark the "central" node of a reified triple:

```
ex:theory     rdf:type        rdf:Statement .
```

If the reified proposition is to be referenced only locally, it can be represented by a blank node. Note also that this way of modeling also allows for multiply nested propositions. An example of both modeling aspects is depicted in Fig. 2.12. With the knowledge acquired in this section you are certainly capable of decoding its content.[7]

2.6 An Example

In order to illustrate the essential modeling capabilities of RDFS, we give a small ontology as an example. For the sake of simplicity, we omit literals and datatypes. Suppose that an RDF document contains the following triples:

---

[7]Hint: It's also some sort of detective story; see Genesis 4:1-16 or Qur'an at 5:26-32 or Moses 5:16-4.

```
ex:vegetableThaiCurry    ex:thaiDishBasedOn    ex:coconutMilk .
ex:sebastian             rdf:type              ex:AllergicToNuts .
ex:sebastian             ex:eats               ex:vegetableThaiCurry .

ex:AllergicToNuts        rdfs:subClassOf       ex:Pitiable .
ex:thaiDishBasedOn       rdfs:domain           ex:Thai .
ex:thaiDishBasedOn       rdfs:range            ex:Nutty .
ex:thaiDishBasedOn       rdfs:subPropertyOf    ex:hasIngredient .
ex:hasIngredient         rdf:type      rdfs:ContainerMembershipProperty.
```

This RDFS specification models the existence of "vegetable thai curry", a Thai dish based on coconut milk.[8] Moreover we learn about a resource "Sebastian" belonging to the class of individuals allergic to nuts. The third triple states that Sebastian eats the vegetable Thai curry. These statements constitute the so-called *assertional knowledge* making propositions about the concrete entities of our domain of interest.

As *terminological knowledge*, our tiny ontology expresses that the class of nut-allergic individuals is a subclass of the class of pitiable things, that any Thai dish (based on something) belongs to the class of Thai things, and (reflecting the personal experience of the afflicted author) that any Thai dish is based only on ingredients belonging to the class of nutty things. Finally, we learn that whenever a (Thai) dish is based on something it also contains that "something" and that "having something as ingredient" constitutes a containedness property. Figure 2.13 shows the same ontology depicted as a graph and once more illustrates the distinction between terminological (or schema) knowledge and assertional (also: factual) knowledge. From knowledge specified in this way, it is now possible to derive implicit knowledge. In the next chapter, we provide the theoretical foundations for this and give an example showing how to automatically draw conclusions from the ontology introduced here.

---

[8] The usage of the property ex:thaiDishBasedOn is rather questionable from the perspective of a good modeling practice, as arguably too much information is squeezed into one property which thereby becomes overly specific. However, we used it for the sake of a small yet informative example. Moreover, we employed it to circumvent a modeling weakness of RDF: if the example were paraphrased using a ex:ThaiDish class and a ex:basedOn property, we would no longer be able to express the proposition "Everything a Thai dish is based on is nutty".

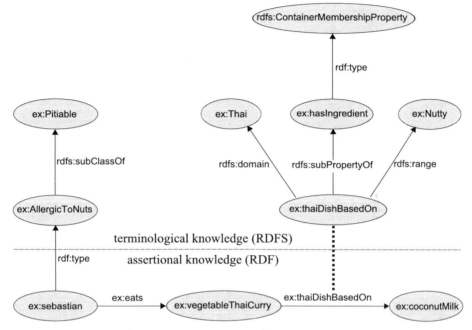

FIGURE 2.13:   Graph representation of a simple RDFS ontology

2.7   Summary

In this chapter, we have introduced the description language RDF and its extension RDFS. Both rely on a data model of graph structures consisting of basic elements called triples, which are also used for encoding more complex data structures like lists. URIs admit the unique identification of nodes and edges in those triples. While RDF essentially serves the purpose of making propositions about the relationships of singular objects (individuals), RDFS provides means for specifying terminological knowledge in the form of class and property hierarchies and their semantic interdependencies.

2.7.1   Overview of RDF(S) Language Constructs

RDF(S) classes

rdfs:Class	rdf:Property
rdfs:Resource	rdfs:Literal
rdfs:Datatype	rdf:XMLLiteral

RDF(S) properties

rdfs:range	rdfs:domain
rdf:type	rdfs:subClassOf
rdfs:subPropertyOf	rdfs:label
rdfs:comment	

RDF lists

rdfs:Container	rdf:Bag
rdf:Seq	rdf:Alt
rdf:li	rdf:_1
rdf:_2	...
rdfs:ContainerMembershipProperty	rdfs:member
rdf:List	rdf:first
rdf:rest	rdf:nil

reification

rdf:Statement	rdf:subject
rdf:predicate	rdf:object

RDF attributes

rdf:about	rdf:ID
rdf:resource	rdf:nodeID
rdf:datatype	

XML attributes

xml:base	xmlns
xml:lang	

RDF(S) further constructs

rdf:RDF	rdfs:seeAlso
rdfs:isDefinedBy	rdf:value

2.8 Exercises

Exercise 2.1 Consider the following RDF document:

```
<rdf:RDF
  xmlns:rdf="http://www.w3.org/1999/02/22-rdf-syntax-ns#"
  xmlns:rdfs="http://www.w3.org/2000/01/rdf-schema#"
  xmlns:iswww="http://sw.edu/#"
>

<rdf:Description rdf:about="http://sw.edu/#germany">
  <rdf:type rdf:resource="http://sw.edu/#country" />
</rdf:Description>

<rdf:Description rdf:about="http://sw.edu/#capital_of">
  <rdf:type
   rdf:resource="http://www.w3.org/1999/02/22-rdf-syntax-ns#Property"/
  >
  <rdfs:domain rdf:resource="http://sw.edu/#city" />
  <rdfs:range rdf:resource="http://sw.edu/#country" />
</rdf:Description>

<rdf:Description rdf:about="http://sw.edu/#country">
  <rdf:type rdf:resource="http://www.w3.org/2000/01/rdf-schema#Class" />
  <rdfs:label xml:lang="de">Land</rdfs:label>
</rdf:Description>

<rdf:Description rdf:about="http://sw.edu/#berlin">
  <rdfs:label xml:lang="en">Berlin</rdfs:label>
  <rdf:type rdf:resource="http://sw.edu/#city" />
  <iswww:capital_of rdf:resource="http://sw.edu/#germany" />
</rdf:Description>

<rdf:Description rdf:about="http://sw.edu/#city">
  <rdf:type rdf:resource="http://www.w3.org/2000/01/rdf-schema#Class" />
  <rdfs:label xml:lang="de">Stadt</rdfs:label>
</rdf:Description>

</rdf:RDF>
```

- Describe in natural language the content of this document.

- Draw the graph representation of the above document.

Exercise 2.2 Write down the modeled list of authors of this book from page 63 in Turtle syntax.

Exercise 2.3 Translate the culinary-allergic example ontology presented in Section 2.6 into RDF/XML syntax.

Exercise 2.4 Represent the following sentences graphically by means of reified triples:

- Romeo thought that Juliet was dead.

- John believes that Mary wants to marry him.

- The dwarf noticed that somebody had been eating from his plate.

Exercise 2.5 Decide whether the following propositions can be satisfactorily modeled in RDFS and, if so, give the corresponding RDF(S) specification.

- Every pizza is a meal.

- Pizzas always have at least two toppings.

- Every pizza from the class `PizzaMargarita` has a `Tomato` topping.

- Everything having a topping is a pizza.

- No pizza from the class `PizzaMargarita` has a topping from the class `Meat`.

- "Having a topping" is a containedness relation.

2.9   Further Reading

The documents of the RDF(S) specification of 2004 are

- "RDF Primer" [MM04], which gives a first overview and introduction to the Resource Description Framework,

- "RDF Concepts and Abstract Syntax" [KC04], where the basic concepts and data model of RDF are introduced,

- "RDF Vocabulary Description Language 1.0: RDF Schema" [BG04], introducing the RDFS vocabulary and its intended meaning,

- "RDF/XML Syntax Specification" [Bec04], defining the XML serialization of RDF,

- "RDF Semantics" [Hay04], which details the formal semantics of RDF and RDFS,

- "RDF Test Cases" [GB04], which specifies the design and usage of the RDF test suite that can be used to check the conformance of RDF tools.

These documents have replaced the initial RDF specification "RDF Model and Syntax" [LS99] which was published as a W3C recommendation in 1999, and the first RDF Schema candidate recommendation [BG00] of 2000. The early version of RDF that is described in those older documents is not compatible with the updated specifications of 2004.

The Turtle syntax for RDF is defined online at [BBL08]. A very restricted subset of Turtle is N-Triples, which is introduced as part of the RDF test case document [GB04]. A much more extensive formalism is Notation3 (also known as N3) [BLa], which does not only encompass all of Turtle, but also further expressive features that go beyond what can be expressed in RDF. However, the available online resources currently provide only an "early draft of a semi-formal semantics of the N3 logical properties" [BLb] instead of a complete specification.

Chapter 3

RDF Formal Semantics

After having dealt with the RDF(S) language in the previous sections, we now attend to its semantics. Our explanations closely follow the official W3C RDF semantics specification document [Hay04].

Before that, we will briefly explain why the definition of a formal semantics became necessary (note that in the early days of RDF, there was no explicit, mathematically defined semantics) and the advantages it brings about.

3.1 Why Semantics?

The term *semantics* (from Greek σημαντικος "significant") is used in many different contexts (like logic, linguistics, or programming languages to name just three). Probably the most appropriate corresponding English term is "meaning."

In this chapter, we mainly focus on the *logical* dimension of the notion of semantics, frequently referred to by the less ambiguous term *formal semantics*.

Introducing a formal semantics for RDF(S) became necessary because the previous informal RDF(S) specification – though successful in conveying some intuition – left plenty of room for interpretation about what conclusions can be drawn from a given specification. Indeed, first implementations of RDF(S) storage and reasoning tools (so-called *triple stores*) provided differing results to posed queries, a situation severely obstructing interoperability of tools and interchangeability of specifications, aims the RDF(S) standard actually was designed for.

While providing sets of examples for valid and invalid conclusions might clarify some singular cases, this can never ensure that each of the infinitely many entailments in question will be agreed upon. The most convenient way to resolve this problem is to avoid the vagueness of an informal specification by providing a well-defined formal semantics.

For our further considerations, it is necessary to define the notion of semantics in a mathematically precise way. As mentioned before, the central purpose of mathematical logic is to formalize correct reasoning. Hence, we first need a notion for statements as the basic elements of our reasoning process. Those elementary constituents are usually referred to as *propositions*.

What exactly the propositions are depends on the specific logic under consideration. In our case, for instance, the propositions are RDF triples. In the appendix you can find another example of logic propositions in the context of first-order predicate logic. Given a specific logic, let us denote the set of all propositions by $\mathbb{P}$. Furthermore, we need a notation to state that, e.g., propositions p_3 and p_4 are logical consequences of the propositions p_1, and p_2. Most commonly, this is expressed by $\{p_1, p_2\} \models \{p_3, p_4\}$, where $\models$ is called *entailment relation* and relates sets of propositions with sets of propositions (hence: $\models \subseteq 2^{\mathbb{P}} \times 2^{\mathbb{P}}$). A logic L is therefore composed of a set of propositions together with an entailment relation and can be described by $L = (\mathbb{P}, \models)$ on an abstract level.

There are numerous ways to define the entailment relation of a specific logic. In the following, we will attend to a rather frequently employed method that is also used in the case of RDF(S).

3.2   Model-Theoretic Semantics for RDF(S)

We start by giving a high-level perspective of the notion of *model-theoretic semantics*. Thereby, one central notion is that of an *interpretation*. Interpretations might be conceived as potential "realities" or "worlds." In particular, interpretations need in no way comply with the actual reality. In formal logic, one usually chooses certain mathematical structures as interpretations in order to work in a formally correct way. Which structures to choose in particular depends on the considered logic.

After stipulating what the interpretations of a logic are, one proceeds by defining how to decide whether a specific interpretation I *satisfies* a specific proposition $p \in \mathbb{P}$ (in which case we call I *model* of p and write $I \models p$, using the same symbol as for the entailment relation). Moreover, for a set $P \subseteq \mathbb{P}$ of propositions, one says that I is a model of P (written $I \models P$), if it is a model for every $p \in P$.

Based on this "model relation" the actual entailment relation is defined in the following (also intuitively plausible) way: a proposition set $P' \subseteq \mathbb{P}$ is entailed by a set of propositions $P \subseteq \mathbb{P}$ (written: $P \models P'$) if and only if every interpretation I satisfying *all* sentences p from P (formally: $I \models P$) is also a model of every sentence p' from P' (i.e., $I \models P'$). Figure 3.1 depicts this correspondence graphically. To further illustrate the basic concept of this definition, consider the following (only halfway formal) analogy: "light green" entails "green," because all light green things are also just green. Using the terminology just introduced and thinking of interpretations as single real world objects, this can be expressed as follows: $\{light\_green\} \models green$, because every thing (every interpretation) I that satisfies $light\_green$ (i.e., $I \models light\_green$)

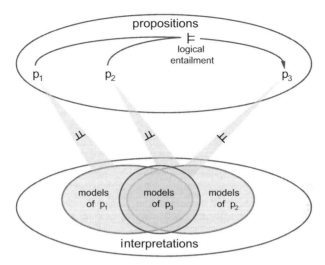

FIGURE 3.1: Definition of the entailment relation via models

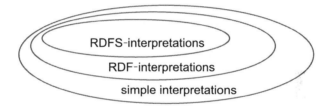

FIGURE 3.2: Correspondence of interpretations

is automatically also a model of the proposition *green* (i.e., $I \models green$).

We define the model-theoretic semantics for RDF(S) in several steps: we start by the comparably easy definition of simple interpretations of graphs. After that, we provide additional criteria which qualify these interpretations as RDF-interpretations. Finally we give further constraints to be fulfilled by an RDF-interpretation in order to be acknowledged as an RDFS-interpretation. As a natural consequence of this approach, every RDFS-interpretation is a valid RDF-interpretation and every RDF-interpretation constitutes a simple interpretation. This correspondency is depicted in Fig. 3.2.

3.2.1 Simple Interpretations

So, let us first have a look at the so-called *simple interpretations*. We shall use the Turtle syntax introduced in Section 2.2 in order to represent RDF graphs, presuming the two conventionally used prefix definitions

```
@prefix rdf: <http://www.w3.org/1999/02/22-rdf-syntax-ns#>
@prefix rdfs: <http://www.w3.org/2000/01/rdf-schema#>
```

Our starting point for the definition of interpretations is the notion of vocabulary, introduced in Section 2.2.6 and further elaborated in Section 2.4. Formally, a vocabulary is just an arbitrary set containing URIs and literals.

Of course, the aim of the introduced semantics is to correctly reflect the intuition behind RDF graphs; hence the interpretations to be defined in the sequel should – although more abstract – in a certain sense be similar to the "possible worlds" resp. "realities" described by the graphs.

As pointed out in Chapter 2, triples are employed to describe how *resources* are interrelated via *properties*. Consequently, an interpretation contains two sets *IR* and *IP*, the elements of which can be understood as abstract resources resp. properties, as well as a function I_{EXT} that tells which resources are interconnected by which properties. So, "resource" and "property" are notions which are purely semantic and to be used on the interpretation side only, whence – in the strict sense – it would be wrong to say that URIs (or literals) *are* resources. More precisely, one should state that (syntactic) URIs or literals *stand for* or *represent* (semantic) resources. And exactly this kind of representation is encoded by further functions that assign a semantic counterpart to every URI and literal. In the case of simple interpretations, all URIs are treated equally as there is no "semantic special treatment" for the RDF and the RDFS vocabulary.

So we define: a *simple interpretation* $\mathcal{I}$ of a given vocabulary V consists of

- *IR*, a non-empty set of *resources*, alternatively called domain or universe of discourse of $\mathcal{I}$,

- *IP*, the set of *properties* of $\mathcal{I}$ (which may overlap with *IR*),

- I_{EXT}, a function assigning to each property a set of pairs from *IR*, i.e. $I_{EXT} : IP \rightarrow 2^{IR \times IR}$, where $I_{EXT}(p)$ is called the *extension* of the property p,

- I_S, a function, mapping URIs from V into the union of the sets *IR* and *IP*, i.e. $I_S : V \rightarrow IR \cup IP$,

- I_L, a function from the typed literals from V into the set *IR* of resources and

- *LV*, a particular subset of *IR*, called the set of *literal values*, containing (at least) all untyped literals from V.

Based on the sets *IR*, *IP*, and *LV* as well as the functions I_{EXT}, I_S, and I_L, we now define an interpretation function $\cdot^{\mathcal{I}}$ that in the first place maps all literals and URIs contained in the vocabulary V to resources and properties:

- every untyped literal "a" is mapped to a, formally: $("a")^{\mathcal{I}} = a$,

- every untyped literal carrying language information "a"@t is mapped to the pair $\langle a, t \rangle$, i.e. $("a"@t)^{\mathcal{I}} = \langle a, t \rangle$,

- every typed literal $\mathfrak{l}$ is mapped to $I_L(\mathfrak{l})$, formally: $\mathfrak{l}^{\mathcal{I}} = I_L(\mathfrak{l})$, and

- every URI u is mapped to $I_S(u)$, i.e. $u^{\mathcal{I}} = I_S(u)$.

Note that, as mentioned in Section 2.1.3, untyped literals without language information are essentially mapped to themselves, while untyped literals with language information are assigned to pairs consisting of the pure literal and the language identifier. Figure 3.3 graphically illustrates this part of the definition of a simple interpretation.

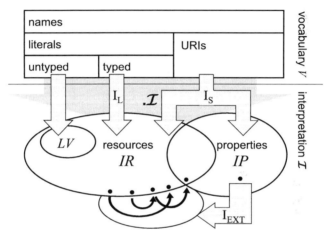

FIGURE 3.3: Schematic representation of a simple interpretation

Now, starting from the definition of the interpretation function with respect to single basic RDF elements, we further extend this function in a way that it assigns a truth value (*true* or *false*) to every *grounded* triple (i.e. every triple not containing blank nodes): the truth value $\texttt{s p o.}^{\mathcal{I}}$ of a grounded triple $\texttt{s p o.}$ will be true exactly if all of its constituents $\texttt{s}$, $\texttt{p}$, and $\texttt{o}$ are contained in the vocabulary V and additionally $\langle \texttt{s}^{\mathcal{I}}, \texttt{o}^{\mathcal{I}} \rangle \in I_{\text{EXT}}(\texttt{p}^{\mathcal{I}})$ holds. Verbally, the latter condition demands that the pair constructed from the resources assigned to $\texttt{s}$ and $\texttt{o}$ is within the extension of the property denoted by $\texttt{p}$. Figure 3.4 graphically displays this condition. If one of these mentioned conditions is violated, the truth value will be *false*.

Finally, the interpretation function $\cdot^{\mathcal{I}}$ also assigns a truth value to every grounded graph G: $G^{\mathcal{I}}$ is true if and only if every triple contained in the graph G is true, i.e. $G^{\mathcal{I}} = true$ exactly if $T^{\mathcal{I}} = true$ for all $T \in G$.

Mark that the notion of interpretation which we have introduced so far only covers grounded graphs, i.e. those not containing blank nodes. In order to enable an interpretation to deal with blank nodes, we have to further generalize our technical notion of interpretation. For this, the essential idea

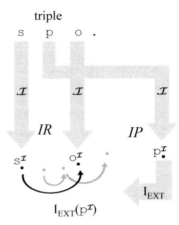

FIGURE 3.4: Criterion for the validity of a triple with respect to an interpretation

is to let a graph that contains blank nodes be valid, if everyone of these blank nodes can be replaced by a resource, such that the resulting bnode-free graph is valid. Hence, let A be a function assigning a resource from IR to every blank node occurring in G. Moreover, we define for such a mapping A and a given interpretation $\mathcal{I}$ a sort of combined interpretation $\mathcal{I}+A$ that behaves exactly like $\mathcal{I}$ on the URIs and literals but additionally uses A to assign resources to all blank nodes: $(b)^{\mathcal{I}+A} = A(b)$. Accordingly $\mathcal{I}+A$ can be extended to triples and further to graphs.

Eventually, we have to abstract from the concrete blank node assignments by stipulating that a (non-combined) interpretation $\mathcal{I}$ be a model of a graph G if there exists a function A', such that $G^{\mathcal{I}+A'} = true$. By this trick, we have extended our original notion of an interpretation to non-grounded graphs. An example of such a simple interpretation is given in Fig. 3.5.

In full compliance with the idea of model-theoretic semantics, we now say that a graph G_1 (simply) entails a graph G_2, if every simple interpretation that is a model of G_1 is also a model of G_2.

3.2.2 RDF-Interpretations

As mentioned earlier, simple interpretations essentially treat all URIs occurring in the vocabulary in the same way, irrespective of their namespace and their intended special meaning. For example, a simple interpretation does not semantically distinguish between the URIs ex:publishedBy and rdf:type. In order to restore the fixed vocabulary to its intended meaning, the set of admissible interpretations has to be further restricted by additional constraints.

The RDF vocabulary V_{RDF} consists of the URIs

Let us consider as an example the graph from Fig. 2.7. The corresponding vocabulary V consists of all names of nodes and edges of the graph.

A simple interpretation $\mathcal{I}$ for this vocabulary would now be given by:

$$IR = \{\chi, \upsilon, \tau, \nu, \epsilon, \iota, 1lb\}$$

$$IP = \{\tau, \nu, \iota\}$$

$$LV = \{1lb\}$$

$$I_{EXT} = \tau \mapsto \{\langle \chi, \epsilon \rangle\}$$
$$\nu \mapsto \{\langle \epsilon, \upsilon \rangle\}$$
$$\iota \mapsto \{\langle \epsilon, 1lb \rangle\}$$

$I_S =$
ex:chutney	$\mapsto \chi$
ex:greenMango	$\mapsto \upsilon$
ex:hasIngredient	$\mapsto \tau$
ex:ingredient	$\mapsto \nu$
ex:amount	$\mapsto \iota$

I_L is the "empty function," since there are no typed literals.

Letting $A : \_{:}\mathtt{id1} \mapsto \epsilon$, we note that the interpretation $\mathcal{I} + A$ valuates all three triples of our considered graph with *true*:

$$\langle \mathtt{ex{:}chutney}^{\mathcal{I}+A}, \_{:}\mathtt{id1}^{\mathcal{I}+A} \rangle = \langle \chi, \epsilon \rangle \in I_{EXT}(\tau) = I_{EXT}(\mathtt{ex{:}hasIngredient}^{\mathcal{I}+A})$$
$$\langle \_{:}\mathtt{id1}^{\mathcal{I}+A}, \mathtt{ex{:}greenMango}^{\mathcal{I}+A} \rangle = \langle \epsilon, \upsilon \rangle \in I_{EXT}(\nu) = I_{EXT}(\mathtt{ex{:}ingredient}^{\mathcal{I}+A})$$
$$\langle \_{:}\mathtt{id1}^{\mathcal{I}+A}, \mathtt{"1lb"}^{\mathcal{I}+A} \rangle = \langle \epsilon, 1lb \rangle \in I_{EXT}(\iota) = I_{EXT}(\mathtt{ex{:}amount}^{\mathcal{I}+A})$$

Therefore, the described graph as a whole is also valued with *true*. Hence, the simple interpretation $\mathcal{I}$ is a model of the graph.

FIGURE 3.5: Example of an interpretation

```
rdf:type rdf:Property rdf:XMLLiteral rdf:nil rdf:List rdf:Statement
rdf:subject rdf:predicate rdf:object rdf:first rdf:rest rdf:Seq
rdf:Bag rdf:Alt rdf:value
```

plus an infinite number of URIs rdf_i for every positive integer i.

Recall the intuitive semantics for this vocabulary: rdf:type is used to assign a type to a URI; in other words, it declares that the resource associated to this URI belongs to a certain class. The name rdf:Property denotes such a class and characterizes all those URIs that may serve as a triple's predicate, i.e. those URIs whose assigned resources have an extension (i.e. which are in *IP* in terms of simple interpretations). Consequently, only interpretations satisfying those conditions will be admitted.

As we learned in Section 2.3.1, there is exactly one predefined datatype in RDF, namely, rdf:XMLLiteral. As opposed to other (externally defined) datatypes, the special characteristics of this one are explicitly taken care of in the RDF semantics definition. In order to do this, it is necessary to distinguish between *well-typed* and *ill-typed* XML literals. An XML literal is categorized as well-typed if it satisfies the syntactic conditions for being contained in the lexical space of rdf:XMLLiteral; otherwise it is ill-typed.

This distinction is relevant for the subsequent definition, because well-typed literals are mapped to literal values (i.e. elements of *LV*), whereas ill-typed ones are mapped to resources that are not literal values.

An *RDF-interpretation* of a vocabulary V is a simple interpretation of the vocabulary $V \cup V_{\mathrm{RDF}}$ that additionally satisfies the following conditions:

- $x \in IP$ exactly if $\langle x, \mathtt{rdf:Property}^{\mathcal{I}} \rangle \in I_{\mathrm{EXT}}(\mathtt{rdf:type}^{\mathcal{I}})$.

  x is a property exactly if it is connected to the resource denoted by rdf:Property via the rdf:type-property (this automatically causes $IP \subseteq IR$ for any RDF-interpretation).

- if "s"^^rdf:XMLLiteral is contained in V and s is a well-typed XML-Literal, then

    - $I_L("s"\text{^^}\mathtt{rdf:XMLLiteral})$ is the XML value[1] of s;

    - $I_L("s"\text{^^}\mathtt{rdf:XMLLiteral}) \in LV$;

    - $\langle I_L("s"\text{^^}\mathtt{rdf:XMLLiteral}), \mathtt{rdf:XMLLiteral}^{\mathcal{I}} \rangle$
        $\in I_{\mathrm{EXT}}(\mathtt{rdf:type}^{\mathcal{I}})$

---

[1]The value space of the datatype assigned to rdf:XMLLiteral contains, for every well-typed XML string (from the lexical space), exactly one so-called XML value. The RDF specification does not give further information about the nature of XML values; it only requires that an XML value is not an XML string, nor a data value, nor a Unicode string. For our purposes and the intuitive usage, however, it does no harm to suppose that XML values are just XML strings.

- if `"s"^^rdf:XMLLiteral` is contained in V and s is an ill-typed XML literal, then

    - $I_L("s"\hat{}\hat{}\texttt{rdf:XMLLiteral}) \notin LV$ and
    - $\langle I_L("s"\hat{}\hat{}\texttt{rdf:XMLLiteral}), \texttt{rdf:XMLLiteral}^{\mathcal{I}} \rangle$
      $$\notin I_{EXT}(\texttt{rdf:type}^{\mathcal{I}}).$$

In addition to those semantic restrictions, RDF-interpretations have to satisfy the condition that all of the subsequent triples (called *axiomatic triples*) must be valued as true:

rdf : type	rdf : type	rdf : Property.
rdf : subject	rdf : type	rdf : Property.
rdf : predicate	rdf : type	rdf : Property.
rdf : object	rdf : type	rdf : Property.
rdf : first	rdf : type	rdf : Property.
rdf : rest	rdf : type	rdf : Property.
rdf : value	rdf : type	rdf : Property.
rdf : _i	rdf : type	rdf : Property.
rdf : nil	rdf : type	rdf : List.

Again, the i in `rdf:_i` is to be replaced by all positive integers; therefore we actually have infinitely many axiomatic triples.

Except for the last one, all those triples serve the purpose of marking resources that are assigned to particular RDF URIs as properties. This is done in the usual way by typing them with `rdf:type rdf:Property` which due to the above definition of RDF-interpretations has exactly the desired effect.

Together, the listed restrictions ensure that an RDF-interpretation complies with the intended meaning.

In exact analogy to the definition of the simple entailment, we now say that a graph G_1 RDF-entails a graph G_2 if every RDF-interpretation that is a model of G_1 is also a model of G_2.

3.2.3 RDFS Interpretations

As pointed out in Section 2.4, RDFS enriches the RDF vocabulary by further constructs which have to be interpreted in a special way. For example, new class names are introduced that allow us to mark a URI as referring to a resource, to an untyped literal, or to a class via `rdf:type`. New URIs for properties allow for characterizing domain and range of a property by typing them with classes. Moreover class names as well as property names can be put into hierarchical relations. This set of modeling options enables us to express schematic or terminological knowledge in the form of triples.

The RDFS vocabulary V_{RDFS} to be specifically interpreted consists of the following names:

```
rdfs:domain rdfs:range rdfs:Resource rdfs:Literal rdfs:Datatype
rdfs:Class rdfs:subClassOf rdfs:subPropertyOf rdfs:member
rdfs:Container rdfs:ContainerMembershipProperty rdfs:comment
rdfs:seeAlso rdfs:isDefinedBy rdfs:label
```

For the sake of a simpler presentation, we introduce a new function I_{CEXT} which, given a fixed RDF-interpretation, maps resources to sets of resources (formally: $I_{\text{CEXT}} : IR \rightarrow 2^{IR}$). We define $I_{\text{CEXT}}(y)$ to contain exactly those elements x for which $\langle x, y \rangle$ is contained in $I_{\text{EXT}}(\texttt{rdf:type}^{\mathcal{I}})$. The set $I_{\text{CEXT}}(y)$ is then also called the *(class) extension* of y.

Moreover we let IC denote the class extension of the URI $\texttt{rdfs:Class}$, formally: $IC = I_{\text{CEXT}}(\texttt{rdfs:Class}^{\mathcal{I}})$. Note that both I_{CEXT} as well as IC are uniquely determined by $\cdot^{\mathcal{I}}$ and I_{EXT}.

We now employ the newly introduced function in order to specify the semantic requirements on an RDFS-interpretation:

An *RDFS-interpretation* of a vocabulary V is an RDF-interpretation of the vocabulary $V \cup V_{\text{RDFS}}$ that in addition satisfies the following criteria:

- $IR = I_{\text{CEXT}}(\texttt{rdfs:Resource}^{\mathcal{I}})$

  Every resource has the type $\texttt{rdfs:Resource}$.

- $LV = I_{\text{CEXT}}(\texttt{rdfs:Literal}^{\mathcal{I}})$

  Every untyped or well-typed literal has the type $\texttt{rdfs:Literal}$.

- If $\langle x, y \rangle \in I_{\text{EXT}}(\texttt{rdfs:domain}^{\mathcal{I}})$ and $\langle u, v \rangle \in I_{\text{EXT}}(x)$, then $u \in I_{\text{CEXT}}(y)$.

  If x and y are interconnected by the property $\texttt{rdfs:domain}$ and the property x connects the resources u and v, then u has the type y.

- If $\langle x, y \rangle \in I_{\text{EXT}}(\texttt{rdfs:range}^{\mathcal{I}})$ and $\langle u, v \rangle \in I_{\text{EXT}}(x)$, then $v \in I_{\text{CEXT}}(y)$.

  If x and y are interconnected by the property $\texttt{rdfs:range}$ and the property x connects the resources u and v, then v has the type y.

- $I_{\text{EXT}}(\texttt{rdfs:subPropertyOf}^{\mathcal{I}})$ is reflexive and transitive on IP.

  The $\texttt{rdfs:subPropertyOf}$ property connects every property with itself.

  Moreover: if $\texttt{rdfs:subPropertyOf}$ links property x with property y and also y with the property z, then $\texttt{rdfs:subPropertyOf}$ also links x directly with z.

- If $\langle x, y \rangle \in I_{\text{EXT}}(\texttt{rdfs:subPropertyOf}^{\mathcal{I}})$, then $x, y \in IP$ and $I_{\text{EXT}}(x) \subseteq I_{\text{EXT}}(y)$.

  Whenever x and y are interlinked by $\texttt{rdfs:subPropertyOf}$, then both x and y are properties and every pair of resources contained in x's extension is also contained in the extension of y.

- If $x \in IC$,
  then $\langle x, \texttt{rdfs:Resource}^{\mathcal{I}} \rangle \in \mathrm{I_{EXT}}(\texttt{rdfs:subClassOf}^{\mathcal{I}})$.

  Every class x is a subclass of the class of all resources, i.e. the pair constructed from x and `rdfs:Resource` is in the extension of `rdfs:subClassOf`.

- If $\langle x, y \rangle \in \mathrm{I_{EXT}}(\texttt{rdfs:subClassOf}^{\mathcal{I}})$,
  then $x, y \in IC$ and $\mathrm{I_{CEXT}}(x) \subseteq \mathrm{I_{CEXT}}(y)$.

  If x and y are in the `rdfs:subClassOf` relation, then both x and y are classes and the (class) extension of x is a subset of the (class) extension of y.

- $\mathrm{I_{EXT}}(\texttt{rdfs:subClassOf}^{\mathcal{I}})$ is reflexive and transitive on IC.

  The `rdfs:subClassOf` property connects each class with itself.

  Moreover if the `rdfs:subClassOf` property connects a class x with a class y and y with some class z, it also connects x with z directly.

- If $x \in \mathrm{I_{CEXT}}(\texttt{rdfs:ContainerMembershipProperty}^{\mathcal{I}})$,
  then $\langle x, \texttt{rdfs:member}^{\mathcal{I}} \rangle \in \mathrm{I_{EXT}}(\texttt{rdfs:subPropertyOf}^{\mathcal{I}})$.

  Any property typed with `rdfs:ContainerMembershipProperty` is in the `rdfs:subPropertyOf` relation to the `rdfs:member` property.

- If $x \in \mathrm{I_{CEXT}}(\texttt{rdfs:Datatype}^{\mathcal{I}})$,
  then $\langle x, \texttt{rdfs:Literal}^{\mathcal{I}} \rangle \in \mathrm{I_{EXT}}(\texttt{rdfs:subClassOf}^{\mathcal{I}})$

  Any x typed as `rdfs:Datatype` must be a subclass of the class of all literal values (denoted by `rdfs:Literal`).

In analogy to the definition of RDF-interpretations, we name a list of axiomatic triples which (in addition to the aforementioned constraints) have to be satisfied by an RDF-interpretation in order to render it an RDFS-interpretation:

rdf:type	rdfs:domain	rdfs:Resource .
rdfs:domain	rdfs:domain	rdf:Property .
rdfs:range	rdfs:domain	rdf:Property .
rdfs:subPropertyOf	rdfs:domain	rdf:Property .
rdfs:subClassOf	rdfs:domain	rdfs:Class .
rdf:subject	rdfs:domain	rdf:Statement .
rdf:predicate	rdfs:domain	rdf:Statement .
rdf:object	rdfs:domain	rdf:Statement .
rdfs:member	rdfs:domain	rdfs:Resource .
rdf:first	rdfs:domain	rdf:List .
rdf:rest	rdfs:domain	rdf:List .
rdfs:seeAlso	rdfs:domain	rdfs:Resource .
rdfs:isDefinedBy	rdfs:domain	rdfs:Resource .

rdfs:comment	rdfs:domain	rdfs:Resource .
rdfs:label	rdfs:domain	rdfs:Resource .
rdf:value	rdfs:domain	rdfs:Resource .
rdf:type	rdfs:range	rdfs:Class .
rdfs:domain	rdfs:range	rdfs:Class .
rdfs:range	rdfs:range	rdfs:Class .
rdfs:subPropertyOf	rdfs:range	rdf:Property .
rdfs:subClassOf	rdfs:range	rdfs:Class .
rdf:subject	rdfs:range	rdfs:Resource .
rdf:predicate	rdfs:range	rdfs:Resource .
rdf:object	rdfs:range	rdfs:Resource .
rdfs:member	rdfs:range	rdfs:Resource .
rdf:first	rdfs:range	rdfs:Resource .
rdf:rest	rdfs:range	rdf:List .
rdfs:seeAlso	rdfs:range	rdfs:Resource .
rdfs:isDefinedBy	rdfs:range	rdfs:Resource .
rdfs:comment	rdfs:range	rdfs:Literal .
rdfs:label	rdfs:range	rdfs:Literal .
rdf:value	rdfs:range	rdfs:Resource .
rdfs:ContainerMembershipProperty		
	rdfs:subClassOf	rdf:Property .
rdf:Alt	rdfs:subClassOf	rdfs:Container .
rdf:Bag	rdfs:subClassOf	rdfs:Container .
rdf:Seq	rdfs:subClassOf	rdfs:Container .
rdfs:isDefinedBy	rdfs:subPropertyOf	rdfs:seeAlso .
rdf:XMLLiteral	rdf:type	rdfs:Datatype .
rdf:XMLLiteral	rdfs:subClassOf	rdfs:Literal .
rdfs:Datatype	rdfs:subClassOf	rdfs:Class .
rdf:_i	rdf:type	
	rdfs:ContainerMembershipProperty .	
rdf:_i	rdfs:domain	rdfs:Resource .
rdf:_i	rdfs:range	rdfs:Resource .

Again, i can be replaced by any positive integer. Obviously this set of triples can be divided into several groups. The first group contains triples with predicate rdfs:domain. The declarative purpose of such a triple p rdfs:domain c is to associate the URI p with a class name c. Basically, this enforces a class membership (realized via rdf:type) for every URI s occurring as a subject together with the predicate p in a triple s p o . For example, the fifth triple in this list just states that whenever a triple c rdfs:subclassOf d is encountered, an immediate consequence is that c denotes a class, expressed by the triple c `rdf:type rdfs:Class`.

Similarly, the triples gathered in the second group and having the predicate `rdfs:range` cause class memberships of triple objects.

As to containers, the axiomatic triples specify the class of all containedness properties as subclass of the class of all properties. Additionally, the class denoted by `rdfs:Container` is declared as the superclass of all kinds of open lists.

Moreover, the `rdfs:isDefinedBy` property is classified as a special case of the `rdfs:seeAlso` property. The class of XML values is marked as a datatype and subclass of all literal values, and the class of all datatypes is identified as a class of classes.

Finally the predefined containedness properties for lists are characterized as such.

Based on the introduced notion of an RDFS-interpretation and in analogy to the previous two cases, we now define that a graph G_1 RDFS entails a graph G_2 if every RDFS-interpretation that is a model of G_1 is also a model of G_2.

3.2.4 Interpretation of Datatypes

We already know that there is just one predefined datatype in RDFS, namely, `rdf:XMLLiteral`, the semantic characteristics of which are fully covered by the definition of RDFS-interpretation in the previous section. Nevertheless, other externally defined datatypes can be used in RDF(S).

In Section 2.3.1 we learned that a datatype d is composed of a *value space* Val_d, a *lexical space* Lex_d and a function $\mathrm{Lex2Val}_d$, assigning a value to every element of the lexical space, formally: $d = \langle Val_d, Lex_d, \mathrm{Lex2Val}_d \rangle$ with $\mathrm{Lex2Val}_d : Lex_d \to Val_d$.

In the same section we also mentioned that when employing external datatypes, one can have URIs referring to those datatypes within the vocabulary. This allows for making statements about datatypes within an RDF(S) specification. For example, it might be reasonable to specify that the natural numbers are a subset of the integers.

In order to capture the entirety of all datatypes used in an RDF(S) description, we introduce the notion of a *datatype map* D, a function assigning the datatypes to their URIs: $D : \mathbf{u} \mapsto d$. Of course, the predefined datatype has to be treated accordingly; hence we require every datatype map to satisfy $D(\texttt{rdf:XMLLiteral}) = d_{\mathrm{XMLLiteral}}$.

Given a datatype map D, we now define a D-*interpretation* of the vocabulary V as an RDFS-interpretation $\mathcal{I}$ of $V \cup \{\mathbf{a} \mid$ there is a d with $D(\mathbf{a}) = d\}$ (that means the vocabulary V extended by the domain of D) that for every $\mathbf{a}$ and d with $D(\mathbf{a}) = d$ additionally satisfies the following properties:

- $\mathbf{a}^{\mathcal{I}} = D(\mathbf{a})$.

For URIs denoting datatypes, the interpretation function $\cdot^{\mathcal{I}}$ coincides with the datatype map D.

- $\mathrm{I}_{\mathrm{CEXT}}(d) = Val_d \subseteq LV$.

  The class extension of a datatype d is the value space of d and is a subset of the literal values.

- For every typed literal $"s"\verb|^^|d \in V$ with $d^{\mathcal{I}} = d$ the following hold:

  - if $s \in Lex_d$, then $\mathrm{I}_{\mathrm{L}}("s"\verb|^^|d) = \mathrm{Lex2Val}_d(s)$,
  - if $s \notin Lex_d$, then $\mathrm{I}_{\mathrm{L}}("s"\verb|^^|d) \notin LV$.

  Every well-typed literal (i.e. one contained in the lexical space of its associated datatype) is mapped into the literal values in accordance with this datatype's lexical-to-value mapping, whereas every ill-typed literal is mapped to a resource outside the literal values.

- $a^{\mathcal{I}} \in \mathrm{I}_{\mathrm{CEXT}}(\texttt{rdfs:Datatype}^{\mathcal{I}})$.

  Every datatype (i.e. every resource assigned to a datatype URI) is a member of the $\texttt{rdfs:Datatype}$ class.

3.2.5   Worked Example

Let us have a closer look at the definitions of models for RDF and RDFS documents by working through them for the example ontology from Section 2.6. This is going to be a bit tedious, but it helps to understand the definitions. Usually, you would not do this manually, but rather use systems based on algorithms like that from Section 3.3.

Let us start by defining a simple interpretation, as given in Fig. 3.6. These assignments define a simple interpretation which is a model of the example ontology. You can check this easily yourself.

Next, we define an RDF-interpretation starting from the simple interpretation just given. To do this, we need to augment the simple interpretation by adding mappings for all elements of V_{RDF} and by redefining $\mathrm{I}_{\mathrm{EXT}}(y)$.

It does not really matter how we set $\mathrm{I}_{\mathrm{S}}(x)$ for those $x \in V_{\mathrm{RDF}}$ which the I_{S} from the simple interpretation does not map, so pick anything that is not yet in $IR \cup IP$ and extend I_{S} accordingly. Note that we could also reuse the elements from $IR \cup IP$ because the unique name assumption is not imposed, but we want to construct a model which is intuitively feasible, and so we avoid reuse. Let's do the settings as given in Fig. 3.7.

Now redefine $\mathrm{I}_{\mathrm{EXT}}(y)$ from the simple interpretation to the following:
$$\mathrm{I}_{\mathrm{EXT}}(y) = \{\langle s, a\rangle, \langle h, i\rangle, \langle d, \pi\rangle, \langle e, \pi\rangle, \langle h, \pi\rangle, \langle b, \pi\rangle, \langle m, \pi\rangle, \langle o, \pi\rangle, \langle r, \pi\rangle, \langle y, \pi\rangle,$$
$$\langle \rho_1, \rho_2\rangle, \langle \rho_4, \pi\rangle, \langle \rho_5, \pi\rangle, \langle \rho_6, \pi\rangle, \langle \rho_7, \pi\rangle, \langle \rho_8, \pi\rangle, \langle \rho_{12}, \pi\rangle, \langle \delta_k, \pi\rangle \mid k \in \mathbb{N}\}.$$
This way, we satisfy the first condition on page 80. The other conditions are not important for us since we have no such elements in V.

$$
\begin{aligned}
IR &= \{a, c, i, n, p, s, t, v, y, d, h\} \\
IP &= \{d, e, h, b, m, o, r, y\} \\
LV &= \emptyset
\end{aligned}
$$

I_S =

`ex:AllergicToNuts`	$\mapsto a$
`ex:coconutMilk`	$\mapsto c$
`ex:Nutty`	$\mapsto n$
`ex:Pitiable`	$\mapsto p$
`ex:sebastian`	$\mapsto s$
`ex:Thai`	$\mapsto t$
`ex:vegetableThaiCurry`	$\mapsto v$
`ex:thaiDishBasedOn`	$\mapsto d$
`ex:eats`	$\mapsto e$
`ex:hasIngredient`	$\mapsto h$
`rdfs:subPropertyOf`	$\mapsto b$
`rdfs:ContainerMembershipProperty`	$\mapsto i$
`rdfs:domain`	$\mapsto m$
`rdfs:subClassOf`	$\mapsto o$
`rdfs:range`	$\mapsto r$
`rdf:type`	$\mapsto y$

$$
\begin{aligned}
I_{\text{EXT}} = {}& d \mapsto \{\langle v, c \rangle\} \\
& e \mapsto \{\langle s, v \rangle\} \\
& h \mapsto \emptyset \\
& b \mapsto \{\langle d, h \rangle\} \\
& m \mapsto \{\langle d, t \rangle\} \\
& o \mapsto \{\langle a, p \rangle\} \\
& r \mapsto \{\langle d, n \rangle\} \\
& y \mapsto \{\langle s, a \rangle, \langle h, i \rangle\} \\
I_L = {}& \emptyset
\end{aligned}
$$

FIGURE 3.6: Example of a simple interpretation

$$
\begin{aligned}
\text{I}_\text{S} : \text{rdf:Property} \quad &\mapsto \pi \\
\text{rdf:XMLLiteral} \quad &\mapsto \rho_0 \\
\text{rdf:nil} \quad &\mapsto \rho_1 \\
\text{rdf:List} \quad &\mapsto \rho_2 \\
\text{rdf:Statement} \quad &\mapsto \rho_3 \\
\text{rdf:subject} \quad &\mapsto \rho_4 \\
\text{rdf:predicate} \quad &\mapsto \rho_5 \\
\text{rdf:object} \quad &\mapsto \rho_6 \\
\text{rdf:first} \quad &\mapsto \rho_7 \\
\text{rdf:rest} \quad &\mapsto \rho_8 \\
\text{rdf:Seq} \quad &\mapsto \rho_9 \\
\text{rdf:Bag} \quad &\mapsto \rho_{10} \\
\text{rdf:Alt} \quad &\mapsto \rho_{11} \\
\text{rdf:value} \quad &\mapsto \rho_{12} \\
\text{rdf:\_n} \quad &\mapsto \delta_n \qquad \text{for all } n \in \mathbb{N}
\end{aligned}
$$

FIGURE 3.7:   Example of an RDF-interpretation

Note that we now also need to adjust *IR* and *IP* to take the new elements into account. We set them as follows.

$$
IR = \{a, c, i, n, p, s, t, v, d, e, h, b, m, o, r, y, \pi, \rho_k, \delta_j \mid k \in \{0, \dots, 12\}, j \in \mathbb{N}\}
$$
$$
IP = \{d, e, h, b, m, o, r, y, \rho_4, \dots, \rho_8, \rho_{12}, \delta_k \mid k \in \mathbb{N}\}
$$

Finally, set $\text{I}_\text{EXT}(\rho_4) = \text{I}_\text{EXT}(\rho_5) = \text{I}_\text{EXT}(\rho_6) = \text{I}_\text{EXT}(\rho_7) = \text{I}_\text{EXT}(\rho_8) = \text{I}_\text{EXT}(\rho_{12}) = \text{I}_\text{EXT}(\delta_k)$ for all $k \in \mathbb{N}$. This completes the definition of an RDF-interpretation which is actually also a model of the given ontology. Check it yourself from the definitions in Section 3.2.2.

We will now finally attempt to extend this to an RDFS-interpretation which is a model of the ontology. Actually, we will see that this is too tedious a task to be done manually, but let's at least have a start to see how it would work in principle. We first extend I_S, for example, as given in Fig. 3.8.

We now redefine *IR* to contain all those things I_S maps to, and *IP* to contain all elements of *IR* which are properties. *LV* and I_L are obviously empty for this example.

$$
IR = \{a, c, i, n, p, s, t, v, d, e, h, b, m, o, r, y, \pi, \rho_0, \dots \rho_{12}, \sigma_0, \dots, \sigma_9, \delta_n \mid n \in \mathbb{N}\}
$$
$$
IP = \{d, e, h, b, m, o, r, y, \rho_4, \dots, \rho_8, \rho_{12}, \sigma_4, \sigma_6, \sigma_7, \sigma_8, \sigma_9, \delta_k \mid k \in \mathbb{N}\}
$$
$$
LV = \emptyset
$$
$$
\text{I}_\text{L} = \emptyset
$$

We finally have to define $\text{I}_\text{EXT}(x)$ for all $x \in IP$. This can in principle be done by starting from the RDF-interpretation above and going through the

$$
\begin{aligned}
I_S = \text{ex:AllergicToNuts} &\mapsto a \\
\text{ex:coconutMilk} &\mapsto c \\
\text{ex:Nutty} &\mapsto n \\
\text{ex:Pitiable} &\mapsto p \\
\text{ex:sebastian} &\mapsto s \\
\text{ex:Thai} &\mapsto t \\
\text{ex:vegetableThaiCurry} &\mapsto v \\
\text{ex:thaiDishBasedOn} &\mapsto d \\
\text{ex:eats} &\mapsto e \\
\text{ex:hasIngredient} &\mapsto h \\
\text{rdfs:subPropertyOf} &\mapsto b \\
\text{rdfs:ContainerMembershipProperty} &\mapsto i \\
\text{rdfs:domain} &\mapsto m \\
\text{rdfs:subClassOf} &\mapsto o \\
\text{rdfs:range} &\mapsto r \\
\text{rdf:type} &\mapsto y \\
\text{rdf:Property} &\mapsto \pi \\
\text{rdf:XMLLiteral} &\mapsto \rho_0 \\
\text{rdf:nil} &\mapsto \rho_1 \\
\text{rdf:List} &\mapsto \rho_2 \\
\text{rdf:Statement} &\mapsto \rho_3 \\
\text{rdf:subject} &\mapsto \rho_4 \\
\text{rdf:predicate} &\mapsto \rho_5 \\
\text{rdf:object} &\mapsto \rho_6 \\
\text{rdf:first} &\mapsto \rho_7 \\
\text{rdf:rest} &\mapsto \rho_8 \\
\text{rdf:Seq} &\mapsto \rho_9 \\
\text{rdf:Bag} &\mapsto \rho_{10} \\
\text{rdf:Alt} &\mapsto \rho_{11} \\
\text{rdf:value} &\mapsto \rho_{12} \\
\text{rdf:\_}n &\mapsto \delta_n \quad \text{for all } n \in \mathbb{N} \\
\text{rdfs:Resource} &\mapsto \sigma_0 \\
\text{rdfs:Literal} &\mapsto \sigma_1 \\
\text{rdfs:Datatype} &\mapsto \sigma_2 \\
\text{rdfs:Class} &\mapsto \sigma_3 \\
\text{rdfs:member} &\mapsto \sigma_4 \\
\text{rdfs:Container} &\mapsto \sigma_5 \\
\text{rdfs:comment} &\mapsto \sigma_6 \\
\text{rdfs:seeAlso} &\mapsto \sigma_7 \\
\text{rdfs:isDefinedBy} &\mapsto \sigma_8 \\
\text{rdfs:label} &\mapsto \sigma_9
\end{aligned}
$$

FIGURE 3.8: Example of I_S

list of requirements on an RDFS-interpretation from pages 82 through 83. While going through the list, we add to I_{EXT} to fulfill all of the requirements. Note, however, that some additions may necessitate going back to one of the earlier requirements and making more additions. Also, don't forget to watch the conditions on RDF-interpretations from page 80 which also need to be satisfied.

You should try this yourself, just to get a feeling for it. In fact, if you do this manually you will soon notice that it's a rather extensive and tedious task. In fact, we refrain from giving the complete I_{EXT}, which would be a bit pointless – it's better to do this automatically, e.g., by means discussed in Section 3.3.

3.3　Syntactic Reasoning with Deduction Rules

In the preceding sections, we introduced a model theoretic semantics for RDF(S) that defines the entailment relation, i.e. we specified in a mathematically precise way when an RDF(S) graph entails another RDF(S) graph. Yet, while a model-theoretic approach is very well suited to theoretically specify a logic's desired behavior with respect to what conclusions can be drawn, it provides no direct algorithmic means for actually doing the reasoning. In order to directly use the model theoretic semantics definition for deciding whether a given graph is entailed by a set of graphs, in principle *all* interpretations would have to be considered. However, as there are always infinitely many such interpretations, this is simply impossible – an essential problem occurring in the context of any sufficiently expressive logic.

Consequently, one strives for methods to decide the validity of conclusions syntactically. These methods would operate only on the given propositions of a logic without directly recurring to interpretations. Of course, any such method would have to be justified by mathematically proving that the results it yields (i.e. its so-called *operational semantics*) are exactly those expected from the model-theoretic semantics.

One option for describing such a syntactic method consists of providing so-called *deduction rules* (also known as inference rules or derivation rules) which in general have the form:

$$\frac{p_1 \ \cdots \ p_n}{p}$$

Such a deduction rule states that, given the validity of the propositions $p_1, \ldots, p_n$, we can deduce that p must also be valid. The whole set of deduction rules given for a logic (usually there are several) is called *deduction calculus*, and the fact that all propositions of a set P' can be derived from a proposition set P by some sequence of applications of the deduction rules is often expressed by writing $P \vdash P'$.

When comparing such a set of inference rules to the semantics of a logic (mediated by its entailment relation $\models$), there are two central notions: *soundness* and *completeness*. A deduction calculus is *sound* with respect to a given semantics if every proposition set P' that can be derived from a set of propositions P by means of the deduction rules is a semantic consequence; formally $P \vdash P'$ implies $P \models P'$. On the other hand, a deduction calculus is called *complete* if every proposition set P' that is semantically entailed by a proposition set P can also be deduced by means of the provided deduction rules, i.e. if $P \models P'$ implies $P \vdash P'$.

Note, however, that the existence of a (sound and complete) deduction calculus does not directly lead to a decision procedure, i.e. an algorithm that, given two proposition sets P and P', terminates after some time and correctly answers the question whether $P \models P'$. Clearly, there are infinitely many possibilities to apply the deduction rules (in the simplest case, the same rule might be applied over and over again), so simply trying out all of them does not work. In order to turn a deduction calculus into a decision procedure, one has to come up with a strategy telling what rules to apply when and when to stop. This is not always possible: there are even logics with a sound and complete deduction calculus that are undecidable, i.e. they lack a decision procedure. Therefore, one should be aware that a deduction calculus provides a way to syntactically characterize a logic's semantics and in the best case provides some hints on how to algorithmize inferencing but it is usually not a ready-to-implement blueprint of a reasoner.

We now consider the case for RDF(S). The different kinds of interpretations introduced previously (simple, RDF-, and RDFS-interpretations) lead to different entailment relations (according to the model-theoretic way of defining entailment relations introduced in Section 3.2). Consequently, we will in the following provide three different sets of deduction rules for triples. Applying a deduction rule in our special case just means adding the triple below the line to the graph under consideration.

By means of those derivation rules, the three distinct entailment relations (simple, RDF, and RDFS-entailment) can be characterized syntactically, although we need some special care in the RDFS case.

As the deduction rules that we will consider in the sequel usually do not only refer to single URIs or literals but, for instance, to all URIs or all literals, the following notations will come in handy:

- a and b can refer to arbitrary URIs (i.e. anything admissible for the predicate position in a triple),

- $\_{:}n$ will be used for the ID of a blank node,

- u and v refer to arbitrary URIs or blank node IDs (i.e. any possible subject of a triple),

- x and y can be used for arbitrary URIs, blank node IDs or literals (i.e. anything admissible for the object position in a triple), and

- l may be any literal.

Other symbols will be explained where they occur.

3.3.1 Deduction Rules for Simple Entailment

As suggested by its name, simple entailment can be characterized comparatively easily. Since all occurring URIs are treated equally, the question whether one graph entails another can be decided based on simple structural considerations which are captured by the following two deduction rules

$$\frac{u \quad a \quad x \quad .}{u \quad a \quad \_:n \quad .} \text{ se1}$$

$$\frac{u \quad a \quad x \quad .}{\_:n \quad a \quad x \quad .} \text{ se2}$$

However, one has to be careful when "weakening" a subject or object by applying either of these rules: The rules can safely be applied if the blank node identified by $\_:n$ is not contained at all in the graph the rule is applied to. If $\_:n$ is already contained, then the the rules are applicable only if $\_:n$ has been introduced by weakening the same URI, literal, or blank node identifier (via rule se1 or se2) as the current application of the rule does. In other words, se1 and se2 must not be used to turn distinct URIs, literals or bnodes into the same bnode. An example is given in Fig. 3.9.

It can be formally proven that those two deduction rules indeed capture the semantics of the simple entailment. More specifically, the following theorem holds:

THEOREM 3.1
A graph G_1 simply entails a graph G_2, if G_1 can be extended to a graph G_1' by virtue of the rules se1 and se2 such that G_2 is contained in G_1'.

Recalling that graphs are just sets of triples, the fact that G_2 is contained in G_1' just means $G_2 \subseteq G_1'$ (i.e. every triple from G_2 is contained in G_1').

In Fig. 3.11, we give an example that illustrates how this theorem can be used to show simple entailment.

3.3.2 Deduction Rules for RDF-Entailment

As opposed to simple entailment, RDF-entailment presumes a special meaning of particular URIs since it is defined via RDF-interpretations. In order to

In order to illustrate why this constraint to the applicability of the above deduction rules is essential, consider the following deduction:

$$\frac{\texttt{ex:heidrun ex:motherOf ex:sebastian .}}{\texttt{\_:id1 ex:motherOf ex:sebastian .}}\ \text{se2}$$

Essentially, the proposition "Heidrun is the mother of Sebastian" is weakened to the proposition "Sebastian has a mother." Furthermore, it would be possible to make the following deduction

$$\frac{\texttt{ex:wolfgang ex:marriedTo ex:heidrun .}}{\texttt{ex:wolfgang ex:marriedTo \_:id1 .}}\ \text{se1}$$

as `id1` is introduced by "weakening" the same URI `ex:heidrun` as in the previous deduction. Together the two generated triples can be read as "Sebastian's mother is married to Wolfgang."
However, imagine there was another triple

```
_:id1        ex:motherOf        ex:markus .
```

(i.e. "Markus has a mother") present in the graph to be reasoned about. Then, by violating the additional applicability constraint above, the first deduction would lead to the erroneous conclusion that Markus and Sebastian have the same mother.

FIGURE 3.9: Example of simple entailment

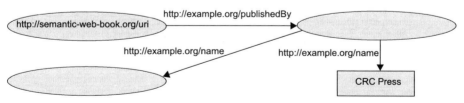

FIGURE 3.10: Graph that is simply entailed by the graph from Fig. 2.3

Suppose we want to find out whether the graph in Fig. 2.3 (let's call it G_1) entails the graph G_2 depicted in Fig. 3.10. To this end, we first represent G_1 as a set of triples:

```
book:uri   ex:publishedBy   crc:uri .
book:uri   ex:title         "Foundations of Semantic Web Technologies" .
crc:uri    ex:name          "CRC Press" .
```

We now have to find out whether and – if yes – how the given deduction rules se1 and se2 can be applied to this set such that the resulting graph G_1' contains the graph G_2 (again understood as a set of triples).

Indeed, applying rule se1 to the first of G_1's three triples allows us to add the triple

```
book:uri   ex:publishedBy   _:blank1 .
```

with a blank node to our graph. Moreover, by applying se2 to the third of the original triples, we can also add the triple

```
_:blank1   ex:name          "CRC Press" .
```

to the graph, since the empty node referenced by `_:blank1` has been introduced by rule se1 exactly for `crc:uri` (and no other URI). Finally, the application of rule se1 to the triple that has just been generated yields the triple

```
_:blank1   ex:name          _:blank2 .
```

By now, we have created a graph G_1' containing all triples from the original graph G_1 and three additional ones. Its not hard to see that exactly these three new triples together form the graph G_2 from Fig. 3.10. Hence, because of $G_2 \subseteq G_1'$, we have shown that G_1 simply entails G_2.

FIGURE 3.11:   Example deduction illustrating Theorem 3.1

account for this, the deduction rules have to be amended. In the sequel, we will introduce the deduction rules for RDF-entailment.

First, we provide a number of rules having no preconditions and therefore being always applicable. Essentially, those rules ensure that the RDF axiomatic triples (whose validity is explicitly demanded in the definition of RDF-interpretations) can always be derived. Hence, they have the form

$$\frac{}{u \quad a \quad x} \text{ rdfax}$$

for all RDF axiomatic triples "u a x." introduced in Section 3.2.2.[2]

Moreover, we need a specialized version of rule se1:

$$\frac{u \quad a \quad l \quad .}{u \quad a \quad \_{:}n \quad .} \text{ lg}$$

The same applicability restrictions as for rule se1 apply: lg must not be used to introduce a blank node that is already present in the graph and has not itself been created out of l. The deduction rule

$$\frac{u \quad a \quad y \quad .}{a \ \texttt{rdf:type rdf:Property} \ .} \text{ rdf1}$$

ensures that for every URI occurring anywhere in predicate position, one can deduce that it is of type `rdf:Property`. The last rule

$$\frac{u \quad a \quad l \quad .}{\_{:}n \ \texttt{rdf:type rdf:XMLLiteral}} \text{ rdf2}$$

allows us to deduce the existence of a literal if a concrete witness (namely, l) is present in the graph. Note that we have again the applicability condition that $\_{:}n$ must not be previously present in the considered graph unless it has been introduced for that very literal by a preceding application of the lg rule.

By means of these deduction rules and based on the characterization of simple entailment introduced in the preceding chapter, we can now also capture the RDF-entailment in a syntactic way.

THEOREM 3.2

A graph G_1 RDF entails a graph G_2 if and only if there is a graph G_1' that can be derived from G_1 by virtue of the rules lg, rdf1, rdf2, as well as rdfax such that G_1' simply entails G_2.

---

[2] Note that, technically, rdfax is a rule scheme comprising infinitely many rules, as there are infinitely many axiomatic triples due to the infinitely many URIs `rdf:_1`, `rdf:_2` and so forth. This fact needs special care when addressing decidability and implementation issues.

Observe that the syntactic deduction process is divided into two steps: initially the rules mentioned in the theorem (but not se1 and se2) are used to derive the graph G'_1 and thereafter the rules se1 and se2 (but only those) are employed to show simple entailment.

3.3.3   Deduction Rules for RDFS-Entailment

Beyond the RDF constructs, the RDFS vocabulary contains further URIs that come with a special interpretation. This necessitates the introduction of a variety of further deduction rules:

RDFS axiomatic triples

Also for RDFS-entailment, each of the (again infinitely many) axiomatic triples must be derivable without preconditions. Hence we have the rule

$$\frac{}{u\ \ a\ \ x}\ \text{rdfsax}$$

for all RDFS axiomatic triples "$u\ \ a\ \ x$." listed in Section 3.2.3. Note that this rule covers (in combination with rules rdfs2 and rdfs3) all the domain and range restrictions specified by those triples.

Treatment of literals

$$\frac{u\ \ a\ \ l\ \ .}{\texttt{\_:}n\ \texttt{rdf:type rdfs:Literal}\ .}\ \text{rdfs1}$$

where l is an untyped literal (with or without language tag) and $\_:n$ again identifies a blank node with the usual novelty restriction. Essentially this rule allows us to deduce an existence statement with respect to literals from their occurrence.

Effects of property restrictions

$$\frac{a\ \texttt{rdfs:domain}\ x\ .\qquad u\ \ a\ \ y\ .}{u\ \texttt{rdf:type}\ x\ .}\ \text{rdfs2}$$

As pointed out in the previous chapter, `rdfs:domain` is used to stipulate that if an individual is the start of a given property then we can deduce that it must be a member of a certain class. If we now encounter a triple containing the corresponding property URI as predicate, we can conclude that this triple's subject must be in this class. This type of deduction is realized by rule rdfs2.

$$\frac{a\ \texttt{rdfs:range}\ x\ .\qquad u\ \ a\ \ v\ .}{v\ \texttt{rdf:type}\ x\ .}\ \text{rdfs3}$$

In an analogue manner, `rdfs:range` is used to infer class memberships for a property's target resources, allowing us to draw corresponding conclusions about a triple's object (rule rdfs3).

Everything is a resource

The following deduction rules ensure that every URI occurring in a triple can also be formally identified to refer to a resource. They ensure that the type "resource" can be explicitly assigned to any subject and any object that is not a literal.

$$\frac{u \quad a \quad x \quad .}{u \ \texttt{rdf:type rdfs:Resource} \ .} \ \text{rdfs4a}$$

$$\frac{u \quad a \quad v \quad .}{v \ \texttt{rdf:type rdfs:Resource} \ .} \ \text{rdfs4b}$$

Note that we do not need an extra deduction rule for enabling the same typing for triple predicates, since this can be derived from the other deduction rules:

$$\frac{\dfrac{u \quad a \quad x}{a \ \texttt{rdf:type rdf:Property}}\text{rdf1}}{a \ \texttt{rdf:type rdfs:Resource}}\text{rdfs4a}$$

Subproperties

The next two deduction rules make sure that the special characteristics of the `rdfs:subPropertyOf` property, by definition demanded for every RDFS-interpretation, are accessible for syntactic deduction: transitivity (rdfs5) and reflexivity (rdfs6).

$$\frac{u \ \texttt{rdfs:subPropertyOf} \ v \ . \qquad v \ \texttt{rdfs:subPropertyOf} \ x \ .}{u \ \texttt{rdfs:subPropertyOf} \ x \ .} \ \text{rdfs5}$$

$$\frac{u \ \texttt{rdf:type rdf:Property} \ .}{u \ \texttt{rdfs:subPropertyOf} \ u \ .} \ \text{rdfs6}$$

The third deduction rule dedicated to `rdfs:subPropertyOf` operationalizes its actual "encoding purpose," namely that all pairs of resources that are interlinked by a property are also connected by any superproperty of this property.

$$\frac{a \ \texttt{rdfs:subPropertyOf} \ b \ . \qquad u \quad a \quad y \quad .}{u \quad b \quad y \quad .} \ \text{rdfs7}$$

By this rule, subproperty specifications (which can be conceived as a kind of macro) can be applied to concrete triples (by executing the macro).

An example of an application of this rule would be

$$\frac{\texttt{ex:motherOf rdfs:subPropertyOf ex:ancestorOf .} \quad \texttt{ex:heidrun ex:motherOf ex:sebastian .}}{\texttt{ex:heidrun ex:ancestorOf ex:sebastian .}} \; \text{rdfs7}$$

Subclasses

The following deduction rules capture the semantic characteristics of the `subClassOf` property.

$$\frac{u \;\; \texttt{rdf:type rdfs:Class .}}{u \;\; \texttt{rdfs:subClassOf rdfs:Resource .}} \; \text{rdfs8}$$

By means of this rule, every URI typed as a class can be concluded to denote a subclass of the class of all resources.

$$\frac{u \;\; \texttt{rdfs:subClassOf} \;\; x \;\; . \qquad v \;\; \texttt{rdf:type} \;\; u \;\; .}{v \;\; \texttt{rdf:type} \;\; x \;\; .} \; \text{rdfs9}$$

This rule allows us to "inherit" a resource's membership in a class to the superclasses of this class.

$$\frac{u \;\; \texttt{rdf:type rdfs:Class .}}{u \;\; \texttt{rdfs:subClassOf} \;\; u \;\; .} \; \text{rdfs10}$$

Hereby we can deduce that every class is its own subclass, in other words: this rule realizes the reflexivity of the `rdfs:subClassOf` property.

$$\frac{u \;\; \texttt{rdfs:subClassOf} \;\; v \;\; . \qquad v \;\; \texttt{rdfs:subClassOf} \;\; x \;\; .}{u \;\; \texttt{rdfs:subClassOf} \;\; x \;\; .} \; \text{rdfs11}$$

Accordingly, the rule rdfs11 implements the `rdfs:subClassOf` property's transitivity.

Container

The following rule identifies the `rdfs:member` property as superproperty of all properties contained in the `rdfs:ContainerMembershipProperty` class.

$$\frac{u \;\; \texttt{rdf:type rdfs:ContainerMembershipProperty .}}{u \;\; \texttt{rdfs:subPropertyOf rdfs:member .}} \; \text{rdfs12}$$

Datatypes

Eventually, by the last rule, any resource that has been identified as data-type (which is equated with its value space) can be inferred to be a subclass of all literal values.

$$\frac{u \text{ rdf:type rdfs:Datatype .}}{u \text{ rdfs:subClassOf rdfs:Literal .}} \text{ rdfs13}$$

Reliteralizing blank nodes

The following rule can be seen as a kind of inverse of the rule gl:

$$\frac{u \; a \; \_{:}n \; .}{u \; a \; l \; .} \text{ gl}$$

where $\_{:}n$ identifies a blank node introduced by an earlier "weakening" of the literal l via the rule lg.

In fact, the necessity of this rule is not at all obvious. It has been added to the calculus at a rather late stage in the approval phase of the respective W3C document in order to ensure deductions that are required by the RDFS semantics. To demonstrate why it is indeed needed, consider the following example:

```
ex:Even        ex:lastDigits    "02468"  .
ex:lastDigits  rdfs:range       rdfs:Class   .
```

It takes a little effort to verify that the triple

```
_:id1          rdfs:subClassOf  "02468"  .
```

is RDFS-entailed. However, gl is necessary to come up with a corresponding deduction:

$$\frac{\cfrac{\cfrac{\cfrac{\cfrac{\text{ex:Even ex:lastDigits ¨02468¨ .}}{\text{ex:Even ex:lastDigits \_:id1 .}} \text{lg}}{\text{ex:lastDigits rdfs:range rdfs:Class .}}}{\text{\_:id1 rdf:type rdf:Class}} \text{rdfs3}}{\text{\_:id1 rdfs:SubClassOf \_:id1}} \text{rdfs8}}{\text{\_:id1 rdfs:SubClassOf ¨02468¨}} \text{gl}$$

Now, prior to framing how RDFS-entailment can be captured by deduction rules, we have to address a somewhat peculiar special case. If a given graph G is inconsistent (which means that there is no interpretation that is a model of

G), it entails *any arbitrary* graph (which can be easily understood by considering the model-theoretic semantics definition). As opposed to other logics, such as predicate logic (see Appendix C) or OWL (which will be dealt with in the next chapter), in RDFS the opportunities to cause inconsistencies are rather restricted.

As an example of such an inconsistency in RDFS, consider the following two triples:

```
ex:hasSmiley        rdfs:range      rdf:Literal .
ex:viciousRemark    ex:hasSmiley    ">:->"^^XMLLiteral .
```

Therein, on the one hand, all targets of the `ex:hasSmiley` property are required to be literal values (i.e. elements of LV). On the other hand, an ill-typed XML literal (due to the imbalanced occurrences of ">"), which by definition must *not* be interpreted as a literal value, is in the object position of a triple containing `ex:hasSmiley` as predicate. Hence there can be no RDFS-interpretation valuing both triples as *true*.

However, such an enforced type mismatch can be diagnosed relatively easy: it occurs as soon as a triple of the form

```
x rdf:type rdfs:Literal .
```

can be derived, where x has been assigned to an ill-typed XML literal by rule lg. Such a case is called an *XML clash*.

Informed about this special case, we can now give a sufficient syntactic criterion for RDFS-entailment in the following theorem.

THEOREM 3.3
A graph G_1 RDFS entails a graph G_2 if there is a graph G_1' which can be derived from G_1 via the rules lg, gl, rdfax, rdf1, rdf2 as well as rdfs1 to rdfs13 and rdfsax such that

- G_1' *simply entails G_2 or*

- G_1' *contains an XML clash.*

Note that the preceding theorem just guarantees soundness of the given deduction calculus. When the calculus was provided in the RDF semantics specification, it was also considered complete, but a bit later that turned out not to be the case.

As an example of the calculus' incompleteness, consider the following set of triples:

```
ex:isHappilyMarriedTo    rdfs:subPropertyOf    _:bnode .
_:bnode                  rdfs:domain           ex:Person .
ex:markus                ex:isHappilyMarriedTo ex:anja .
```

It is not hard to show that the triple

```
ex:markus                rdf:type              ex:Person .
```

is a semantic consequence of the above. However, it cannot be derived by means of the given deduction calculus.

One option to deal with this problem is to extend the definition of RDF: it has been shown that allowing blank nodes in the predicate position of triples overcomes this problem.

It remains to consider the issue mentioned in Section 3.3: even the existence of a sound and complete set of deduction rules does not ensure that semantic entailment of two proposition sets (or in our case, graphs) can be decided by an automatic procedure.[3] In our case, it can be shown that the set of (relevant) inferable triples cannot become arbitrary large and therefore a kind of saturation is certainly reached. However, showing this is not trivial: in principle, arbitrarily many blank node triples can be created by the rules se1 and se2 in the simple entailment case. As to RDF and RDFS entailment, there are infinitely many rules involved (due to the infinitely many axiomatic triples). So one has to carefully consider how to restrict the application of rules without losing relevant consequences. Moreover, even if a terminating algorithm has been found, it might still not be efficient at all. Summing up, the design of efficient RDF(S) reasoning tools for possibly large data sets is an extremely challenging task requiring both theoretical expertise and profound software engineering skills. This is also substantiated by the fact that simple, RDF, and RDFS entailment are NP-complete problems.[4]

---

[3] Put into terms of theoretical computer science: there are problems which are recursively enumerable but not decidable. Entailment in first order predicate logic is a prominent example of this.

[4] The reason for this complexity is the blank nodes. Checking whether an RDF graph simply entails an RDF graph containing blank nodes allows us to solve the graph homomorphism problem which is known to be NP-complete. By disallowing blank nodes, all three entailment problems become polynomial.

3.3.4   Additional Rules for Datatypes

The deduction rules introduced so far only addressed the compatibility with RDFS-interpretations which only take care of the correct semantic characterization of `rdf:XMLLiteral`. External datatypes may be introduced by name (by typing them as class members of the `rdfs:datatype` class); however, it is impossible to completely characterize their semantic behavior only by RDFS-internal means.

Of course, additional deduction rules capturing the functionality of specific datatypes would have to depend on the intended semantics of the latter. Still, it is possible to state how frequently occurring interdependencies related to datatypes should be expressed by deduction rules.

For instance, if a literal s is known to be well-formed with respect to a datatype d being represented by the URI d (i.e., $D(d) = d$ and s is contained in d's lexical space Lex_d), the following deduction rule yields valid triples

$$\frac{d \text{ rdf:type rdfs:Datatype . } \qquad u \text{ } a\,"s\,"\hat{\ }\hat{\ }d \text{ .}}{\_:n \text{ rdf:type } d \text{ .}} \text{ rdfD1}$$

Here, $\_:n$ denotes a blank node which has not been assigned to any other entity than the literal $"s\,"\hat{\ }\hat{\ }d$. In the end, this deduction rule just allows us to infer the existence of a resource of some type, if a well-typed individual of this type is explicitly mentioned.

As another frequently occurring case, the value spaces of certain datatypes might overlap, e.g., there are numbers being both natural and floating point numbers (obviously, the typed literals $"2"\hat{\ }\hat{\ }$`xsd:nonNegativeInteger` and $"2.00"\hat{\ }\hat{\ }$`xsd:decimal` should be recognized to represent the same values). Now suppose that the lexical expression s of a datatype denoted by the URI d is expected to represent the same value as the lexical expression t of a datatype denoted by e. Then the following rule can be applied

$$\frac{\begin{array}{c} d \text{ rdf:type rdfs:Datatype .} \\ e \text{ rdf:type rdfs:Datatype .} \\ u \text{ } a \text{ } "s\,"\hat{\ }\hat{\ }d \text{ .} \end{array}}{u \text{ } a \text{ } "t\,"\hat{\ }\hat{\ }e \text{ .}} \text{ rdfD2}$$

It essentially allows us to substitute any occurrence of one typed literal in object position (the only place where it is allowed to show up syntactically) by the other one. Mark that this rule covers the case $s = t$ (as for instance, for $"2"\hat{\ }\hat{\ }$`xsd:nonNegativeInteger` and $"2"\hat{\ }\hat{\ }$`xsd:Integer`).

Another frequent piece of information about datatypes is that one includes the other (e.g., any natural number is an integer). If the value space of the datatype d is known to be contained in the value space of another datatype e, the deduction rule

$$\frac{}{d \text{ rdfs:subClassOf } e \text{ .}} \text{ rdfDAx}$$

can be used to add the respective subclass relation to the set of axiomatic triples.

If the mentioned preconditions are satisfied, the above deduction rules lead to valid conclusions. However, there is no guarantee that all semantic consequences can be created by virtue of those deduction rules.

For instance, in any D-interpretation that supports all XML datatypes admissible for RDF and that satisfies the triples

```
u    rdf:type    xsd:nonNegativeInteger .
u    rdf:type    xsd:nonPositiveInteger .
```

also the triple

```
u    rdf:type    xsd:byte .
```

must hold. Yet, it cannot be derived from the given rules.

Likewise it would be possible to use the characteristics of particular datatypes to cause inconsistencies by assigning two datatypes with disjoint value spaces to one resource, e.g.:

```
u    rdf:type    xsd:integer .
u    rdf:type    xsd:string .
```

All those and many more consequences that arise from the special semantics of D-interpretations with particular datatypes would have to be realized by software systems which claim to support those datatypes in a logically complete way. Note, however, that for RDF(S) compliance as prescribed by the W3C specification, only the support of `rdf:XMLLiteral` is required.

3.3.5 Example of an RDFS Deduction

Now, as we have treated the deduction rules for RDFS-entailment, we will illustrate their usage by a small example. We start with the example ontology introduced in Section 2.6 and would like to logically detect whether an emergency will occur, i.e. whether a person allergic to nuts consumes something having nutty ingredients. Translated into graph notation this would mean checking whether the graph G_1 depicted in Fig. 2.13 entails the graph G_2 from Fig. 3.12.

To start with, let's list the triples of G_1:

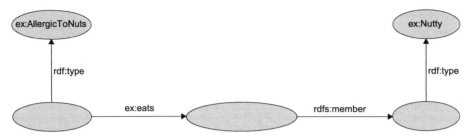

FIGURE 3.12:   Graph G_2, possibly RDFS-entailed by G_1

```
ex:vegetableThaiCurry   ex:thaiDishBasedOn   ex:coconutMilk .
ex:sebastian            rdf:type             ex:AllergicToNuts .
ex:sebastian            ex:eats              ex:vegetableThaiCurry .

ex:AllergicToNuts       rdfs:subClassOf      ex:Pitiable .
ex:thaiDishBasedOn      rdfs:domain          ex:Thai .
ex:thaiDishBasedOn      rdfs:range           ex:Nutty .
ex:thaiDishBasedOn      rdfs:subPropertyOf   ex:hasIngredient .
ex:hasIngredient        rdf:type     rdfs:ContainerMembershipProperty.
```

Next, we apply several deduction rules to G_1. We exploit the classification of objects via range restrictions, the fact that `rdfs:member` comprises all containedness relations, the transitivity of the subproperty relation and the generalization of a triple by subproperties. This is shown in Fig. 3.13.

This way, we have obtained the graph G_1' by enriching the graph G_1. In order to prove the RDF-entailment in question, it remains to show that G_1' simply entails G_2. It is easy to see that this can be achieved by manifold application of se1 and se2, in analogy to the example given in Fig. 3.11.

3.4   The Semantic Limits of RDF(S)

The semantics presented in the previous sections is not the only "reasonable" semantics for RDF(S). Further logical consequences that do not arise from the standard semantics (which is sometimes also called *intensional semantics*) might be desirable in some cases. This can be realized by an alternative *extensional semantics* for RDFS which imposes stronger constraints on RDFS-interpretations. The reason for choosing the weaker semantics as the standard is the following: for the intensional semantics, there are deduction rules that can be implemented rather easily, which facilitates the development of tools supporting RDFS. Hence, it is reasonable to define the standard as a kind of rule rdfs3:

$$\frac{\begin{array}{c} \texttt{ex:vegetableThaiCurry ex:thaiDishBasedOn ex:coconutMilk .} \\ \texttt{ex:thaiDishBasedOn rdfs:range ex:Nutty .} \end{array}}{\texttt{ex:coconutMilk rdf:type ex:Nutty .}}$$

rule rdfs12:

$$\frac{\texttt{ex:hasIngredient rdf:type rdfs:ContainerMembershipProperty .}}{\texttt{ex:hasIngredient rdfs:subPropertyOf rdfs:member .}}$$

rule rdfs5:

$$\frac{\begin{array}{c} \texttt{ex:thaiDishBasedOn rdfs:subPropertyOf ex:hasIngredient .} \\ \texttt{ex:hasIngredient rdfs:subPropertyOf rdfs:member .} \end{array}}{\texttt{ex:thaiDishBasedOn rdfs:subPropertyOf rdfs:member .}}$$

rule rdfs7:

$$\frac{\begin{array}{c} \texttt{ex:thaiDishBasedOn rdfs:subPropertyOf rdfs:member .} \\ \texttt{ex:vegetableThaiCurry ex:thaiDishBasedOn ex:coconutMilk .} \end{array}}{\texttt{ex:vegetableThaiCurry rdfs:member ex:coconutMilk .}}$$

FIGURE 3.13: Example of an RDFS deduction

minimal requirement for RDF(S)-compatible systems.

As an example of a seemingly reasonable inference not supported by the standard RDF(S) semantics consider the triples

```
ex:speaksWith    rdfs:domain     ex:Homo .
ex:Homo          rdfs:subClassOf ex:Primates .
```

which should allow us to deduce the following triple:

```
ex:speaksWith    rdfs:domain     ex:Primates .
```

Irrespective of the question whether the intensional or the extensional semantics is employed, the modeling capabilities of RDFS are fundamentally restricted. As one of the most significant shortcomings, it is impossible to express negated statements: the fact that some statement is not true cannot be described in RDFS.[5] Of course, it is possible to incorporate negation into class or property names and simply introduce URIs like ex:NonSmoker or ex:notMarriedTo. However, there is no way to enforce that those vocabulary elements are interpreted in accordance with their intended semantics. For instance, the two triples

```
ex:sebastian   rdf:type   ex:NonSmoker .
ex:sebastian   rdf:type   ex:Smoker .
```

do not cause an inconsistency (as one might expect) as there is no way to specify in RDFS that the two classes denoted by ex:NonSmoker and ex:Smoker must not contain common elements. In the next chapter we will introduce an ontology language which provides those capabilities, and many more, the cost being that automated inferencing becomes much harder in the worst case.

3.5 Summary

By introducing a model-theoretic semantics of RDF(S), a binding standard for tools processing RDF(S) data is created. We distinguish simple, RDF- and RDFS-entailment, which are defined via respective interpretations. Moreover,

---

[5]Note also that the absence of a triple in a graph does not imply that the corresponding statement does not hold as the RDF(S) semantics is based on the open world assumption.

we discussed how any of those entailments can be characterized in terms of a deduction calculus, whereby in the case of RDFS, some amendments would be required. In addition, we investigated how external datatypes may be introduced into the semantics. Finally, we pointed out that the ontology language RDFS is insufficient for certain modeling purposes.

3.6 Exercises

Exercise 3.1 Describe a very simple RDFS-interpretation that is a model of the example ontology from Section 2.6.

Exercise 3.2 Consider the ontology from Exercise 3.1 and find

- a simply entailed triple,

- an RDF-entailed triple, which is not simply entailed,

- an RDFS-entailed triple, which is not RDF-entailed.

Exercise 3.3 As you know, the *unique name assumption* does not hold in RDF(S), i.e. in a model, several URIs might be assigned to the same resource. Contemplate whether (and if so, how) it is possible to specify in RDFS that two given URIs refer to the same resource.

Exercise 3.4 The *empty graph* does not contain any triples (i.e. it corresponds to the empty set). Give derivations showing that the empty graph RDFS-entails the following triples:

```
rdfs:Resource rdf:type rdfs:Class .
rdfs:Class rdf:type rdfs:Class .
rdfs:Literal rdf:type rdfs:Class .
rdf:XMLLiteral rdf:type rdfs:Class .
rdfs:Datatype rdf:type rdfs:Class .
rdf:Seq rdf:type rdfs:Class .
rdf:Bag rdf:type rdfs:Class .
rdf:Alt rdf:type rdfs:Class .
rdfs:Container rdf:type rdfs:Class .
rdf:List rdf:type rdfs:Class .
rdfs:ContainerMembershipProperty rdf:type rdfs:Class .
rdf:Property rdf:type rdfs:Class .
rdf:Statement rdf:type rdfs:Class .
rdfs:domain rdf:type rdf:Property .
rdfs:range rdf:type rdf:Property .
```

```
rdfs:subPropertyOf rdf:type rdf:Property .
rdfs:subClassOf rdf:type rdf:Property .
rdfs:member rdf:type rdf:Property .
rdfs:seeAlso rdf:type rdf:Property .
rdfs:isDefinedBy rdf:type rdf:Property .
rdfs:comment rdf:type rdf:Property .
rdfs:label rdf:type rdf:Property .
```

3.7 Further Reading

There is comparatively little literature about the RDF(S) semantics. The W3C document "Semantics" [Hay04] constitutes the normative standard reference.

An article of Herman J. ter Horst [tH05] provides further information on the incompleteness of the RDFS deduction rules and complexity of RDFS reasoning.

"A Semantic Web Primer" [AvH08] provides one way to define the extensional semantics of RDFS via a translation into first-order predicate logic. Another approach for expressing the simple, RDF, and RDFS semantics in terms of first-order logic is described in Section 6.4.6.

Part II

Web Ontology Language OWL

Chapter 4

Ontologies in OWL

In this chapter, we introduce the ontology language OWL. We focus on an introduction to the syntax and on conveying an intuitive understanding of the semantics. We will also discuss the forthcoming OWL 2 standard. A formal treatment of the semantics will be done later in Chapter 5, and a discussion of OWL software tools can be found in Section 8.5.

We have seen at the end of Chapter 3 that RDF(S) is suitable for modeling simple ontologies and allows the derivation of implicit knowledge. But we have also seen that RDF(S) provides only very limited expressive means and that it is not possible to represent more complex knowledge. For example, it is not possible to model the meaning of the sentences from Fig. 4.1 in RDF(S) in a sufficiently precise way.

For modeling such complex knowledge, expressive representation languages based on formal logic are commonly used. This also allows us to do logical reasoning on the knowledge, and thereby enables the access to knowledge which is only implicitly modeled. OWL is such a language.

The acronym OWL stands for *Web Ontology Language*.[1] Since 2004 OWL is a W3C recommended standard for the modeling of ontologies, and since then has seen a steeply rising increase in popularity in many application domains. Central for the design of OWL was to find a reasonable balance between expressivity of the language on the one hand, and efficient reasoning, i.e. scalability, on the other hand. This was in order to deal with the general observation that complex language constructs for representing implicit knowledge usually yield high computational complexities or even undecidability of

---

[1] There exist a number of speculations about the origin of the distorted acronym. In particular, it is often said that the acronym was a reference to a character appearing in the book *Winnie the Pooh* by Alan Alexander Milne: the character is an owl which always misspells its name as wol instead of owl.

Historically correct, however, is that the acronym was originally proposed by Tim Finin in an email to www-webont-wg@w3.org, dated 27th of December 2001, which can be found under http://lists.w3.org/Archives/Public/www-webont-wg/2001Dec/0169.html: "I prefer the three letter WOL .... How about OWL as a variation. ...it has several advantages: (1) it has just one obvious pronunciation which is easy on the ear; (2) it opens up great opportunities for logos; (3) owls are associated with wisdom; (4) it has an interesting back story."

The mentioned background story concerns an MIT project called *One World Language* by William A. Martin from the 1970s, which was an early attempt at developing a universal language for knowledge representation.

Every project has at least one participant.
Projects are always internal or external projects.
Gisela Schillinger and Anne Eberhardt are the secretaries of Rudi Studer.
The superior of my superior is also my superior.

FIGURE 4.1: Sentences which cannot be modeled in RDF(S) in a sufficiently precise way

reasoning, and therefore unfavorable scalability properties. In order to give the user a choice between different degrees of expressivity, three sublanguages of OWL – called *species* of OWL – have been designed: OWL Full, OWL DL, and OWL Lite. OWL Full contains both OWL DL and OWL Lite, and OWL DL contains OWL Lite. The main differences between the sublanguages are summarized in Fig. 4.2. We will discuss this in more detail in Section 4.2.

We introduce OWL in this chapter by means of a syntax based on RDF. While most of the contents of this chapter should be accessible without any in-depth knowledge about RDF, the reader may occasionally want to refer to Chapter 2, and in particular to Sections 2.1 to 2.3.

4.1   OWL Syntax and Intuitive Semantics

OWL documents are used for modeling OWL ontologies. Two different syntaxes have been standardized in order to express these. One of them is based on RDF and is usually used for data exchange. It is also called *OWL RDF syntax* since OWL documents in RDF syntax are also valid RDF documents. The other syntax is called the *OWL abstract syntax* and is somewhat more readable for humans. However, it is only available for OWL DL, and it will undergo some major changes in the transition to OWL 2. In this chapter, we introduce the RDF syntax since it is more widely used. In Chapter 5 we will present yet another syntax for OWL DL which is very popular among researchers due to its conciseness and because it is stripped of some technicalities. Indeed in later chapters, we will mostly use this latter syntax. The RDF syntax which we now introduce, though, is suitable for data exchange on the Web, which is why it is so important.

An OWL ontology is basically expressed in terms of classes and properties, which we already know from RDF(S). In OWL, however, much more complex relationships between these classes and properties can be described. The sentences in Fig. 4.1 are examples of such complex relationships. We will see how they can be modeled by means of a number of constructors taken from

OWL Full

- contains OWL DL and OWL Lite,
- is the only OWL sublanguage containing all of RDFS,
- very expressive,
- semantically difficult to understand and to work with,
- undecidable,
- supported by hardly any software tools.

OWL DL

- contains OWL Lite and is contained in OWL Full,
- decidable,
- fully supported by most software tools,
- worst-case computational complexity: NExpTime.

OWL Lite

- contained in OWL DL and OWL Full,
- decidable,
- less expressive,
- worst-case computational complexity: ExpTime.

FIGURE 4.2:   The three sublanguages of OWL and their most important general properties. Further details can be found in Section 4.2

formal logic. We will introduce them on an intuitive level in this chapter, and will give an in-depth formal treatment of the underlying logical aspects in Chapter 5.

4.1.1 The Header of an OWL Ontology

The header of an OWL document contains information about namespaces, versioning, and so-called annotations. This information has no direct impact on the knowledge expressed by the ontology.

Since every OWL document is an RDF document, it contains a root element. Namespaces are specified in the opening tag of the root, as in the following example.

```
<rdf:RDF
    xmlns    ="http://www.example.org/"
    xmlns:rdf ="http://www.w3.org/1999/02/22-rdf-syntax-ns#"
    xmlns:xsd ="http://www.w3.org/2001/XMLSchema#"
    xmlns:rdfs="http://www.w3.org/2000/01/rdf-schema#"
    xmlns:owl ="http://www.w3.org/2002/07/owl#">
```

The second line in this example defines the namespace used for objects without prefix. Note the namespace which should be used for `owl`.

An OWL document may furthermore contain some general information about the ontology. This is done within an `owl:Ontology` element. We give an example.

```
<owl:Ontology rdf:about="">
  <rdfs:comment
      rdf:datatype="http://www.w3.org/2001/XMLSchema#string">
    SWRC ontology, version of June 2007
  </rdfs:comment>
  <owl:versionInfo>v0.7.1</owl:versionInfo>
  <owl:imports rdf:resource="http://www.example.org/foo" />
  <owl:priorVersion
      rdf:resource="http://ontoware.org/projects/swrc" />
</owl:Ontology>
```

Note the first line of this example: it states that the current base URI – usually given by `xml:base` – identifies an instance of the class `owl:Ontology`. Some header elements are inherited from RDFS, for example the following:

```
rdfs:comment
rdfs:label
rdfs:seeAlso
rdfs:isDefinedBy
```

For versioning, the following elements can be used:

    owl:versionInfo
    owl:priorVersion
    owl:backwardCompatibleWith
    owl:incompatibleWith
    owl:DeprecatedClass
    owl:DeprecatedProperty

owl:versionInfo usually has a string as object. With the statements owl:DeprecatedClass and owl:DeprecatedProperty, parts of the ontology can be described which are still supported, but should not be used any longer. The other versioning elements contain pointers to other ontologies, with the obvious meaning.

It is also possible to import other OWL ontologies using the owl:imports element as given in the example above. The content of the imported ontology is then understood as being part of the importing ontology.

4.1.2 Classes, Roles, and Individuals

The basic building blocks of OWL are classes and properties, which we already know from RDF(S), and individuals, which are declared as RDF instances of classes. OWL properties are also called *roles*, and we will use both notions interchangeably.

Classes are defined in OWL using owl:Class. The following example states the RDF triple Professor rdf:type owl:Class.[2]

```
<rdf:Description rdf:about="Professor">
  <rdf:type rdf:resource="&owl;Class" />
</rdf:Description>
```

Equivalently, the following short form can be used:

```
<owl:Class rdf:about="Professor" />
```

Via rdf:about="Professor", the class gets assigned the name Professor, which can be used for references to the class. Instead of rdf:about it is also possible to use rdf:ID, if the conditions given on page 33 are observed.[3]

---

[2] We assume that <!ENTITY owl 'http://www.w3.org/2002/07/owl#'> has been declared – see Section 2.2.5.

[3] For better readability, we assume that http://www.example.org/ is the namespace used in all our examples, as declared on page 114.

There are two predefined classes, called `owl:Thing` and `owl:Nothing`. The class `owl:Thing` is the most general class, and has every individual as an instance. The class `owl:Nothing` has no instances by definition.

`owl:Class` is a subclass of `rdfs:Class`. There are some differences, however, which we will discuss in Section 4.2 on the different sublanguages of OWL.

As in RDF, individuals can be declared to be instances of classes. This is called *class assignment.*

```
<rdf:Description rdf:about="rudiStuder">
  <rdf:type rdf:resource="Professor" />
</rdf:Description>
```

Equivalently, the following short form can be used.

```
<Professor rdf:about="rudiStuder" />
```

There are two different kinds of roles in OWL: abstract roles and concrete roles. Abstract roles connect individuals with individuals. Concrete roles connect individuals with data values, i.e. with elements of datatypes. Both kinds of roles are subproperties of `rdf:Property`. However, there are again some differences which we will discuss in Section 4.2 on the different sublanguages of OWL.

Roles are declared similarly as classes.

```
<owl:ObjectProperty rdf:about="hasAffiliation" />
<owl:DatatypeProperty rdf:about="firstName" />
```

The first of these roles is abstract and shall express which organization(s) a given person is affiliated with. The second role is concrete and assigns first names to persons. Domain and range of roles can be declared via `rdfs:domain` and `rdfs:range` as in RDFS.[4]

---

[4]We assume that `<!ENTITY xsd 'http://www.w3.org/2001/XMLSchema#'>` has been declared – see Section 2.2.5.

xsd:string	xsd:boolean	xsd:decimal
xsd:float	xsd:double	xsd:dateTime
xsd:time	xsd:date	xsd:gYearMonth
xsd:gYear	xsd:gMonthDay	xsd:gDay
xsd:gMonth	xsd:hexBinary	xsd:base64Binary
xsd:anyURI	xsd:token	xsd:normalizedString
xsd:language	xsd:NMTOKEN	xsd:positiveInteger
xsd:NCName	xsd:Name	xsd:nonPositiveInteger
xsd:long	xsd:int	xsd:negativeInteger
xsd:short	xsd:byte	xsd:nonNegativeInteger
xsd:unsignedLong	xsd:unsignedInt	xsd:unsignedShort
xsd:unsignedByte	xsd:integer	

FIGURE 4.3: XML datatypes for OWL

```
<owl:ObjectProperty rdf:about="hasAffiliation">
  <rdfs:domain rdf:resource="Person" />
  <rdfs:range rdf:resource="Organization" />
</owl:ObjectProperty>
<owl:DatatypeProperty rdf:about="firstName">
  <rdfs:domain rdf:resource="Person" />
  <rdfs:range  rdf:resource="&xsd;string" />
</owl:DatatypeProperty>
```

Besides xsd:string it is also possible to use xsd:integer in OWL. Indeed all XML datatypes from Fig. 4.3 can in principle be used in OWL, but the standard does not require their support. Concrete tools typically support only a selected set of datatypes. rdfs:Literal can also be used as datatype.

Just as in RDF, it is also possible to explicitly declare two individuals connected by a role, as in the following example. This is called a *role assignment*. The example also shows that roles may not be functional,[5] as it is possible to give two affiliations for rudiStuder.

```
<Person rdf:about="rudiStuder">
  <hasAffiliation rdf:resource="aifb" />
  <hasAffiliation rdf:resource="ontoprise" />
  <firstName rdf:datatype="&xsd;string">Rudi</firstName>
</Person>
```

---

[5]Functionality of roles will be treated on page 135.

The class inclusions

```
<owl:Class rdf:about="Professor">
  <rdfs:subClassOf rdf:resource="FacultyMember" />
</owl:Class>
<owl:Class rdf:about="FacultyMember">
  <rdfs:subClassOf rdf:resource="Person" />
</owl:Class>
```

allow us to infer that `Professor` is a subclass of `Person`.

FIGURE 4.4:   Logical inference by transitivity of `rdfs:subClassOf`

In this book, we adhere to a common notational convention that names of classes start with uppercase letters, while names for roles and individuals start with lowercase letters. This is not required by the W3C recommendation, but it is good practice and enhances readability.

4.1.3 Simple Class Relations

OWL classes can be put in relation to each other via `rdfs:subClassOf`. A simple example of this is the following.

```
<owl:Class rdf:about="Professor">
  <rdfs:subClassOf rdf:resource="FacultyMember" />
</owl:Class>
```

The construct `rdfs:subClassOf` is considered to be transitive as in RDFS. This allows us to draw simple inferences, as in Fig. 4.4. Also, every class is a subclass of `owl:Thing`, and `owl:Nothing` is a subclass of every other class.

Two classes can be declared to be disjoint using `owl:disjointWith`. This means that they do not share any individual, i.e. their intersection is empty. This allows corresponding inferences, as exemplified in Fig. 4.5.

Two classes can be declared to be equivalent using `owl:equivalentClass`. Equivalently, this can be achieved by stating that two classes are subclasses of each other. Further examples for corresponding inferences are given in Figs. 4.6 and 4.7.

4.1.4 Relations Between Individuals

We have already seen how to declare class memberships of individuals and role relationships between them. OWL also allows us to declare that two individuals are in fact the same.

The class inclusions

```
<owl:Class rdf:about="Professor">
  <rdfs:subClassOf rdf:resource="FacultyMember" />
</owl:Class>
<owl:Class rdf:about="Book">
  <rdfs:subClassOf rdf:resource="Publication" />
</owl:Class>
```

together with the statement that `FacultyMember` and `Publication` are disjoint,

```
<owl:Class rdf:about="FacultyMember">
  <owl:disjointWith rdf:resource="Publication" />
</owl:Class>
```

allow us to infer that `Professor` and `Book` are also disjoint.

FIGURE 4.5:   Example of an inference with `owl:disjointWith`

The class inclusion

```
<owl:Class rdf:about="Man">
  <rdfs:subClassOf rdf:resource="Person" />
</owl:Class>
```

together with the class equivalence

```
<owl:Class rdf:about="Person">
  <owl:equivalentClass rdf:resource="Human" />
</owl:Class>
```

allows us to infer that `Man` is a subclass of `Human`.

FIGURE 4.6:   Example of an inference with `owl:equivalentClass`

From

```
<Book rdf:about="http://semantic-web-book.org/uri">
  <author rdf:resource="markusKroetzsch" />
  <author rdf:resource="sebastianRudolph" />
</Book>
<owl:Class rdf:about="Book">
 <rdfs:subClassOf rdf:resource="Publication" />
</owl:Class>
```

we can infer that `http://semantic-web-book.org/uri` is a `Publication`.

FIGURE 4.7:   Example of an inference with individuals

From

```
<Professor rdf:about="rudiStuder" />
<rdf:Description rdf:about="rudiStuder">
  <owl:sameAs rdf:resource="professorStuder" />
</rdf:Description>
```

we can infer that `professorStuder` is in the class `Professor`.

FIGURE 4.8:   Example inference with `owl:sameAs`

```
<rdf:Description rdf:about="rudiStuder">
  <owl:sameAs rdf:resource="professorStuder" />
</rdf:Description>
```

An example of an inference with `owl:sameAs` is given in Fig. 4.8.

Let us remark that the possible identification of differently named individuals via `owl:sameAs` distinguishes OWL from many other knowledge representation languages, which usually impose the so-called *Unique Name Assumption* (UNA), i.e. in these languages it is assumed that differently named individuals are indeed different. In OWL,[6] however, differently named individuals can denote the same thing. `owl:sameAs` allows us to declare this explicitly, but it is also possible that such an identification is implicit, i.e. can be inferred from the knowledge base without being explicitly stated.

---

[6]RDF(S) does also *not* impose the Unique Name Assumption.

With `owl:differentFrom`, it is possible to declare that individuals are different. In order to declare that several individuals are mutually different, OWL provides a shortcut, as follows. Recall from Section 2.5.1.3 that we can use `rdf:parseType="Collection"` for representing closed lists.

```
<owl:AllDifferent>
  <owl:distinctMembers rdf:parseType="Collection">
    <Person rdf:about="rudiStuder" />
    <Person rdf:about="dennyVrandecic" />
    <Person rdf:about="peterHaase" />
  </owl:distinctMembers>
</owl:AllDifferent>
```

4.1.5   Closed Classes

A declaration like

```
<SecretariesOfStuder rdf:about="giselaSchillinger" />
<SecretariesOfStuder rdf:about="anneEberhardt" />
```

states that `giselaSchillinger` and `anneEberhardt` are secretaries of Studer. However, it does not say anything about the question whether he has more secretaries, or only those two. In order to state that a class contains only the explicitly stated individuals, OWL provides closed classes as in Fig. 4.9.

It is also possible that a closed class contains data values, i.e. elements of a datatype, which are collected into a list using `rdf:List` (cf. Section 2.5.1.3). Figure 4.10 gives an example using email addresses as strings.

The use of these constructors is restricted in OWL Lite, and we will come back to that in Section 4.2.

4.1.6   Boolean Class Constructors

The language elements described so far allow us to model simple ontologies. But their expressivity hardly surpasses that of RDFS. In order to express more complex knowledge, OWL provides logical class constructors. In particular, OWL provides language elements for logical *and*, *or*, and *not*, i.e. conjunction, disjunction, and negation. They are expressed via `owl:intersectionOf`, `owl:unionOf`, and `owl:complementOf`, respectively. These constructors allow us to combine *atomic classes* – i.e. class names – to *complex classes*. Let us remark that the use of these constructors is restricted in OWL Lite, and we will come back to that in Section 4.2.

The declaration

```
<owl:Class rdf:about="SecretariesOfStuder">
  <owl:oneOf rdf:parseType="Collection">
    <Person rdf:about="giselaSchillinger" />
    <Person rdf:about="anneEberhardt" />
  </owl:oneOf>
</owl:Class>
```

states that `giselaSchillinger` and `anneEberhardt` are the only individuals in the class `SecretariesOfStuder`. If we also add

```
<Person rdf:about="anupriyaAnkolekar" />
<owl:AllDifferent>
  <owl:distinctMembers rdf:parseType="Collection">
    <Person rdf:about="anneEberhardt" />
    <Person rdf:about="giselaSchillinger" />
    <Person rdf:about="anupriyaAnkolekar" />
  </owl:distinctMembers>
</owl:AllDifferent>
```

then it can also be inferred, e.g., that `anupriyaAnkolekar` is not in the class `SecretariesOfStuder`. Without the latter statement, such an inference is not possible, since the knowledge that the individuals are different is needed to exclude identification of `anupriyaAnkolekar` with `giselaSchillinger` or `anneEberhardt`.

FIGURE 4.9:   Example inference with closed classes

```
<owl:Class rdf:about="emailsAuthor">
  <owl:DataRange>
    <owl:oneOf>
      <rdf:List>
        <rdf:first rdf:datatype="&xsd;string"
          >pascal@pascal-hitzler.de</rdf:first>
        <rdf:rest>
          <rdf:List>
            <rdf:first rdf:datatype="&xsd;string"
              >markus@korrekt.org</rdf:first>
            <rdf:rest>
              <rdf:List>
                <rdf:first rdf:datatype="&xsd;string"
                  >mail@sebastian-rudolph.de</rdf:first>
                <rdf:rest rdf:resource="&rdf;nil" />
              </rdf:List>
            </rdf:rest>
          </rdf:List>
        </rdf:rest>
      </rdf:List>
    </owl:oneOf>
  </owl:DataRange>
</owl:Class>
```

FIGURE 4.10:   Classes via `oneOf` and datatypes

The conjunction `owl:intersectionOf` of two classes consists of exactly those objects which belong to both classes. The following example states that `SecretariesOfStuder` consists of exactly those objects which are both `Secretaries` and `MembersOfStudersGroup`.

```
<owl:Class rdf:about="SecretariesOfStuder">
  <owl:intersectionOf rdf:parseType="Collection">
    <owl:Class rdf:about="Secretaries" />
    <owl:Class rdf:about="MembersOfStudersGroup" />
  </owl:intersectionOf>
</owl:Class>
```

An example of an inference which can be drawn from this is that all instances of the class `SecretariesOfStuder` are also in the class `Secretaries`. The example just given is a short form of the following statement.

```
<owl:Class rdf:about="SecretariesOfStuder">
  <owl:intersectionOf rdf:parseType="Collection">
    <owl:Class rdf:about="Secretaries" />
    <owl:Class rdf:about="MembersOfStudersGroup" />
  </owl:intersectionOf>
</owl:Class>
```

Certainly, it is also possible to use Boolean class constructors together with `rdfs:subClassOf`. The following example with `owl:unionOf` describes that professors are actively teaching or retired. Note that it also allows the possibility that a retired professor is still actively teaching. Also, it allows for the possibility that there are teachers who are not professors.

```
<owl:Class rdf:about="Professor">
  <rdfs:subClassOf>
    <owl:Class>
      <owl:unionOf rdf:parseType="Collection">
        <owl:Class rdf:about="ActivelyTeaching" />
        <owl:Class rdf:about="Retired" />
      </owl:unionOf>
    </owl:Class>
  </rdfs:subClassOf>
</owl:Class>
```

The use of `owl:unionOf` together with `rdfs:subClassOf` in the example just given thus states only that every `Professor` is in at least one of the classes `ActivelyTeaching` and `Retired`.

The complement of a class can be declared via `owl:complementOf`, which corresponds to logical negation: The complement of a class consists of exactly those objects which are *not* members of the class itself. The following example states that no faculty member can be a publication. It is thus equivalent to the statement made using `owl:disjointWith` in Fig. 4.5, that the classes `FacultyMember` and `Publication` are disjoint.

```
<owl:Class rdf:about="FacultyMember">
  <rdfs:subClassOf>
    <owl:Class>
      <owl:complementOf rdf:resource="Publication" />
    </owl:Class>
  </rdfs:subClassOf>
</owl:Class>
```

Correct use of `owl:complementOf` can be tricky. Consider, for instance, the following example.

```
<owl:Class rdf:about="Male">
  <owl:complementOf rdf:resource="Female" />
</owl:Class>
<Penguin rdf:about="tweety" />
```

From these statements it cannot be concluded that `tweety` is an instance of `Female`. However, it can also not be concluded that `tweety` is *not* `Female`, and hence it cannot be concluded that `tweety` is `Male`.

Now add the following statements to the ones just given, which state the obvious facts that `Furniture` is not `Female`, and that `myDesk` is a `Furniture`.

```
<owl:Class rdf:about="Furniture">
  <rdfs:subClassOf>
    <owl:Class>
      <owl:complementOf rdf:resource="Female" />
    </owl:Class>
  </rdfs:subClassOf>
</owl:Class>
<Furniture rdf:about="myDesk" />
```

From the combined statements, however, we can now conclude that `myDesk` is `Male` – because it is known *not* to be `Female`. If you contemplate this, then you will come to the conclusion that it is usually incorrect to model `Male` as the complement of `Female`, simply because there are things which are neither

From the declarations

```
<owl:Class rdf:about="Professor">
  <rdfs:subClassOf>
    <owl:Class>
      <owl:unionOf rdf:parseType="Collection">
        <owl:intersectionOf rdf:parseType="Collection">
          <owl:Class rdf:about="Person" />
          <owl:Class rdf:about="FacultyMember" />
        </owl:intersectionOf>
        <owl:intersectionOf rdf:parseType="Collection">
          <owl:Class rdf:about="Person" />
          <owl:complementOf rdf:resource="PhDStudent">
        </owl:intersectionOf>
      </owl:Class>
    </owl:intersectionOf>
  </rdfs:subClassOf>
</owl:Class>
```

we can infer that every `Professor` is a `Person`.

FIGURE 4.11:   Example inference using nested Boolean class constructors

`Male` nor `Female` – such as `myDesk`. It would be more appropriate to simply declare `Male` and `Female` to be disjoint, or alternatively, to declare `Male` to be equivalent to the intersection of `Human` and the complement of `Female`.

Boolean class constructors can be nested arbitrarily deeply; see Fig. 4.11 for an example.

4.1.7   Role Restrictions

By role restrictions we understand another type of logic-based constructors for complex classes. As the name suggests, role restrictions are constructors involving roles.

The first role restriction is derived from the universal quantifier in predicate logic and defines a class as the set of all objects for which the given role only attains values from the given class. This is best explained by an example, like the following which states that examiners must always be professors. More precisely, it states that *all* examiners of an exam must be professors.[7]

---

[7]This actually includes those exams which have *no* examiner.

```
<owl:Class rdf:about="Exam">
  <rdfs:subClassOf>
    <owl:Restriction>
      <owl:onProperty rdf:resource="hasExaminer" />
      <owl:allValuesFrom rdf:resource="Professor" />
    </owl:Restriction>
  </rdfs:subClassOf>
</owl:Class>
```

In order to declare that any exam must have at least one examiner, OWL provides role restrictions via `owl:someValuesFrom`, which is closely related to the existential quantifier in predicate logic.

```
<owl:Class rdf:about="Exam">
  <rdfs:subClassOf>
    <owl:Restriction>
      <owl:onProperty rdf:resource="hasExaminer" />
      <owl:someValuesFrom rdf:resource="Person" />
    </owl:Restriction>
  </rdfs:subClassOf>
</owl:Class>
```

Using `owl:allValuesFrom`, we can say something about *all* of the examiners. Using `owl:someValuesFrom`, we can say something about *at least one* of the examiners. In a similar way we can also make statements about the number of examiners. The following example declares an upper bound on the number; more precisely it states that an exam must have a maximum of two examiners.

```
<owl:Class rdf:about="Exam">
  <rdfs:subClassOf>
    <owl:Restriction>
      <owl:onProperty rdf:resource="hasExaminer" />
      <owl:maxCardinality rdf:datatype="&xsd;nonNegativeInteger">
        2
      </owl:maxCardinality>
    </owl:Restriction>
  </rdfs:subClassOf>
</owl:Class>
```

It is also possible to declare a lower bound, e.g., that an exam must cover at least three subject areas.

```
<owl:Class rdf:about="Exam">
  <rdfs:subClassOf>
    <owl:Restriction>
      <owl:onProperty rdf:resource="hasTopic" />
      <owl:minCardinality rdf:datatype="&xsd;nonNegativeInteger">
        3
      </owl:minCardinality>
    </owl:Restriction>
  </rdfs:subClassOf>
</owl:Class>
```

Some combinations of restrictions are needed frequently, so that OWL provides shortcuts. If we want to declare that an exam covers *exactly* three subject areas, then this can be done via `owl:cardinality`.

```
<owl:Class rdf:about="Exam">
  <rdfs:subClassOf>
    <owl:Restriction>
      <owl:onProperty rdf:resource="hasTopic" />
      <owl:cardinality rdf:datatype="&xsd;nonNegativeInteger">
        3
      </owl:cardinality>
    </owl:Restriction>
  </rdfs:subClassOf>
</owl:Class>
```

Obviously, this can also be expressed by combining `owl:minCardinality` with `owl:maxCardinality` as in Fig. 4.12.

The restriction `owl:hasValue` is a special case of `owl:someValuesFrom`, for which a particular individual can be given as value for the role. The following example declares that `ExamStuder` consists of those things which have `rudiStuder` as examiner.

```
<owl:Class rdf:about="ExamStuder">
  <owl:equivalentClass>
    <owl:Restriction>
      <owl:onProperty rdf:resource="hasExaminer" />
      <owl:hasValue rdf:resource="rudiStuder" />
    </owl:Restriction>
  </owl:equivalentClass>
</owl:Class>
```

```
<owl:Class rdf:about="Exam">
  <rdfs:subClassOf>
    <owl:intersectionOf rdf:parseType="Collection">
      <owl:Restriction>
        <owl:onProperty rdf:resource="hasTopic" />
        <owl:minCardinality rdf:datatype="&xsd;nonNegativeInteger">
          3
        </owl:minCardinality>
      </owl:Restriction>
      <owl:Restriction>
        <owl:onProperty rdf:resource="hasTopic" />
        <owl:maxCardinality rdf:datatype="&xsd;nonNegativeInteger">
          3
        </owl:maxCardinality>
      </owl:Restriction>
    </owl:intersectionOf>
  </rdfs:subClassOf>
</owl:Class>
```

FIGURE 4.12: `owl:cardinality` expressed using `owl:minCardinality` and `owl:maxCardinality`

In this case an exam belongs to the class `ExamStuder` even if it has another examiner besides `rudiStuder`.

The example just given can also be expressed using `owl:someValuesFrom` and `owl:oneOf`.

```
<owl:Class rdf:about="ExamStuder">
  <owl:equivalentClass>
    <owl:Restriction>
      <owl:onProperty rdf:resource="hasExaminer" />
      <owl:someValuesFrom>
        <owl:oneOf rdf:parseType="Collection">
          <owl:Thing rdf:about="rudiStuder" />
        </owl:oneOf>
      </owl:someValuesFrom>
    </owl:Restriction>
  </owl:equivalentClass>
</owl:Class>
```

We give an extended example with role restriction in order to display the expressivity of these language constructs. We consider three colleagues and the role `likesToWorkWith`. Figure 4.13 shows the example ontology. If we now additionally define

```
<Person rdf:about="anton">
  <likesToWorkWith rdf:resource="doris" />
  <likesToWorkWith rdf:resource="dagmar" />
</Person>
<Person rdf:about="doris">
  <likesToWorkWith rdf:resource="dagmar" />
  <likesToWorkWith rdf:resource="bernd" />
</Person>
<Person rdf:about="gustav">
  <likesToWorkWith rdf:resource="bernd" />
  <likesToWorkWith rdf:resource="doris" />
  <likesToWorkWith rdf:resource="desiree" />
</Person>
<Person rdf:about="charles" />
<owl:Class rdf:about="FemaleColleagues">
  <owl:oneOf rdf:parseType="Collection">
    <Person rdf:about="dagmar" />
    <Person rdf:about="doris" />
    <Person rdf:about="desiree" />
  </owl:oneOf>
</owl:Class>
<owl:AllDifferent>
  <owl:distinctMembers rdf:parseType="Collection">
    <Person rdf:about="anton" />
    <Person rdf:about="bernd" />
    <Person rdf:about="charles" />
    <Person rdf:about="dagmar" />
    <Person rdf:about="desiree" />
    <Person rdf:about="doris" />
  </owl:distinctMembers>
</owl:AllDifferent>
```

FIGURE 4.13:   Example ontology for role restrictions

```
<owl:Class rdf:about="Class1">
  <owl:equivalentClass>
    <owl:Restriction>
      <owl:onProperty rdf:resource="likesToWorkWith" />
      <owl:someValuesFrom rdf:resource="FemaleColleagues" />
    </owl:Restriction>
  </owl:equivalentClass>
</owl:Class>
```

then we can infer that `anton`, `doris` and `gustav` are in `Class1`.

Note that we cannot infer that `charles` is in `Class1`. At the same time, we also cannot infer that he is *not* in `Class1`. In fact we cannot infer any statement about `charles` belonging to `Class1` or not. The reason for this lies in the so-called *Open World Assumption* (OWA): It is implicitly assumed that a knowledge base may always be incomplete. In our example this means that `charles` *could* be in the relation `likesToWorkWith` to an instance of the class `FemaleColleagues`, but this relation is simply not (or not yet) known.

Let us dwell for a moment on this observation, because the OWA can easily lead to mistakes in the modeling of knowledge. In other paradigms, like databases, usually the *Closed World Assumption* (CWA) is assumed, which means that the knowledge base is considered to be complete concerning all relevant knowledge. Using the CWA, one could infer that `charles` is indeed *not* in `Class1`, because there is no known female colleague `charles` `likesToWorkWith`. The choice of OWA for OWL, however, is reasonable since the World Wide Web is always expanding rapidly, i.e. new knowledge is added all the time.

The OWA obviously also impacts on other situations. If, for example, an ontology contains the statements

```
<Professor rdf:about="rudiStuder" />
<Philosopher rdf:about="mikeStange" />
```

then we cannot infer anything about the membership (or non-membership) of `mikeStange` in the class `Professor`, because further knowledge, which may not yet be known to us, could state or allow us to infer such membership (or non-membership).

Now consider the following `Class2`.

```
<owl:Class rdf:about="Class2">
  <owl:equivalentClass>
    <owl:Restriction>
      <owl:onProperty rdf:resource="likesToWorkWith" />
      <owl:allValuesFrom rdf:resource="FemaleColleagues" />
    </owl:Restriction>
  </owl:equivalentClass>
</owl:Class>
```

We can infer that doris and gustav do *not* belong to Class2. Because of the OWA we cannot say anything about the membership of anton or charles in Class2.

If we define

```
<owl:Class rdf:about="Class3">
  <owl:equivalentClass>
    <owl:Restriction>
      <owl:onProperty rdf:resource="likesToWorkWith" />
      <owl:hasValue rdf:resource="doris" />
    </owl:Restriction>
  </owl:equivalentClass>
</owl:Class>
```

then anton and gustav belong to Class3 because both like to work with doris (among others).

If we define

```
<owl:Class rdf:about="Class4">
  <owl:equivalentClass>
    <owl:Restriction>
      <owl:onProperty rdf:resource="likesToWorkWith" />
      <owl:minCardinality rdf:datatype="&xsd;nonNegativeInteger">
        3
      </owl:minCardinality>
    </owl:Restriction>
  </owl:equivalentClass>
</owl:Class>
```

then gustav belongs to Class4 because he is the only one we know has at least three colleagues he likesToWorkWith.

If we define

```
<owl:Class rdf:about="Class5">
  <owl:equivalentClass>
    <owl:Restriction>
      <owl:onProperty rdf:resource="likesToWorkWith" />
      <owl:maxCardinality rdf:datatype="&xsd;nonNegativeInteger">
        0
      </owl:maxCardinality>
    </owl:Restriction>
  </owl:equivalentClass>
</owl:Class>
```

then due to the OWA we cannot infer that `charles` is in `Class5`.

`Class5` could equivalently be defined as follows – note that there are different ways to say the same thing.

```
<owl:Class rdf:about="Class5">
  <owl:equivalentClass>
    <owl:Restriction>
      <owl:onProperty rdf:resource="likesToWorkWith" />
      <owl:allValuesFrom rdf:resource="&owl;Nothing" />
    </owl:Restriction>
  </owl:equivalentClass>
</owl:Class>
```

The use of the constructs `owl:minCardinality`, `owl:maxCardinality` and `owl:cardinality` is restricted in OWL Lite; see Section 4.2 for details.

4.1.8   Role Relationships

Roles can be related in various ways. In particular, `rdfs:subPropertyOf` can also be used in OWL. The following example states: examiners of an event are also present at the event.

```
<owl:ObjectProperty rdf:about="hasExaminer">
  <rdfs:subPropertyOf rdf:resource="hasParticipant" />
</owl:ObjectProperty>
```

Similarly it is possible to state that two roles are in fact identical. This is done by using `owl:equivalentProperty` instead of `rdfs:subPropertyOf`.

Two roles can also be inverse to each other, i.e. can state the same relationship but with arguments exchanged. This is declared using `owl:inverseOf`.

```
<Exam rdf:about="semanticWebExam">
  <hasExaminer rdf:resource="rudiStuder" />
</Exam>
<owl:ObjectProperty rdf:about="hasExaminer">
  <rdfs:subPropertyOf rdf:resource="hasParticipant" />
</owl:ObjectProperty>
<owl:ObjectProperty rdf:about="hasParticipant">
  <owl:equivalentProperty rdf:resource="hasAttendee" />
</owl:ObjectProperty>
<owl:ObjectProperty rdf:about="hasAttendee">
  <owl:inverseOf rdf:resource="participatesIn" />
</owl:ObjectProperty>
```

FIGURE 4.14:   Example using role relationships

```
<owl:ObjectProperty rdf:about="hasExaminer">
  <owl:inverseOf rdf:resource="examinerOf" />
</owl:ObjectProperty>
```

Figure 4.14 shows another example of the use of role relations. In this case `semanticWebExam` and `rudiStuder` are in the relation `hasParticipant` and also in the equivalent relation `hasAttendee`. Consequently, `rudiStuder` and `semanticWebExam` can be inferred to be in the relation `participatesIn`.

The use of role relationships is restricted in OWL DL and OWL Lite; see Section 4.2 for details.

4.1.9   Role Characteristics

OWL allows us to declare that roles have certain characteristics. This includes the specification of domain and range as well as characteristics like transitivity and symmetry.

We have already talked briefly about using `rdfs:range` and `rdfs:domain`. Let us now have a closer look at their semantics. Consider the statement

```
<owl:ObjectProperty rdf:about="isMemberOf">
  <rdfs:range rdf:resource="Organization" />
</owl:ObjectProperty>
```

which is equivalent to the following.

```
<owl:Class rdf:about="&owl;Thing">
  <rdfs:subClassOf>
    <owl:Restriction>
      <owl:onProperty rdf:resource="isMemberOf" />
      <owl:allValuesFrom rdf:resource="Organization" />
    </owl:Restriction>
  </rdfs:subClassOf>
</owl:Class>
```

Now what happens if we also declare that `five isMemberOf PrimeNumbers`?

```
<number rdf:about="five">
  <isMemberOf rdf:resource="PrimeNumbers" />
</number>
```

From this, OWL allows us to infer that `PrimeNumbers` is an `Organization`! This is obviously an undesired result, which comes from the use of `isMemberOf` within two very different contexts: the first statement declares `isMemberOf` as a role which is used for making statements about memberships in organizations, while the second statement talks about a different domain, namely, numbers. The example is comparable to the one given at the end of Section 2.4.5.

Please note that the example just given does not yield a formal contradiction. In order to arrive at an inconsistency, one could additionally declare that `PrimeNumbers` are not in the class `Organization`.

Similar considerations also hold for `rdfs:domain`.

Let us now return to the characteristics which roles in OWL can be declared to have. They are transitivity, symmetry, functionality, and inverse functionality. We explain their meaning using the examples in Fig. 4.15.

Symmetry states: if A and B are in a symmetric role relationship, then B and A (in reverse order) are also in the same role relationship. In the example `peterHaase` is in a `hasColleague` relationship with `steffenLamparter`, i.e. `peterHaase` has `steffenLamparter` as colleague, and by symmetry we obtain that `steffenLamparter` has `peterHaase` as colleague.

Transitivity means: if A and B are in some transitive role relationship, and B and C are in the same role relationship, then A and C are also related via the same role. In the example, since we know that `steffenLamparter` `hasColleague` `peterHaase` and `peterHaase` `hasColleague` `philippCimiano`, we obtain by transitivity of the role `hasColleague` that `steffenLamparter` also `hasColleague` `philippCimiano`.

Functionality of a role means: if A and B are related via a functional role, and A and C are related by the same role, then B and C are identical in the

```
<owl:ObjectProperty rdf:about="hasColleague">
  <rdf:type rdf:resource="&owl;TransitiveProperty" />
  <rdf:type rdf:resource="&owl;SymmetricProperty" />
</owl:ObjectProperty>
<owl:ObjectProperty rdf:about="hasProjectLeader">
  <rdf:type rdf:resource="&owl;FunctionalProperty" />
</owl:ObjectProperty>
<owl:ObjectProperty rdf:about="isProjectLeaderFor">
  <rdf:type rdf:resource="&owl;InverseFunctionalProperty" />
</owl:ObjectProperty>
<Person rdf:about="peterHaase">
  <hasColleague rdf:resource="philippCimiano" />
  <hasColleague rdf:resource="steffenLamparter" />
  <isProjectLeaderFor rdf:resource="neOn" />
</Person>
<Project rdf:about="x-Media">
  <hasProjectLeader rdf:resource="philippCimiano" />
  <hasProjectLeader rdf:resource="cimianoPhilipp" />
</Project>
```

FIGURE 4.15:   Role characteristics

sense of `owl:sameAs`. In the example we can conclude that `philippCimiano` and `cimianoPhilipp` are identical since `hasProjectLeader` is functional.

Inverse functionality of a role R is equivalent to the inverse of R being functional. In the example, we could have omitted the declaration of inverse functionality of `isProjectLeaderFor` and instead state the following.

```
<owl:ObjectProperty rdf:about="isProjectLeaderFor">
  <owl:inverseOf rdf:resource="hasProjectLeader" />
</owl:ObjectProperty>
```

Since it is declared that the role `hasProjectLeader` is functional, the inverse role `isProjectLeaderFor` would automatically be inverse functional.

Note that it does usually not make sense to declare transitive roles to be functional. It is, however, not explicitly forbidden in OWL.

The use of role characteristics is restricted in OWL DL and OWL Lite; see Section 4.2 for details.

4.1.10   Types of Inferences

To date, there is no standardized query language for OWL. While we discuss proposals for expressive query languages for OWL in Chapter 7, we briefly discuss here what types of simple queries are commonly considered to be important when working with OWL. These are also supported by the usual software tools, as listed in Section 8.5. It is customary to distinguish between two types of simple queries, those involving individuals, and those using only schema knowledge.

Queries not involving individuals are concerned with classes and their relationships. We can distinguish between querying about the *equivalence* of two classes in the sense of `owl:equivalentClass` and querying about a subclass relationship in the sense of `rdfs:subClassOf`. We have given examples for this in Figs. 4.4, 4.6 and 4.11. Computing all subclass relationships between named classes is called *classifying* the ontology. Figure 4.5 gives an example asking about the *disjointness* of classes in the sense of `owl:disjointWith`.

We will see in Chapter 5 that querying for *global consistency*, i.e. for *satisfiability* of a knowledge base, is of central importance. Global consistency means the absence of contradictions.

Checking for *class consistency* is usually done in order to debug an ontology. A class is called *inconsistent*[8] if it is equivalent to `owl:Nothing`, which usually happens due to a modeling error. The following is a simple example of a class inconsistency caused by erroneous modeling.

```
<owl:Class rdf:about="Book">
  <rdfs:subClassOf rdf:resource="Publication" />
  <owl:disjointWith rdf:resource="Publication" />
</owl:Class>
```

Note that the knowledge base is not inconsistent: if there are no books, (and only in this case), the knowledge is consistent. That is because if we had a book, then it would also be a `Publication` by the `rdfs:subclassOf` statement. But this is impossible because `Publication` and `Book` are disjoint by the other statement. So, since there can be no book, `Book` is equivalent to `owl:Nothing`.

Queries involving individuals are of particular importance for practical applications. Such queries usually ask for all *known instances of a given class*, also known as *instance retrieval*. We have given examples for this in Figs. 4.7 and 4.8, and also in Section 4.1.7. Instance retrieval is closely related to *instance checking* which, given a class and an individual, decides whether the individual belongs to the class.

---

[8]In this case it is sometimes said that the class or ontology is *incoherent*.

4.2 OWL Species

We have remarked that there are three official sublanguages of OWL, and we have mentioned some of their conceptual differences in Fig. 4.2. We will now discuss the syntactic differences and their significance.

4.2.1 OWL Full

In OWL Full, all OWL language constructs can be used and mixed freely with all RDF(S) language constructs, as long as the resulting document is valid RDF(S).

Due to the unrestricted use of OWL and RDF(S) constructs in OWL Full, several problems arise, which suggest the design of more restrictive sublanguages. These problems are caused by the fact that OWL has been designed for the modeling of expressive knowledge and the resulting ability to access implicit knowledge by logical inference. For OWL Full, however, drawing inferences is in general undecidable, and indeed there is no software tool which supports the entire unwieldy semantics of OWL Full.

One of the reasons for the undecidability of OWL Full is that type separation is not enforced, i.e. in OWL Full individuals, classes, and roles can be mixed freely, and it is, e.g., possible to use an identifier as an individual in one statement, and as a role in the next statement. Consequently, the classes `owl:Thing` and `rdfs:Resource` are equivalent in OWL Full, as are `owl:Class` and `rdfs:Class`. Further, `owl:DatatypeProperty` is a subclass of `owl:ObjectProperty`, which in turn is equivalent to `rdf:Property`.

Complete type separation, however, is not desired in all cases, and OWL Full accommodates this. To give an example, it is sometimes necessary to make statements about a class, in which this class appears syntactically as an individual. In the following, we use roles to assign linguistic information to the class `Book`, thereby providing the basis for a multilingual system.

```
<owl:Class rdf:about="Book">
  <germanName rdf:datatype="&xsd;string">Buch</germanName>
  <frenchName rdf:datatype="&xsd;string">livre</frenchName>
</owl:Class>
```

The use of classes (or roles) as individuals is called *metamodeling*, and it allows us to talk about classes of classes.

Hardly any of the current inference engines support OWL Full, and in particular these do not provide its complete semantics. It would be unreasonable to expect this to change any time soon. This has only little impact on practical applications since for metamodeling and other constructs not supported in OWL DL it is easy to provide workarounds outside the knowledge base: In the example just given, metamodeling is only used for providing background information, e.g., for multi-language user dialogues. In this case, the multi-lingual data could still be stored in and extracted from the OWL knowledge base, while inferencing over this knowledge is not needed.

Despite the lack of automated reasoning support, OWL Full is used for conceptual modeling in cases where automated reasoning support is not required.

4.2.2 OWL DL

The use of some language elements from OWL Full is restricted in OWL DL. This concerns mainly type separation and the use of RDF(S) language constructs, but also other restrictions. OWL DL was designed to be decidable, i.e. for any inference problem from Section 4.1.10 there exists an always terminating algorithm for deciding it. We discuss this in more detail in Chapter 5.

The following conditions must be satisfied such that an OWL Full document is a valid OWL DL document.

- Restricted use of RDF(S) language constructs: Only those RDF(S) language constructs may be used which are specifically allowed for OWL DL. These are essentially all those RDF(S) language constructs which we have used in our examples throughout this chapter. The use of `rdfs:Class` and `rdf:Property` is forbidden.

- Type separation and declaration: Type separation must be respected in OWL DL, i.e. it must be clearly distinguished between individuals, classes, abstract roles, concrete roles, datatypes, and the ontology characteristics specified in the header. In addition, classes and roles must be declared explicitly.

- Restricted use of concrete roles: The role characteristics `owl:inverseOf`, `owl:TransitiveProperty`, `owl:InverseFunctionalProperty`, as well as `owl:SymmetricProperty` must not be used for concrete roles.

- Restricted use of abstract roles: Cardinality restrictions expressed via `owl:cardinality`, `owl:minCardinality`, or via `owl:maxCardinality` must not be used with transitive roles, inverses of transitive roles, or superroles of transitive roles.[9]

---

[9]This somewhat strange restriction – which in exact form is a bit more complicated than this – is necessary to ensure decidability of OWL DL; see Section 5.1.4.3.

4.2.3 OWL Lite

OWL Lite was intended to be an easy to implement sublanguage containing the most important language constructs. However, it turned out that OWL Lite is essentially as difficult to deal with as OWL DL, and so it does not come as a surprise that it plays only a minor role in practice.

The following conditions must be satisfied such that an OWL Full document is a valid OWL Lite document.

- All restrictions imposed for OWL DL must be respected.

- Restricted use of class constructors: `owl:unionOf`, `owl:complementOf`, `owl:hasValue`, `owl:oneOf`, `owl:disjointWith`, `owl:DataRange` must not be used.

- Restricted use of cardinality restrictions: They can only be used with the numbers 0 and 1.

- Mandatory use of class names: In some situations, class names must be used:
  in the subject of `owl:equivalentClass` and `rdfs:subClassOf`,
  in the object of `rdfs:domain`.

- Mandatory class names or role restrictions: In some situations, class names or role restrictions must be used:
  in the object of `owl:equivalentClass`, `rdfs:subClassOf`, `rdf:type`, `owl:allValuesFrom`, `owl:someValuesFrom`, `rdfs:range`.
  Additionally, `owl:intersectionOf` must be used only for class names and role restrictions.

4.3 The Forthcoming OWL 2 Standard

The Web Ontology Language is currently undergoing a revision by means of a working group of the World Wide Web Consortium.[10] The forthcoming revision, originally called OWL 1.1 and now christened OWL 2, is essentially a small extension of the original version, which we will call OWL 1 in the following. At the time of this writing (June 2009), the working group has produced so-called Candidate Recommendations of the standard, which are very likely to be close to the final outcome. However, some things may still change, and so the following introduction to OWL 2 can only reflect the current state of the standardization process.

---

[10]http://www.w3.org/2007/OWL/

Let us first note that OWL 2 introduces a new syntax, called the *functional style syntax*, which will replace the OWL 1 abstract syntax. However, OWL 2 also comes with an RDF syntax, and we use this for the introduction. There will probably also be an XML syntax for OWL 2, which we do not discuss here.

4.3.1   OWL 2 DL

We introduce OWL 2 DL, which is backward compatible with OWL 1 DL, but extends it with some additional features. We thus describe only the new language features.

4.3.1.1   Type Separation, Punning and Declarations

OWL 1 DL imposes type separation, as discussed in Section 4.2.2, i.e. class names, role names, and individual names must be distinct. OWL 2 relaxes this requirement such that a class name, for example, may also occur as a role name. However, they are treated as distinct.[11] This is called *punning*.

Consider the following example.

```
<owl:Class rdf:about="Professor" />
<Professor rdf:about="rudiStuder" />
<owl:Class rdf:about="Institute" />
<owl:ObjectProperty rdf:about="Professor" />
<Institute rdf:about="aifb">
  <Professor rdf:resource="rudiStuder" />
</Institute>
```

In this example, `Professor` occurs both as class name and as abstract role name. This is not allowed in OWL 1 DL, but possible in OWL 1 Full. Intuitively, however, it seems reasonable to treat the role `Professor`[12] as distinct from the class `Professor`.

In OWL 2 DL, it is possible to use `Professor` both as role and as class name, and these are assumed to be distinct. Thus, the example code above is valid OWL 2 DL. However, it is not allowed that a name stands for both an abstract and a concrete role. Likewise, it is not allowed that a name stands for both a class and a datatype.

In OWL 2, classes, datatypes and roles must be declared as such. Individuals can also be declared, as follows, though this is optional.

---

[11] Note that if a class name is also used as a role name, they are identified by the same URI, i.e. they are *the same resource* in the sense of RDF. Nevertheless, in OWL 2 DL we consider them *semantically distinct*, i.e. we have two different views on the same resource.

[12] In this case, we cannot maintain our notational convention from page 118 to write roles lowercase and classes uppercase.

```
<rdf:Description rdf:about="rudiStuder">
  <rdf:type rdf:resource="&owl;NamedIndividual" />
</rdf:Description>
```

Alternatively, declaration of an individual can be done via the following shortcut.

```
<owl:NamedIndividual rdf:about="rudiStuder" />
```

4.3.1.2 Disjoint Classes

In OWL 1, `owl:disjointWith` can be used to declare two classes to be disjoint. If several classes should be declared to be mutually disjoint, however, a lot of `owl:disjointWith` statements are needed. Hence OWL 2 introduces `owl:AllDisjointClasses` as a shortcut which allows us to declare several classes to be mutually disjoint. Say, for example, that the classes `UndergraduateStudent`, `GraduateStudent` and `OtherStudent` should be declared as mutually disjoint. Then this can be done as follows.

```
<owl:AllDisjointClasses>
  <owl:members rdf:parseType="Collection">
    <owl:Class rdf:about="UndergraduateStudent" />
    <owl:Class rdf:about="GraduateStudent" />
    <owl:Class rdf:about="OtherStudent" />
  </owl:members>
</owl:AllDisjointClasses>
```

In OWL 1 the union of classes can be described using `owl:unionOf`. OWL 2 allows us to use `owl:disjointUnionOf` to declare a class the disjoint union of some other classes. Consider, for example, the situation that each `Student` is exactly in one of `UndergraduateStudent`, `GraduateStudent`, `OtherStudent`. Then this can be written in OWL 2 DL as follows.

```
<owl:Class rdf:about="Student">
  <owl:disjointUnionOf rdf:parseType="Collection">
    <owl:Class rdf:about="UndergraduateStudent" />
    <owl:Class rdf:about="GraduateStudent" />
    <owl:Class rdf:about="OtherStudent" />
  </owl:disjointUnionOf>
</owl:Class>
```

Obviously, the same effect can be obtained using `owl:unionOf` together with an `owl:AllDisjointClasses` statement.

4.3.1.3 Role Characteristics and Relationships

In OWL 1, it is possible to declare roles to be transitive, symmetric, functional or inverse functional. OWL 2 furthermore allows declarations of roles to be

- asymmetric, via `owl:AsymmetricProperty`, meaning that if A is related to B via such a role, then B is never related to A via this a role,

- reflexive, via `owl:ReflexiveProperty`, meaning that every individual A is related to itself via such a role, and

- irreflexive, via `owl:IrreflexiveProperty`, meaning that no individual is related to itself via such a role.

Recall that in OWL 1, as discussed in Section 4.2.2, transitivity, symmetry and inverse functionality must not be used for concrete roles. Likewise, asymmetry, reflexivity and irreflexivity must not be used for concrete roles. This leaves only functionality for both concrete and abstract roles.

It should be noted that reflexivity is a very strong statement since it refers to *every* possible individual, not just to individuals of a particular class. In many applications, it is more appropriate to use a more "local" notion of reflexivity, as provided by the Self construct that is introduced in Section 4.3.1.7 below.

Related to inverse functionality is `owl:hasKey`, which allows us to say that certain roles are keys for named instances of classes. More precisely, given a class `AClass`, a set of roles `r1,...,rn` is said to be a *key* for `AClass`, if no two named instances of `AClass` coincide on all values of all the (concrete or abstract) roles `r1,...,rn`. The syntax is the following.

```
<owl:Class rdf:about="AClass">
  <owl:hasKey rdf:parseType="Collection">
    <owl:ObjectProperty rdf:about="key1" />
    <owl:ObjectProperty rdf:about="key2" />
    <owl:DatatypeProperty rdf:about="key3" />
  </owl:hasKey>
</owl:Class>
```

Note the differences between using a key and using inverse functionality: Keys apply only to explicitly named instances of a class, while inverse functionality is also applicable to instances whose existence may only be implied, e.g., by means of `owl:someValuesFrom`. Another difference is that keys can involve several roles. Also note that concrete roles can be used for keys, while inverse functionality is forbidden for them.

Roles can also be declared to be disjoint, which means that two individuals *A* and *B* cannot be in relationship with respect to both roles. The following states, for example, that it is impossible that somebody teaches and attends a course at the same time.

```
<owl:ObjectProperty rdf:about="attendsCourse">
  <owl:propertyDisjointWith rdf:resource="teachesCourse" />
</owl:ObjectProperty>
```

As for classes, there is a shortcut notation to declare a number of roles to be mutually disjoint. The syntax is as follows.

```
<owl:AllDisjointProperties>
  <owl:members rdf:parseType="Collection">
    <owl:ObjectProperty rdf:about="attendsCourse" />
    <owl:ObjectProperty rdf:about="teachesCourse" />
    <owl:ObjectProperty rdf:about="skipsCourse" />
  </owl:members>
</owl:AllDisjointProperties>
```

Both `owl:propertyDisjointWith` and `owl:AllDisjointProperties` can also be used with concrete roles. Stating disjointness of an abstract and a concrete role is not useful (and not allowed) since abstract and concrete roles are always disjoint.[13]

OWL 2 furthermore sports four predefined roles:

- `owl:topObjectProperty`, called the top abstract role. It connects all possible pairs of individuals. Every abstract role is related to this role via `rdfs:subPropertyOf`.

- `owl:topDataProperty`, called the top concrete role. It connects all possible individuals with all datatype literals. Every concrete role is related to this role via `rdfs:subPropertyOf`.

- `owl:bottomObjectProperty`, called the bottom abstract role. It does not connect any pair of individuals. This role is related to any other abstract role via `rdfs:subPropertyOf`.

- `owl:bottomDataProperty`, called the bottom concrete role. It does not connect any individual with a literal. This role is related to any other concrete role via `rdfs:subPropertyOf`.

---

[13]Some further restrictions apply, which we discuss in Section 5.1.4.

4.3.1.4 Inverse Roles

OWL 1 allows the declaration of a role as the inverse of another role. In OWL 2, we can also refer to the inverse of a role without naming it. The following example states that if the event A has the person B as examiner (i.e. A is an exam), then B participates in A. Note that not every B participating in some event A implies that B is an examiner in A.

```
<owl:ObjectProperty rdf:about="hasExaminer">
  <rdfs:subPropertyOf>
    <owl:ObjectProperty>
      <owl:inverseOf rdf:resource="participatesIn" />
    </owl:ObjectProperty>
  </rdfs:subPropertyOf>
</owl:ObjectProperty>
```

This construction is not allowed for concrete roles.

4.3.1.5 Role Chains

OWL 2 allows us to express role chains, in the sense of concatenation of roles.[14] The classic example would be to express that whenever a person's parent has a brother, then that brother is the person's uncle. The syntax for this is as follows.

```
<owl:ObjectProperty rdf:about="hasUncle">
  <owl:propertyChainAxiom rdf:parseType="Collection">
    <owl:ObjectProperty rdf:resource="hasParent" />
    <owl:ObjectProperty rdf:about="hasBrother" />
  </owl:propertyChainAxiom>
</owl:ObjectProperty>
```

It is certainly possible to include more roles in the chain. However, concrete roles must not be used.

From a logical perspective, role chains are the most substantial improvement of OWL 2 compared to OWL 1. They can be understood as a broad generalization of transitivity, since, e.g.,

---

[14]Some restrictions apply, which we discuss in Section 5.1.4.

```
<owl:ObjectProperty rdf:about="hasAncestor">
  <owl:propertyChainAxiom rdf:parseType="Collection">
    <owl:ObjectProperty rdf:resource="hasAncestor" />
    <owl:ObjectProperty rdf:about="hasAncestor" />
  </owl:propertyChainAxiom>
</owl:ObjectProperty>
```

is equivalent to stating that the role hasAncestor is transitive.

4.3.1.6   Qualified Cardinality Restrictions

OWL 1 allows cardinality restrictions which are called *unqualified*, since they do not allow us to declare the target class of the role onto which the cardinality restriction is imposed. Have a look at the example on page 127, which states that Exam is a subclass of those things which have at most two objects attached via the hasExaminer role. With qualified cardinality restrictions we can say also something about the class these objects belong to. The following example states that each Exam has at most two elements from the class Professor related to it via the hasExaminer role. Note that this would allow further things to be related to an Exam via the hasExaminer role – as long as they are not in the class Professor.

```
<owl:Class rdf:about="Exam">
  <rdfs:subClassOf>
    <owl:Restriction>
      <owl:onProperty rdf:resource="hasExaminer" />
      <owl:maxQualifiedCardinality
          rdf:datatype="&xsd;nonNegativeInteger">
        2
      </owl:maxQualifiedCardinality>
      <owl:onClass rdf:resource="Professor" />
    </owl:Restriction>
  </rdfs:subClassOf>
</owl:Class>
```

Similar constructions can be made with owl:minQualifiedCardinality and owl:qualifiedCardinality. They can also be used for concrete roles, using owl:onDataRange instead of owl:onClass.

4.3.1.7 The Self Construct

With the Self construct it can be stated that some individuals are related to themselves under a given role.[15] The typical example is that of persons committing suicide: they can be characterized by stating that these are all those people who killed themselves, as in the following example.

```
<owl:Class rdf:about="PersonCommittingSuicide">
  <owl:equivalentClass>
    <owl:Restriction>
      <owl:onProperty rdf:resource="hasKilled" />
      <owl:hasSelf rdf:datatype="&xsd;boolean">true</owl:hasSelf>
    </owl:Restriction>
  </owl:equivalentClass>
</owl:Class>
```

4.3.1.8 Negated Role Assignments

OWL 1 allows us to express that two individuals are related by some role. OWL 2 furthermore allows us to express that two individuals are *not* related by some role. The following example states that `anupriyaAnkolekar` and `sebastianRudolph` are *not* colleagues.

```
<owl:NegativePropertyAssertion>
  <owl:sourceIndividual rdf:about="anupriyaAnkolekar" />
  <owl:assertionProperty rdf:about="hasColleague" />
  <owl:targetIndividual rdf:about="sebastianRudolph" />
</owl:NegativePropertyAssertion>
```

The same is possible with concrete roles, where `owl:targetIndividual` is replaced by `owl:targetValue`.

4.3.1.9 Datatypes

Most XML Schema datatypes from Fig. 4.3 are supported in OWL 2 DL. Exceptions are some types relating to date and time: not supported are `xsd:time`, `xsd:date`, `xsd:gYear`, `xsd:gMonth`, `xsd:gDay`, `xsd:gMonthDay`, and `xsd:gYearMonth`. Furthermore, OWL 2 introduces the following new datatypes.[16]

---

[15]Some restrictions apply, which we discuss in Section 5.1.4.

[16]The datatypes `owl:rational` and `rdf:XMLLiteral` are currently *at risk*, i.e. they may be dropped in the final version.

- `owl:real`: the set of all real numbers

- `owl:rational`: the set of all rational numbers

- `rdf:PlainLiteral`: a string enriched with a language tag following BCP 47.[17]

- `rdf:XMLLiteral`: borrowed from RDF

- `xsd:dateTimeStamp`: based on `xsd:dateTime` but requires the specification of time zones.

It is not possible to explicitly write down literals for the datatype `owl:real`. However, such values can come about implicitly when dealing with integers and rationals, which is why they were included.

In addition to these basic datatypes, OWL 2 supports the use of *constraining facets*, which are actually borrowed from XML Schema, to further restrict datatype values. The example in Fig. 4.16 describes the class `Teenager` as the intersection of the class `Person` with all things which have an age between 12 and 19, where 19 is included in the range, but 12 is not. Other constraining facets for numeric datatypes are `xsd:maxInclusive` and `xsd:minExclusive`. Constraining facets for string datatypes are `xsd:minLength`, `xsd:maxLength`, `xsd:length`, and `xsd:pattern`. The latter refers to a selection based on matching a regular expression. Further information on constraining facets can be found in literature on XML Schema.

OWL 2 furthermore allows us to refer to the complement of a datatype, using `owl:datatypeComplementOf`. The following example specifies that the deficit on a bank account cannot be a positive integer.

```
<owl:DatatypeProperty rdf:about="deficit">
  <rdfs:domain rdf:resource="BankAccount" />
  <rdfs:range>
    <rdfs:Datatype>
      <owl:datatypeComplementOf rdf:resource="&xsd;positiveInteger" />
    </rdfs:Datatype>
  </rdfs:range>
</owl:DatatypeProperty>
```

The range then includes all negative integers and zero, but it also contains all strings and other values from other datatypes which are not positive integers.

Similarly, datatypes can be intersected using `owl:intersectionOf` with a list of datatypes in the object place. Likewise, `owl:unionOf` can be used for datatypes. These expressions can be nested.

---

[17]http://www.rfc-editor.org/rfc/bcp/bcp47.txt

```
<owl:Class rdf:about="Teenager">
  <owl:equivalentClass>
    <owl:Class>
      <owl:intersectionOf rdf:parseType="Collection">
        <rdf:Description rdf:about="Person" />
        <owl:Restriction>
          <owl:onProperty rdf:resource="hasAge" />
          <owl:someValuesFrom>
            <rdfs:Datatype>
              <owl:onDataType rdf:resource="&xsd;integer" />
              <owl:withRestrictions rdf:parseType="Collection">
                <xsd:minExclusive rdf:datatype="&xsd;integer">
                  12
                </xsd:minExclusive>
                <xsd:maxInclusive rdf:datatype="&xsd;integer">
                  19
                </xsd:maxInclusive>
              </owl:withRestrictions>
            </rdfs:Datatype>
          </owl:someValuesFrom>
        </owl:Restriction>
      </owl:intersectionOf>
    </owl:Class>
  </owl:equivalentClass>
</owl:Class>
```

FIGURE 4.16: Datatype constraining facets: restricting the allowed range of an integer value

4.3.2 OWL 2 Profiles

OWL 2 profiles are sublanguages of OWL 2. In this sense, OWL 2 DL, OWL 1 DL and OWL 1 Lite could be understood as profiles of OWL 2. The forthcoming standard will furthermore comprise three designated profiles which have been chosen for their favorable computational properties. We briefly present them in the following, but it should be noted that we omit details of the definitions, since our goal is to provide a rough intuition about them, rather than a comprehensive treatment.

4.3.2.1 OWL 2 EL

OWL 2 EL allows polynomial time algorithms for all standard inference types, such as satisfiability checking, classification, and instance checking. It was designed as a language that is particularly suitable for defining ontologies that include very large class and role hierarchies while using only a limited amount of OWL features. A typical example application is the large medical ontology SNOMED CT (see Section 9.5) that defines more than one hundred thousand classes and roles.

The following language elements can be used in OWL 2 EL.

- `owl:Class`, `owl:Thing`, and `owl:Nothing`

- `rdfs:subClassOf`, `owl:equivalentClass`, `owl:disjointWith`, `owl:AllDisjointClasses`, and `owl:intersectionOf`

- `owl:someValuesFrom`, `owl:hasValue`, `owl:hasSelf`, and `owl:oneOf` (with exactly one individual or value)

- `owl:ObjectProperty`, `owl:DatatypeProperty`, `rdfs:domain`, `rdfs:range` (subject to some restrictions when using role chains), `owl:topObjectProperty`, `owl:topDataProperty`, `owl:bottomObjectProperty`, and `owl:bottomDataProperty`

- `rdfs:subPropertyOf`, `owl:equivalentProperty`, `owl:propertyChainAxiom`, `owl:TransitiveProperty`, `owl:ReflexiveProperty`, `owl:hasKey`, and for concrete roles also `owl:FunctionalProperty`

- all language elements needed for stating class and role relationship assignments for individuals using `owl:sameAs`, `owl:differentFrom` and `owl:AllDifferent`, `owl:NegativePropertyAssertion`, and for stating the basic assignment of an individual to a class, of two individuals to be related by an abstract role, and an individual and a datatype literal to be related by a concrete role

- class, role, and individual declarations

- many of the predefined OWL 2 datatypes

Note that in particular the use of `owl:allValuesFrom`, `owl:unionOf`, and `owl:complementOf` is disallowed. Cardinality restrictions also must not be used. Most role characteristics, including disjointness and inverses of roles, are also not allowed. For preserving its good computational properties, the datatypes supported by OWL 2 EL have been chosen to ensure that their intersection is either empty or infinite. This specifically excludes a number of numerical datatypes such as `xsd:int`, `xsd:byte`, and `xsd:double`. The usage of constraining facets is disallowed for the same reason.

4.3.2.2 OWL 2 QL

OWL 2 QL allows conjunctive query answering (see Section 7.2) to be implemented using conventional relational database systems. It also features polynomial time algorithms for all standard inference types. OWL 2 QL has been designed for data-driven applications, and offers a convenient option for vendors of RDF stores to include some amount of OWL support without sacrificing the advantages of a database-like implementation.

- All predefined classes and roles can be used.

- OWL 2 QL imposes different restrictions on the subject and the object part of `rdfs:subClassOf` statements.

  - On the subject side, it is only allowed to use class names and `owl:someValuesFrom`, though in the latter case the target class must be `owl:Thing`.
  - On the object side, it is allowed to use class names. It is also allowed to use `owl:someValuesFrom` with target class as on the object side, `owl:complementOf` with target class as on the subject side, and `owl:intersectionOf` with the intersecting classes as on the object side.

- `owl:equivalentClass`, `owl:disjointWith`, `owl:AllDisjointClasses` can only be used with class expressions as allowed on the subject side of `rdfs:subClassOf`.

- `rdfs:subPropertyOf` and `owl:equivalentProperty` are allowed, as well as `rdfs:domain` (restricted to object side class expressions for concrete roles), `rdfs:range`, `owl:inverseOf`, and expressions involving `owl:propertyDisjointWith` and `owl:AllDisjointProperties`. Abstract roles can be declared to be symmetric, asymmetric, and reflexive.

- Assignments of individuals to be members of a class, and of individuals to be related to individuals or datatype literals via roles are allowed.

- `owl:differentFrom` and `owl:AllDifferent` can be used.

- Many of the predefined OWL 2 datatypes can be used.

Note that in addition to the subject and object side restrictions on the use of `rdfs:subClassOf`, it is not allowed to use `owl:allValuesFrom`, `owl:oneOf`, `owl:hasValue`, `owl:unionOf`, `owl:hasSelf`, `owl:hasKey`, and cardinality restrictions including functional and inverse functional roles. Transitivity and `owl:propertyChainAxiom`, `owl:sameAs`, and negative property assignments must not be used. The available datatypes and the use of facets are restricted in a similar way as for OWL 2 EL.

4.3.2.3 OWL 2 RL

OWL 2 RL allows standard inference types to be implemented with polynomial time algorithms using rule-based reasoning engines in a relatively straightforward way. It has been designed to allow the easy adoption of OWL by vendors of rule-based inference tools, and it provides some amount of interoperability with knowledge representation languages based on rules (see Chapter 6).

OWL 2 RL is defined as a restriction of OWL 2 DL which mainly impacts on the use of `rdfs:subClassOf`. We present the main restrictions in the following.

- `owl:Thing` and `owl:Nothing` can be used. Top and bottom roles are disallowed.

- As for OWL 2 QL, the subject and the object sides of `rdfs:subClassOf` bear different restrictions.

  - On the subject side, we can use class names, `owl:Nothing` (but not `owl:Thing`), `owl:oneOf` and `owl:hasValue`. It is allowed to use `owl:intersectionOf`, `owl:unionOf`, `owl:someValuesFrom`; however, the involved class expressions must again be subject side class expressions; if `owl:someValuesFrom` is used with a concrete role, only datatype literals can be used.

  - On the object side, we can use class names and `owl:Nothing` (but not `owl:Thing`). It is allowed to use `owl:hasValue` and also `owl:allValuesFrom` for concrete roles, but it is restricted to object side class expressions for abstract roles. The only cardinality restriction allowed is `owl:maxCardinality`, and it is furthermore restricted to the cardinalities 0 and 1. For abstract roles, qualified cardinality restrictions can only be used with subject side class expressions as the target class.

- `owl:equivalentClass` can only be used with class expressions which are both subject and object side class expressions. `owl:disjointWith` and `owl:AllDisjointClasses` are restricted to subject side class expressions. `owl:disjointUnionOf` is disallowed.

- `owl:hasKey` can only be used with subject side class expressions.

- `rdfs:domain` and `rdfs:range` can only be used with object side class expressions. There are almost no further restrictions on using language elements for roles. `rdfs:subPropertyOf` and `owl:equivalentProperty`, inverse roles, and `owl:propertyChainAxiom` are supported. Roles can be declared transitive, symmetric, asymmetric, irreflexive, functional, and inverse functional.

- Many of the predefined OWL 2 datatypes can be used.

- Assignments of class membership of individuals can only be used with object side class expressions. `owl:NegativePropertyAssertion` is disallowed. There are no further restrictions on assignments and on the use of `owl:sameAs`, `owl:differentFrom` and `owl:AllDifferent`.

Note that top roles and reflexive roles are specifically excluded. This restriction is not motivated by computational properties (inferencing would still be polynomial if they were included), but by implementation-specific considerations: various rule-based systems are based on pre-computing and storing all logical consequences that can be expressed as assertional facts – a method known as *materialization* – and this approach works less well if some language constructs entail a very large number of such consequences. The available datatypes and the use of facets are restricted in a similar way as for OWL 2 EL.

4.3.3   OWL 2 Full

OWL 2 Full, syntactically, is the union of OWL 2 DL and RDFS. Semantically, i.e. in terms of inferences derivable from such ontologies, OWL 2 Full is compatible with OWL 2 DL in the sense that the OWL 2 Full semantics allows us to draw all inferences which can be drawn using the OWL 2 DL semantics (which is presented in the next chapter).

It can be expected that OWL 2 Full will play a similar role as OWL 1 Full for applications, i.e. it will probably be mainly used for conceptual modeling in cases where automated reasoning is not required.

4.4   Summary

In this chapter we have introduced the Web Ontology Language OWL using the normative RDFS syntax following the W3C recommendation from 2004. We put the focus on modeling with OWL DL, since this sublanguage is currently the most important one. We have also presented the other sublanguages OWL Full and OWL Lite and discussed their differences.

Besides introducing the syntax of the language constructs, we have also exemplified in all cases how logical inferences can be drawn from OWL ontologies. We will give this a thorough and formal treatment in Chapter 5.

We briefly mentioned important types of queries for OWL, and we will follow up on this in Chapter 7. We also presented the forthcoming revision of OWL, called OWL 2.

An introductory text like this cannot and may not present all the details of a rich language such as OWL, and so we have omitted several aspects the understanding of which is not central for an introduction to the language. The most important of our omissions are the following.

- Besides `owl:ObjectProperty` and `owl:DatatypeProperty`, there also exists `owl:AnnotationProperty`, instances of which can be used to annotate the whole ontology, single statements, or single entities. They do not affect the logical meaning of OWL ontologies, i.e. they do not infringe on the semantics which is presented in the next chapter. A typical example would be `rdfs:comment`, and also the other header elements which can be used. In particular OWL 2 provides rich support for annotation properties, which can be freely defined, for example to give additional human-readable information, such as comments or provenance information, to statements and entities.

- There are some global syntactic constraints concerning the use of transitive roles and subrole relationships. We actually explain them in detail in the next chapter, when we discuss the semantics of OWL. In a nutshell, cyclic dependencies of subrole relationships are problematic if they involve OWL 2 role chains. Transitive roles must not occur in cardinality restrictions or the OWL 2 Self construct.

Advice on engineering ontologies can be found in Chapter 8, which also contains a discussion of available OWL Tools.

4.4.1   Overview of OWL 1 Language Constructs

Language constructs with restricted use in OWL Lite are marked by a $\star$. Note that this does not cover all the restrictions listed in Section 4.2.3.

4.4.1.1   Header

`rdfs:comment`	`rdfs:label`
`rdfs:seeAlso`	`rdfs:isDefinedBy`
`owl:versionInfo`	`owl:priorVersion`
`owl:backwardCompatibleWith`	`owl:incompatibleWith`
`owl:DeprecatedClass`	`owl:DeprecatedProperty`
`owl:imports`	

4.4.1.2   Relations Between Individuals

`owl:sameAs` `owl:differentFrom`
`owl:AllDifferent` together with `owl:distinctMembers`

4.4.1.3   Class Constructors and Relationships

`owl:Class`	`owl:Thing`	`owl:Nothing`
`rdfs:subClassOf`	`owl:disjointWith`$\star$	`owl:equivalentClass`
`owl:intersectionOf`	`owl:unionOf`$\star$	`owl:complementOf`$\star$

Role restrictions using `owl:Restriction` and `owl:onProperty`:

`owl:allValuesFrom`	`owl:someValuesFrom`	`owl:hasValue`
`owl:cardinality`$\star$	`owl:minCardinality`$\star$	`owl:maxCardinality`$\star$
`owl:oneOf`$\star$, for datatypes together with `owl:DataRange`$\star$		

4.4.1.4 Role Constructors, Relationships and Characteristics

owl:ObjectProperty	owl:DatatypeProperty
rdfs:subPropertyOf	owl:equivalentProperty
rdfs:domain	rdfs:range
owl:TransitiveProperty	owl:SymmetricProperty
owl:FunctionalProperty	owl:InverseFunctionalProperty
owl:inverseOf	

4.4.1.5 Allowed Datatypes

The standard only requires the support of xsd:string and xsd:integer.

xsd:string	xsd:boolean	xsd:decimal
xsd:float	xsd:double	xsd:dateTime
xsd:time	xsd:date	xsd:gYearMonth
xsd:gYear	xsd:gMonthDay	xsd:gDay
xsd:gMonth	xsd:hexBinary	xsd:base64Binary
xsd:anyURI	xsd:token	xsd:normalizedString
xsd:language	xsd:NMTOKEN	xsd:positiveInteger
xsd:NCName	xsd:Name	xsd:nonPositiveInteger
xsd:long	xsd:int	xsd:negativeInteger
xsd:short	xsd:byte	xsd:nonNegativeInteger
xsd:unsignedLong	xsd:unsignedInt	xsd:unsignedShort
xsd:unsignedByte	xsd:integer	

4.4.2 Overview of Additional OWL 2 Language Constructs

4.4.2.1 Declaring Individuals

owl:NamedIndividual

4.4.2.2 Class Relationships

owl:disjointUnionOf owl:AllDisjointClasses owl:members

4.4.2.3 Role Characteristics and Relationships

owl:AsymmetricProperty	owl:ReflexiveProperty	
owl:IrreflexiveProperty		
owl:topObjectProperty	owl:topDataProperty	
owl:bottomObjectProperty	owl:bottomDataProperty	
owl:propertyDisjointWith	owl:AllDisjointProperties	
owl:propertyChainAxiom	owl:hasKey	owl:inverseOf

4.4.2.4   Role Restrictions

owl:maxQualifiedCardinality	owl:minQualifiedCardinality
owl:qualifiedCardinality	owl:onClass
owl:onDataRange	owl:hasSelf

4.4.2.5   Role Assignments

owl:NegativePropertyAssertion	owl:sourceIndividual
owl:assertionProperty	owl:targetIndividual
owl:targetValue	

4.4.2.6   Datatype Restrictions

owl:onDataType	owl:withRestrictions
owl:datatypeComplementOf	

4.4.2.7   Additional Datatypes

owl:real	owl:rational	rdf:PlainLiteral
rdf:XMLLiteral	xsd:dateTimeStamp	

4.5   Exercises

Exercise 4.1 Use OWL DL to model the following sentences:

- The class Vegetable is a subclass of PizzaTopping.

- The class PizzaTopping does not share any elements with the class Pizza.

- The individual aubergine is an element of the class Vegetable.

- The abstract role hasTopping is only used for relationships between elements of the classes Pizza and PizzaTopping.

- The class VegPizza consists of those elements which are in the class NoMeatPizza and in the class NoFishPizza.

- The role hasTopping is a subrole of hasIngredient.

Exercise 4.2 Decide which of the following statements would be reasonable in the context of the ontology from Exercise 4.1.

- The role `hasIngredient` is transitive.

- The role `hasTopping` is functional.

- The role `hasTopping` is inverse functional.

Exercise 4.3 Use OWL DL to model the following sentences.

- Every pizza has at least two toppings.

- Every pizza has `tomato` as topping.

- Every pizza in the class `PizzaMargarita` has exactly `tomato` and `cheese` as toppings.

Exercise 4.4 Consider the example in Fig. 4.7. Show that the given inference can be drawn using the formal semantics of RDFS.

Exercise 4.5 Install Protégé and KAON2 on your computer. Use Protégé to input the example from Fig. 4.11. Then use KAON2 to show that the given inference is correct.

4.6   Further Reading

We will give a thorough treatment of OWL semantics in Chapter 5, and also further literature references on semantics. So for the time being we will simply give pointers to the original documents with the W3C specification.

- [OWL] is the central website for OWL.

- [MvH04] gives an overview of OWL.

- [SD04] contains a complete description of all OWL language constructs.

- [SMW04] shows how to use OWL for knowledge representation.

- [HHPS04] describes the semantics of OWL, which we will cover in Chapter 5. It also presents the abstract syntax for OWL, which we do not treat in this book.

The current state of discussion on the forthcoming OWL 2 standard can be found on the Web pages of the W3C OWL working group.[18] The current key documents are the following.

---

[18]http://www.w3.org/2007/OWL

- [MPSP09] is the central document which introduces OWL 2 in functional style syntax.

- [PSM09] describes how the functional style syntax translates from and to the RDF syntax.

- [MCGH⁺09] specifies the different profiles of OWL 2.

- [SHK09] describes conformance conditions for OWL 2 and introduces the format of OWL 2 test cases which are provided along with the OWL 2 documents.

- [HKP⁺09] is a general introduction to OWL 2.

Exercises 4.1 to 4.3 were inspired by [RDH⁺04].

Chapter 5

OWL Formal Semantics

In Chapter 4 we introduced OWL syntactically, and have discussed intuitively how to derive logical inferences from OWL ontologies. This derivation of implicit knowledge is at the heart of logic-based semantics, and we give this a thorough and formal treatment in this chapter. We start with description logics in Section 5.1, which provide a logical view on OWL. In Section 5.2, we then present two equivalent ways of defining the formal semantics of OWL. In Section 5.3 we present the most successful algorithmic approach, the so-called tableaux method, for automated reasoning with OWL ontologies. In this chapter, the reader will benefit from some background in predicate logic, which can be found in Appendix C.

5.1 Description Logics

OWL DL can be identified with a decidable fragment of first-order predicate logic and thus OWL draws on the long history of philosophical and mathematical logic, which is a well-established and well-understood theory. As such, it is also in the tradition of logic-based artificial intelligence research, where the development of suitable knowledge representation formalisms plays an important part.

Historically, OWL DL can be traced back to so-called *semantic networks*, which can be used for the modeling of simple relationships between individuals and classes via roles, roughly comparable to RDFS. In the beginning, the meaning of such semantic networks was vague, which necessitated a formalization of their semantics. Eventually, this led to the development of *description logics* which we will deal with prominently in this chapter. OWL DL is essentially a description logic, which in turn can be understood as a fragment of first-order predicate logic.

Description logics have been designed in order to achieve favorable trade-offs between expressivity and scalability. Also, they are usually decidable and there exist efficient algorithms for reasoning with them.

To make this introduction more accessible, we will sometimes refrain from a complete treatment of OWL DL, and instead restrict our attention to sublanguages which suffice for conveying the key insights.

5.1.1   The Description Logic $\mathcal{ALC}$

By *description logics* we understand a family of logics for knowledge representation, derived from semantic networks and related to so-called *frame logics*. Description logics are usually fragments of first-order predicate logic, and their development is usually driven by considerations concerning computational complexity: Given a complexity class, find a description logic which is as expressive as possible concerning its language constructs, but remains within the given complexity class. We will return to computational complexity later.

Researchers have developed a simple and useful notation for description logics which makes working with them much easier. We will use it in the following. We start by introducing the basic description logic $\mathcal{ALC}$.

5.1.1.1   Building Blocks of $\mathcal{ALC}$

Just as in OWL, the basic building blocks of $\mathcal{ALC}$ are classes, roles, and individuals, which can be put into relationships with each other. The expression

$$\texttt{Professor(rudiStuder)}$$

describes that the individual `rudiStuder` belongs to the class `Professor`. The expression

$$\texttt{hasAffiliation(rudiStuder, aifb)}$$

describes that `rudiStuder` is affiliated with `aifb`. The role `hasAffiliation` is an abstract role – we will discuss concrete roles later.

Subclass relations are expressed using the symbol $\sqsubseteq$. The expression

$$\texttt{Professor} \sqsubseteq \texttt{FacultyMember}$$

says that `Professor` is a subclass of the class `FacultyMember`. Equivalence between classes is expressed using the symbol $\equiv$, e.g., as

$$\texttt{Professor} \equiv \texttt{Prof}.$$

In order to express complex class relationships, $\mathcal{ALC}$ provides logical class constructors which we already know from OWL. The symbols for conjunction, disjunction, and negation are $\sqcap$, $\sqcup$, and $\neg$, respectively. The constructors can be nested arbitrarily, as in the following example.

$$\text{Professor} \sqsubseteq (\text{Person} \sqcap \text{FacultyMember}) \sqcup (\text{Person} \sqcap \neg \text{PhDStudent})$$

These logical constructors correspond to class constructors we already know from the OWL RDF syntax, namely, `owl:intersectionOf`, `owl:unionOf`, and `owl:complementOf`, respectively. The example just given corresponds to that from Fig. 4.11.

Complex classes can also be defined by using quantifiers, which correspond to role restrictions in OWL. If R is a role and C a class expression, then $\forall R.C$ and $\exists R.C$ are also class expressions.

The statement
$$\text{Exam} \sqsubseteq \forall \text{hasExaminer.Professor}$$

states that all examiners of an exam must be professors, and corresponds to the example from page 127 using `owl:allValuesFrom`. The statement

$$\text{Exam} \sqsubseteq \exists \text{hasExaminer.Professor}$$

says that every exam must have at least one examiner who is a professor, and corresponds to the example using `owl:someValuesFrom` from page 127.

Quantifiers and logical constructors can be nested arbitrarily.

5.1.1.2 Modeling Part of OWL in $\mathcal{ALC}$

We have already seen that many OWL DL language constructs can be expressed directly in $\mathcal{ALC}$. Some others can be expressed indirectly, as we will now demonstrate.

The empty class `owl:Nothing`, denoted in $\mathcal{ALC}$ using the symbol $\perp$, can be expressed by
$$\perp \equiv C \sqcap \neg C,$$

where C is some arbitrary class. Analogously, the class $\top$, which corresponds to `owl:Thing`, can be expressed by

$$\top \equiv C \sqcup \neg C,$$

or equivalently by

$$\top \equiv \neg \perp.$$

Disjointness of two classes C and D can be expressed using

$$C \sqcap D \sqsubseteq \bot,$$

or equivalently by

$$C \sqsubseteq \neg D,$$

corresponding to `owl:disjointWith`.

Domain and range of roles can also be expressed: The expression

$$\top \sqsubseteq \forall R.C$$

states that C is the `rdfs:range` of R, and the expression

$$\exists R.\top \sqsubseteq C$$

states that C is the `rdfs:domain` of R.

5.1.1.3 Formal Syntax of $\mathcal{ALC}$

Formally, the following syntax rules define $\mathcal{ALC}$. We first define how complex classes are constructed. Let A be an *atomic class*, i.e. a class name, and let R be an (abstract) role. Then *class expressions* C, D are constructed using the following rule.

$$C, D ::= A \mid \top \mid \bot \mid \neg C \mid C \sqcap D \mid C \sqcup D \mid \forall R.C \mid \exists R.C$$

Another common name for class expressions in description logics is "concept" or "concept expression" but we will adhere to the terminology that is used in OWL. Statements in $\mathcal{ALC}$ – and in other description logics – are divided into two groups, namely into *TBox* statements and *ABox* statements. The TBox is considered to contain terminological (or schema) knowledge, while the ABox contains assertional knowledge about instances (i.e. individuals). Remember that we distinguished between these two types of knowledge already in the case of RDFS (cf. the example in Section 2.6). Separating TBox and ABox becomes a bit academic when considering certain more expressive description logics, but it is still useful, and the distinction is well-defined for $\mathcal{ALC}$. Statements of either kind are often called *axioms* in description logics.[1]

Formally, a *TBox* consists of statements of the form $C \equiv D$ or $C \sqsubseteq D$, where C and D are class expressions. Statements $C \sqsubseteq D$ are called *(general) class inclusion axioms*. An *ABox* consists of statements of the form $C(a)$ and $R(a, b)$, where C is a class expression, R is a role, and a, b are individuals. An $\mathcal{ALC}$ *knowledge base* consists of an ABox and a TBox.

---

[1]The term "formula" would be more accurate than "axiom" in cases where a statement is not required to be true, but "axiom" is widely used in the literature.

5.1.2 OWL DL as Description Logic

We have already seen that the following OWL DL language constructs can be represented in $\mathcal{ALC}$:

- classes, roles, and individuals

- class membership and role instances

- owl:Thing and owl:Nothing

- class inclusion, class equivalence, and class disjointness

- conjunction, disjunction, and negation of classes

- role restrictions using owl:allValuesFrom and owl:someValuesFrom

- rdfs:domain and rdfs:range

The other OWL DL language constructs cannot be expressed in $\mathcal{ALC}$. Instead, we need to extend $\mathcal{ALC}$ to the description logic $\mathcal{SHOIN}(D)$, which encompasses $\mathcal{ALC}$ and also provides further expressive means. We will present them in the following.

5.1.2.1 Class Constructors and Relationships

Closed class expressions using owl:oneOf can be expressed in $\mathcal{SHOIN}(D)$ as follows: The class containing exactly the individuals $a_1, \ldots, a_n$ is written as $\{a_1, \ldots, a_n\}$. When talking about description logics, closed classes are called *nominals*.[2]

We have already seen on page 129 that owl:hasValue can be expressed by making use of owl:someValuesFrom and owl:oneOf, i.e. owl:hasValue is expressible in $\mathcal{SHOIN}(D)$.

$\mathcal{SHOIN}(D)$ further provides cardinality restrictions via the following notation: The statement

$$\text{Exam} \sqsubseteq \leq 2\text{hasExaminer}$$

says that each exam has at most two examiners. More generally, we can express owl:maxCardinality via $\leq nR$, where n is a non-negative integer, and R is an (abstract) role. Likewise, owl:minCardinality is written using $\geq nR$. As already exemplified in Fig. 4.12, owl:cardinality can be expressed using the intersection of owl:minCardinality and owl:maxCardinality.

---

[2]To be precise, a nominal is a class which contains exactly one individual. Closed classes correspond to unions of nominals then.

5.1.2.2 Relationships Between Individuals

Equality of individuals a and b is expressed indirectly as $\{a\} \equiv \{b\}$ using nominals and class equivalence. Inequality of individuals a and b is expressed likewise by saying that the classes $\{a\}$ and $\{b\}$ are disjoint, i.e. by stating $\{a\} \sqcap \{b\} \sqsubseteq \bot$.

5.1.2.3 Role Constructors, Role Relationships, and Role Characteristics

The statement that R is a subrole of S is written as $R \sqsubseteq S$, and is called a *role inclusion axiom*. Equivalence between these roles is written as $R \equiv S$. The inverse role to R is denoted by R^-, i.e. $S \equiv R^-$ states that S is the inverse of R. In $\mathcal{SHOIN}(\mathrm{D})$, inverse role descriptions may be used in all the places where roles may occur, basically as in OWL 2.

Transitivity of a role R is stated as $\mathrm{Trans}(R)$. Symmetry of R can be declared indirectly using $R \equiv R^-$. Functionality of R is stated as $\top \sqsubseteq \leq 1R$ while inverse functionality of R is stated as $\top \sqsubseteq \leq 1R^-$.

5.1.2.4 Datatypes

$\mathcal{SHOIN}(\mathrm{D})$ allows the use of data values, i.e. of elements of datatypes, in the second argument of concrete roles. It is also possible to form closed classes using such data values. This straightforward use of datatypes does not have any significant impact on the logical underpinnings, so we will not go into more detail here.

There exist more powerful uses of datatypes, known as *concrete domains*, in the theory of description logics. But concrete domains are not part of the OWL standard, so we only refer the interested reader to the literature given in Section 5.6.

5.1.2.5 $\mathcal{SHOIN}(\mathrm{D})$ and OWL DL

Let us summarize the expressive means available in $\mathcal{SHOIN}(\mathrm{D})$, as they cover OWL DL. We have

- all language constructs from $\mathcal{ALC}$,

- equality and inequality between individuals,

- closed classes (i.e. disjunctions of nominals),

- cardinality restrictions,

- role inclusion axioms and role equivalences (i.e. role hierarchies),

- inverse roles,

- transitivity, symmetry, functionality, and inverse functionality of roles,

- datatypes.

5.1.3 Naming Description Logics – and How They Relate to the OWL Sublanguages

We have already introduced and used some of the strange names description logics have, such as $\mathcal{ALC}$ or $\mathcal{SHOIN}$(D). The terminology behind these names is in fact systematic: the letters describe which language constructs are allowed in a particular description logic. $\mathcal{ALC}$ is short for *Attributive Language with Complement*, and has its name for historical reasons. $\mathcal{ALC}$ is considered to be the most fundamental description logic,[3] and is usually the starting point for theoretical investigations. We have formally defined $\mathcal{ALC}$ in Section 5.1.1.3.

Expressive means beyond $\mathcal{ALC}$ are now indicated by certain letters. The following explains $\mathcal{SHOIN}$(D).

- $\mathcal{S}$ stands for $\mathcal{ALC}$ plus role transitivity.

- $\mathcal{H}$ stands for role hierarchies, i.e. for role inclusion axioms.

- $\mathcal{O}$ stands for nominals, i.e. for closed classes with one element.

- $\mathcal{I}$ stands for inverse roles.

- $\mathcal{N}$ stands for cardinality restrictions.

- D stands for datatypes.

We also give the letters for some other language constructs which are of particular importance, and will explain them below.

- $\mathcal{F}$ stands for role functionality.

- $\mathcal{Q}$ stands for qualified cardinality restrictions.

- $\mathcal{R}$ stands for generalized role inclusion axioms.

- $\mathcal{E}$ stands for the use of existential role restrictions.

---

[3]$\mathcal{ALC}$ is often said to be *Boolean closed*, which means that conjunction, disjunction, negation and both quantifiers can be used without any restrictions. Description logics without this feature are called *sub-Boolean*.

5.1.3.1 Role Functionality

We have already said that OWL DL corresponds to $\mathcal{SHOIN}$(D). But functionality of roles can be declared in OWL DL, so why didn't we say that it corresponds to $\mathcal{SHOINF}$(D)? The reason is that redundant letters are usually left out. We have seen on page 164 that functionality can be expressed by means of cardinality restrictions, so functionality is implicit in $\mathcal{SHOIN}$(D), i.e. the letter $\mathcal{F}$ is omitted. Likewise, there is no letter for inverse functionality simply because it can be expressed using cardinality restrictions and inverse roles. Likewise, symmetry of roles can be expressed using inverse roles and role hierarchies.

So why do we need the letter $\mathcal{F}$ at all? Because having description logics with functionality but without, e.g., cardinality restrictions can be meaningful. Indeed, OWL Lite corresponds to the description logic $\mathcal{SHIF}$(D).

5.1.3.2 Qualified Cardinality Restrictions

Qualified cardinality restrictions are a generalization of the cardinality restrictions which we already know from $\mathcal{SHOIN}$. They allow us to make declarations like $\leq nR.C$ and $\geq nR.C$ which are similar to $\leq nR$ and $\geq nR$ (sometimes called *unqualified* cardinality restrictions) but furthermore allow us to specify to which class the second arguments in the role R belong – we have already encountered them in our discussion of OWL 2 in Section 4.3.1.6. This usage of qualified cardinality restrictions is thus analogous to the role restrictions $\forall R.C$ or $\exists R.C$.

Qualified cardinality restrictions encompass unqualified ones: $\geq nR$, for example, can be expressed using $\geq nR.\top$. It is also a fact that extending from unqualified to qualified cardinality restrictions hardly makes a difference in terms of theory, algorithms, or system runtimes. Description logic literature is thus usually concerned with $\mathcal{SHIQ}$ or $\mathcal{SHOIQ}$ rather than $\mathcal{SHIN}$ or $\mathcal{SHOIN}$.

5.1.3.3 Generalized Role Inclusions

We have already encountered generalized role inclusions in our discussion of OWL 2 in Section 4.3.1.5. The notation used for description logics is $R_1 \circ \cdots \circ R_n \sqsubseteq R$, meaning that the concatenation of $R_1, \ldots, R_n$ is a subrole of R. A typical example of this would be

$$\texttt{hasParent} \circ \texttt{hasBrother} \sqsubseteq \texttt{hasUncle}.$$

OWL 2 DL is essentially the description logic $\mathcal{SROIQ}$(D). Note that generalized role inclusions encompass role hierarchies, so that $\mathcal{SROIQ}$(D) contains $\mathcal{SHOIN}$(D), i.e. OWL 2 DL contains OWL DL.

OWL Full	is not a description logic
OWL DL	$\mathcal{SHOIN}(D)$
OWL Lite	$\mathcal{SHIF}(D)$
OWL 2 Full	is not a description logic
OWL 2 DL	$\mathcal{SROIQ}(D)$
OWL 2 EL	$\mathcal{EL}^{++}$
OWL 2 QL	DL-Lite
OWL 2 RL	DLP

FIGURE 5.1: Correspondence between OWL variants and description logics

5.1.3.4 Existential Role Restrictions

Since existential role restrictions are contained in $\mathcal{ALC}$, this symbol is only useful when discussing sub-Boolean description logics which are *properly* contained in $\mathcal{ALC}$. This is the case for the description logics corresponding to some of the tractable profiles of OWL 2, as discussed in Section 4.3.2: The description logic $\mathcal{EL}$ allows conjunction and existential role restrictions.[4] $\mathcal{EL}^{++}$ additionally allows generalized role inclusions and nominals. It corresponds to the OWL 2 EL profile from Section 4.3.2.1. The tractable fragment DL-Lite imposes more complicated restrictions on the use of language constructs, and we will not treat it in more detail here. It corresponds to the OWL 2 QL profile from Section 4.3.2.2. The OWL 2 RL profile from Section 4.3.2.3 corresponds to a naive intersection between $\mathcal{SROIQ}$ and datalog (see Section 6.2) and is very closely related to so-called Description Logic Programs (DLP). DLP is also a tractable fragment of $\mathcal{SROIQ}$, but we refrain from covering it in more detail here: we will have much more to say about OWL and Rules in Chapter 6.

5.1.3.5 OWL Sublanguages and Description Logics

The mentioned letters for describing description logics have to be taken carefully, since minor modifications are imposed in some cases. It is therefore necessary to revert to the formal definitions when details matter. We have given a formal definition of $\mathcal{ALC}$ in Section 5.1.1.3 above, and will give the formal definition of $\mathcal{SROIQ}$ and $\mathcal{SHIQ}$ in Section 5.1.4 below.

We summarize the relationships between different versions and sublanguages of OWL and description logics in Fig. 5.1.

---

[4]The letter $\mathcal{L}$ does not really carry a specific meaning.

5.1.4   Formal Syntax of $\mathcal{SROIQ}$

We will now formally define the complete syntax of the $\mathcal{SROIQ}$ description logic. By doing this, we will encounter some details which we have not mentioned so far in our rather intuitive treatment. The definition we will give is one of several possible logically equivalent definitions. It is the one most convenient for the rest of our treatment in this chapter. Its formal semantics will be presented in Section 5.2.

For $\mathcal{SROIQ}$, it is customary and convenient to distinguish between RBox, for roles, TBox, for terminological knowledge, and ABox, for assertional knowledge.

5.1.4.1 $\mathcal{SROIQ}$ RBoxes

A $\mathcal{SROIQ}$ *RBox* is based on a set **R** of *atomic roles*, which contains all role names, all inverses of role names (i.e. R^- for any role name R), and the *universal role* U. The universal role is something like the $\top$ element for roles: It is a superrole of all roles and all inverse roles, and can intuitively be understood as relating all possible pairs of individuals. It is the top abstract role which we have already encountered in Section 4.3.1.3.

A *generalized role inclusion axiom* is a statement of the form $S_1 \circ \cdots \circ S_n \sqsubseteq R$, and a set of such axioms is called a *generalized role hierarchy*. Such a role hierarchy is called *regular* if there exists a strict partial order[5] $\prec$ on **R**, such that the following hold:

- $S \prec R$ if and only if $S^- \prec R$

- every role inclusion axiom is of one of the forms

$$R \circ R \sqsubseteq R, \qquad R^- \sqsubseteq R, \qquad S_1 \circ \cdots \circ S_n \sqsubseteq R,$$
$$R \circ S_1 \circ \cdots \circ S_n \sqsubseteq R, \qquad S_1 \circ \cdots \circ S_n \circ R \sqsubseteq R$$

such that R is a non-inverse role name, and $S_i \prec R$ for $i = 1, \ldots, n$.

Regularity is a way to restrict the occurrence of cycles in generalized role hierarchies. It needs to be imposed in order to guarantee decidability of $\mathcal{SROIQ}$.

---

[5]A *partial order* $\leq$ on a set X satisfies the following conditions for all $x, y, z \in X$: $x \leq x$; if $x \leq y$ and $y \leq x$, then $x = y$; and if $x \leq y$ and $y \leq z$, then $x \leq z$. If $\leq$ is a partial order, then we can define a *strict partial order* $<$ by setting $x < y$ if and only if $x \leq y$ and $x \neq y$.

We give an example of a role hierarchy which is *not* regular:

$$\texttt{hasParent} \circ \texttt{hasHusband} \sqsubseteq \texttt{hasFather}$$
$$\texttt{hasFather} \sqsubseteq \texttt{hasParent}$$

This role hierarchy is not regular because regularity would enforce both `hasParent` $\prec$ `hasFather` and `hasFather` $\prec$ `hasParent`, which is impossible because $\prec$ must be strict.

Note that regular role hierarchies must not contain role equivalences: If we had $R \sqsubseteq S$ and $S \sqsubseteq R$, then regularity would enforce $R \prec S$ and $S \prec R$, which is impossible because $\prec$ must be strict. Formally, however, this restriction is not severe, since it basically means that we do not allow roles to have synonyms, i.e. if a knowledge base would contain two roles S and R which are equivalent, then we could simply replace all occurrences of S by R without losing any substantial information.

We now turn to the notion of *simple* role, which is also needed in order to guarantee decidability. Given a role hierarchy, the set of simple roles of this hierarchy is defined inductively, as follows.

- If a role does not occur on the right-hand side of a role inclusion axiom – and neither does the inverse of this role –, then it is simple.

- The inverse of a simple role is simple.

- If a role R occurs only on the right-hand side of role inclusion axioms of the form $S \sqsubseteq R$ with S being simple, then R is also simple.

Simplicity of a role essentially means that it does not occur on the right-hand side of a role inclusion axiom containing a role concatenation $\circ$.

To give an example, the set of simple roles of the role hierarchy $\{R \sqsubseteq R_1; R_1 \circ R_2 \sqsubseteq R_3; R_3 \sqsubseteq R_4\}$ is $\{R, R^-, R_1, R_1^-, R_2, R_2^-\}$.

Note that regular role hierarchies allow us to express transitivity ($R \circ R \sqsubseteq R$) and symmetry ($R^- \sqsubseteq R$). In $\mathcal{SROIQ}$, we additionally allow the explicit declaration of reflexivity of a role by $\text{Ref}(R)$, of antisymmetry of a role by $\text{Asy}(S)$, and of disjointness of two roles S_1 and S_2 by $\text{Dis}(S_1, S_2)$. However, we have to impose the condition that S, S_1 and S_2 are simple in order to ascertain decidability. These declarations are called *role characteristics*.[6]

---

[6]In the description logic literature, role characteristics are often called *role assertions*.

Let us explain the intuition behind the three new $\mathcal{SROIQ}$ role characteristics which we have already encountered in Section 4.3.1.3. Reflexivity of a role means that everything is related to itself by this role; a typical example would be isIdenticalTo. Antisymmetry of a role R means that whenever a is related to b via R, then b is *not* related to a via R. Most roles are antisymmetric; an example would be the role hasParent. Disjointness of two roles means that they do not share any pair of instances. The two roles hasParent and hasChild, for example, would be disjoint, while hasParent and hasFather would not be disjoint.

A $\mathcal{SROIQ}$ *RBox* is the union of a set of role characteristics and a role hierarchy. A $\mathcal{SROIQ}$ RBox is *regular* if its role hierarchy is regular.

5.1.4.2 $\mathcal{SROIQ}$ Knowledge Bases

Given a $\mathcal{SROIQ}$ RBox $\mathcal{R}$, we now define the set of class expressions **C** inductively as follows.

- Every class name is a class expression.

- $\top$ and $\bot$ are class expressions.

- If C, D are class expressions, $R, S \in \mathbf{R}$ with S being simple, a is an individual, and n is a non-negative integer, then the following are class expressions:

$$\neg C \qquad C \sqcap D \qquad C \sqcup D \qquad \{a\} \qquad \forall R.C \qquad \exists R.C$$
$$\exists S.\text{Self} \qquad \leq nS.C \qquad \geq nS.C$$

From our discussion of $\mathcal{SHOIN}$(D), these language constructs are already familiar. An exception is the $\exists S.\text{Self}$ expression, which we have already encountered for OWL 2 in Section 4.3.1.7. Intuitively, an individual a is an instance of $\exists S.\text{Self}$ if a is related to itself via the S role. A typical example would be the class inclusion

$$\text{PersonCommittingSuicide} \sqsubseteq \exists \text{kills.Self.}$$

Concerning nominals, i.e. the use of the construct $\{a\}$, note that closed classes with more than one individual can be constructed using disjunction, i.e. $\{a_1, \ldots, a_n\}$ can be written as $\{a_1\} \sqcup \cdots \sqcup \{a_n\}$.

A $\mathcal{SROIQ}$ *TBox* is a set of *class inclusion axioms* of the form $C \sqsubseteq D$, where C and D are class expressions.

A $\mathcal{SROIQ}$ *ABox* is a set of *individual assignments* – of one of the forms $C(a)$, $R(a, b)$, or $\neg R(a, b)$, where $C \in \mathbf{C}$, $R \in \mathbf{R}$ and a, b are individuals.

Note that $\mathcal{SROIQ}$ allows negated role assignments $\neg R(a, b)$, which we also know from OWL 2 and Section 4.3.1.8. This allows us to state explicitly, e.g., that John is *not* the father of Mary, namely by $\neg$hasFather(Mary, John).

A $\mathcal{SROIQ}$ *knowledge base* is the union of a regular RBox $\mathcal{R}$, an ABox, and a TBox for $\mathcal{R}$.

5.1.4.3 $\mathcal{SHIQ}$

The description logic $\mathcal{SHIQ}$ is of particular importance for research around OWL. From the perspective of computational complexity, which we discuss more closely in Section 5.3.5, $\mathcal{SHIQ}$ is not more complicated than $\mathcal{ALC}$. At the same time, only nominals are missing from $\mathcal{SHIQ}$ in order to encompass OWL DL.[7] $\mathcal{SHOIN}$, however, which is essentially OWL DL, is much more complex than $\mathcal{SHIQ}$, and $\mathcal{SROIQ}$ is even worse.

For research into reasoning issues around OWL, methods and algorithms are often first developed for $\mathcal{ALC}$, and then lifted to $\mathcal{SHIQ}$, before attempting $\mathcal{SHOIQ}$ or even $\mathcal{SROIQ}$. We do the same in Section 5.3, and require a formal definition of $\mathcal{SHIQ}$.

We define $\mathcal{SHIQ}$ by restricting $\mathcal{SROIQ}$. $\mathcal{SHIQ}$ RBoxes are $\mathcal{SROIQ}$ RBoxes restricted to axioms of the form $R \circ R \sqsubseteq R$ (written as Trans(R)), $R^- \sqsubseteq R$ (written as Sym(R)), and $S \sqsubseteq R$. Regularity does not need to be imposed for $\mathcal{SHIQ}$. Simplicity of roles is defined as for $\mathcal{SROIQ}$, but note that we can give a simpler definition of simplicity for $\mathcal{SHIQ}$: A role is simple unless it is transitive, its inverse is transitive, it has a transitive subrole, or its inverse has a transitive subrole. Note that we do not allow any of the additional role characteristics from $\mathcal{SROIQ}$.

$\mathcal{SHIQ}$ TBoxes are $\mathcal{SROIQ}$ TBoxes where Self and nominals of the form $\{a\}$, for a an individual, do not occur.

$\mathcal{SHIQ}$ ABoxes contain statements of the form $C(a)$, $R(a, b)$, or $a \neq b$, where $C \in \mathbf{C}$, $R \in \mathbf{R}$, and a, b are individuals, i.e. $\mathcal{SHIQ}$ ABoxes are $\mathcal{SROIQ}$ ABoxes where $\neg$ does not occur and where inequality of individuals may be explicitly stated. Note that there is no need to explicitly allow inequality of individuals in $\mathcal{SROIQ}$ ABoxes, since a statement like $a \neq b$ can be expressed in a $\mathcal{SROIQ}$ TBox using nominals as $\{a\} \sqcap \{b\} \sqsubseteq \bot$.

A $\mathcal{SHIQ}$ *knowledge base* is the union of a $\mathcal{SHIQ}$ RBox, a $\mathcal{SHIQ}$ TBox, and a $\mathcal{SHIQ}$ Abox.

For completeness, let us remark that the only difference between $\mathcal{SHIQ}$ and $\mathcal{SHOIQ}$ is that nominals are allowed in class expressions.

---

[7]Datatypes are also missing, but they do not pose any particular difficulties to the theory.

5.2   Model-Theoretic Semantics of OWL

We now define formally the semantics of $\mathcal{SROIQ}$, i.e. for OWL 2 DL. Since $\mathcal{SROIQ}$ encompasses $\mathcal{SHOIN}$, this also means that we essentially define the formal semantics of OWL DL.

We present the semantics in two versions, which are equivalent. In Section 5.2.1 we give the extensional semantics, sometimes also called the direct model-theoretic semantics. In Section 5.2.2, we define the semantics by a translation into first-order predicate logic.

5.2.1   Extensional Semantics of $\mathcal{SROIQ}$

The direct model-theoretic semantics which we now define is similar to the model-theoretic semantics of RDF(S) given in Chapter 3. We will make remarks about similarities and differences at the appropriate places.

5.2.1.1   Interpreting Individuals, Classes, and Roles

As for RDF(S), we first need to fix notation for the vocabulary used. We assume

- a set **I** of symbols for individuals,

- a set **C** of symbols for class names, and

- a set **R** of symbols for roles.

There is a significant difference from the situation for RDF(S) (and OWL Full): The sets **I**, **C**, and **R** must be mutually disjoint. This means that we enforce type separation as discussed for OWL DL on page 139. OWL 2 punning as in Section 4.3.1.1 is not needed, although this would not change the theory. We avoid the issue of punning here simply for convenience.

We next define the notion of $\mathcal{SROIQ}$ interpretation. As for RDF(S), we start with a set of entities, which can be thought of as resources, individuals, or single objects. We denote this set, called the *domain of the interpretation*, by Δ. We now declare how individuals, class names, and roles are interpreted, namely, by means of the functions

- $I_{\mathbf{I}}$, which maps individuals to elements of the domain: $I_{\mathbf{I}} : \mathbf{I} \to \Delta$,

- $I_{\mathbf{C}}$, which maps class names to subsets of the domain: $I_{\mathbf{C}} : \mathbf{C} \to 2^{\Delta}$ (the *class extension*), and

- $I_{\mathbf{R}}$, which maps roles to binary relations on the domain, i.e. to sets of pairs of domain elements: $I_{\mathbf{R}} : \mathbf{R} \to 2^{\Delta \times \Delta}$ (the *property extension*).

There are many choices possible, which we do not further restrict: The set Δ may be arbitrary, and how exactly the functions I_I, I_C, and I_R assign their values also bears a lot of freedom.

We note that we do not map class names and role names to single elements as done in RDF(S). The function I_C, however, could be understood as the concatenation of the functions I_S and I_{CEXT} from an RDF(S) interpretation. Likewise, I_R could be understood as the concatenation of the functions I_S and I_{EXT}. Figure 5.2 graphically depicts a DL interpretation.

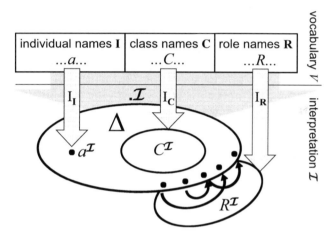

FIGURE 5.2: Schematic representation of a DL interpretation

We next define an interpretation function $\cdot^{\mathcal{I}}$, which lifts the interpretation of individuals, class names, and role names just given to complex class and role expressions.

- We set $\top^{\mathcal{I}} = \Delta$ and $\bot^{\mathcal{I}} = \emptyset$.

- $\neg C$ describes those things which are not in C, i.e. $(\neg C)^{\mathcal{I}} = \Delta \setminus C^{\mathcal{I}}$.

- $C \sqcap D$ describes those things which are both in C and in D, i.e. $(C \sqcap D)^{\mathcal{I}} = C^{\mathcal{I}} \cap D^{\mathcal{I}}$.

- $C \sqcup D$ describes those things which are in C or in D, i.e. $(C \sqcup D)^{\mathcal{I}} = C^{\mathcal{I}} \cup D^{\mathcal{I}}$.

- $\exists R.C$ describes those things which are connected via R with something in C, i.e. $(\exists R.C)^{\mathcal{I}} = \{x \mid \text{there is some } y \text{ with } (x, y) \in R^{\mathcal{I}} \text{ and } y \in C^{\mathcal{I}}\}$.

- $\forall R.C$ describes those things x for which every y which connects from x via a role R is in the class C, i.e. $(\forall R.C)^{\mathcal{I}} = \{x \mid \text{for all } y \text{ with } (x, y) \in R^{\mathcal{I}} \text{ we have } y \in C^{\mathcal{I}}\}$.

- $\leq nR.C$ describes those things which are connected via R to at most n things in C, i.e.[8] $(\leq nR.C)^{\mathcal{I}} = \{x \mid \#\{(x,y) \in R^{\mathcal{I}} \mid y \in C^{\mathcal{I}}\} \leq n\}$.

- $\geq nR.C$ describes those things which are connected via R to at least n things in C, i.e. $(\geq nR.C)^{\mathcal{I}} = \{x \mid \#\{(x,y) \in R^{\mathcal{I}} \mid y \in C^{\mathcal{I}}\} \geq n\}$.

- $\{a\}$ describes the class containing only a, i.e. $\{a\}^{\mathcal{I}} = \{a^{\mathcal{I}}\}$.

- $\exists S.\mathrm{Self}$ describes those things which are connected to themselves via S, i.e. $(\exists S.\mathrm{Self})^{\mathcal{I}} = \{x \mid (x,x) \in S^{\mathcal{I}}\}$.

- For $R \in \mathbf{R}$, we set $(R^-)^{\mathcal{I}} = \{(b,a) \mid (a,b) \in R^{\mathcal{I}}\}$.

- For the universal role U, we set $U^{\mathcal{I}} = \Delta \times \Delta$.

Given a $\mathcal{SROIQ}$ knowledge base, an *interpretation* consists of a domain Δ and an interpretation function which satisfies the constraints just given. Note that due to the many degrees of freedom in choosing Δ and the functions I_I, I_C, and I_R, it is not necessary that interpretations are intuitively meaningful.

If we consider, for example, the knowledge base consisting of the axioms

$$\mathtt{Professor} \sqsubseteq \mathtt{FacultyMember}$$
$$\mathtt{Professor(rudiStuder)}$$
$$\mathtt{hasAffiliation(rudiStuder, aifb)}$$

then we could set

$$\Delta = \{a, b, \mathrm{Ian}\}$$
$$I_I(\mathtt{rudiStuder}) = \mathrm{Ian}$$
$$I_I(\mathtt{aifb}) = b$$
$$I_C(\mathtt{Professor}) = \{a\}$$
$$I_C(\mathtt{FacultyMember}) = \{a, b\}$$
$$I_R(\mathtt{hasAffiliation}) = \{(a, b), (b, \mathrm{Ian})\}$$

Intuitively, these settings are nonsense, but they nevertheless determine a valid interpretation.

Let us dwell for a bit on the point that the interpretation just given is intuitively nonsense. There are actually two aspects to this. The first is the choice of names for the elements in Δ, e.g., that $\mathtt{rudiStuder}$ is interpreted as Ian, which seems to be quite far-fetched. Note, however, that this aspect

---

[8]Recall from Appendix B that $\#A$ denotes the cardinality of the set A.

relates only to the names of elements in a set, while in logic we would usually abstract from concrete names, i.e. we would usually be able to rename things without compromising logical meanings. The second aspect is more severe, as it is structural: It is about the question whether the interpretation faithfully captures the relations between entities as stated in the knowledge base. This is not the case in this example: $I_I(\texttt{rudiStuder})$ is not contained in $I_C(\texttt{Professor})$, although the knowledge base states that it should. Similarly, $I_R(\texttt{hasAffiliation})$ does not contain the pair $(I_I(\texttt{rudiStuder}), I_I(\texttt{aifb}))$, although it should according to the knowledge base.

Interpretations which *do* make sense for a knowledge base in the structural manner just described are called *models* of the knowledge base, and we introduce them formally next. Note, however, that we ignore the first aspect, as commonly done in logic.

5.2.1.2   Interpreting Axioms

Models capture the structure of a knowledge base in the sense that they give a truthful representation of the axioms in terms of sets. Formally, models of a knowledge base are interpretations which satisfy additional constraints which are determined by the axioms of the knowledge base. The constraints are as follows: An interpretation $\mathcal{I}$ of a $\mathcal{SROIQ}$ knowledge base K is a *model* of K, written $\mathcal{I} \models K$, if the following hold.

- If $C(a) \in K$, then $a^{\mathcal{I}} \in C^{\mathcal{I}}$.

- If $R(a, b) \in K$, then $(a^{\mathcal{I}}, b^{\mathcal{I}}) \in R^{\mathcal{I}}$.

- If $\neg R(a, b) \in K$, then $(a^{\mathcal{I}}, b^{\mathcal{I}}) \notin R^{\mathcal{I}}$.

- If $C \sqsubseteq D \in K$, then $C^{\mathcal{I}} \subseteq D^{\mathcal{I}}$.

- If $S \sqsubseteq R \in K$, then $S^{\mathcal{I}} \subseteq R^{\mathcal{I}}$.

- If $S_1 \circ \cdots \circ S_n \sqsubseteq R \in K$, then $\{(a_1, a_{n+1}) \in \Delta \times \Delta \mid \text{there are } a_2, \ldots, a_n \in \Delta \text{ such that } (a_i, a_{i+1}) \in S_i^{\mathcal{I}} \text{ for all } i = 1, \ldots, n\} \subseteq R^{\mathcal{I}}$.

- If $\mathrm{Ref}(R) \in K$, then $\{(x, x) \mid x \in \Delta\} \subseteq R^{\mathcal{I}}$.

- If $\mathrm{Asy}(R) \in K$, then $(x, y) \notin R^{\mathcal{I}}$ whenever $(y, x) \in R^{\mathcal{I}}$.

- If $\mathrm{Dis}(R, S) \in K$, then $R^{\mathcal{I}} \cap S^{\mathcal{I}} = \emptyset$.

	Model 1	Model 2	Model 3
Δ	$\{a, r, s\}$	$\{1, 2\}$	$\{\spadesuit\}$
I_I(rudiStuder)	r	1	$\spadesuit$
I_I(aifb)	a	2	$\spadesuit$
I_C(Professor)	$\{r\}$	$\{1\}$	$\{\spadesuit\}$
I_C(FacultyMember)	$\{a, r, s\}$	$\{1, 2\}$	$\{\spadesuit\}$
I_R(hasAffiliation)	$\{(r, a)\}$	$\{(1, 1), (1, 2)\}$	$\{(\spadesuit, \clubsuit)\}$

FIGURE 5.3: Models for the example knowledge base from page 174

We can now see that the example interpretation from page 174 is not a model: For it to be a model, we would need to have $(\text{rudiStuder}^{\mathcal{I}}, \text{aifb}^{\mathcal{I}}) \in$ hasAffiliation$^{\mathcal{I}}$, i.e. we would need to have

$$(\text{Ian}, b) \in \{(a, b), (b, \text{Ian})\},$$

which is not the case.

The following determines an interpretation which is also a model of the example knowledge base from page 174.

$$\Delta = \{a, r, s\}$$
$$I_I(\text{rudiStuder}) = r$$
$$I_I(\text{aifb}) = a$$
$$I_C(\text{Professor}) = \{r\}$$
$$I_C(\text{FacultyMember}) = \{r, s\}$$
$$I_R(\text{hasAffiliation}) = \{(r, a)\}$$

Let us remark on a difference to RDF(S): for the $\mathcal{SROIQ}$ (i.e. OWL) semantics, we need to consider many different kinds of axioms. For RDF(S), however, we had to consider only one kind of axiom, namely triples.

5.2.1.3   Logical Consequences

Models capture the structure of a knowledge base in set-theoretic terms. However, a knowledge base can still have many models. Each of these models describes a meaningful interpretation of the knowledge base. Figure 5.3 lists several example models for the knowledge base from page 174.

So how do we make the step from models to a notion of logical consequence, i.e. how do we define what *implicit knowledge* a knowledge base entails? Figure 5.3 shows that it does not suffice to consider one or a few models.

$K \models C \sqsubseteq D$	iff $(C \sqsubseteq D)^{\mathcal{I}}$ f.a. $\mathcal{I} \models K$	iff $C^{\mathcal{I}} \subseteq D^{\mathcal{I}}$ f.a. $\mathcal{I} \models K$
$K \models C(a)$	iff $(C(a))^{\mathcal{I}}$ f.a. $\mathcal{I} \models K$	iff $a^{\mathcal{I}} \in C^{\mathcal{I}}$ f.a. $\mathcal{I} \models K$
$K \models R(a,b)$	iff $(R(a,b))^{\mathcal{I}}$ f.a. $\mathcal{I} \models K$	iff $(a^{\mathcal{I}}, b^{\mathcal{I}}) \in R^{\mathcal{I}}$ f.a. $\mathcal{I} \models K$
$K \models \neg R(a,b)$	iff $(\neg R(a,b))^{\mathcal{I}}$ f.a. $\mathcal{I} \models K$	iff $(a^{\mathcal{I}}, b^{\mathcal{I}}) \notin R^{\mathcal{I}}$ f.a. $\mathcal{I} \models K$

FIGURE 5.4: Logical consequences of a knowledge base. The first line states that $C \sqsubseteq D$ is a logical consequence of K if and only if $(C \sqsubseteq D)^{\mathcal{I}}$ holds for all models $\mathcal{I}$ of K, which is the case if and only if $C^{\mathcal{I}} \subseteq D^{\mathcal{I}}$ holds for all models $\mathcal{I}$ of K.

For example, we have $\mathtt{aifb}^{\mathcal{I}} \in \mathtt{FacultyMember}^{\mathcal{I}}$ in all three models in Fig. 5.3, but we would not expect the conclusion from the knowledge base that aifb is a faculty member.

The right perspective on different models is the following: Each model of a knowledge base provides a *possible view* or *realization* of the knowledge base. The model captures all necessary structural aspects of the knowledge base, but it may add additional relationships which are not generally intended. In order to get rid of these additional relationships, we consider *all* models of a knowledge base when defining the notion of logical consequence. The rationale behind this idea is the following: If the models capture all possible views, or possible realizations, of a knowledge base, then those things common to *all* models must be universally valid logical consequences from the knowledge base. This leads us to the following formal definition.

Let K be a $\mathcal{SROIQ}$ knowledge base and α be a general inclusion axiom or an individual assignment. Then α is a *logical consequence* of K, written $K \models \alpha$, if $\alpha^{\mathcal{I}}$, as defined in Fig. 5.4, holds in every model I of K. Figure 5.5 contains an example related to logical consequence.

Let us introduce some further notions which are useful when dealing with model-theoretic semantics. A knowledge base is called *satisfiable* or *consistent* if it has at least one model. It is *unsatisfiable*, or *contradictory*, or *inconsistent*, if it is not satisfiable. A class expression C is called *satisfiable* if there is a model $\mathcal{I}$ of the knowledge base such that $C^{\mathcal{I}} \neq \emptyset$, and it is called *unsatisfiable* otherwise. Examples of these notions are given in Fig. 5.6.

Unsatisfiability of a knowledge base or of a named class usually points to modeling errors. But unsatisfiability also has other uses, which we will encounter in Section 5.3.

Returning to our running example knowledge base, let us show formally that FacultyMember(aifb) is not a logical consequence. This can be done by giving a model M of the knowledge base where $\text{aifb}^M \notin \text{FacultyMember}^M$. The following determines such a model.

$$\Delta = \{a, r\}$$
$$I_I(\text{rudiStuder}) = r$$
$$I_I(\text{aifb}) = a$$
$$I_C(\text{Professor}) = \{r\}$$
$$I_C(\text{FacultyMember}) = \{r\}$$
$$I_R(\text{hasAffiliation}) = \{(r, a)\}$$

FIGURE 5.5:   Example of logical consequence

We give examples of these notions. The knowledge base consisting of the axioms

$$\text{Unicorn(beautyTheUnicorn)}$$
$$\text{Unicorn} \sqsubseteq \text{Fictitious}$$
$$\text{Unicorn} \sqsubseteq \text{Animal}$$
$$\text{Fictitious} \sqcap \text{Animal} \sqsubseteq \bot$$

is inconsistent because beautyTheUnicorn would be a Fictitious Animal, which is forbidden by the last axiom. If we leave out the first individual assignment, then the resulting knowledge base is consistent, but Unicorn is unsatisfiable (i.e. is necessarily empty), as the existence of a Unicorn would lead to a contradiction.

FIGURE 5.6:   Examples of notions of consistency and satisfiability

5.2.2 $\mathcal{SROIQ}$ Semantics via Predicate Logic

We now briefly present an alternative perspective on the semantics of OWL, namely by translating $\mathcal{SROIQ}$ knowledge bases into first-order predicate logic. This perspective serves two purposes:

- it shows that the formal semantics of OWL is based on the long-standing tradition of mathematical logic, and

- it helps to convey the semantics of OWL to those readers who already have some background in formal logic.

More precisely, the translation is into first-order predicate logic with equality, which is a mild generalization of first-order predicate logic with an equality predicate $=$ and with the unary $\top$ and $\bot$ predicates, with the obvious meaning and formal semantics. Every $\mathcal{SROIQ}$ knowledge base thus translates to a theory in first-order predicate logic with equality.

We give the translation of a $\mathcal{SROIQ}$ knowledge base K by means of a function π which is defined by $\pi(K) = \bigcup_{\alpha \in K} \pi(\alpha)$. How $\pi(\alpha)$ is defined depends on the type of the axiom α, and is specified in the following.

5.2.2.1 Translating Class Inclusion Axioms

If α is a class inclusion axiom of the form $C \sqsubseteq D$, then $\pi(\alpha)$ is defined inductively as in Fig. 5.7, where A is a class name.

5.2.2.2 Translating Individual Assignments

If α is an individual assignment, then $\pi(\alpha)$ is defined as

$$\pi(C(a)) = C(a),$$
$$\pi(R(a,b)) = R(a,b),$$
$$\pi(\neg R(a,b)) = \neg R(a,b),$$

i.e. the translation does nothing, due to the notational similarity of individual assignments in $\mathcal{SROIQ}$ to standard predicate logic notation.

5.2.2.3 Translating RBoxes

If α is an RBox statement, then $\pi(\alpha)$ is defined inductively as stated in Fig. 5.8, where S is a role name.

5.2.2.4 Properties of the Translation and an Example

The function π translates $\mathcal{SROIQ}$ knowledge bases to first-order predicate logic theories in such a way that K and $\pi(K)$ are very intimately related. Indeed, K and $\pi(K)$ have essentially identical models, where the models of $\pi(K)$ are defined as usual for first-order predicate logic. This means that we

$$\pi(C \sqsubseteq D) = (\forall x)(\pi_x(C) \rightarrow \pi_x(D))$$
$$\pi_x(A) = A(x)$$
$$\pi_x(\neg C) = \neg \pi_x(C)$$
$$\pi_x(C \sqcap D) = \pi_x(C) \wedge \pi_x(D)$$
$$\pi_x(C \sqcup D) = \pi_x(C) \vee \pi_x(D)$$
$$\pi_x(\forall R.C) = (\forall x_1)(R(x, x_1) \rightarrow \pi_{x_1}(C))$$
$$\pi_x(\exists R.C) = (\exists x_1)(R(x, x_1) \wedge \pi_{x_1}(C))$$

$$\pi_x(\geq nS.C) = (\exists x_1) \ldots (\exists x_n) \left(\bigwedge_{i \neq j}(x_i \neq x_j) \wedge \bigwedge_i (S(x, x_i) \wedge \pi_{x_i}(C)) \right)$$

$$\pi_x(\leq nS.C) = \neg(\exists x_1) \ldots (\exists x_{n+1}) \left(\bigwedge_{i \neq j}(x_i \neq x_j) \wedge \bigwedge_i (S(x, x_i) \wedge \pi_{x_i}(C)) \right)$$

$$\pi_x(\{a\}) = (x = a)$$
$$\pi_x(\exists S.\mathrm{Self}) = S(x, x)$$

FIGURE 5.7: Translating $\mathcal{SROIQ}$ general inclusion axioms into first-order predicate logic with equality. Note that $\pi_x(\geq 0S.C) = \top(x)$. We use auxiliary functions π_x, π_{x_1}, etc., where x, x_1, etc. are variables. Also note that variables $x_1 \ldots, x_{n+1}$ introduced on the right-hand sides should always be variables which are new, i.e. which have not yet been used in the knowledge base. Obviously, renamings are possible – and indeed advisable for better readability. The axiom $D \sqsubseteq \exists R.\exists S.C$, for example, could be translated to $(\forall x)((D(x)) \rightarrow (\exists y)(R(x, y) \wedge (\exists z)(S(y, z) \wedge C(z))))$.

$$\pi(R_1 \sqsubseteq R_2) = (\forall x)(\forall y)(\pi_{x,y}(R_1) \to \pi_{x,y}(R_2))$$
$$\pi_{x,y}(S) = S(x,y)$$
$$\pi_{x,y}(R^-) = \pi_{y,x}(R)$$
$$\pi_{x,y}(R_1 \circ \cdots \circ R_n) = (\exists x_1) \ldots (\exists x_{n-1})$$
$$\left(\pi_{x,x_1}(R_1) \wedge \bigwedge_{i=1}^{n-2} \pi_{x_i,x_{i+1}}(R_{i+1}) \wedge \pi_{x_{n-1},y}(R_n) \right)$$
$$\pi(\mathrm{Ref}(R)) = (\forall x)\pi_{x,x}(R)$$
$$\pi(\mathrm{Asy}(R)) = (\forall x)(\forall y)(\pi_{x,y}(R) \to \neg\pi_{y,x}(R))$$
$$\pi(\mathrm{Dis}(R_1,R_2)) = \neg(\exists x)(\exists y)(\pi_{x,y}(R_1) \wedge \pi_{x,y}(R_2))$$

FIGURE 5.8:   Translating $\mathcal{SROIQ}$ RBoxes into first-order predicate logic

can understand $\mathcal{SROIQ}$ essentially as a fragment of first-order predicate logic, which means that it is in the tradition of mathematical logic, and results which have been achieved in this mathematical field can be carried over directly.

We have left out the treatment of datatypes in the translation, since it is unusual to consider predicate logic with datatypes. However, adding datatypes to predicate logic does not pose any particular problems unless complex operators on the datatype are allowed – which is not the case for OWL.

We close our discussion of the translation to predicate logic with an example, given in Fig. 5.9. It also shows that the established description logic notation is much easier to read than the corresponding first-order logic formulae.

5.3   Automated Reasoning with OWL

The formal model-theoretic semantics which we presented in Section 5.2 provides us with the logical underpinnings of OWL. At the heart of the formal semantics is that it provides means for accessing implicit knowledge, by the notion of logical consequence.

The definition of *logical consequence* given on page 177, however, does not lend itself easily to casting into an algorithm. Taken literally, it would necessitate examining *every* model of a knowledge base. Since there might be many models, and in general even infinitely many, a naive algorithmization of the definition of logical consequence is not feasible.

With OWL being a fragment of first-order predicate logic,it appears natural

Let K be the knowledge base containing the following axioms.

$$\text{Professor} \sqsubseteq \text{FacultyMember}$$
$$\text{Professor} \sqsubseteq (\text{Person} \sqcap \text{FacultyMember})$$
$$\sqcup (\text{Person} \sqcap \neg \text{PhDStudent})$$
$$\text{Exam} \sqsubseteq \forall \text{hasExaminer.Professor}$$
$$\text{Exam} \sqsubseteq \leq 2 \text{hasExaminer}$$
$$\text{hasParent} \circ \text{hasBrother} \sqsubseteq \text{hasUncle}$$
$$\text{Professor}(\text{rudiStuder})$$
$$\text{hasAffiliation}(\text{rudiStuder}, \text{aifb})$$

Then $\pi(K)$ contains the following logical formulae.

$$(\forall x)(\text{Professor}(x) \rightarrow \text{FacultyMember}(x)),$$
$$(\forall x)(\text{Professor}(x) \rightarrow ((\text{Person}(x) \wedge \text{FacultyMember}(x)) \vee (\text{Person}(x)$$
$$\wedge \neg \text{PhDStudent})(x))),$$
$$(\forall x)(\text{Exam}(x) \rightarrow (\forall y)(\text{hasExaminer}(x, y) \rightarrow \text{Professor}(y))),$$
$$(\forall x)(\text{Exam}(x) \rightarrow \neg (\exists x_1)(\exists x_2)(\exists x_3)((x_1 \neq x_2) \wedge (x_2 \neq x_3) \wedge (x_1 \neq x_3)$$
$$\wedge \text{hasExaminer}(x, x_1) \wedge \text{hasExaminer}(x, x_2) \wedge \text{hasExaminer}(x, x_3))),$$
$$(\forall x)(\forall y)(((\exists x_1)(\text{hasParent}(x, x_1) \wedge \text{hasBrother}(x_1, y)))$$
$$\rightarrow \text{hasUncle}(x, y)),$$
$$\text{Professor}(\text{rudiStuder}),$$
$$\text{hasAffiliation}(\text{rudiStuder}, \text{aifb})$$

FIGURE 5.9: Example of translation from description logic syntax to first-order predicate logic syntax

to employ deduction algorithms from predicate logic and to simply adjust them to the description logic setting. This has indeed been done for all the major inference systems from predicate logic.

By far the most successful approach for description logics to date is based on tableaux algorithms, suitably adjusted to OWL. We present this in the following. Since these algorithms are somewhat sophisticated, we do this first for $\mathcal{ALC}$, and then extend the algorithm to $\mathcal{SHIQ}$. We refrain from presenting the even more involved algorithm for $\mathcal{SROIQ}$, as $\mathcal{SHIQ}$ allows us to convey the central ideas.

But before coming to the algorithms, we need some preparation.

5.3.1 Inference Problems

In Section 4.1.10 we introduced the typical types of inferences which are of interest in the context of OWL. Let us recall them here from a logical perspective.

- *Subsumption.* To find out whether a class C is a subclass of D (i.e. whether C is *subsumed* by D), we have to find out whether $C \sqsubseteq D$ is a logical consequence of the given knowledge base.

- *Class equivalence.* To find out whether a class C is equivalent to a class D, we have to find out if $C \equiv D$ is a logical consequence of the given knowledge base.

- *Class disjointness.* To find out whether two classes C and D are disjoint, we have to find out whether $C \sqcap D \sqsubseteq \bot$ is a logical consequence of the given knowledge base.

- *Global consistency.* To find out whether the given knowledge base is globally consistent, we have to show that it has a model.

- *Class consistency.* To find out whether a given class D is consistent, we have to show that $C \sqsubseteq \bot$ is *not* a logical consequence of the given knowledge base.

- *Instance checking.* To find out if an individual a belongs to a class C, we have to check whether $C(a)$ is a logical consequence of the knowledge base.

- *Instance retrieval.* To find all individuals belonging to a class C, we have to check for all individuals whether they belong to C.

It would be very inconvenient if we had to devise a separate algorithm for each inference type. Fortunately, description logics allow us to reduce these inference problems to each other. For the tableaux algorithms, we need to reduce them to the checking of knowledge base satisfiability, i.e. to the question whether a knowledge base has at least one model. This is done as follows, where K denotes a knowledge base.

- *Subsumption.* $K \models C \sqsubseteq D$ if and only if $K \cup \{(C \sqcap \neg D)(a)\}$ is unsatisfiable, where a is a new individual not occurring in K.

- *Class equivalence.* $K \models C \equiv D$ if and only if we have $K \models C \sqsubseteq D$ and $K \models D \sqsubseteq C$.

- *Class disjointness.* $K \models C \sqcap D \sqsubseteq \bot$ if and only if $K \cup \{(C \sqcap D)(a)\}$ is unsatisfiable, where a is a new individual not occurring in K.

- *Global consistency.* K is globally consistent if it has a model.

- *Class consistency.* $K \models C \sqsubseteq \bot$ if and only if $K \cup \{C(a)\}$ is unsatisfiable, where a is a new individual not occurring in K.

- *Instance checking.* $K \models C(a)$ if and only if $K \cup \{\neg C(a)\}$ is unsatisfiable

- *Instance retrieval.* To find all individuals belonging to a class C, we have to check for all individuals a whether $K \models C(a)$.

Note that, strictly speaking, statements such as $\neg C(a)$ or $(C \sqcap \neg D)(a)$ are not allowed according to our definition of ABox in Section 5.1.1.3. However, complex class expressions like $C(a)$ in the ABox, where C is an arbitrary class expression, can easily be transformed to comply with our formal definition, namely, by introducing a new class name, say A, and rewriting $C(a)$ to the two statements $A(a)$ and $A \equiv C$. This technique is known as *ABox reduction*, and can also be applied to $\mathcal{SROIQ}$. The knowledge bases before and after the reduction are essentially equivalent. Without loss of generality, we will therefore allow complex classes in the ABox in this chapter.

We have now reduced all inference types to satisfiability checking. In principle, we could now use the transformation into predicate logic from Section 5.2.2 and do automated reasoning on OWL using predicate logic reasoning systems. This approach, however, is not very efficient, so special-purpose algorithms tailored to description logics are preferable. But there is also a more fundamental problem with the translational approach: $\mathcal{SROIQ}$, and also the description logics it encompasses, are decidable, while first-order predicate logic is not. This means that, in general, termination of description logic reasoning cannot be guaranteed by using reasoning algorithms for first-order predicate logic.

Nevertheless, the tableaux algorithms which we present in the following are derived from the corresponding first-order predicate logic proof procedures. And we will return to the termination issue later.

5.3.2 Negation Normal Form

Before presenting the actual algorithms, we do a preprocessing on the knowledge base known as negation normal form transformation, i.e. we transform the knowledge base into a specific syntactic form known as negation normal

$$\text{NNF}(K) = \mathcal{A} \cup \mathcal{R} \cup \bigcup_{C \sqsubseteq D \in K} \text{NNF}(C \sqsubseteq D) \qquad \text{where } \mathcal{A} \text{ and } \mathcal{R}$$

are the ABox and the RBox of K

$$\text{NNF}(K)(C \sqsubseteq D) = \text{NNF}(\neg C \sqcup D)$$

$$\text{NNF}(C) = C \qquad \text{if } C \text{ is a class name}$$

$$\text{NNF}(\neg C) = \neg C \qquad \text{if } C \text{ is a class name}$$

$$\text{NNF}(\neg\neg C) = \text{NNF}(C)$$

$$\text{NNF}(C \sqcup D) = \text{NNF}(C) \sqcup \text{NNF}(D)$$

$$\text{NNF}(C \sqcap D) = \text{NNF}(C) \sqcap \text{NNF}(D)$$

$$\text{NNF}(\neg(C \sqcup D)) = \text{NNF}(\neg C) \sqcap \text{NNF}(\neg D)$$

$$\text{NNF}(\neg(C \sqcap D)) = \text{NNF}(\neg C) \sqcup \text{NNF}(\neg D)$$

$$\text{NNF}(\forall R.C) = \forall R.\text{NNF}(C)$$

$$\text{NNF}(\exists R.C) = \exists R.\text{NNF}(C)$$

$$\text{NNF}(\neg\forall R.C) = \exists R.\text{NNF}(\neg C)$$

$$\text{NNF}(\neg\exists R.C) = \forall R.\text{NNF}(\neg C)$$

$$\text{NNF}(\leq nR.C) = \leq nR.\text{NNF}(C)$$

$$\text{NNF}(\geq nR.C) = \geq nR.\text{NNF}(C)$$

$$\text{NNF}(\neg\leq nR.C) = \geq(n+1)R.\text{NNF}(C)$$

$$\text{NNF}(\neg\geq(n+1)R.C) = \leq nR.\text{NNF}(C)$$

$$\text{NNF}(\neg\geq 0R.C) = \bot$$

FIGURE 5.10: Transformation of a $\mathcal{SHIQ}$ knowledge base K into negation normal form

form. It is not absolutely necessary to do this, and the algorithms could also be presented without this preprocessing step, but they are already complicated enough as they are, and restricting our attention to knowledge bases in negation normal form eases the presentation considerably.

In a nutshell, the negation normal form $\text{NNF}(K)$ of a knowledge base K is obtained by first rewriting all $\sqsubseteq$ symbols in an equivalent way, and then moving all negation symbols down into subformulae until they only occur directly in front of class names. How this is done formally is presented in Fig. 5.10 for $\mathcal{SHIQ}$. Note that only the TBox is transformed.

In the negation normal form transformation, subclass relationships like $C \sqsubseteq D$ become class expressions $\neg C \sqcup D$ which, intuitively, may look strange at first sight. Cast into first-order predicate logic, however, they become

$(\forall x)(C(x) \rightarrow D(x))$ and $(\forall x)(\neg C(x) \vee D(x))$ – and these two formulae are logically equivalent.

By slight abuse of terminology, we will henceforth refer to NNF($C \sqsubseteq D$) as a *TBox statement* whenever $C \sqsubseteq D$ is contained in the TBox of the knowledge base currently under investigation.

The knowledge bases K and NNF(K) are logically equivalent, i.e. they have identical models. We assume for the rest of this chapter that all knowledge bases are given in negation normal form.

5.3.3   Tableaux Algorithm for $\mathcal{ALC}$

The tableaux algorithm determines if a knowledge base is satisfiable. It does this by attempting to construct a generic representation of a model. If this construction fails, the knowledge base is unsatisfiable.

Obviously, it requires formal proofs to verify that such an algorithm indeed does what it claims. In this book, however, we do not have the space or the means to present this verification, which is based on comprehensive mathematical proofs. We refer the interested reader to the literature listed in Section 5.6. Nevertheless, by keeping in mind that tableaux algorithms essentially attempt to construct models, it should become intuitively clear why they indeed implement automated reasoning.

We now start with the description logic $\mathcal{ALC}$. The presentation of the corresponding tableaux algorithm is done in three stages to make this introduction easier to follow. We first informally discuss some examples. Then we formally define the *naive* tableaux algorithm for $\mathcal{ALC}$. It only is a small step then to provide the full tableaux algorithm.

5.3.3.1   Initial Examples

Consider a very simple case, where we have only class names, conjunction, disjunction, negation, and only one individual. We are given such a knowledge base and we are to determine whether it is satisfiable. Let us have a look at an example.

Assume the knowledge base K consists of the following two statements.

$$C(a) \qquad (\neg C \sqcap D)(a)$$

Then obviously $C(a)$ is a logical consequence of K. From the statement $(\neg C \sqcap D)(a)$ we also obtain $\neg C(a)$ as logical consequence – this is due to the semantics of conjunction. But this means that we have been able to derive $C(a)$ and $\neg C(a)$, which is a contradiction. So K cannot have a model and is therefore unsatisfiable.

What we have just constructed is essentially a part of a tableau. Informally speaking, a tableau is a structured way of deriving and representing logical consequences of a knowledge base. If in this process a contradiction is found, then the initial knowledge base is unsatisfiable.

Let us consider a slightly more difficult case. Assume the negation normal form of a knowledge base K consists of the following three statements.

$$C(a) \qquad \neg C \sqcup D \qquad \neg D(a)$$

We are now going to derive knowledge about class membership for a, as done in the previous example. The set of all classes for which we have derived class membership of a will be called $\mathcal{L}(a)$. We use the notation $\mathcal{L}(a) \leftarrow C$ to indicate that $\mathcal{L}(a)$ is updated by adding C. For example, if $\mathcal{L}(a) = \{D\}$ and we update via $\mathcal{L}(a) \leftarrow C$, then $\mathcal{L}(a)$ becomes $\{C, D\}$. Similarly, $\mathcal{L}(a) \leftarrow \{C, D\}$ denotes the subsequent application of $\mathcal{L}(a) \leftarrow C$ and $\mathcal{L}(a) \leftarrow D$, i.e. both C and D get added to $\mathcal{L}(a)$.

From the example knowledge base just given, we immediately obtain $\mathcal{L}(a) = \{C, \neg D\}$. The TBox statement $\neg C \sqcup D$ corresponds to $C \sqsubseteq D$ and must hold for all individuals, i.e. in particular for a, so we obtain $\mathcal{L}(a) \leftarrow \neg C \sqcup D$. Now consider the expression $(\neg C \sqcup D) \in \mathcal{L}(a)$, which states that we have $\neg C(a)$ or $D(a)$. So we distinguish two cases. (1) In the first case we assume $\neg C(a)$ and obtain $\mathcal{L}(a) \leftarrow \neg C = \{C, \neg D, \neg C \sqcup D, \neg C\}$, which is a contradiction. (2) In the second case we assume $D(a)$ and obtain $\mathcal{L}(a) \leftarrow D = \{C, \neg D, \neg C \sqcup D, D\}$, which is also a contradiction. In either case, we arrive at a contradiction which indicates that K is unsatisfiable.

Note the *branching* we had to do in the example in order to deal with disjunction. This and similar situations lead to nondeterminism of the tableaux algorithm, and we will return to this observation later.

In the previous section we have provided examples of how to deal with class membership information for individuals in a tableau, i.e. how to derive contradictions from this information. Our examples were restricted to single individuals, and we did not use any roles.

So how do we represent role information? We represent it graphically as arrows between individuals. Consider an ABox consisting of the assignments $R(a, b)$, $S(a, a)$, $R(a, c)$, $S(b, c)$. This would be represented as the following figure.

Likewise, we use arrows to represent roles between unknown individuals, the existence of which is ascertained by the knowledge base: Consider the single statement $\exists R.\exists S.C(a)$. Then there is an arrow labeled with R leading from a to an unknown individual x, from which in turn there is an arrow labeled with S to a second unknown individual y. The corresponding picture would be the following.

Let us give an example tableau involving roles. Consider the knowledge base $K = \{C(a), C \sqsubseteq \exists R.D, D \sqsubseteq E\}$, so that $\mathrm{NNF}(K) = \{C(a), \neg C \sqcup \exists R.D, \neg D \sqcup$

$E\}$. We would like to know if $(\exists R.E)(a)$ is a logical consequence of K.

We first reduce the instance checking problem to a satisfiability problem as described in Section 5.3.1: $\neg\exists R.E$ in negation normal form becomes $\forall R.\neg E$, and we obtain the knowledge base $\{C(a), \neg C \sqcup \exists R.D, \neg D \sqcup E, \forall R.\neg E(a)\}$, of which we have to show that it is unsatisfiable. We start with the node a with label $\mathcal{L}(a) = \{C, \forall R.\neg E\}$, which is information we take from the ABox. The first TBox statement results in $\mathcal{L}(a) \leftarrow \neg C \sqcup \exists R.D$. We can now resolve the disjunction as we have done above, i.e. we have to consider two cases. Adding $\neg C$ to $\mathcal{L}(a)$, however, results in a contradiction since $C \in \mathcal{L}(a)$, so we do not have to consider this case, i.e. we end up with $\mathcal{L}(a) \leftarrow \exists R.D$. So, since $\exists R.D \in \mathcal{L}(a)$, we create a new individual x and a connection labeled R from a to x, and we set $\mathcal{L}(x) = \{D\}$. The situation is as follows.

$$a \qquad \mathcal{L}(a) = \{C, \forall R.\neg E, \neg C \sqcup \exists R.D, \exists R.D\}$$

$$\downarrow R$$

$$x \qquad \mathcal{L}(x) = \{D\}$$

The TBox information $\neg D \sqcup E$ can now be added to $\mathcal{L}(x)$, i.e. $\mathcal{L}(x) \leftarrow \neg D \sqcup E$, and expanded using the already known case distinction because of the disjunction. As before, however, selecting the left hand side $\neg D$ results in a contradiction because $D \in \mathcal{L}(x)$, so we have to put $\mathcal{L}(x) \leftarrow E$. The situation is now as follows.

$$a \qquad \mathcal{L}(a) = \{C, \forall R.\neg E, \neg C \sqcup \exists R.D, \exists R.D\}$$

$$\downarrow R$$

$$x \qquad \mathcal{L}(x) = \{D, \neg D \sqcup E, E\}$$

Now note that $\forall R.\neg E \in \mathcal{L}(a)$, which means that everything to which a connects using the R role must be contained in $\neg E$. Since a connects to x via an arrow labeled R, we set $\mathcal{L}(x) \leftarrow \neg E$, which results in a contradiction because we already have $E \in \mathcal{L}(x)$. Thus, the knowledge base is unsatisfiable, and the instance checking problem is solved, i.e. $(\exists R.E)(a)$ is indeed a logical consequence of K. The final tableau is depicted below.

$$a \qquad \mathcal{L}(a) = \{C, \forall R.\neg E, \neg C \sqcup \exists R.D, \exists R.D\}$$

$$\downarrow R$$

$$x \qquad \mathcal{L}(x) = \{D, \neg D \sqcup E, E, \neg E\}$$

It is now time to leave the intuitive introduction and to formalize the tableau procedure.

5.3.3.2 The Naive Tableaux Algorithm for $\mathcal{ALC}$

A tableau for an $\mathcal{ALC}$ knowledge base consists of

- a set of nodes, labeled with individual names or variable names,

FIGURE 5.11: Example of an initial tableau given the knowledge base
$K = \{A(a), (\exists R.B)(a), R(a,b), R(a,c), S(b,b), (A \sqcup B)(c), \neg A \sqcup (\forall S.B)\}$

- directed edges between some pairs of nodes,

- for each node labeled x, a set $\mathcal{L}(x)$ of class expressions, and

- for each pair of nodes x and y, a set $\mathcal{L}(x, y)$ of role names.

When we depict a tableau, we omit edges which are labeled with the empty
set. Also, we make the agreement that $\top$ is contained in $\mathcal{L}(x)$, for any x, but
we often do not write it down, and in fact the algorithm does not explicitly
derive this.

Given an $\mathcal{ALC}$ knowledge base K in negation normal form, the *initial
tableau* for K is defined by the following procedure.

1. For each individual a occurring in K, create a node labeled a and set
   $\mathcal{L}(a) = \emptyset$.

2. For all pairs a, b of individuals, set $\mathcal{L}(a, b) = \emptyset$.

3. For each ABox statement $C(a)$ in K, set $\mathcal{L}(a) \leftarrow C$.

4. For each ABox statement $R(a, b)$ in K, set $\mathcal{L}(a, b) \leftarrow R$.

An example of an initial tableau can be found in Fig. 5.11.

After initialization, the tableaux algorithm proceeds by nondeterministically applying the rules from Fig. 5.12. This means that at each step one of
the rules is selected and executed. The algorithm terminates if

- either there is a node x such that $\mathcal{L}(x)$ contains a contradiction, i.e. if
  there is $C \in \mathcal{L}(x)$ and at the same time $\neg C \in \mathcal{L}(x)$,[9]

---

[9]This includes the case when both $\bot$ and $\top$ are contained in $\mathcal{L}(x)$, which is also a contradiction as $\top \equiv \neg\bot$.

⊓-**rule:** If $C \sqcap D \in \mathcal{L}(x)$ and $\{C, D\} \not\subseteq \mathcal{L}(x)$, then set $\mathcal{L}(x) \leftarrow \{C, D\}$.

⊔-**rule:** If $C \sqcup D \in \mathcal{L}(x)$ and $\{C, D\} \cap \mathcal{L}(x) = \emptyset$, then set $\mathcal{L}(x) \leftarrow C$ or $\mathcal{L}(x) \leftarrow D$.

∃-**rule:** If $\exists R.C \in \mathcal{L}(x)$ and there is no y with $R \in L(x, y)$ and $C \in \mathcal{L}(y)$, then

      1. add a new node with label y (where y is a new node label),

      2. set $\mathcal{L}(x, y) = \{R\}$, and

      3. set $\mathcal{L}(y) = \{C\}$.

∀-**rule:** If $\forall R.C \in \mathcal{L}(x)$ and there is a node y with $R \in \mathcal{L}(x, y)$ and $C \notin \mathcal{L}(y)$, then set $\mathcal{L}(y) \leftarrow C$.

TBox-rule: If C is a TBox statement and $C \notin \mathcal{L}(x)$, then set $\mathcal{L}(x) \leftarrow C$.

FIGURE 5.12: Expansion rules for the naive $\mathcal{ALC}$ tableaux algorithm

- or none of the rules from Fig. 5.12 is applicable.

The knowledge base K is satisfiable if the algorithm terminates without producing a contradiction, i.e. if there is a selection of subsequent rule applications such that no contradiction is produced and the algorithm terminates. Otherwise, K is unsatisfiable. Note that due to the nondeterminism of the algorithm we do not know which choice of subsequent rule applications leads to termination without producing a contradiction. Implementations of this algorithm thus have to guess the choices, and possibly have to backtrack to choice points if a choice already made has led to a contradiction.

Let us explain this point in more detail since it is critical to understanding the algorithm. There are two sources of nondeterminism, namely (1) which expansion rule to apply next and (2) the choice which has to be made when applying the ⊔-rule, namely whether to set $\mathcal{L}(x) \leftarrow C$ or $\mathcal{L}(x) \leftarrow D$ (using the notation from Fig. 5.12). There is a fundamental difference between these two: The choice made in (1) is essentially a choice about the sequence in which the rules are applied, i.e. whatever results from such a choice could also be obtained by doing the same expansion later. Intuitively speaking, we cannot get "on the wrong track" by a bad choice, although some choices will cause the algorithm to take more steps before termination. Hence, if such a choice causes a contradiction, then this contradiction cannot be avoided by making a different choice, simply because the original choice can still be made later – and entries are never removed from node labels during execution. This kind of nondeterminism is usually called *don't care* nondeterminism. In contrast to this, (2) is a *don't know* nondeterminism, since a bad choice can indeed get us "on the wrong track." This is because, if we choose to set $\mathcal{L}(x) \leftarrow C$, then it is no longer possible to also add $\mathcal{L}(x) \leftarrow D$ by applying the same rule – the condition $\{C, D\} \cap \mathcal{L}(x) = \emptyset$ prevents this. So if we have chosen to add $\mathcal{L}(x) \leftarrow C$ and this leads to a contradiction, then we have to go back to this choice and try the other alternative as well, because this other alternative may not lead to a contradiction.

To sum this up, note the following. If the sequence of choices (of both types) leads to termination without producing a contradiction, then the original knowledge base is satisfiable. However, if the algorithm produces a contradiction, then we do not yet know if there is a sequence of choices which avoids the contradiction. Hence, we have to check on all choices made due to (2) and see if we also get contradictions if we alter these choices – in other words, we have to *backtrack* to these *choice points*. But it is not necessary to reconsider the choices made due to (1). We recommend the reader to go back to the initial examples in Section 5.3.3.1 and observe how we have done this: It occurs in all the cases where we have dismissed one of the choices from applying the ⊔-rule because it would lead to a contradiction.

We will see in the next section that the naive tableaux algorithm does not necessarily terminate. This will be fixed then. But we first present, in Fig. 5.13, another worked example.

5.3.3.3 The Tableaux Algorithm with Blocking for $\mathcal{ALC}$

We have already remarked that the naive tableaux algorithm for $\mathcal{ALC}$ does not always terminate. To see this, consider $K = \{\exists R.\top, \top(a_1)\}$. First note that K is satisfiable: consider the interpretation $\mathcal{I}$ with infinite domain $\{a_1, a_2, \dots\}$ such that $a_1^{\mathcal{I}} = a_1$ and $(a_i, a_{i+1}) \in R^{\mathcal{I}}$ for all $i = 1, 2, \dots$. Then $\mathcal{I}$ is obviously a model.

Now we construct a tableau for K, as depicted below. Initialization leaves us with one node a_1 and $\mathcal{L}(a_1) = \{\top\}$. Applying the TBox-rule yields $\mathcal{L}(a_1) \leftarrow \exists R.\top$. Then we apply the $\exists$-rule and create a node x with $\mathcal{L}(a_1, x) = \{R\}$ and $\mathcal{L}(x) = \{\top\}$. Again we apply the TBox-rule which yields $\mathcal{L}(x) \leftarrow \exists R.\top$, and then the $\exists$-rule allows us to create yet another new node y with $\mathcal{L}(x, y) = \{R\}$ and $\mathcal{L}(y) = \{\top\}$. Obviously, this process repeats and does not terminate.

$$a_1 \xrightarrow{\quad R \quad} x \xrightarrow{\quad R \quad} y \xrightarrow{\quad R \quad} \cdots$$

$$\mathcal{L}(a_1) = \{\top, \exists R.\top\} \qquad \mathcal{L}(x) = \{\top, \exists R.\top\} \qquad \mathcal{L}(y) = \{\top, \exists R.\top\}$$

But we remarked earlier that $\mathcal{ALC}$ (and actually also $\mathcal{SROIQ}$) is decidable, i.e. algorithms exist which allow reasoning with $\mathcal{ALC}$ and which are always guaranteed to terminate! To ensure termination in all cases, we have to modify the naive tableaux algorithm. The technique used for this purpose is called *blocking*, and rests on the observation that in the above example, the process is essentially repeating itself: The newly created node x has the same properties as the node a_1, so instead of expanding x to a new node y it should be possible to "reuse" a_1 in some sense.

Consider the following knowledge base K.

$$\text{Human} \sqsubseteq \exists \text{hasParent.Human}$$
$$\text{Orphan} \sqsubseteq \text{Human} \sqcap \forall \text{hasParent.} \neg \text{Alive}$$
$$\text{Orphan(harrypotter)}$$
$$\text{hasParent(harrypotter, jamespotter)}$$

We want to know if $\alpha = \neg \text{Alive(jamespotter)}$ is a logical consequence of K.

We first add $\neg\neg\text{Alive(jamespotter)}$ to K and call the result K'. In order to show that α is a logical consequence of K, we have to show that K' is unsatisfiable. We now transform K' into negation normal form. We also use some straightforward shortcuts to ease the notation. So $\text{NNF}(K')$ is the following.

$$\neg H \sqcup \exists P.H$$
$$\neg O \sqcup (H \sqcap \forall P.\neg A)$$
$$O(h)$$
$$P(h,j)$$
$$A(j)$$

The initial tableau for $\text{NNF}(K')$ is depicted below.

$$h \qquad \mathcal{L}(h) = \{O\}$$
$$\Big\downarrow P$$
$$j \qquad \mathcal{L}(j) = \{A\}$$

We now apply the TBox-rule and set $\mathcal{L}(h) \leftarrow \neg O \sqcup (H \sqcap \forall P.\neg A)$. Applying the $\sqcup$-rule to the same TBox axiom leaves us with a choice how to resolve the disjunction. However, choosing the left hand side $\neg O$ immediately results in a contradiction since $O \in \mathcal{L}(h)$, so, backtracking, we choose to set $\mathcal{L}(h) \leftarrow H \sqcap \forall P.\neg A$. Applying the $\sqcap$-rule results in $\mathcal{L}(h) \leftarrow \{H, \forall P.\neg A\}$. Finally, we apply the $\forall$-rule to $\forall P.\neg A \in \mathcal{L}(h)$, which results in $\mathcal{L}(j) \leftarrow \neg A$. Since $A \in \mathcal{L}(j)$, we have thus arrived at an unavoidable contradiction, i.e. K' is unsatisfiable, and therefore $\neg A(j)$ is a logical consequence of K. The final tableau is depicted below.

$$h \qquad \mathcal{L}(h) = \{O, \neg O \sqcup (H \sqcap \forall P.\neg A), H \sqcap \forall P.\neg A, H, \forall P.\neg A\}$$
$$\Big\downarrow P$$
$$j \qquad\qquad \mathcal{L}(j) = \{A, \neg A\}$$

FIGURE 5.13: Worked example of $\mathcal{ALC}$ tableau

The formal definition is as follows: A node with label x is *directly blocked* by a node with label y if

- x is a variable (i.e. not an individual),

- y is an ancestor of x, and

- $\mathcal{L}(x) \subseteq \mathcal{L}(y)$.

The notion of *ancestor* is defined inductively as follows: Every z with $\mathcal{L}(z, x) \neq \emptyset$ is called a *predecessor* of x. Every predecessor of x, which is not an individual, is an ancestor of x, and every predecessor of an ancestor of x, which is not an individual, is also an ancestor of x.

A node with label x is *blocked* if it is directly blocked or one of its ancestors is blocked.

The naive tableaux algorithm for $\mathcal{ALC}$ is now modified as follows, resulting in the (full) tableaux algorithm for $\mathcal{ALC}$: The rules in Fig. 5.12 may only be applied *if x is not blocked*. Otherwise, the algorithm is exactly the naive algorithm.

Returning to the example above, we note that $\mathcal{L}(x) \subseteq \mathcal{L}(a_1)$, so x is blocked by a_1. This means that the algorithm terminates with the following tableau, and therefore shows that the knowledge base is satisfiable.

$$a_1 \xrightarrow{\quad R \quad} x$$

$$\mathcal{L}(a_1) = \{\top, \exists R.\top\} \qquad \mathcal{L}(x) = \{\top\}$$

Recall the model for this knowledge base which we gave on page 191. Intuitively, the blocked node x is a representative for the infinite set $\{a_2, a_3, \dots\}$. Alternatively, we could view the tableau as standing for the model $\mathcal{J}$ with domain $\{a_1, a\}$ such that $a_1^{\mathcal{J}} = a_1$, $x^{\mathcal{J}} = a$ and $R^{\mathcal{J}} = \{(a_1, a), (a, a)\}$, i.e. the model would be cyclic.

5.3.3.4 Worked Examples

We give a number of worked examples which show some aspects of the algorithm in more detail.

5.3.3.4.1 Blocking Consider $K = \{H \sqsubseteq \exists P.H, B(t)\}$ as knowledge base, which stands for

$$\textsf{Human} \sqsubseteq \exists \textsf{hasParent.Human}$$

$$\textsf{Bird(tweety)}$$

We try to show that `tweety` is *not* in the class ¬**Human**, i.e. that $\neg H(t)$ is *not* a logical consequence of K. To do this, we add $\neg\neg H(t)$ to K, resulting in K', and attempt to show that K' is unsatisfiable. Obviously, this attempt will not be successful, which shows that `tweety` *could* be in the class `Human` according to the knowledge base.

We obtain $\text{NNF}(K') = \{\neg H \sqcup \exists P.H, B(t), H(t)\}$. The tableau is initialized with one node t and $\mathcal{L}(t) = \{B, H\}$. Applying the TBox rule yields $\mathcal{L}(t) \leftarrow \neg H \sqcup \exists P.H$. Expanding this TBox axiom using the $\sqcup$-rule results in $\mathcal{L}(t) \leftarrow \exists P.H$ since the addition of $\neg H$ to $\mathcal{L}(t)$ would immediately yield a contradiction. We now apply the $\exists$-rule and create a node with label x, $\mathcal{L}(t, x) = \{P\}$, and $\mathcal{L}(x) = \{H\}$. At this stage, the node x is blocked by t, and no further expansion of the tableau is possible.

$$t \qquad \mathcal{L}(t) = \{H, B, \neg H \sqcup \exists P.H, \exists P.H\}$$

$$\Big\downarrow P$$

$$x \qquad\qquad\quad \mathcal{L}(x) = \{H\}$$

5.3.3.4.2 Open World Consider the knowledge base

$$K = \{h(j, p), h(j, a), m(p), m(a)\},$$

which consists only of an ABox. The knowledge base stands for the following.

$$\text{hasChild(john, peter)}$$
$$\text{hasChild(john, alex)}$$
$$\text{Male(peter)}$$
$$\text{Male(alex)}$$

We want to show that $\forall\text{hasChild.male(john)}$ is *not* a logical consequence of the knowledge base. We do this by adding the negation of the statement, $\neg\forall h.m(j)$, resulting in the knowledge base K'. We then need to show that K' is satisfiable.

Let us first try to understand why K' is satisfiable. Due to the Open World Assumption as discussed on page 131, the knowledge base contains no information whether or not `john` has only `peter` and `alex` as children. It is entirely possible that `john` has additional children who are not listed in the knowledge base. Therefore, it is not possible to infer that all of `john`'s children are `Male`. We will see how the tableaux algorithm mimics this.

Transformation into negation normal form yields

$$\text{NNF}(K') = \{h(j, p), h(j, a), m(p), m(a), \exists h.\neg m(j)\}.$$

The initial tableau for $\text{NNF}(K')$ can be depicted as follows.

$$p \qquad \mathcal{L}(p) = \{m\}$$

$$\mathcal{L}(j) = \{\exists h.\neg m\} \qquad j \xrightarrow{\ h\ } a \qquad \mathcal{L}(a) = \{m\}$$

Now, application of the ∃-rule yields a new node x with $\mathcal{L}(j, x) = \{h\}$ and $\mathcal{L}(x) = \{\neg m\}$, as depicted below.

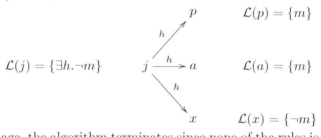

$\mathcal{L}(p) = \{m\}$

$\mathcal{L}(j) = \{\exists h. \neg m\}$

$\mathcal{L}(a) = \{m\}$

$\mathcal{L}(x) = \{\neg m\}$

At this stage, the algorithm terminates since none of the rules is applicable. This means that K' is satisfiable.

The new node x represents a potential child of john who is not male. Note how the constructed tableau indeed corresponds to a model of the knowledge base K'.

5.3.3.4.3 A Sophisticated Example

We close our discussion of the $\mathcal{ALC}$ tableaux algorithm with a more sophisticated example. We start with the knowledge base K containing the statements

$$C(a), \quad C(c), R(a,b), \quad R(a,c), \quad S(a,a), \quad S(c,b),$$
$$C \sqsubseteq \forall S.A, \quad A \sqsubseteq \exists R.\exists S.A, \quad A \sqsubseteq \exists R.C,$$

and want to show that $\exists R.\exists R.\exists S.A(a)$ is a logical consequence of K.

We first add $\neg \exists R.\exists R.\exists S.A(a)$, which results in K'. The knowledge base $\text{NNF}(K')$ then consists of

$$C(a), \quad C(c), R(a,b), \quad R(a,c), \quad S(a,a), \quad S(c,b),$$
$$\neg C \sqcup \forall S.A, \quad \neg A \sqcup \exists R.\exists S.A, \quad \neg A \sqcup \exists R.C, \quad \forall R.\forall R.\forall S.\neg A(a),$$

and the initial tableau for $\text{NNF}(K')$ is the following.

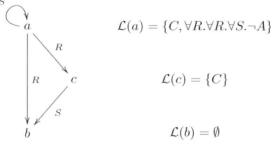

$\mathcal{L}(a) = \{C, \forall R.\forall R.\forall S.\neg A\}$

$\mathcal{L}(c) = \{C\}$

$\mathcal{L}(b) = \emptyset$

At this stage, there are many choices of which rules to apply and at which node. We urge the reader to attempt solving the tableau by herself before reading on. Indeed, the tableau can grow considerably larger if the expansion rules are chosen more or less randomly.

We choose to first use the TBox-rule and set $\mathcal{L}(c) \leftarrow \neg C \sqcup \forall S.A$. Expanding this TBox axiom using the $\sqcup$-rule gives us a choice, but we refrain from adding $\neg C$ to $\mathcal{L}(c)$ as this would contradict $C \in \mathcal{L}(c)$. So we set $\mathcal{L}(c) \leftarrow \forall S.A$.

As the next step, we choose $\forall S.A \in \mathcal{L}(c)$ and apply the $\forall$-rule, resulting in $\mathcal{L}(b) \leftarrow A$. Then we choose $\forall R.\forall R.\forall S.\neg A \in \mathcal{L}(a)$ and again apply the $\forall$-rule, resulting in $\mathcal{L}(b) \leftarrow \forall R.\forall R.\forall S.\neg A$. Applying the TBox-rule we set $\mathcal{L}(b) \leftarrow \neg A \sqcup \exists R.\exists S.A$. The following picture shows the current situation.

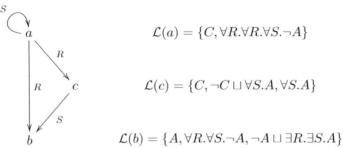

$$\mathcal{L}(a) = \{C, \forall R.\forall R.\forall S.\neg A\}$$

$$\mathcal{L}(c) = \{C, \neg C \sqcup \forall S.A, \forall S.A\}$$

$$\mathcal{L}(b) = \{A, \forall R.\forall S.\neg A, \neg A \sqcup \exists R.\exists S.A\}$$

The node b is now going to be the key to finding a contradiction. Using the $\sqcup$-rule on $\neg A \sqcup \exists R.\exists S.A \in \mathcal{L}(b)$ yields $\mathcal{L}(b) \leftarrow \exists R.\exists S.A$ since the addition of $\neg A$ would already result in a contradiction. We apply the $\exists$-rule to $\exists R.\exists S.A \in \mathcal{L}(b)$, creating a new node x with $\mathcal{L}(b, x) = \{R\}$ and $\mathcal{L}(x) = \{\exists S.A\}$. The $\forall$-rule for $\forall R.\forall S.\neg A$ yields $\mathcal{L}(x) \leftarrow \forall S.\neg A$.

Finally, we use the $\exists$-rule on $\exists S.A \in \mathcal{L}(x)$, resulting in a new node y with $\mathcal{L}(x, y) = \{S\}$ and $\mathcal{L}(y) = \{A\}$. Application of the $\forall$-rule to $\forall S.\neg A \in \mathcal{L}(x)$ yields $\mathcal{L}(y) \leftarrow \neg A$. We end up with $\mathcal{L}(y) = \{A, \neg A\}$, i.e. with a contradiction. The final tableau is depicted in Fig. 5.14.

5.3.4   Tableaux Algorithm for $\mathcal{SHIQ}$

The algorithm which we have presented in Section 5.3.3 displays the central concepts of tableaux algorithms for description logics. In order to convey an idea about the modifications to the $\mathcal{ALC}$ algorithm which need to be made to generalize it to more expressive description logics, we now provide the tableaux algorithm for $\mathcal{SHIQ}$.

We give a self-contained presentation of the $\mathcal{SHIQ}$ tableaux algorithm, and at the same time discuss the differences to the $\mathcal{ALC}$ algorithm.

A tableau for a $\mathcal{SHIQ}$ knowledge base consists of

- a set of nodes, labeled with individual names or variable names,

- directed edges between some pairs of nodes,

- for each node labeled x, a set $\mathcal{L}(x)$ of class expressions,

- for each pair of nodes x and y, a set $\mathcal{L}(x, y)$ containing role names or inverses of role names, and

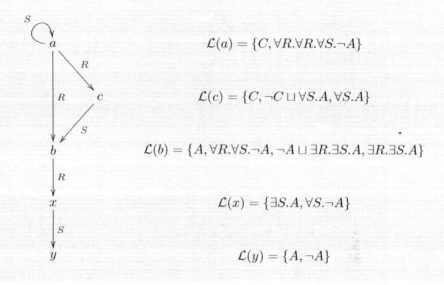

$$\mathcal{L}(a) = \{C, \forall R.\forall R.\forall S.\neg A\}$$

$$\mathcal{L}(c) = \{C, \neg C \sqcup \forall S.A, \forall S.A\}$$

$$\mathcal{L}(b) = \{A, \forall R.\forall S.\neg A, \neg A \sqcup \exists R.\exists S.A, \exists R.\exists S.A\}$$

$$\mathcal{L}(x) = \{\exists S.A, \forall S.\neg A\}$$

$$\mathcal{L}(y) = \{A, \neg A\}$$

FIGURE 5.14: Final tableau for the example from Section 5.3.3.4.3

- two relations between nodes, denoted by $\approx$ and $\not\approx$.

The relations $\approx$ and $\not\approx$ are implicitly assumed to be symmetrical, i.e. whenever $x \approx y$, then $y \approx x$ also holds, and likewise for $\not\approx$. When we depict a tableau, we omit edges which are labeled with the empty set. We indicate the relations $\approx$ and $\not\approx$ by drawing undirected edges, labeled with $\approx$ or $\not\approx$.

There are only two differences to $\mathcal{ALC}$ tableaux. The first is that edges may be labeled with inverse role names, which accommodates the use of inverse roles in $\mathcal{SHIQ}$. The second is the presence of the relations $\approx$ and $\not\approx$, which are used to keep track of equality or inequality of nodes.[10] This accommodates the fact that $\mathcal{SHIQ}$, when translated to predicate logic as in Section 5.2.2, actually translates to predicate logic with equality. From the discussion in Section 5.2.2 it can easily be seen that $\mathcal{ALC}$ translates into equality-free predicate logic, so $\approx$ and $\not\approx$ are not needed for the $\mathcal{ALC}$ algorithm.

Given a $\mathcal{SHIQ}$ knowledge base K in negation normal form, the *initial tableau* for K is defined by the following procedure, which differs from the $\mathcal{ALC}$ procedure only in the final two steps.

1. For each individual a occurring in K, create a node labeled a and set $\mathcal{L}(a) = \emptyset$. These nodes are called *root nodes*.

---

[10]In fact, the relation $\approx$ used for equality is not really needed. It can easily be removed from the algorithm description, where it occurs only once. We keep it, though, because it makes understanding the algorithm a bit easier.

2. For all pairs a, b of individuals, set $\mathcal{L}(a, b) = \emptyset$.

3. For each ABox statement $C(a)$ in K, set $\mathcal{L}(a) \leftarrow C$.

4. For each ABox statement $R(a, b)$ in K, set $\mathcal{L}(a, b) \leftarrow R$.

5. For each ABox statement $a \neq b$ in K, set $a \not\approx b$.

6. Set $\approx$ to be the empty relation, i.e. initially, no two nodes are considered to be equal.

Again, we make the agreement that $\top$ is contained in $\mathcal{L}(x)$, for any x, but we will often not write it down, and in fact the algorithm will not explicitly derive this.

We exemplify the visualization of initial tableaux by considering the knowledge base

$$K = \{R^-(a, b), S(a, b), S(a, c), c \neq b, C(a), C(b), D(b), D(c)\}.$$

$$\mathcal{L}(a) = \{C\}$$
$$\mathcal{L}(b) = \{C, D\}$$
$$\mathcal{L}(c) = \{D\}$$

For convenience, we use the following notation: If $R \in \mathbf{R}$ (i.e. if R is a role name), then set $\mathrm{Inv}(R) = R^-$ and $\mathrm{Inv}(R^-) = \mathrm{Inv}(R)$. Furthermore, call $R \in \mathbf{R}$ *transitive* if $R \circ R \sqsubseteq R$ or $\mathrm{Inv}(R) \circ \mathrm{Inv}(R) \sqsubseteq R$. This, and the following somewhat involved definitions, are needed to accommodate inverse roles.

Consider a tableau for a knowledge base K. Let H_K be the set of all statements of the form $R \sqsubseteq S$ and $\mathrm{Inv}(R) \sqsubseteq \mathrm{Inv}(S)$, where $R, S \in \mathbf{R}$ and $R \sqsubseteq S \in K$. We now call R a *subrole* of S if $R = S$, if $R \sqsubseteq S \in H_K$, or if there are $S_1, \ldots, S_n \in \mathbf{R}$ with $\{R \sqsubseteq S_1, S_1 \sqsubseteq S_2, \ldots, S_{n-1} \sqsubseteq S_n, S_n \sqsubseteq S\} \subseteq H_K$. In other words, R is a subrole of S if and only if R and S are related via the reflexive-transitive closure of $\sqsubseteq$ in H_K.

If $R \in \mathcal{L}(x, y)$ for two nodes x and y, and if R is a subrole of S, then y is called an *S-successor* of x, and x is called an *S-predecessor* of y. If y is an S-successor or an $\mathrm{Inv}(S)$-predecessor of x, then y is called an *S-neighbor* of x. Furthermore, inductively, every predecessor of x, which is not an individual, is called an *ancestor* of x, and every predecessor of an ancestor of x, which is not an individual, is also called an *ancestor* of x. Examples of these notions are given in Fig. 5.15.

Consider a knowledge base $H = \{R \sqsubseteq S^-, S \sqsubseteq S_1^-, S_1 \sqsubseteq S_2\}$ which consists only of a role hierarchy. Then $H_K = H \cup \{R^- \sqsubseteq S, S^- \sqsubseteq S_1, S_1^- \sqsubseteq S_2^-\}$. Furthermore, R is a subrole of S^-, S_1, and S_2. S is a subrole of S_1^- and S_2^-; S_1 is a subrole of S_2; R^- is a subrole of S, S_1^- and S_2^-, etc. Now consider the knowledge base

$$K = \{R^-(a,b), R(b,c), S(c,d), S^-(d,e), S_1(e,f), R \sqsubseteq S\},$$

which, apart from $R \sqsubseteq S$, can be depicted by the following diagram.

$$a \xrightarrow{R^-} b \xrightarrow{R} c \xrightarrow{S} d \xrightarrow{S^-} e \xrightarrow{S_1} f$$

Then a is an R^--predecessor of b, and hence also an S^--predecessor of b. At the same time, c is an R-successor of b, and hence also an S-successor of b. We thus have that the S-neighbors of b are a and c. Also, we have that c is an S-predecessor of d and e is an S^--successor of d. Hence d has S^--neighbors c and e. Note that f has no ancestors because ancestors must not be individuals.

FIGURE 5.15: Example of notions of successor, predecessor, neighbor and ancestor

5.3.4.1 Blocking for $\mathcal{SHIQ}$

The blocking mechanism we used for $\mathcal{ALC}$ in Section 5.3.3.3 is not sufficient for $\mathcal{SHIQ}$, and we will give an example of this in Section 5.3.4.3.5 below. For $\mathcal{SHIQ}$, we need to employ *pairwise blocking*: While in $\mathcal{ALC}$, a node x is blocked by a node y if y essentially repeats x, in $\mathcal{SHIQ}$ a node x is blocked if it has a predecessor x' and there exists a node y with predecessor y', such that the *pair* (y', y) essentially repeats the pair (x', x). We formalize this as follows.

A node x is *blocked* if it is not a root node and any one of the following hold.

- There exist ancestors x', y, and y' of x such that
  - y is not a root node,
  - x is a successor of x' and y is a successor of y',
  - $\mathcal{L}(x) = \mathcal{L}(y)$ and $\mathcal{L}(x') = \mathcal{L}(y')$, and
  - $\mathcal{L}(x', x) = \mathcal{L}(y', y)$.

- An ancestor of x is blocked.

- There is no node y with $\mathcal{L}(y, x) \neq \emptyset$.

If only the first case applies, then x is called *directly blocked* by y. In all other cases, x is called *indirectly blocked*. Note that we require $\mathcal{L}(x) = \mathcal{L}(y)$ if x is (directly) blocked by y, which is stronger than the required $\mathcal{L}(x) \subseteq \mathcal{L}(y)$ in the case of $\mathcal{ALC}$.

As an example of blocking, consider the following part of a tableau.

$$a \xrightarrow{\;\;R\;\;} x \xrightarrow{\;\;R\;\;} y \xrightarrow{\;\;R\;\;} z \xrightarrow{\;\;R\;\;} w$$

$$\mathcal{L}(a) = \{D\} \qquad \mathcal{L}(x) = \{C\} \qquad \mathcal{L}(y) = \{C\} \qquad \mathcal{L}(z) = \{C\} \qquad \mathcal{L}(w) = \{D\}$$

Then z is directly blocked by y, since the pair (y, z) essentially repeats the pair (x, y). The node w is indirectly blocked because its ancestor z is blocked.

5.3.4.2 The Algorithm

The $\mathcal{SHIQ}$ tableaux algorithm is a nondeterministic algorithm which essentially extends the $\mathcal{ALC}$ algorithm. It decides whether a given knowledge base K is satisfiable.

Given a $\mathcal{SHIQ}$ knowledge base K, the tableaux algorithm first constructs the initial tableau as given above. Then the initial tableau is expanded by nondeterministically applying the rules from Figs. 5.16 and 5.17. The algorithm terminates if

- there is a node x such that $\mathcal{L}(x)$ contains a contradiction, i.e. if there is $C \in \mathcal{L}(x)$ and at the same time $\neg C \in \mathcal{L}(x)$,

- or there is a node x with $\leq nS.C \in \mathcal{L}(x)$, and x has $n + 1$ S-neighbors $y_1, \ldots, y_{n+1}$ with $C \in \mathcal{L}(y_i)$ and $y_i \not\approx y_j$ for all $i, j \in \{1, \ldots, n+1\}$ with $i \neq j$,

- or none of the rules from Figs. 5.16 and 5.17 is applicable.

In the first two cases, we say that the tableau *contains a contradiction*. In the third case, we say that the tableau is *complete*. The knowledge base K is satisfiable if and only if there is a selection of subsequent expansion rule applications which leads to a complete and contradiction-free tableau. Otherwise, K is unsatisfiable.

5.3.4.3 Worked Examples

We continue with some worked examples which help to explain the different expansion rules.

5.3.4.3.1 Cardinalities
We first give an example of the application of the $\leq$-rule. Consider the knowledge base

$$K = \{h(j, p), h(j, a), m(p), m(a), \leq 2h.\top(j)\},$$

⊓-**rule:** If x is not indirectly blocked, $C \sqcap D \in \mathcal{L}(x)$, and $\{C, D\} \not\subseteq \mathcal{L}(x)$, then set $\mathcal{L}(x) \leftarrow \{C, D\}$.

⊔-**rule:** If x is not indirectly blocked, $C \sqcup D \in \mathcal{L}(x)$ and $\{C, D\} \sqcap \mathcal{L}(x) = \emptyset$, then set $\mathcal{L}(x) \leftarrow C$ or $\mathcal{L}(x) \leftarrow D$.

∃-**rule:** If x is not blocked, $\exists R.C \in \mathcal{L}(x)$, and there is no y with $R \in \mathcal{L}(x, y)$ and $C \in \mathcal{L}(y)$, then

    1. add a new node with label y (where y is a new node label),

    2. set $\mathcal{L}(x, y) = \{R\}$ and $\mathcal{L}(y) = \{C\}$.

∀-**rule:** If x is not indirectly blocked, $\forall R.C \in \mathcal{L}(x)$, and there is a node y with $R \in \mathcal{L}(x, y)$ and $C \notin \mathcal{L}(y)$, then set $\mathcal{L}(y) \leftarrow C$.

TBox-rule: If x is not indirectly blocked, C is a TBox statement, and $C \notin \mathcal{L}(x)$, then set $\mathcal{L}(x) \leftarrow C$.

FIGURE 5.16: Expansion rules (part 1) for the $\mathcal{SHIQ}$ tableaux algorithm

which extends the example from Section 5.3.3.4.2 by adding the statement $\leq 2\mathtt{hasChild}.\top(\mathtt{john})$. We will show that $\forall h.m(j)$ is still *not* a logical consequence of K.

As before, we add $\exists h.\neg m(j)$ to the knowledge base, resulting in K'. The initial tableau now looks as follows.

$$\mathcal{L}(j) = \{\exists h.\neg m, \leq 2h.\top\} \qquad j \xrightarrow{h} a$$

with node p ($\mathcal{L}(p) = \{m\}$) connected from j by h, and $\mathcal{L}(a) = \{m\}$.

Now, application of the ∃-rule yields

$$\mathcal{L}(j) = \{\exists h.\neg m, \leq 2h.\top\} \qquad j \xrightarrow{h} a$$

with node p ($\mathcal{L}(p) = \{m\}$) connected from j by h, $\mathcal{L}(a) = \{m\}$, and a new node x connected from j by h with $\mathcal{L}(x) = \{\neg m\}$.

and subsequent application of the $\leq$-root-rule allows us to identify p and a, resulting in the following.

trans-rule: If x is not indirectly blocked, $\forall S.C \in \mathcal{L}(x)$, S has a transitive subrole R, and x has an R-neighbor y with $\forall R.C \notin \mathcal{L}(y)$, then set $\mathcal{L}(y) \leftarrow \forall R.C$.

choose-rule: If x is not indirectly blocked, $\leq nS.C \in \mathcal{L}(x)$ or $\geq nS.C \in \mathcal{L}(x)$, and there is an S-neighbor y of x with $\{C, \mathrm{NNF}(\neg C)\} \cap \mathcal{L}(y) = \emptyset$, then set $\mathcal{L}(y) \leftarrow C$ or $\mathcal{L}(y) \leftarrow \mathrm{NNF}(\neg C)$.

$\geq$-rule: If x is not blocked, $\geq nS.C \in \mathcal{L}(x)$, and there are no n S-neighbors $y_1, \dots, y_n$ of x with $C \in \mathcal{L}(y_i)$ and $y_i \not\approx y_j$ for $i, j \in \{1, \dots, n\}$ and $i \neq j$, then

1. create n new nodes with labels $y_1, \dots, y_n$ (where the labels are new),
2. set $\mathcal{L}(x, y_i) = \{S\}$, $\mathcal{L}(y_i) = \{C\}$, and $y_i \not\approx y_j$ for all $i, j \in \{1, \dots, n\}$ with $i \neq j$.

$\leq$-rule: If x is not indirectly blocked, $\leq nS.C \in \mathcal{L}(x)$, there are more than n S-neighbors y_i of x with $C \in \mathcal{L}(y_i)$, and x has two S-neighbors y, z such that y is neither a root node nor an ancestor of z, $y \not\approx z$ does not hold, and $C \in \mathcal{L}(y) \cap \mathcal{L}(z)$, then

1. set $\mathcal{L}(z) \leftarrow \mathcal{L}(y)$,
2. if z is an ancestor of x, then $\mathcal{L}(z, x) \leftarrow \{\mathrm{Inv}(R) \mid R \in \mathcal{L}(x, y)\}$,
3. if z is not an ancestor of x, then $\mathcal{L}(x, z) \leftarrow \mathcal{L}(x, y)$,
4. set $\mathcal{L}(x, y) = \emptyset$, and
5. set $u \not\approx z$ for all u with $u \not\approx y$.

$\leq$-root-rule: If $\leq nS.C \in \mathcal{L}(x)$, there are more than n S-neighbors y_i of x with $C \in \mathcal{L}(y_i)$, and x has two S-neighbors y, z which are both root nodes, $y \not\approx z$ does not hold, and $C \in \mathcal{L}(y) \cap \mathcal{L}(z)$, then

1. set $\mathcal{L}(z) \leftarrow \mathcal{L}(y)$,
2. for all directed edges from y to some w, set $\mathcal{L}(z, w) \leftarrow \mathcal{L}(y, w)$,
3. for all directed edges from some w to y, set $\mathcal{L}(w, z) \leftarrow \mathcal{L}(w, y)$,
4. set $\mathcal{L}(y) = \mathcal{L}(w, y) = \mathcal{L}(y, w) = \emptyset$ for all w,
5. set $u \not\approx z$ for all u with $u \not\approx y$, and
6. set $y \approx z$.

FIGURE 5.17: Expansion rules (part 2) for the $\mathcal{SHIQ}$ tableaux algorithm

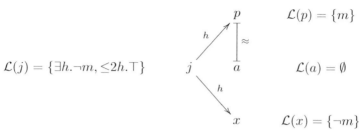

None of the expansion rules is now applicable, so the tableau is complete and K' is satisfiable.

5.3.4.3.2   Choose   We do a variant of the example just given in order to show how the choose-rule is applied. Consider the knowledge base $K = \{\geq 3h.\top(j), \leq 2h.m\}$. We want to find out if K is satisfiable. The initial tableau for K consists of a single node j with $\mathcal{L}(j) = \{\geq 3h.\top, \leq 2h.m\}$. Application of the $\geq$-rule yields three new nodes x, y and z with $\mathcal{L}(x) = \mathcal{L}(y) = \mathcal{L}(z) = \{\top\}$, $x \not\approx y$, $x \not\approx z$, and $y \not\approx z$. The choose-rule then allows us to assign classes to these new nodes, e.g., by setting $\mathcal{L}(x) \leftarrow m$, $\mathcal{L}(y) \leftarrow m$, and $\mathcal{L}(z) \leftarrow \neg m$. The resulting tableau, depicted below, is complete.

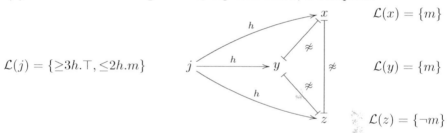

5.3.4.3.3   Inverse Roles   The next example displays the handling of inverse roles. Consider the knowledge base $K = \{\exists C.h(j), \neg h \sqcup \forall P.h, C \sqsubseteq P^-\}$, which stands for

$$\exists \mathtt{hasChild.Human(john)}$$
$$\mathtt{Human} \sqsubseteq \forall \mathtt{hasParent.Human}$$
$$\mathtt{hasChild} \sqsubseteq \mathtt{hasParent}^-$$

We show that $\mathtt{Human(john)}$ is a logical consequence from K, i.e. we start by adding $\neg h(j)$ to K, which is already in negation normal form.

In the initial tableau, we apply the $\exists$-rule to $\exists C.h \in \mathcal{L}(j)$, which yields the following.

$$\mathcal{L}(j) = \{\exists C.h, \neg h\} \qquad j \xrightarrow{C} x \qquad \mathcal{L}(x) = \{h\}$$

We now use the TBox rule and set $\mathcal{L}(x) \leftarrow \neg h \sqcup \forall P.h$. The $\sqcup$-rule on this yields $\mathcal{L}(x) \leftarrow \forall P.h$, since the addition of $\neg h$ would yield a contradiction.

$$\mathcal{L}(j) = \{\exists C.h, \neg h\} \qquad j \xrightarrow{C} x \qquad \mathcal{L}(x) = \{h, \neg h \sqcup \forall P.h, \forall P.h\}$$

We now apply the $\forall$-rule to $\forall P.h \in \mathcal{L}(x)$: j is a C-predecessor of x, and hence a P^--predecessor of x due to $C \sqsubseteq P^-$. So j is a P^--neighbor of x, and the $\forall$-rule yields $\mathcal{L}(j) \leftarrow h$. Since we already have $\neg h \in \mathcal{L}(j)$, the algorithm terminates with the tableau containing a contradiction.

$$\mathcal{L}(j) = \{\exists C.h, \neg h, h\} \qquad j \xrightarrow{\ C\ } x \qquad \mathcal{L}(x) = \{h, \neg h \sqcup \forall P.h, \forall P.h\}$$

5.3.4.3.4 Transitivity and Blocking

The next example displays blocking and the effect of the trans-rule. Consider the knowledge base $K = \{h \sqsubseteq \exists F.\top, F \sqsubseteq A, \forall A.h(j), h(j), \geq F.\top(j), A \circ A \sqsubseteq A\}$, which stands for the following.

$$\text{Human} \sqsubseteq \exists\text{hasFather}.\top$$
$$\text{hasFather} \sqsubseteq \text{hasAncestor}$$
$$\forall\text{hasAncestor}.\text{Human(john)}$$
$$\text{Human(john)}$$
$$\geq 2\text{hasFather}.\top(\text{john})$$
$$\text{hasAncestor} \circ \text{hasAncestor} \sqsubseteq \text{hasAncestor}$$

Since the knowledge base states that john has at least two fathers, we attempt to show unsatisfiability of K, which will not be possible.[11] We first get $\text{NNF}(K) = \{\neg h \sqcup \exists F.\top, F \sqsubseteq A, \forall A.h(j), h(j), \geq F.\top(j), A \circ A \sqsubseteq A\}$. From the initial tableau, we apply the $\geq$-rule to $\geq 2F.\top$, which results in the following tableau.

$$j \qquad \mathcal{L}(j) = \{h, \geq 2F.\top, \forall A.h\}$$

$$\mathcal{L}(y) = \{\top\} \quad y \quad x \qquad \mathcal{L}(x) = \{\top\}$$

We now perform the following steps.

1. Apply the TBox-rule and set $\mathcal{L}(j) = \{\neg h \sqcup \exists F.\top\}$.

2. Apply the $\sqcup$-rule to the axiom just added, which yields $\mathcal{L}(j) \leftarrow \exists F.\top$ because adding $\neg h$ would result in a contradiction.

3. Apply the $\forall$-rule to $\forall A.h \in \mathcal{L}(j)$, which yields $\mathcal{L}(x) \leftarrow h$.

4. Apply the trans-rule to $\forall A.h \in \mathcal{L}(j)$, setting $\mathcal{L}(x) \leftarrow \forall A.h$.

5. Apply the TBox-rule and set $\mathcal{L}(x) \leftarrow \neg h \sqcup \exists F.\top$.

6. Apply the $\sqcup$-rule to the axiom just added, which yields $\mathcal{L}(x) \leftarrow \exists F.\top$ because adding $\neg h$ would result in a contradiction.

---

[11]There is no information in the knowledge base which forbids anybody having two fathers.

$$j \qquad \mathcal{L}(j) = \{h, \geq 2F.\top, \forall A.h, \neg h \sqcup \exists F.\top, \exists F.\top\}$$

$$\mathcal{L}(y) = \{\top\} \quad y \qquad x \qquad \mathcal{L}(x) = \{\top, h, \forall A.h, \neg h \sqcup \exists F.\top, \exists F.\top\}$$

We can now perform the following steps.

7. Apply the $\exists$-rule to $\exists F.\top \in \mathcal{L}(x)$, creating a new node x_1 with $\mathcal{L}(x_1) = \top$.

8. Apply the $\forall$-rule to $\forall A.h \in \mathcal{L}(x)$, resulting in $\mathcal{L}(x_1) \leftarrow h$.

9. Apply the TBox rule and set $\mathcal{L}(x_1) \leftarrow \neg h \sqcup \exists F.\top$.

10. Apply the $\sqcup$-rule to the axiom just added, which yields $\mathcal{L}(x_1) \leftarrow \exists F.\top$ because adding $\neg h$ would result in a contradiction.

$$j \qquad \mathcal{L}(j) = \{h, \geq 2F.\top, \forall A.h, \neg h \sqcup \exists F.\top, \exists F.\top\}$$

$$\mathcal{L}(y) = \{\top\} \quad y \qquad x \qquad \mathcal{L}(x) = \{\top, h, \forall A.h, \neg h \sqcup \exists F.\top, \exists F.\top\}$$

$$x_1 \qquad \mathcal{L}(x_1) = \{\top, h, \forall A.h, \neg h \sqcup \exists F.\top, \exists F.\top\}$$

Note that $\mathcal{L}(x_1) = \mathcal{L}(x)$, so we can apply steps 7 to 10 to x_1 in place of x, creating a node x_2 in step 7. Likewise, we can do for y exactly what we have done for x, starting at step 1, creating two new nodes y_1 and y_2 in the process. The resulting tableau is as follows.

$$j \qquad \mathcal{L}(j) = \{h, \geq 2F.\top, \forall A.h, \neg h \sqcup \exists F.\top, \exists F.\top\}$$

$$\mathcal{L}(y) = \mathcal{L}(x) \quad y \qquad x \qquad \mathcal{L}(x) = \{\top, h, \forall A.h, \neg h \sqcup \exists F.\top, \exists F.\top\}$$

$$\mathcal{L}(y_1) = \mathcal{L}(x) \quad y_1 \qquad x_1 \qquad \mathcal{L}(x_1) = \mathcal{L}(x)$$

$$\mathcal{L}(y_2) = \mathcal{L}(x) \quad y_2 \qquad x_2 \qquad \mathcal{L}(x_2) = \mathcal{L}(x)$$

At this stage, x_2 is directly blocked by x_1 since the pair (x_1, x_2) repeats the pair (x, x_1). Likewise, y_2 is directly blocked by y_1 since the pair (y_1, y_2) repeats the pair (y, y_1). There is no expansion rule applicable, so the tableau is complete, showing that K is satisfiable.

5.3.4.3.5 Why We Need Pairwise Blocking The next example shows that the more complicated pairwise blocking is indeed needed for $\mathcal{SHIQ}$.

Consider the knowledge base K consisting of the statements $R \circ R \sqsubseteq R$, $F \sqsubseteq R$, and $\neg C \sqcap (\leq 1F) \sqcap \exists F^-.D \sqcap \forall R^-.(\exists F^-.D)(a)$, where D is short for the class expression $C \sqcap (\leq 1F) \sqcap \exists F.\neg C$.

K is unsatisfiable, which is not easy to see by simply inspecting the knowledge base. So let us construct the tableau, which will help us to understand the knowledge base. From the initial tableau, we repeatedly apply the $\sqcap$-rule to break down the class expression in $\mathcal{L}(a)$. Then we apply the $\exists$-rule to $\exists F^-.D$, creating a node y with $\mathcal{L}(y) = \{D\}$. $D \in \mathcal{L}(y)$ can be broken down by applying the $\sqcap$-rule repeatedly. Applying the $\forall$-rule to $\forall R^-.(\exists F^-.D) \in \mathcal{L}(a)$ yields $\mathcal{L}(y) \leftarrow \exists F^-.D$ due to $F \sqsubseteq R$, and the trans-rule applied to $\forall R^-.(\exists F^-.D) \in \mathcal{L}(a)$ yields $\mathcal{L}(y) \leftarrow \forall R^-.(\exists F^-.D)$. The following picture shows the current state; note that we have omitted some elements of $\mathcal{L}(a)$ and $\mathcal{L}(y)$.

$$a \qquad \mathcal{L}(a) \supseteq \{\neg C, \leq 1F, \exists F^-.D, \forall R^-.(\exists F^-.D)\}$$

$$\big\downarrow F^-$$

$$y \qquad \mathcal{L}(y) \supseteq \{D, \exists F^-.D, \forall R^-.(\exists F^-.D), C, \leq 1F, \exists F.\neg C\}$$

Similar arguments applied to y instead of a leave us with a new node z and the following situation.

$$a \qquad \mathcal{L}(a) \supseteq \{\neg C, \leq 1F, \exists F^-.D, \forall R^-.(\exists F^-.D)\}$$

$$\big\downarrow F^-$$

$$y \qquad \mathcal{L}(y) \supseteq \{D, \exists F^-.D, \forall R^-.(\exists F^-.D), C, \leq 1F, \exists F.\neg C\}$$

$$\big\downarrow F^-$$

$$z \qquad \mathcal{L}(z) = \mathcal{L}(y)$$

Since the $\mathcal{SHIQ}$ tableau requires pairwise blocking, the node z is not blocked in this situation. If it were blocked, then the tableau would be complete, and K would be satisfiable. Since z is not blocked, however, we can expand $\exists F.\neg C \in \mathcal{L}(z)$ via the $\exists$-rule, creating a new node x with $\mathcal{L}(x) = \{\neg C\}$. Application of the $\leq$-rule to $\leq 1F \in \mathcal{L}(z)$ forces us to identify y and x, and yields the following.

$$a \qquad \mathcal{L}(a) \supseteq \{\neg C, \leq 1F, \exists F^-.D, \forall R^-.(\exists F^-.D)\}$$

$$\big\downarrow F^-$$

$$x \longmapsto^{\approx} y \qquad \mathcal{L}(y) \supseteq \{D, \exists F^-.D, \forall R^-.(\exists F^-.D), C, \leq 1F, \exists F.\neg C, \neg C\}$$

$$\big\downarrow F^-$$

$$z \qquad \mathcal{L}(z) \supseteq \{D, \exists F^-.D, \forall R^-.(\exists F^-.D), C, \leq 1F, \exists F.\neg C\}$$

Since $\{C, \neg C\} \subseteq \mathcal{L}(y)$, the tableau contains a contradiction and the algorithm terminates.

description logic	combined complexity	data complexity
$\mathcal{ALC}$	ExpTime-complete	NP-complete
$\mathcal{SHIQ}$	ExpTime-complete	NP-complete
$\mathcal{SHOIN}$(D)	NExpTime-complete	NP-hard
$\mathcal{SROIQ}$	N2ExpTime-complete	NP-hard
$\mathcal{EL}^{++}$	P-complete	P-complete
DLP	P-complete	P-complete
DL-Lite	In P	In LOGSPACE

FIGURE 5.18: Worst-case complexity classes of some description logics

5.3.5 Computational Complexities

Considerations of computational complexities of reasoning with various description logics have been a driving force in their development.[12] The rationale behind this is that understanding the computational complexity of a knowledge representation language aids avoiding language constructs which are too expensive to deal with in practice. This is an arguable position, and objections against the emphasis on computational complexity by description logic developers has been criticized from application perspectives. Nevertheless, it appears that the approach has been successful in the sense that it has indeed helped to produce paradigms with a favorable trade-off between expressivity and scalability. Complexities of description logics, more precisely of the underlying decision problems, are usually measured in terms of the size of the knowledge base. This is sometimes called the *combined complexity* of a description logic. If complexity is measured in terms of the size of the ABox only, then it is called the *data complexity* of the description logic. These notions are in analogy to database theory.

Figure 5.18 lists the complexity classes for the most important description logics mentioned in this chapter. It should be noted that despite the emphasis on complexity issues in developing description logics, their complexities are very high, usually exponential or beyond. This means that reasoning even with relatively small knowledge bases could prove to be highly intractable in the worst case. However, this is not a fault of the design of description logics: Dealing with complex logical knowledge is inherently difficult.

At the same time, it turns out that average-case complexity, at least for real existing knowledge bases, is not so bad, and state of the art reasoning systems, as discussed in Section 8.5, can deal with knowledge bases of considerable size. Such performance relies mainly on optimization techniques and intelligent

---

[12]Introducing complexity theory is beyond the scope of this book. See [Pap94] for a comprehensive overview.

heuristics which can be added to tableau reasoners in order to improve their performance on real data.

5.4   Summary

In this chapter we have presented the logical underpinnings of OWL. We have introduced description logics and explained their formal semantics. In particular, we have given two alternative but equivalent ways of describing the formal semantics of $\mathcal{SROIQ}$, and therefore of OWL DL and of OWL 2 DL, namely the direct extensional model-theoretic semantics, and the predicate logic semantics which is obtained by a translation to first-order predicate logic with equality.

We then moved on to discuss the major paradigm for automated reasoning in OWL, namely tableaux algorithms. We have formally specified the algorithms for $\mathcal{ALC}$ and $\mathcal{SHIQ}$. We have also given many examples explaining the algorithms, and briefly discussed issues of computational complexity for description logics.

5.5   Exercises

Exercise 5.1 Translate the ontology which you created as a solution for Exercise 4.1 into DL syntax.

Exercise 5.2 Translate the ontology which you created as a solution for Exercise 4.1 into predicate logic syntax.

Exercise 5.3 Express the following sentences in $\mathcal{SROIQ}$, using the individual names bonnie and clyde, the class names Honest and Crime, and the role names reports, commits, suspects, and knows.

1. Everybody who is honest and commits a crime reports himself.

2. Bonnie does not report Clyde.

3. Clyde has committed at least 10 crimes.

4. Bonnie and Clyde have committed at least one crime together.

5. Everybody who knows a suspect is also a suspect.

Exercise 5.4 Translate the knowledge base

$$\text{Human} \sqsubseteq \exists\text{hasMother}.\text{Human}$$
$$\exists\text{hasMother}.(\exists\text{hasMother}.\text{Human}) \sqsubseteq \text{Grandchild}$$
$$\text{Human}(\text{anupriyaAnkolekar})$$

into RDFS syntax.

Exercise 5.5 Validate the logical inferences drawn in Fig. 4.11 by arguing with extensional semantics.

Exercise 5.6 Consider the two RDFS triples
$$\texttt{r rdfs:domain B . and A rdfs:subClassOf B .}$$
Understood as part of an OWL knowledge base, they can be expressed as $B \sqsubseteq \forall r.\top$ and $A \sqsubseteq B$.

Give a triple which is RDFS-entailed by the two given triples, but which cannot be derived from the OWL DL semantics.

Furthermore, give an OWL DL statement which is a logical consequence of the two OWL statements but cannot be derived using the RDFS semantics.

Exercise 5.7 Show using the $\mathcal{ALC}$ tableaux algorithm that the knowledge base

$$\text{Student} \sqsubseteq \exists\text{attends}.\text{Lecture}$$
$$\text{Lecture} \sqsubseteq \exists\text{attendedBy}.(\text{Student} \sqcap \text{Eager})$$
$$\text{Student}(\text{aStudent})$$
$$\neg\text{Eager}(\text{aStudent})$$

is satisfiable.

Exercise 5.8 Show using the $\mathcal{ALC}$ tableaux algorithm that $(\exists r.E)(a)$ is a logical consequence of the knowledge base $K = \{C(a), C \sqsubseteq \exists r.D, D \sqsubseteq E \sqcup F, F \sqsubseteq E\}$.

Exercise 5.9 Show using the $\mathcal{ALC}$ tableaux algorithm that the knowledge base $K = \{\neg H \sqcup \exists p.H, B(t), \neg H(t)\}$ is satisfiable.

Exercise 5.10 Validate the logical inferences drawn in Fig. 4.11 using the $\mathcal{ALC}$ tableaux algorithm.

Exercise 5.11 Show using the $\mathcal{ALC}$ tableaux algorithm that the following knowledge base is unsatisfiable.

$$\text{Bird} \sqsubseteq \text{Flies}$$
$$\text{Penguin} \sqsubseteq \text{Bird}$$
$$\text{Penguin} \sqcap \text{Flies} \sqsubseteq \bot$$
$$\text{Penguin}(\text{tweety})$$

Exercise 5.12 Show using the $\mathcal{SHIQ}$ tableaux algorithm that the statement $\forall$hasChild.Male(john) is a logical consequence of the following knowledge base.

$$\text{hasChild}(\text{john}, \text{peter})$$
$$\text{hasChild}(\text{john}, \text{alex})$$
$$\text{Male}(\text{peter})$$
$$\text{Male}(\text{alex})$$
$$\leq 2\text{hasChild}.\text{Male}(\text{john})$$
$$\text{peter} \neq \text{alex}$$

Exercise 5.13 Show using the $\mathcal{SHIQ}$ tableaux algorithm that the statement ≥ 2hasChild.$\top$(john) is a logical consequence of the following knowledge base.

$$\geq 2\text{hasSon}.\top(\text{john})$$
$$\text{hasSon} \sqsubseteq \text{hasChild}$$

5.6 Further Reading

[HHPS04] is the normative document for the semantics of OWL 1, while [MPSCG09] is the current version describing the semantics of the forthcoming OWL 2 DL.

The Description Logic Handbook [BCM+07] is a comprehensive reference for description logics.

[HPSvH03] gives an overview of OWL 1 in relation to RDF and $\mathcal{SHIQ}$.

The $\mathcal{SHIQ}$ tableaux algorithms have been introduced in [HST00, HS99]. Our presentation differs slightly for didactic purposes, but there is no substantial difference.

A tableaux algorithm for $\mathcal{SHOIQ}$ can be found in [HS07]. Nominals basically add another element of nondeterminism which is very difficult to deal with efficiently in automated reasoning systems.

$\mathcal{SROIQ}$ as an extension of OWL DL was proposed in [HKS06]. The extensions are uncritical in terms of realization in tableaux algorithms; in this sense, $\mathcal{SROIQ}$ is only a minor extension of $\mathcal{SHOIQ}$.

$\mathcal{EL}^{++}$ was introduced in [BBL05] and has recently sparked a considerable interest in studying polynomial description logics.

DL-Lite is covered in [CGL+07].

For DLP, see [GHVD03].

Complexities for many description logics, including appropriate literature references, can be retrieved from http://www.cs.man.ac.uk/~ezolin/dl/.

Part III

Rules and Queries

Chapter 6

Ontologies and Rules

This chapter introduces "rules" as an alternative way of modeling knowledge which complements the means of specifying knowledge we have already learned about. In the broadest sense, a rule could be any statement which says that a certain *conclusion* must be valid whenever a certain *premise* is satisfied, i.e. any statement that could be read as a sentence of the form "if ... then ..."[1] We will soon confine ourselves to concrete types of rules that will be defined more accurately. Yet it is worth noting that the term "rule" as such refers rather to a knowledge modeling paradigm than to a particular formalism or language. And it is this paradigm that makes rules attractive in many applications, since users sometimes find it more natural to formulate knowledge in terms of rules than in terms of other kinds of ontological axioms.

But the difference between rules and ontologies is not merely pedagogical. In the cases we consider, rules typically can help to express knowledge that cannot be formulated in RDFS or OWL. At the same time, there are also various features of OWL that rule languages do not provide, so a natural question to ask is how the strengths of OWL and of rules can be combined. It turns out that this is indeed possible, but that the added power often also comes at the price of higher complexity and more difficult implementation. The rule languages discussed in this chapter have therefore been chosen to be the ones for which a combination with RDF and OWL is not just possible in principle, but for which this combination is also practically supported by software tools and, in some cases, by upcoming standards.

We begin this chapter with a general discussion of the concept "rule" to clarify our use of this rather vague term. Thereafter, Section 6.2 introduces datalog as a basic rule language. The semantics given there is based on first-order logic, which further allows us to combine datalog with OWL DL in Section 6.3. We explain the semantics of this combination and discuss two possible restrictions that can each be used to ensure decidability of reasoning with OWL and rules. The latter is desirable as a basic prerequisite for arriving at sound and complete implementations. Section 6.4 presents the Rule Interchange Format (RIF) as an upcoming standard for encoding and exchanging

---

[1]Instead of the terms "premise" and "conclusion" it is sometimes also common to speak of "precondition" and "postcondition" or "precedent" and "antecedent" of a rule. We use these terms interchangeably.

rules in practical applications. RIF also supports the combined use of rules, OWL, and RDF. While the case of OWL is closely related to our discussion in Section 6.3, the specification of a combined semantics for RDF and rules requires us to encode RDF entailments in first-order logic. This last aspect, which is interesting in its own right, is found in Section 6.4.6 and can be read separately. We close the chapter with a short summary, exercises, and notes on further reading.

6.1 What Is a Rule?

It has been mentioned that rules of any type should consist at least of a premise and a conclusion, with the intuitive meaning that in any situation where the premise applies the conclusion must also hold. Such a general description obviously comprises some, if not all, OWL axioms. Consider, e.g., the "rule" that, if a person is the author of a book then she is a (member of the class) book author. This can surely be expressed in OWL DL: using the more concise description logic syntax introduced in Chapter 5 we could write

$$\text{Person} \sqcap \exists \text{authorOf}.\text{Book} \sqsubseteq \text{Bookauthor}.$$

It has also been explained in Section 5.2.2 that OWL DL can be considered as a sublanguage of first-order predicate logic. Using this knowledge, we can equivalently write the above statement as a predicate logic formula:

$$\forall x.\big(\text{Person}(x) \wedge \exists y.\big(\text{authorOf}(x,y) \wedge \text{Book}(y)\big) \rightarrow \text{Bookauthor}(x)\big).$$

Using standard semantic equivalences of predicate logic, we can make the existential quantifier disappear (exercise: how exactly?):

$$\forall x \forall y.\big(\text{Person}(x) \wedge \text{authorOf}(x,y) \wedge \text{Book}(y) \rightarrow \text{Bookauthor}(x)\big).$$

This formula is a logical implication with universally quantified variables, hence it comes close to our vague idea of a "rule." The universal quantifiers express the fact that the implication is applicable to all individuals that satisfy the premise. So could we indeed consider "predicate logic rules" to mean simply predicate logic formulae that are implications? It turns out that this alone would not say much, simply because every predicate logic formula can be rewritten to fit that syntactic form (exercise: how?). Yet, using the term "rule" as a synonym for "first-order implication" has become common practice in connection with the Semantic Web, as witnessed by formalisms such as the *Semantic Web Rule Language*, *Description Logic Rules*, *DL-safe Rules*, and the *Rule Interchange Format* (RIF-Core), all of which essentially comprise certain kinds of first-order implications. These approaches further restrict us to particular kinds of implications that no longer encompass all possible formulae of predicate logic, and which are thus interesting in their own right. Indeed, it turns out that many such rule languages have expressive and computational properties that distinguish them from first-order logic, thus making them adequate for different application scenarios.

Before going into the details of the Semantic Web rule languages mentioned above, it should be noted that there are a number of rather different interpretations of the term "rule" outside of first-order logic. Among the most popular rule formalisms in Computer Science is certainly logic programming, which is closely associated with the Prolog programming language and its various derivatives and extensions. At first glance, Prolog rules appear to be very similar to first-order logic implications that merely use a slightly different syntax, putting the precondition to the right of the rule. The example above would read as follows in Prolog:

$$\texttt{Bookauthor}(X) \text{ :- } \texttt{Person}(X), \texttt{authorOf}(X, Y), \texttt{Book}(Y).$$

Basic Prolog indeed has the same expressivity as first-order logic, and can equivalently be interpreted under a predicate logic semantics. But there are many extensions of Prolog that introduce features beyond first-order logic, such as operational plug-ins (e.g., for arithmetic functions) and so-called *non-monotonic* inferences which derive new results from the fact that something else can *not* be derived. Logic programming in this form, as the name suggests, has been conceived as a way of specifying and controlling powerful computations, and not as an ontology language for direct interchange on the Web. Two ontologies from different sources can usually be merged simply by taking the union of their axioms (meaningful or not), whereas two independent Prolog programs can hardly be combined without carefully checking manually that the result is still a program that can be successfully executed by the employed logic programming engine. The use of logic programming in combination with ontologies can still be quite useful, but the research that has been conducted in this field is beyond the scope of this book.

Yet another kind of rules that is very relevant in practice is known as *production rules*, such as *Event Condition Action Rules* or *business rules*. Rule languages of this type apply a more *operational* interpretation of rules, i.e.

they view rules as program statements that can be *executed* actively. For ontology languages like OWL, the semantics of an ontology is not affected by the order in which ontological axioms are considered. In contrast, for rules with an operational semantics it can be crucial to know which rule is executed first, and part of the semantics of production rules is concerned with the question of precedence between rules. Many different kinds of production rule engines are used in practice and many rule engines implement their own customized semantic interpretations of rules that do not follow a shared published semantics. As such, production rules again are hard to interchange between different systems, and the ongoing work on the W3C Rule Interchange Format is among the first efforts to allow for the kind of interoperability that a common semantic standard can offer. Yet it is currently unclear how production rule engines should best be combined with ontology-based systems, and we shall not pursue this endeavor in the remainder of this book.

Besides the interpretation of "rule" in these diverse approaches, the term can also have an even more general meaning in the context of (onto)logical knowledge representation. In particular, a "deduction rule" or "rule of inference" is sometimes understood as an instruction of how to derive additional conclusions from a knowledge base. In this sense, the rule is not part of the encoded knowledge, but rather a component of algorithms that are used to process this knowledge. A case in point is the deduction rules for RDF(S) that were discussed in Section 3.3. As we will see in Section 6.4.6, the essence of these rules can actually be captured by first-order logic implications, so that the distinction between deduction rules and rule-like logical formulae is blurred here. More generally, the deduction rules of virtually any calculus could be expressed as logical rules of some suitable logic. But this logic is typically required to be very expressive, making it difficult or impossible to implement general-purpose reasoners that can process the logical theory that was derived from a set of deduction rules. Since we are interested in semantic technologies that represent knowledge in a machine-processable way, the topic of this chapter is rules in the earlier sense, i.e. axioms for representing ontological knowledge in the form of a rule.

Moreover, all rule languages that we consider here can be viewed as fragments of first-order logic. This allows for a close semantic integration with both OWL and RDF, which in turn has helped to advance standardization, implementation, and practical usage of these types of rules. Additionally, simple first-order rule languages can also be extended with non-monotonic features inspired by logic programming. Discussing the various types of extensions that have been considered in this line of research is beyond this book, but the material covered herein is still useful as a basis for further reading (see Section 6.7). The W3C Rule Interchange Format, introduced in Section 6.4, is expected to support non-monotonic features at some future stage, possibly leading to a greater impact of such rules in the field of semantic technologies.

6.2 Datalog as a First-Order Rule Language

We now turn to concrete types of rules that, in essence, are implications of first-order logic. The advantage of this interpretation of rules is that the semantics of first-order predicate logic can be naturally combined with the semantics of OWL DL, since the latter can also be defined as a sublanguage of first-order logic. The rule language that we consider here is known as datalog, and was originally developed in the field of deductive databases.

6.2.1 Introduction to Datalog

In a nutshell, a datalog rule is a logical implication that may only contain conjunctions, constant symbols, and universally quantified variables, but no disjunctions, negations, existential quantifiers, or function symbols. We always consider datalog as a sublanguage of first-order logic to which the classical semantics applies. Both syntax and semantics will be explained in more precise terms below in a fully self-contained way. Some background knowledge in first-order logic can still be handy for understanding datalog (see Appendix C).

Before going into further details, it is worth mentioning that datalog was originally developed for querying databases. Rules and queries indeed have much in common: our example rule from Section 6.1, e.g., is in fact a datalog rule which can also be interpreted as a means of *querying* a given database for all book authors:

$$\forall x \forall y. (\texttt{Person}(x) \land \texttt{authorOf}(x, y) \land \texttt{Book}(y) \rightarrow \texttt{Bookauthor}(x)).$$

In this case, one would assume information about `Person`, `authorOf`, and `Book` to be stored in a database, while `Bookauthor` is derived from this data as a "query result." It is thus always possible to regard single rules as descriptions of relevant "views" on the data. Much work on datalog is related to the use of rules in this sense, and we will return to the topic of querying later in Chapter 7.

When considering datalog as a rule language, however, we also want to allow rules to be applied *recursively*. This means that the result of a rule can again be used by other rules to derive further conclusions, continuing until no further conclusions can be obtained from any rule. This use of recursion has been an important topic in the area of *deductive databases* as well, and semantic technologies can build on the results that were obtained in this field.

Further references on deductive databases are given at the end of this chapter.[2]

Let us now consider the syntax of datalog rules and the intuitive semantics of such rules. Besides logical operators, a datalog rule can feature three kinds of symbols:

- *Constant symbols* are used as names to refer to certain elements of the domain of interest.

- *Variables* are used as place holders for (arbitrary) domain elements to which rules might apply.

- *Predicate symbols*, or simply *predicates*, are used to denote relations between domain elements.

Constant symbols play essentially the role of individual names in OWL or description logics, as explained in Chapters 4 and 5. Predicate symbols may take an arbitrary number of arguments: predicates with one argument are similar to OWL classes, just like `Person` in our earlier example; predicates with two arguments resemble OWL property names, as in the case of `authorOf` above. But datalog also allows for predicates that have three or more, or even zero arguments. It is usually assumed that the number of arguments for each predicate symbol is fixed, and this number is then called the *arity* of this predicate symbol.

Summing up, the syntax of datalog depends on three sets of symbols: a set C of constant symbols, a set V of variable symbols, and a set P of predicate symbols each of which has a fixed natural number as its arity. Together, the sets (C, V, P) are called a *signature* of datalog, and every set of datalog rules is based on some such signature. The sets C and P are usually assumed to be finite, containing only the symbols required for an application. In contrast, one often assumes that there is an arbitrary supply of variables, i.e. that the set V is (countably) infinite. It is common to denote variables by letters x, y, and z, possibly with subscripts.

Now given such a signature we can build datalog rules as follows:

- A datalog *term* is a constant symbol or a variable.

- A datalog *atom* is a formula of the form $p(t_1, \ldots, t_n)$ given that $p \in P$ is a predicate of arity n, and $t_1, \ldots, t_n$ are terms.

---

[2]A notable difference to our treatment is that many database-related applications define datalog based on a logic programming semantics or with certain "closure axioms." This is useful for achieving a *closed-world* semantics that is desirable for a database: if a fact is not in the database, it should be concluded that it is false. Such *non-monotonic* behavior, however, is only obtained when extending datalog with further features, especially with non-monotonic negation. We do not consider any form of non-monotonicity in this chapter. For plain datalog, our definitions lead to exactly the same deductions as the closed-world approach. See [AHV94, Chapter 12] for a discussion and comparison of both approaches.

(1)	$\text{Vegetarian}(x) \wedge \text{FishProduct}(y) \rightarrow \text{dislikes}(x, y)$
(2)	$\text{orderedDish}(x, y) \wedge \text{dislikes}(x, y) \rightarrow \text{Unhappy}(x)$
(3)	$\text{orderedDish}(x, y) \rightarrow \text{Dish}(y)$
(4)	$\text{dislikes}(x, z) \wedge \text{Dish}(y) \wedge \text{contains}(y, z) \rightarrow \text{dislikes}(x, y)$
(5)	$\rightarrow \text{Vegetarian}(\text{markus})$
(6)	$\text{Happy}(x) \wedge \text{Unhappy}(x) \rightarrow$

FIGURE 6.1: Example datalog program

- A *datalog rule* is a formula of the form

$$\forall x_1 \ldots \forall x_m . \big(B_1 \wedge \ldots \wedge B_k \rightarrow H\big),$$

where $B_1, \ldots, B_k$ and H are datalog atoms, and $x_1, \ldots, x_m$ are exactly the variables that occur within these atoms.

Since all variables in datalog are always universally quantified at the level of rules, it is common to omit the $\forall$ quantifiers from datalog rules. We adopt this simplification for the rest of this chapter. The premise of a datalog rule is called the *rule body* while the conclusion is called the *rule head*. A set of datalog rules is sometimes called a *datalog program* which hints at the relationship to logic programming.

Figure 6.1 gives an example of a datalog program based on a datalog signature with set of constant symbols $C = \{\text{markus}\}$ and set of predicate symbols $P = \{\text{Dish}, \text{Vegetarian}, \text{FishProduct}, \text{Happy}, \text{Unhappy}, \text{dislikes}, \text{orderedDish}\}$. Adopting the convention introduced for OWL, we use capital letters for predicates of arity 1 ("class names"); the other predicates are all of arity 2. It is not hard to read the intended meaning from such a set of datalog rules:

(1) "Every vegetarian dislikes all fish products."[3]

(2) "Anyone who ordered a dish that he or she dislikes is unhappy." This rule shows that not all variables occurring in a rule body need to appear in the rule head.

(3) "Everything that can be ordered as a dish actually is a dish."

(4) "If someone dislikes something that is contained in a certain dish, then this person will also dislike the whole dish."

---

[3]Some "pesco-vegetarians" might disagree. We follow the historic definition of the *Vegetarian Society* here.

(5) "Markus is a vegetarian." Empty rule bodies impose no conditions, i.e. they are always true. This is the reason why a rule that consists only of a rule head is also called a *fact*. The implication arrow is sometimes omitted in this case.

(6) "Nobody can be happy and unhappy at the same time." Empty rule heads cannot be concluded, i.e. they are always false. Hence a rule without a head describes a condition that must never occur, and such rules therefore are sometimes called *integrity constraints*.

Note that some of the rules might be more widely applicable than desired. For example, rule (2) does not require that it was a person who ordered the dish. In practice, one might add further preconditions to ensure that such implicit assumptions do really hold. For the purposes of this book, however, we prefer a more simple formalization over a more correct one.

This example also illustrates that rules can often be read and understood rather easily, which is one reason why they might sometimes be preferred over other types of ontological axioms. Yet we must be wary when dealing with rules: while the intention of a single rule can seem obvious, there are still many possibly unexpected conclusions that can be drawn from a set of rules. In particular, we must be aware that rules in first-order logic "work in both directions": if a rule body is true then the rule head must of course also be true, but conversely, if a rule head is false, then the rule body must also be false. In logic, this inverse reading of a rule is known as the *contrapositive* of the implication; it is well-known that both forms – $p \to q$ and $\neg q \to \neg p$ – are logically equivalent. Assume, e.g., that the following facts are added to the program of Fig. 6.1 (we assume that the new constant symbols have been added to the signature):

```
Happy(markus)
orderedDish(markus,crêpeSuzette)
FishProduct(worcestershireSauce)
```

With these additional assertions, we might (rightly) conclude that Crêpe Suzette does *not* contain Worcestershire Sauce: Since Markus is happy, he cannot be unhappy (6), and hence he did not order any dish he dislikes (2). Thus, since he ordered Crêpe Suzette, Markus does not dislike this dish. On the other hand, as a vegetarian (5) Markus dislikes Worcestershire Sauce on account of it being a fish product (1). Thus, since Crêpe Suzette is a dish (3), and since Markus does not dislike it, rule (4) ensures us that the crêpe does not contain any Worcestershire Sauce.

Conclusions like the one we have just drawn are often not obvious, and as soon as we deal with larger datalog programs, we certainly would like to leave it to the computer to draw such conclusions for us. To make this possible, we first need to specify the problem more precisely: which conclusions exactly do we expect the computer to draw? This is the right time to introduce the formal semantics of datalog.

6.2.2 Semantics of Datalog

As mentioned in the previous section, we consider datalog as a sublanguage of first-order logic, and its formal semantics is already determined by this fact. In this section, we give an alternative self-contained presentation of the datalog semantics, which can be slightly simplified due to the fact that function symbols and various first-order logical operators do not need to be addressed. This section can safely be skipped by readers who are familiar with first-order logic or who are content with the intuitive understanding established so far.

As in Chapters 3 and 5, the semantics of datalog is *model-theoretic*, i.e. it is based on defining which "models" a datalog program has. A correct conclusion from a datalog program then is any formula that is satisfied by all models of this program. As usual, a model is a special kind of *interpretation*, one that makes a given datalog program true. Hence we first explain what a datalog interpretation is and what it means for it to satisfy some datalog rule.

A *datalog interpretation* $\mathcal{I}$ consists of an interpretation domain $\Delta^{\mathcal{I}}$ and an interpretation function $\cdot^{\mathcal{I}}$. The domain is an arbitrary set that defines the (abstract) world within which all symbols are interpreted, while the interpretation function establishes the mapping from symbols into this domain:

- If a is a constant, then $a^{\mathcal{I}} \in \Delta^{\mathcal{I}}$, i.e. a is interpreted as an element of the domain.

- If p is a predicate symbol of arity n, then $p^{\mathcal{I}} \subseteq (\Delta^{\mathcal{I}})^n$, i.e. p is interpreted as an n-ary relation over the domain (the *predicate extension*).

In contrast to RDFS and OWL, datalog also contains variables and we must account for the fact that these can take arbitrary values from the domain, even for a fixed interpretation. Therefore they obtain their values from a *variable assignment*. A variable assignment $\mathcal{Z}$ for a datalog interpretation $\mathcal{I}$ is simply a function from the set V of variables to the interpretation domain $\Delta^{\mathcal{I}}$. For an arbitrary term t we write $t^{\mathcal{I},\mathcal{Z}}$ to mean $t^{\mathcal{I}}$ if t is a constant, and $\mathcal{Z}(t)$ if t is a variable. With these additional tools we can define a truth value – *true* or *false* – of a formula by extending $\cdot^{\mathcal{I}}$:

- For a datalog atom $p(t_1, \ldots, t_n)$, we set $p(t_1, \ldots, t_n)^{\mathcal{I},\mathcal{Z}} = true$ if we find that $(t_1^{\mathcal{I},\mathcal{Z}}, \ldots, t_n^{\mathcal{I},\mathcal{Z}}) \in p^{\mathcal{I}}$. We set $p(t_1, \ldots, t_n)^{\mathcal{I},\mathcal{Z}} = false$ otherwise.

- For a conjunction $B_1 \wedge \ldots \wedge B_n$ of datalog atoms $B_1, \ldots, B_n$, we set $(B_1 \wedge \ldots \wedge B_n)^{\mathcal{I},\mathcal{Z}} = true$ if $B_i^{\mathcal{I},\mathcal{Z}} = true$ for all $i = 1, \ldots, n$. We set $(B_1 \wedge \ldots \wedge B_n)^{\mathcal{I},\mathcal{Z}} = false$ otherwise.

$$\begin{aligned}
\mathtt{Vegetarian}^{\mathcal{I}} &= \mathtt{Happy}^{\mathcal{I}} = \{\mathtt{markus}\} \\
\mathtt{FishProduct}^{\mathcal{I}} &= \{\mathtt{worcestershireSauce}\} \\
\mathtt{dislikes}^{\mathcal{I}} &= \{(\mathtt{markus, worcestershireSauce})\} \\
\mathtt{orderedDish}^{\mathcal{I}} &= \{(\mathtt{markus, crêpeSuzette})\} \\
\mathtt{Dish}^{\mathcal{I}} &= \{\mathtt{crêpeSuzette}\} \\
\mathtt{Unhappy}^{\mathcal{I}} &= \mathtt{contains}^{\mathcal{I}} = \emptyset
\end{aligned}$$

FIGURE 6.2:   Example datalog interpretation of predicate symbols

- For a datalog rule $B \to H$, we set $(B \to H)^{\mathcal{I}} = \textit{true}$ if, for all possible variable assignments $\mathcal{Z}$ for $\mathcal{I}$, we find that either $B^{\mathcal{I},\mathcal{Z}} = \textit{false}$ or $H^{\mathcal{I},\mathcal{Z}} = \textit{true}$. We set $(B \to H)^{\mathcal{I}} = \textit{false}$ otherwise. Note that B can be an arbitrary conjunction of datalog atoms in this case.

- For a datalog fact $\to H$, we set $(\to H)^{\mathcal{I}} = \textit{true}$ if, for all possible variable assignments $\mathcal{Z}$ for $\mathcal{I}$, we find that $H^{\mathcal{I},\mathcal{Z}} = \textit{true}$. Otherwise, we set $(\to H)^{\mathcal{I}} = \textit{false}$.

- For a datalog integrity constraint $B \to$, we set $(B \to)^{\mathcal{I}} = \textit{true}$ if, for all possible variable assignments $\mathcal{Z}$ for $\mathcal{I}$, we find that $B^{\mathcal{I},\mathcal{Z}} = \textit{false}$. Otherwise, we set $(B \to)^{\mathcal{I}} = \textit{false}$. Note that B can be an arbitrary conjunction of datalog atoms in this case.

Note that the truth of a rule does not depend on a particular variable assignment, since the (implicit) universal quantifiers bind all variables in all rules. If an interpretation $\mathcal{I}$ maps a datalog rule to *true*, then we say that $\mathcal{I}$ *satisfies* this rule. If $\mathcal{I}$ satisfies all rules of a datalog program, then we say that $\mathcal{I}$ satisfies the program, or that $\mathcal{I}$ is a *model* of that program. A datalog rule is a *conclusion* of a datalog program if the rule is satisfied by all models of the program. Observe that the last sentence includes all types of rules, so in particular it defines in which cases a certain fact is entailed by a datalog program. The entailment of facts is by far the most common reasoning problem for datalog, and many implementations are specifically tailored toward the derivation of facts.

The above finishes the formal definition of the datalog semantics. To illustrate the definitions, we describe a particularly interesting model for the example in Section 6.2.1 (Fig. 6.1 and the related facts on page 219). As a domain of interpretation, we pick the set of constant symbols of the given signature, i.e. $\Delta^{\mathcal{I}} = \{\mathtt{markus, crêpeSuzette, worcestershireSauce}\}$. Next, we need to define the mapping $\cdot^{\mathcal{I}}$. On constant symbols, this is very easy to do: we just map every constant symbol to itself, e.g., $\mathtt{markus}^{\mathcal{I}} = \mathtt{markus}$. The interpretations of the predicate symbols are given in Fig. 6.2. It is straightforward to check that this interpretation is indeed a model for the datalog program we consider. For plain datalog programs that are consistent, it is always possible to construct models in this particularly simple fashion by just taking the constant symbols as interpretation domains, and such models are known as *Herbrand models*.[4] Moreover, it is always possible to find a model that satisfies as few datalog atoms as possible, such that no other model satisfies fewer datalog facts. The existence of such *least Herbrand models* is of great significance and can be exploited for practical implementations – but for our purposes it is enough to note that this feature provides us with a conveniently small example model. Unfortunately, this nice property is lost as soon as we introduce OWL or RDF into the picture.

6.3 Combining Rules with OWL DL

Datalog gives us a basic mechanism for specifying knowledge using rules. Our introduction to datalog so far has intentionally left out technical issues such as a concrete machine-readable syntax for storing and exchanging datalog rules but these details could clearly be added to obtain a full-fledged modeling language that could be used on the Semantic Web. Indeed, the Rule Interchange Format introduced in Section 6.4 achieves this to a certain extent.

The paradigm of rule-based modeling is quite different from the ontological modeling that was introduced with OWL, and it is not obvious how to combine both approaches. Would such a combination of OWL and rules be meaningful at all? Would this combination actually increase the expressive power of either formalism? How difficult would it be to build tools that can process a combination of OWL and rules? We address these questions in this section.

6.3.1 Combined Semantics: Datalog and Description Logics

The first of our initial questions is not hard to answer: a combination of datalog and OWL DL is indeed meaningful. Both languages can be seen as sublanguages of standard first-order logic, so the combination of a datalog program with an OWL DL ontology can always be viewed as a collection of first-order logic formulae with the usual first-order semantics. So, at least conceptually, there are no major problems.[5]

---

[4]After the French mathematician *Jacques Herbrand*, pronounced /ɛrbrã/ with H silent.

[5]The situation for OWL Full is not as clear. A possible combined semantics is proposed in the OWL compatibility document of the Rule Interchange Format; see Section 6.4 for some discussion.

(7) ∃orderedDish.ThaiCurry(markus)
(8) ThaiCurry ⊑ ∃contains.FishProduct

FIGURE 6.3: Description logic axioms extending the datalog program from Fig. 6.1

It is worthwhile to elaborate the details of this combined semantics. The semantics of datalog has just been detailed in Section 6.2.2, where we defined what an interpretation of datalog is, and what it means to say that an interpretation satisfies a given datalog rule. Interpretations in datalog provide an interpretation domain and an interpretation function that accomplish two tasks: it assigns a domain element to every constant symbol, and it assigns an n-ary relation to every predicate symbol. If we compare this to interpretations of OWL (i.e. of description logics, see Section 5.2), we find obvious similarities. Description logic interpretations again specify a domain of interpretation and an interpretation function, which can now be considered to consist of three different mappings: the mapping I_I that assigns a domain element to every individual name, the mapping I_C that assigns a set of individuals to every class name, and the mapping I_R that assigns a binary relation to every role.

It is now easy to see that, as expected, interpretations of datalog and description logics are closely related. In fact, the main differences are simply the names we have used for parts of the syntax. What is called *constant symbol* in datalog is called *individual name* in description logics. Likewise, unary and binary predicates of datalog are the same as class names and role names in description logics. Note in particular that the "unary relation" that a datalog interpretation assigns to unary predicates is just a set of domain elements. Therefore, we can view any datalog interpretation also as a description logic interpretation that simply provides some additional interpretations for predicate symbols that do not occur in description logics. When using the combination of a datalog program with a description logic ontology, we therefore use datalog interpretations over a datalog signature that includes not only all symbols of the datalog program, but which also incorporates individual names, class names, and role names from the description logic part as constant symbols, unary predicates, and binary predicates, respectively.

As an example of such a combined knowledge base, consider again the datalog rules from Fig. 6.1 together with the additional description logic axioms given in Fig. 6.3. By (7), Markus has ordered some Thai curry dish, and, according to this example, all Thai curries contain some fish product. Combining these statements with the rules of Fig. 6.1, we would intuitively expect the conclusion that Markus is now unhappy. Using the above semantics, we can support our intuition with a more formal argument.

Using the semantics of $\exists$ from Section 5.2.1, we find that every interpretation $\mathcal{I}$ that satisfies (7) must have some element e in its domain $\Delta^{\mathcal{I}}$ such that $(\mathtt{markus}^{\mathcal{I}}, e) \in \mathtt{orderedDish}^{\mathcal{I}}$ and $e \in \mathtt{ThaiCurry}^{\mathcal{I}}$. But if $\mathcal{I}$ also satisfies rule (3), then we must have $e \in \mathtt{Dish}^{\mathcal{I}}$ as well. This last conclusion can be obtained as follows: Clearly there is a variable assignment $\mathcal{Z}$ with $\mathcal{Z}(x) = \mathtt{markus}^{\mathcal{I}}$ and $\mathcal{Z}(y) = e$. Since $\mathcal{Z}$ and $\mathcal{I}$ satisfy the body of rule (3), they must also satisfy its head. So we obtain $\mathcal{Z}(y) \in \mathtt{Dish}^{\mathcal{I}}$ as claimed. Normally, it is not required to explain conclusions from rules in that much detail, and one usually just says that $e \in \mathtt{Dish}^{\mathcal{I}}$ follows by *applying* rule (3).

We can continue our derivation as follows. If (8) is satisfied, then $e \in (\exists \mathtt{contains}.\mathtt{FishProduct})^{\mathcal{I}}$. Again this means that there must be some element $f \in \Delta^{\mathcal{I}}$ such that $(e, f) \in \mathtt{contains}^{\mathcal{I}}$ and $f \in \mathtt{FishProduct}^{\mathcal{I}}$. Applying rules (5) and (1), we also know that $(\mathtt{markus}^{\mathcal{I}}, f) \in \mathtt{dislikes}^{\mathcal{I}}$. Hence we can apply rule (4) with a variable assignment $\mathcal{Z}$ with $\mathcal{Z}(x) = \mathtt{markus}^{\mathcal{I}}$, $\mathcal{Z}(y) = e$, and $\mathcal{Z}(z) = f$ to conclude that $(\mathtt{markus}^{\mathcal{I}}, e) \in \mathtt{dislikes}^{\mathcal{I}}$. Thus, we have established that Markus dislikes the (unnamed) dish e which he ordered. Therefore rule (2) can be applied to conclude that $\mathtt{markus}^{\mathcal{I}} \in \mathtt{Unhappy}^{\mathcal{I}}$.

The above conclusions were drawn by assuming merely that $\mathcal{I}$ satisfies the rules and axioms (1)–(9), and they are thus valid for an arbitrary model of our combined knowledge base. In other words, every model of the above rules and axioms must also satisfy $\mathtt{Unhappy}(\mathtt{markus})$, which is therefore a logical conclusion of the knowledge base.

6.3.2 Computing Conclusions

The previous section showed how we can use the formal semantics of datalog and description logics to derive conclusions. The argument we gave there, however, was still somewhat informal and required some amount of thought on our part. It would clearly be desirable to automate this process, i.e. to develop software tools that automatically draw conclusions from description logic knowledge bases in combination with datalog. This section addresses the question of how complicated it is to solve this task.

We have learned in Section 5.3.5 that OWL DL, i.e. the description logic $\mathcal{SHOIN}(D)$, is in a complexity class called NExpTime, the class of all decision problems that a computer can solve in exponential time given that it makes the right (non-deterministic) guesses. This is already quite complex but optimizations still allow implementations to work well in many practical cases. For datalog, it turns out that the complexity of typical reasoning tasks (e.g., solving the question whether a particular conclusion can be drawn from a set of datalog rules) is ExpTime, i.e. that the answer can be computed in time exponential with respect to the size of the input datalog program. This is slightly better than the case of OWL DL and corresponds to OWL Lite, i.e. the description logic $\mathcal{SHIF}(D)$. This might come as a surprise given that, intuitively, drawing conclusions from datalog appears not to be very hard. Roughly speaking, the complexity stems from the large number of different ways in which rules can be applied, especially if they have a great number of variables in their body.

Do these results imply that the combined complexity of OWL DL and datalog is also not harder than NExpTime, the larger of the two individual complexities? The answer is a resounding no. Complexities can in general not be combined in such a naive way, and, in fact, typical reasoning tasks for the combination of datalog and $\mathcal{SHOIN}(D)$ turn out to be *undecidable*. Moreover, this is the case even for much simpler description logics such as $\mathcal{ALC}$. This result might be somewhat disappointing since it assures us that it is impossible to ever devise a software tool that can compute *all* conclusions from *all* possible knowledge bases that consist of a description logic part and a datalog part. But this formulation also hints at two ways of escaping this problem. As a first option, one might be content with a tool that draws at least *some* conclusions which are certain, i.e. an inferencing program that is sound but incomplete. Alternatively, one could try to find reasoning methods that are sound and complete, but that cannot be applied to all possible knowledge bases. In the next sections, we explore these options for two cases that restrict the expressivity of datalog rules to recover decidability: *Description Logic Rules* and *DL-safe Rules*.

6.3.3   Description Logic Rules

We have already noted in the introductory Section 6.1 that some description logic axioms can also be presented as (datalog) rules, and, equivalently, certain datalog rules can be cast into description logic axioms with the same meaning. It is clear that there must still be rules and axioms that cannot be rewritten in this way, or at least that it is not possible to do this rewriting automatically. Otherwise, one could use a rewriting algorithm followed by a standard reasoning algorithm for datalog or description logics, respectively, to obtain a decision procedure for the combined reasoning tasks. Such a procedure cannot exist according to the undecidability result mentioned in the previous section.

In this section, we address the question which datalog rules can be directly represented as description logic axioms, thus deserving the name *Description Logic Rules*. We shall see that the highly expressive description logic $\mathcal{SROIQ}$ (the basis for OWL 2 DL) can express significantly more rules than the description logic $\mathcal{SHOIN}$ (the basis for OWL DL). A comprehensive algorithm for transforming rules into description logic axioms is then provided in Fig. 6.5.

Let us first consider some examples to improve our intuition. The following rule appeared within the introductory section:

$$\text{Person}(x) \wedge \text{authorOf}(x, y) \wedge \text{Book}(y) \rightarrow \text{Bookauthor}(x).$$

We noted that it can eqiuvalently be expressed by the description logic axiom $\text{Person} \sqcap \exists\text{authorOf}.\text{Book} \sqsubseteq \text{Bookauthor}$. The important difference between both representations is that the latter does not use any variables. So where did the variables go? We have learned in previous sections that class descriptions resemble unary predicates of first-order logic. It is not necessary to state the argument of these unary predicates since it is always the same variable on both sides of a class inclusion axiom. In the above case, e.g., we could mix datalog and description logic syntax to write:

$$(\text{Person} \sqcap \exists\text{authorOf}.\text{Book})(x) \rightarrow \text{Bookauthor}(x).$$

This explains the whereabouts of variable x. The variable y in turn appears only in two positions in the rule body. Since it is not referred to in any other part of the rule, it suffices to state that there exists some object with the required relationship to x, so the rule atoms $\text{authorOf}(x, y) \wedge \text{Book}(y)$ are transformed into $\exists\text{authorOf}.\text{Book}(x)$. Rewriting atoms as description logic class expressions in this fashion is sometimes called *rolling-up*, since a "branch" of the rule body is rolled-up into a statement about its first variable. This terminology will become more intuitive in light of a graphical representation that we explain below.

We can try to generalize from this example. We have seen that x in the above case is simply an implicit (and necessary) part of the class inclusion axiom. So for any rule that we wish to rewrite as such an axiom, we need to identify some variable x which plays this special role, and find a way to eliminate all other variables from the rule using a rolling-up method as above. This is not always possible, as rule (2) from Fig. 6.1 illustrates:

$$\text{orderedDish}(x, y) \wedge \text{dislikes}(x, y) \rightarrow \text{Unhappy}(x).$$

The conclusion of this rule suggests that the variable y should be eliminated to obtain a class inclusion axiom. But the premise of the rule cannot be rewritten as above. A class expression like $\exists\text{orderedDish}.\top \sqcap \exists\text{dislikes}.\top$ describes elements with relationships orderedDish and dislikes, but not necessarily to the same element y. Using inverse roles, one could also write $\exists\text{orderedDish}.\exists\text{dislikes}^-.\top$ to describe some x who ordered something that is disliked by someone – but not necessarily by x. It turns out that there is no way to directly express this relationship in any of the major description

FIGURE 6.4:   Examples of simple rule dependency graphs

logics considered in this book.[6] We conclude that rolling-up is only possible if a variable is "reachable" by only a single binary predicate.

We now give a more precise characterization of the rules that can be rewritten as description logic axioms. In order to understand in which cases we can use the rolling-up method, the key is to consider the *dependency graph* of the rule premise. This graph is obtained from the premise by simply taking variables as nodes, and binary predicates as edges between variables. Note that (atoms with) constant symbols do not play a role in this definition; it will be discussed further below why this is desirable. Figure 6.4 shows the dependency graphs of the above example rules, with labels indicating the relationship to binary predicates.

With this visualization in mind, we can speak about "paths" within a rule premise. Intuitively, a path between two nodes is simply a set of edges leading from one node to the other, where we do not care about the direction of the edges. More formally, we can describe a path in some rule premise B as follows:

- if $R(x, y)$ is an atom in B, then $\{R(x, y)\}$ is a path between x and y,

- if p is a path between x and y, then p is also a path between y and x,

- if p is a path between x and y, q is a path between y and z, and no atom occurs both in p and in q, then $p \cup q$ is a path between x and z,

where x, y, and z are all variables. The set $\{\texttt{authorOf}(x, y)\}$, e.g., is a path between x and y, and this is the only path in the first example rule given in this section. In the second example rule, we find the obvious paths of length one, but also the path $\{\texttt{orderedDish}(x, y), \texttt{dislikes}(x, y)\}$ which can be viewed as a path from x to x, or as a path from y to y. Looking at Fig. 6.4, we recognize that paths are really just sets of edges that we can use to get from one node to another. Observe that as a result of defining paths as sets, we are not allowed to use any edge more than once in a single path.

Now a datalog rule can be transformed into a semantically equivalent set of axioms of the description logic $\mathcal{SROIQ}$ if the following conditions hold:

- The rule contains only unary and binary predicates.

---

[6]The required description logic feature in this case is the *conjunction of roles*; see [RKH08].

- For any two variables x and y, there is at most a single path between x and y in the premise of the rule.

We call such datalog rules *Description Logic Rules*, or *DL Rules* for short. Before providing the complete transformation algorithm for Description Logic Rules in Fig. 6.5, we highlight some important cases that the definition allows.

The second item in the above definition is tantamount to the statement that the rule premise's dependency graph contains no (undirected) cycles of length greater than 1. A cycle of length 1 is an atom of the form $R(x, x)$ – a special case that we can address in $\mathcal{SROIQ}$. Indeed, whenever we encounter an atom of the form $R(x, x)$, we can introduce a new class name C_R which we define with an axiom $C_R \equiv \exists R.\mathsf{Self}$. One can then simply replace any atom $R(x, x)$ by $C_R(x)$, and this does not change the conclusions that can be drawn from the knowledge base, as long as we are only interested in conclusions that do not refer to the new class name C_R.

The attentive reader will already have noticed that our above definition admits further types of rules that we did not consider yet. An example is rule (4) of Fig. 6.1: it contains only unary and binary predicates, and its dependency graph has no loops. Yet its conclusion is a binary atom, and hence can certainly not be expressed as a class inclusion axiom. $\mathcal{SROIQ}$ offers two basic forms of role inclusion axioms that we may try to use:

$$R \sqsubseteq S \qquad \text{and} \qquad R_1 \circ \ldots \circ R_n \sqsubseteq S,$$

where the first can be considered as a special case of the second role composition. But both of these axioms can include only role names, while rule (4) also contains a unary (class) atom $\mathsf{Dish}(y)$. As in the above case of role atoms $R(x, x)$, this problem can be addressed by adding an auxiliary axiom to the knowledge base. This time, a new role name R_{Dish} is introduced together with the class inclusion axiom $\mathsf{Dish} \equiv \exists R_{\mathsf{Dish}}.\mathsf{Self}$. Intuitively speaking, this defines the class of dishes to be equivalent to the class of those things which have the relationship R_{Dish} to themselves. With this additional axiom, one can rewrite rule (4) as follows:

$$\mathsf{dislikes}(x, z) \wedge R_{\mathsf{Dish}}(y, y) \wedge \mathsf{contains}(y, z) \rightarrow \mathsf{dislikes}(x, y).$$

This step is the core of the transformation to $\mathcal{SROIQ}$. Using inverse roles, we can now write the rule premise as a chain:

$$\mathsf{dislikes}(x, z) \wedge \mathsf{contains}^-(z, y) \wedge R_{\mathsf{Dish}}(y, y) \rightarrow \mathsf{dislikes}(x, y).$$

This rule can now easily be expressed as a $\mathcal{SROIQ}$ role composition axiom. Together with the auxiliary axiom we have used above, rule (4) is thus represented by the following description logic knowledge base:

$$\text{Dish} \equiv \exists R_{\text{Dish}}.\text{Self}$$
$$\text{dislikes} \circ \text{contains}^- \circ R_{\text{Dish}} \sqsubseteq \text{dislikes}$$

Note that the second axiom no longer contains the requirement that R_{Dish} refers to the same variable in first and second position. The resulting knowledge base therefore is not strictly semantically equivalent to the original rule. Yet, a formula that does not contain the auxiliary name R_{Dish} is entailed by the new knowledge base exactly if it is entailed by the original rule (4). Therefore the transformed knowledge base can be used instead of the original rule for all common reasoning tasks.

While these examples provide us with a significant set of tools for translating rules into axioms, there is still a case that we have not addressed yet. Consider rule (1) of Fig. 6.1. Its dependency graph has no edges and certainly no loops, so it should be possible to transform it. Yet, even if we use the above method for replacing the unary predicates $\text{Vegetarian}(x)$ and $\text{FishProduct}(y)$ with new auxiliary roles, we only obtain the following rule:

$$R_{\text{Vegetarian}}(x, x) \wedge R_{\text{FishProduct}}(y, y) \rightarrow \text{dislikes}(x, y).$$

But this cannot be rewritten as a role composition axiom, since there is a "gap" between x and y. Another special feature of $\mathcal{SROIQ}$ comes to our aid: the universal role U can be added to the rule without changing the semantics:

$$R_{\text{Vegetarian}}(x, x) \wedge U(x, y) \wedge R_{\text{FishProduct}}(y, y) \rightarrow \text{dislikes}(x, y).$$

Since the relation denoted by U is defined to comprise all pairs of individuals, adding the atom $U(x, y)$ does not impose any restrictions on the applicability of the rule. Yet it helps us to bring the rule into the right syntactic shape for being expressed in $\mathcal{SROIQ}$. Together with the required auxiliary axioms, we thus obtain:

$$\text{Vegetarian} \equiv \exists R_{\text{Vegetarian}}.\text{Self}$$
$$\text{FishProduct} \equiv \exists R_{\text{FishProduct}}.\text{Self}$$
$$R_{\text{Vegetarian}} \circ U \circ R_{\text{FishProduct}} \sqsubseteq \text{dislikes}$$

Essentially, this discussion provides us with enough tools for treating all DL Rules in Fig. 6.1. Yet there is one more issue that deserves some attention, even if it does not occur in our example: the definition of DL Rules does not impose any restrictions on the occurrence of constant symbols, since the latter are not taken into account when defining dependency graphs. The reason why this is feasible is that we can replace individual occurrences of constant symbols by arbitrary new variables. If, for example, a rule body has the form $R(x, a) \wedge S(a, y)$, it can equivalently be rewritten as $R(x, z) \wedge \{a\}(z) \wedge S(a, y)$. Here, the new variable z is required to refer to the (unique) member of the nominal class denoted by $\{a\}$, i.e. z must refer to the individual denoted by a. Note that only one occurrence of the constant a has been replaced in this transformation. When replacing the remaining occurrence, we can introduce yet another new variable instead of using z again: $R(x, z) \wedge \{a\}(z) \wedge S(v, y) \wedge \{a\}(v)$. Clearly, this transformation cannot create any new cycles in the rule's dependency graph, so that it is indeed safe to ignore constants when defining DL Rules.

This completes our set of methods for rewriting rules. We sum up our insights in a single transformation algorithm that can be applied to any Description Logic Rule, given in Fig. 6.5. The algorithm is organized in multiple steps, each of which is meant to solve a particular problem that may occur in the shape of the input rule. All but the last step apply to rules with unary and binary head atoms alike, while the last step needs to distinguish between class inclusion axioms and role inclusion axioms. The underlying ideas of steps 2 through 6 have already been explained in the examples above – we only note that the step-wise transformation introduces some description logic syntax into the rule, and that notions like "unary atom" should be assumed to include these additional expressions.

Step 1 has been added to normalize the shape of the rule so as to reduce the cases we need to distinguish in the algorithm. This initial step uses $\top$ and $\bot$ class expressions to normalize rules with empty bodies or heads, i.e. facts and integrity constraints. Moreover, it eliminates constant symbols as discussed above.

Some further characteristics of the transformation algorithm are worth noting. First of all, the algorithm is non-deterministic since there are often multiple ways to complete a step. Step 3, e.g., allows us to pick any pair of unconnected variables to connect them. If the dependency graph consists of two unconnected parts with more than one variable in each, then we can choose any of the occurring variables to be connected. Here and in all other non-deterministic cases, our choice does not influence the correctness of the result, but it might simplify some of the later steps.

Moreover, it must be acknowledged that the transformation algorithm is by far not optimal, and often produces more complicated results than necessary. This is so, since the purpose of the algorithm is to cover all possible cases, and not to yield minimal results whenever possible. As an ex-

Input: A Description Logic Rule $B \to H$
Output: A $\mathcal{SROIQ}$ knowledge base K

Initialize $K := \emptyset$
Repeat each of the following steps until no further changes occur:

Step 1: Normalize rule

- If H is empty, then set $H := \bot(x)$, where x is an arbitrary variable.
- For each variable x in H: If x does not occur in B, then set $B := B \wedge \top(x)$.
- If possible, select a single occurrence of a constant symbol a as a parameter of some predicate of $B \to H$, and pick a variable x not occurring in $B \to H$. Then replace the selected occurrence of a with x, and set $B := B \wedge \{a\}(x)$.

Step 2: Replace reflexive binary predicates

- If possible, select a predicate $R(x,x)$ and replace $R(x,x)$ with $C_R(x)$ where C_R is a new unary predicate symbol. Set $K := K \cup \{C_R \equiv \exists R.\mathrm{Self}\}$.

Step 3: Connect rule premise

- If possible, select two (arbitrary) variables x and y such that there is no path between x and y in B. Then set $B := B \wedge U(x,y)$.

Step 4: Orient binary predicates

- Now H must be of the form $D(z)$ or $S(z,z')$ for some variables z and z'. For every binary predicate $R(x,y)$ in B:
  If the (unique) path from z to y is shorter (has fewer elements) than the path from z to x, then replace $R(x,y)$ in B by $R^-(y,x)$.

Step 5: Roll up side branches

- If B contains an atom $R(x,y)$ or $R^-(x,y)$ such that y does not occur in any other binary atom in B or H then

  - If B contains unary atoms $C_1(y), \ldots, C_n(y)$ that refer to y, then define a new description logic concept $E := C_1 \sqcap \ldots \sqcap C_n$, and delete $C_1(y), \ldots, C_n(y)$ from B. Otherwise define $E := \top$.
  - Replace $R(x,y)$ (or $R^-(x,y)$, respectively) by $\exists R.E(x)$ (or $\exists R^-.E(x)$), where E is the concept just defined.

Step 6a: If H is of the form $D(x)$: Create final class inclusion axiom

- In this case, B must be of the form $C_1(x) \wedge \ldots \wedge C_n(x)$. Set $K := K \cup \{C_1 \sqcap \ldots \sqcap C_n \sqsubseteq D\}$.

Step 6b: If H is of the form $S(x,y)$: Create final role inclusion axiom

- For each unary atom $C(z)$ in B: Replace $C(z)$ by $R_C(z,z)$ where R_C is a new role name, and set $K := K \cup \{C \equiv \exists R_C.\mathrm{Self}\}$.
- Now B contains only one unique path between x and y which is of the form $\{R_1(x,x_2), R_2(x_2,x_3), \ldots, R_n(x_n,y)\}$ (where each of the R_i might be a role name or an inverse role name). Set $K := K \cup \{R_1 \circ \ldots \circ R_n \sqsubseteq S\}$.

FIGURE 6.5: Transforming Description Logic Rules into $\mathcal{SROIQ}$ axioms

treme example, consider the simple fact $\to R(a, b)$ which could directly be expressed as a $\mathcal{SROIQ}$ ABox statement. Instead, the algorithm normalizes the rule to $\{a\}(x) \land \{b\}(y) \to R(x, y)$, and then connects both terms to obtain $\{a\}(x) \land U(x, y) \land \{b\}(y) \to R(x, y)$. Finally, in Step 6b, unary atoms are replaced by auxiliary binary predicates $R_{\{a\}}$ and $R_{\{b\}}$, so that we obtain the following final set of description logic axioms:

$$\{a\} \equiv \exists R_{\{a\}}.\text{Self}$$
$$\{b\} \equiv \exists R_{\{b\}}.\text{Self}$$
$$R_{\{a\}} \circ U \circ R_{\{b\}} \sqsubseteq R$$

While this is clearly not the preferred way of expressing this statement, it still captures the intended semantics. On the other hand, the algorithm also covers cases like $\to R(x, a)$, $C(x) \land D(y) \to$, or $R(x, y) \land S(a, z) \to T(y, z)$ where a proper transformation might be less obvious. When dealing with such transformations – for instance in the exercises later in this chapter – it is therefore left to the reader to either apply exactly the above algorithm to obtain a correct but possibly lengthy solution, or to use shortcuts for obtaining a simplified yet, hopefully, correct result.

When using DL Rules in practice, we should not forget to take into account that the description logic $\mathcal{SROIQ}$ imposes some further restrictions on its knowledge bases. Two such restrictions have been introduced in Section 5.1.4: regularity of RBoxes and simplicity of roles. To ensure decidability, the corresponding conditions must be checked for the knowledge base as a whole, and not just for single axioms. Hence, when adding DL Rules to $\mathcal{SROIQ}$ knowledge bases, we must take care not to violate any such condition. The following DL Rule, e.g., could be useful in practice:

$$\text{Woman}(x) \land \text{hasChild}(x, y) \to \text{motherOf}(x, y).$$

But if, in addition, an axiom $\text{motherOf} \sqsubseteq \text{hasChild}$ is contained in the knowledge base, then the RBox obtained after translating the DL Rule to $\mathcal{SROIQ}$ contains a cyclic dependency between motherOf and hasChild, and hence is no longer regular. Therefore, either of the two statements can be used, but they cannot be combined in one knowledge base if we want to employ common inference algorithms for reasoning. It is conceivable that the restrictions of current algorithms could be relaxed to accommodate some more of the specific axioms that are obtained from Description Logic Rules. Another possible solution is to resort to other kinds of rules, as introduced in the following section.

(1)	$\text{Vegetarian}(x) \wedge \text{FishProduct}(y) \rightarrow \text{dislikes}(x, y)$
(2)	$\text{orderedDish}(x, y) \wedge \text{dislikes}(x, y) \rightarrow \text{Unhappy}(x)$
(3)	$\text{orderedDish}(x, y) \rightarrow \text{Dish}(y)$
(4)	$\text{dislikes}(x, z) \wedge \text{Dish}(y) \wedge \text{contains}(y, z) \rightarrow \text{dislikes}(x, y)$
(5)	$\rightarrow \text{Vegetarian}(\text{markus})$
(6)	$\text{Happy}(x) \wedge \text{Unhappy}(x) \rightarrow$
(7)	$\exists \text{orderedDish.ThaiCurry}(\text{markus})$
(8)	$\text{ThaiCurry} \sqsubseteq \exists \text{contains.FishProduct}$

FIGURE 6.6: DL-safety of rules depends on the given description logic axioms

6.3.4 DL-safe Rules

The previous section considered DL Rules as a kind of datalog rules that could also be represented in description logics. The main application of DL Rules therefore is to simplify ontology editing, especially considering that some of the required encodings can be quite complex. This section, in contrast, introduces a different type of rules that add real expressivity which is not available in $\mathcal{SROIQ}$ yet. These datalog rules are called *DL-safe*, and they are based on the idea of limiting the interaction between datalog and description logics to a "safe" amount that does not endanger decidability.[7]

The restrictions that DL-safe rules impose on datalog to preserve decidability can be viewed from two perspectives. On the one hand, one can give syntactic "safety" conditions that ensure the desired behavior. This corresponds to the original definition of DL-safe rules. On the other hand, one can modify the semantics of datalog rules so as to ensure that every rule is implicitly restricted to allow only "safe" interactions with description logic knowledge bases. This approach has become very common in practice, since it is indeed always possible to evaluate arbitrary datalog rules in a DL-safe way, without requiring the user to adhere to specific syntactic restrictions. We begin with the original definition and explain the second perspective afterwards.

To define DL-safety, we need to consider a concrete description logic knowledge base K. We call a datalog atom a *DL-atom* if its predicate symbol is used as a role name or class name in K, and we call all other datalog atoms *non-DL-atoms*. Then a datalog rule $B \rightarrow H$ is *DL-safe for K* if all variables occurring in $B \rightarrow H$ also occur in a non-DL-atom in the body B. Note that, as before, we use B to abbreviate an arbitrary conjunction of datalog atoms. A set of datalog rules is DL-safe for K if all of its rules are DL-safe for

---

[7]The name "DL-safe" actually originates from a related notion of "safety" that has been considered for datalog in the field of deductive databases.

K. Consider, e.g., the datalog rules and description logic axioms in Fig. 6.6 that we already know from earlier examples. The predicates orderedDish, contains, ThaiCurry, and FishProduct are used in the description logic part. Therefore, rule (1) is not DL-safe since y is used only in the DL-atom FishProduct(y). Rule (3) is not allowed for similar reasons, but all other rules are indeed DL-safe.

DL-safety therefore is rather easy to recognize: we only need to check whether there are enough non-DL-atoms in each rule premise. Some care must still be taken since DL-safety is not an intrinsic feature that a datalog rule may have. Rather, it depends on the accompanying description logic knowledge base and the predicates used therein. To see this, we can take a different perspective on the rules of Fig. 6.6. As we have seen in Section 6.3.3, rule (1) and rules (3) to (6) could similarly be considered as Description Logic Rules, while rule (2) does not meet the requirements. Using DL Rules and DL-safe rules together is no problem since the former are merely a syntactic shortcut for description logic axioms. We just have to treat all predicates that occur in DL Rules as if they were used in the description logic part of the knowledge base. Rule (1) and rule (3), which we found not to be DL-safe above, could thus also be considered as DL Rules. But when doing so, the predicates Dish and dislikes also belong to the description logic part of the knowledge base, and thus rules (2) and (4) are no longer DL-safe.

Summing up, we can treat the rules of Fig. 6.6 in at least two ways: either we use rules (2), (4), (5), and (6) as DL-safe rules, or we use rule (1) and rules (3) to (6) as DL Rules. Neither approach is quite satisfying, since we have to neglect one or the other rule in each of the cases. But the definition of DL-safety shows us a way to get closer to our original rule set. Namely, whenever a rule is not DL-safe for a particular knowledge base, it can be modified to become DL-safe. All we have to do is to add further non-DL-atoms to the rule premise for all variables that did not appear in such an atom yet. Which further non-DL-atoms should this be? In fact, we can simply introduce a new unary non-DL-predicate O and use atoms of the form $O(x)$ to ensure the DL-safety conditions for a variable x. When viewing rules (1) and rules (3) to (6) as DL Rules, e.g., we can modify rule (2) to become DL-safe as follows:

(2') orderedDish$(x, y) \land$ dislikes$(x, y) \land O(x) \land O(y) \rightarrow$ Unhappy(x)

This new rule is indeed DL-safe since both x and y occur in non-DL-atoms, and hence it can be used together with the other (DL) rules. But, unfortunately, this rule does not allow for any additional conclusions! The reason is that there is no information about O, and therefore we can always find an interpretation where O is interpreted as the empty set, so that rule (2') is never applicable. Adding $O(x)$ and $O(y)$ imposes additional conditions for applying the rule. Therefore we would like to ensure that O must encompass

$\texttt{orderedDish}(x,y) \wedge \texttt{dislikes}(x,y) \wedge O(x) \wedge O(y) \rightarrow \texttt{Unhappy}(x)$
$\rightarrow O(\texttt{markus})$
$\rightarrow O(\texttt{anja})$
$\rightarrow O(\texttt{thaiRedCurry})$
$\texttt{Vegetarian}(x) \wedge \texttt{FishProduct}(y) \rightarrow \texttt{dislikes}(x,y)$
$\texttt{orderedDish}(x,y) \rightarrow \texttt{Dish}(y)$
$\texttt{dislikes}(x,z) \wedge \texttt{Dish}(y) \wedge \texttt{contains}(y,z) \rightarrow \texttt{dislikes}(x,y)$
$\texttt{ThaiCurry} \sqsubseteq \exists\texttt{contains}.\texttt{FishProduct}$
$\texttt{Vegetarian}(\texttt{markus})$
$\texttt{Vegetarian}(\texttt{anja})$
$\exists\texttt{orderedDish}.\texttt{ThaiCurry}(\texttt{markus})$
$\texttt{orderedDish}(\texttt{anja}, \texttt{thaiRedCurry})$
$\texttt{ThaiCurry}(\texttt{thaiRedCurry})$

FIGURE 6.7: Combination of DL-safe rules, DL Rules, and description logic axioms

as many elements as possible. A first idea might be to add the rule $\rightarrow O(x)$, i.e. the fact that O encompasses *all* elements. But this rule would not be DL-safe, as x does not occur in a non-DL-atom in the premise. A little reflection shows that the problem cannot be solved by adding some clever rule premise, since this premise would merely face the same problem again. What we can do, however, is to assert that concrete elements belong to O, e.g., by writing $\rightarrow O(\texttt{markus})$. By giving many facts of this kind, we can extend the applicability of rule (2') to further cases.

To illustrate this idea, a modified set of example rules and axioms is given in Fig. 6.7. To clarify the intended semantics of each element, the rules have been reordered, and vertical lines clearly separate the knowledge base into DL-safe rule, DL Rules, terminological description logic axioms, and description logic facts. The knowledge base now also features another vegetarian who ordered a Thai curry dish, and this particular Thai curry is represented by the individual name (constant symbol) $\texttt{thaiRedCurry}$. Further datalog facts for the predicate O have been added to the DL-safe part. Note that we cannot assert more than the given facts about O in a DL-safe way.

What exactly does the knowledge base of Fig. 6.7 entail? The lower three groups of axioms can still be used as in earlier examples (cf. Section 6.3.1). So we can, e.g., still conclude that Markus ordered a dish that he dislikes. This statement corresponds to the description logic assertion

$$(\exists\texttt{orderedDish}.\exists\texttt{dislikes}^-.\{\texttt{markus}\})(\texttt{markus})$$

which we could check with a description logic reasoner. The reader may not find this expression very intuitive, and it is worth taking some time to understand how it encodes the statement we just made. An explicit way to read this expression is as follows: Markus belongs to the class of people who ordered a dish that is disliked by someone in the class {markus}, of which Markus is the only member.

In spite of this conclusion, we cannot infer that Markus is unhappy. The topmost DL-safe rule is applicable only if the variables x and y represent members of the class denoted by O. But we can always find an interpretation where this is not the case for the element that represents the unnamed Thai curry dish that Markus ordered. The rule is really just applicable to elements represented by constant symbols.

On the other hand, we know that Anja ordered a particular Thai curry dish called "Thai Red Curry" and again we may conclude that she dislikes this dish. The situation is similar to the case of Markus, with the only difference being that the domain element that corresponds to Anja's dish is represented by the constant symbol thaiRedCurry. This clearly must be true in any model of the knowledge base that we consider. Thus the initial DL-safe rule is applicable and we conclude that, alas, Anja is unhappy.

After this example, we also get an intuition why the DL-safety restriction is enough to ensure decidability of reasoning. Namely, DL-safety effectively restricts the applicability of rules to those domain elements that are identified by constant symbols, i.e. to the elements for which we can instantiate the predicate O (or any other non-DL-predicate we may use). Since we only ever have a finite number of constant symbols, rules are applicable in only a finite number of cases. The DL-safe part of Fig. 6.7, e.g., could also be replaced by rules without variables that enumerate all the basic cases that are covered:

orderedDish(anja, thaiRedCurry) ∧ dislikes(anja, thaiRedCurry)
   → Unhappy(anja)

orderedDish(markus, thaiRedCurry) ∧ dislikes(markus, thaiRedCurry)
   → Unhappy(markus)

orderedDish(markus, anja) ∧ dislikes(markus, anja)
   → Unhappy(markus)

. . .

While this still yields exponentially many rules, these rules now are easier to deal with for a description logic reasoner. In fact, rules without variables can always be considered as Description Logic Rules, and could thus even be transformed into description logic axioms. This approach, however, is not feasible in practice, since it creates an exponential amount of new axioms that the reasoner must take into account. Reasoners with direct support for DL-safe rules, in contrast, may process such rules rather efficiently, and in an optimized fashion. Examples of systems that currently support DL-safe rules are KAON2 and Pellet (see Section 8.5).

It has been mentioned that there is a second perspective that one may take on DL-safe rules. The above discussions have shown that, intuitively, DL-safe rules are applicable only to elements that are denoted by constant symbols. Instead of imposing a syntactic requirement to ensure this, we may directly build this restriction into the semantics of datalog. One way to do that is to change the definition of variable assignments, requiring that variables can only be assigned to domain elements of the form $a^\mathcal{I}$ for some constant symbol a. Such domain elements are sometimes called *named elements*. Another possible approach is to assume that the premise of every rule (DL-safe or not) is silently extended with conditions $O(x)$ where O is defined by facts $\rightarrow O(a)$ for each constant symbol a. Both approaches are essentially equivalent in that they allow us to write arbitrary datalog rules and use them like DL-safe rules. This is, in fact, what some description logic reasoners that support DL-safe rules will automatically do when presented with a rule that is not DL-safe.

The above perspective is convenient since it allows users to specify arbitrary rules without considering the details of their semantics. However, this approach introduces some confusion, since the term "DL-safe rule" might now be used for two different things. On the one hand, it might refer to a datalog rule that respects the syntactic restrictions explained above. On the other hand, it might denote a rule that is syntactically similar to datalog, but which is evaluated under a modified semantics that restricts its conclusions. The second approach can also be viewed as an incomplete way of reasoning with datalog: all conclusions that the rules entail under the "DL-safe semantics" are also correct conclusions under the standard datalog semantics, but some conclusions might not be found. An example of such a lost conclusion would be Unhappy(markus) which we could derive in datalog in Section 6.3.1 but not with the DL-safe rules above.

While the relationship between the two approaches is straightforward, it is important to clarify the intended meaning when exchanging rules between systems. This is even more the case when Description Logic Rules are also considered, since datalog rules that are not DL-safe may still be suitable as DL Rules. First and foremost, however, the task of exchanging rules requires a unified machine-readable syntax with a standardized semantics. This is the purpose of the Rule Interchange Format that is the topic of the next section.

6.4 Rule Interchange Format RIF

The considerations of the previous sections have provided us with important insights regarding the combination of OWL DL and datalog rules. We have seen how this combination can be endowed with a meaningful semantics, and how either approach contributes modeling power to augment the other one. Moreover, various restrictions were considered to identify cases where the complete implementation of such a merger of OWL and rules is actually possible. Yet, we lack an important ingredient for applying this knowledge in practice: so far, we have not specified any machine-readable format for encoding rules and their combination with OWL. This section considers the *Rule Interchange Format* (RIF) as a possible means to fill this gap.

RIF – currently under development by a W3C working group – is expected to become a standard format for exchanging rules of many different kinds of rule languages, both for the Semantic Web and for various other application areas. Due to the multitude of existing rule languages, the specification of such an overarching exchange framework is a difficult task. At the time of the writing of this book, the RIF working group has not completed the intended specification documents yet. The discussions in this section therefore refer to the most recent working draft documents of 30 July 2008 and 18 December 2008, respectively.

While many parts of RIF may thus still be changed or extended in the future, we concentrate here on core aspects that are likely to remain stable throughout this process. First and foremost, this is the simple core rule language *RIF-Core*. We will see that it is closely related to datalog as discussed in the previous sections. Moreover, we consider the proposed way of combining RIF-Core with RDF and OWL. For the latter case, this shows many parallels to the combination of OWL and datalog discussed before, while the combination of rules and RDF is new.

We omit various aspects of RIF that are not central to our treatment, but we will provide details regarding syntax and semantics of the features we discuss.

6.4.1 RIF-Core

RIF is conceived as a general framework for exchanging rules of many different kinds. One way to approach this ambitious goal is to start with a "least common denominator" of a (possibly large) set of targeted rule languages. Such a shared core language helps to emphasize the commonalities of different formalisms and can be a basis for guiding the extension toward more expressive languages. RIF therefore specifies a language called *RIF-Core* that is supported by a large class of rule-based systems. RIF-Core is defined as a restriction of the more expressive *Basic Logic Dialect* (BLD), but it can similarly be considered as a sublanguage of the *Production Rule Dialect* (PRD) that RIF defines. In this sense, RIF-Core is indeed the basic core of the rule languages considered by RIF.

Semantically, RIF-Core is closely related to datalog as presented in Section 6.2, i.e. to (first-order) logic programming without function symbols or any form of negation. From a semantic viewpoint, the main difference between

RIF-Core and RIF-BLD is that the latter also supports the use of function symbols. Since we have hitherto restricted our attention to plain datalog, we focus on RIF-Core in this chapter. Readers who are familiar with logic programming will find it straightforward – both syntactically and semantically – to add function symbols as done in RIF-BLD.

RIF-Core provides a *presentation syntax* for rules that is useful in understanding their basic features and structure. For actually exchanging rules between machines, an XML-based syntax is proposed as a more robust syntactic format. The latter is described in Section 6.4.4. To illustrate the basics of the BLD presentation syntax, we reconsider rule (1) in Fig. 6.1:

$$\text{Vegetarian}(x) \wedge \text{FishProduct}(y) \rightarrow \text{dislikes}(x, y)$$

A RIF-Core document with this rule could look as follows:

```
Document(
 Prefix(ex http://example.com/)
 Group(
   Forall ?x ?y (
     ex:dislikes(?x ?y) :- And( ex:Vegetarian(?x) ex:FishProduct(?y) )
   )
 )
)
```

Comparing this to the earlier datalog syntax, we immediately observe various differences. First of all, we should familiarize ourselves with the basic syntactic structure of RIF-Core presentation syntax: most structures are described using functional-style operators, such as `Document` or `Forall`, and these operators are often followed by parameters in parentheses. Lists of parameters are separated by spaces, without a comma or any other separating character in between. It is easy to see that the encoded rule is essentially contained in lines 4 to 6, while the rest of the document consists of standard headers and basic declarations. We will omit this outermost part in all future examples.

Looking at the rule in more detail now, we see that all predicates are specified by QNames, i.e. a namespace prefix `ex` is used to abbreviate full URIs. This is not a surprise for a Semantic Web language, and by now we are familiar with the conventions of coining and abbreviating such URIs. The namespace declaration in this case is given by `Prefix`. We also notice that variables are written with an initial question mark ?. Moreover, we observe that the rule has switched its sides: the conclusion, formerly found on the right, is now written on the left, while the rule premise is given subsequently on the right.

We also see that this right-to-left implication arrow ← is encoded by :-. This style of writing rules is common in logic programming.

Finally, logical operators such as ∧ and ∀ are now also replaced by operator names that are written like function symbols with the parameters in parentheses. For example, the sub-formula `And(...)` specifies a conjunction. Every variable is explicitly mentioned in an initial `Forall ?x ?y`. Recall that for datalog, too, all variables are considered to be universally quantified, i.e. rules are always considered to apply to all possible variable assignments. This is also true for RIF-Core, but the universal quantification is now always written in front of all rules.

While we may need a moment for getting used to these modified syntactic conventions, it should be noted that RIF-Core is still very similar to datalog: variables, predicates, and logical operators are still used in exactly the same way; they are just written in a slightly more explicit syntax. With this knowledge, we are able to cast many of the previously considered datalog rules into RIF-Core presentation syntax. If multiple rules are to be stored in one document, they are usually separated by line breaks, though spaces would also suffice.

Naturally it is also possible to use constant symbols for representing individuals:

```
Forall ?y (
    ex:dislikes(ex:markus ?y) :- ex:FishProduct(?y)
)
```

This rule states that the individual represented by `ex:markus` dislikes all fish products. RIF-Core does not require us to declare whether a URI is used as a logical predicate or as an individual name. However, every URI must only be used in one of these two contexts. In addition, a particular predicate must be given the same number of parameters in all places it is used: the *arity* of each predicate is fixed. If these conditions are satisfied, the RIF-Core document is said to be *well-formed*. Both of the following rules are thus *not* allowed in a well-formed document:

```
Forall ?y (
    ex:dislikes(ex:dislikes ?y) :- ex:FishProduct(?y)
)

Forall ?x ?y (
    ex:FishProduct(?x) :- ex:FishProduct(?x ?y)
)
```

The premise of a rule in RIF-Core can be completely omitted if the result follows without precondition, i.e. if a fact is specified:

```
ex:Happy(ex:markus)
```

Here we also do not need to specify a `Forall` quantifier since no variable occurs. The implication operator `:-` must also be omitted in this case.

Finally, RIF-Core also supports data literals of a number of datatypes. These are encoded in a similar fashion as in the RDF Turtle syntax which is already familiar to us:

```
ex:hasName(ex:markus "Markus"^^xsd:string)
```

Here we assume that the namespace prefix `xsd` has been declared to match the usual URI prefix of XML Schema datatypes. For the purposes of this book, it suffices to know that such data literals in RIF are treated rather similarly to RDF data literals, and that standard XML Schema datatypes are compatible with RIF. A main difference is that RIF waives the distinction between URIs and data literals: URIs are considered to be literals of a special "datatype" `rif:iri`,[8] and literals of other datatypes are also considered to represent individuals (though they may never represent logical predicates). Since RIF generalizes the notion of datatypes in RDF, the term *symbol space* is used to refer to entities such as `rif:iri`. For us, these design choices are not essential for understanding RIF. Yet, we should now be able to interpret syntactic variants of RIF as illustrated in the following example:

```
"http://example.org/Happy"^^rif:iri(
    "http://example.org/markus"^^rif:iri
)
```

Unifying the treatment of URIs and data literals may not improve readability on the level of presentation syntax, but it simplifies various parts of the specification.

6.4.2   Object-Oriented Data Structures: Frames in RIF

Even though RIF-Core is conceived as a rather small base language for RIF, it offers various syntactic features which go beyond datalog. One such feature

---

[8]The prefix `rif` commonly abbreviates the URI prefix `http://www.w3.org/2007/rif#`.

is so-called *frames* that provide a convenient syntax for specifying property values of objects. The following example gives a simple fact, reminiscent of the fact shown in Fig. 2.1 on page 20, encoded in a frame (assuming suitable namespace declarations for book and crc):

```
book:uri[ex:publishedBy -> crc:uri]
```

Here, book:uri refers to an object for which attribute-value pairs are specified. When using RIF frames, we thus speak of objects, attributes, and values, where RDF would use the terms subject, predicate, and object. These slight differences in naming should not be a cause for confusion; the next section will confirm that the semantics of both approaches are indeed closely related. Syntactically, frames use the symbols [and] for enclosing a frame's content, and the operator -> for defining value assignments. Further attributes and values can be given by simply adding assignments to the list:

```
book:uri[
    ex:publishedBy -> crc:uri
    ex:title -> "Foundations of Semantic Web Technologies"^^xsd:string
]
```

While the above examples are expressible in RDF, frames can also be used in RIF rules that can be used to derive new facts. For instance, one could define the inverse of a property as follows:

```
Forall ?person ?book (
    ?person[ex:authorOf -> ?book] :- ?book[ex:hasAuthor -> ?person]
)
```

Frames can freely be combined with the predicate-based formulae that we considered before, also within a single rule. All URIs used in a frame are considered to occur as individual names in the RIF-Core document, and can thus also not be used as predicates.

Summing up, the frame syntax provides a simple means for specifying data structures in an "object oriented" fashion. On the other hand, we have also seen that frames are closely related to RDF triples, which can be encoded along the schema

```
subject[predicate -> object].
```

This intuition of considering frames as triples will be substantiated when considering their formal semantics in the following section.

6.4.3 RIF-Core Semantics

In order to fully understand the meaning of a set of RIF rules, we still need to specify its logical semantics. It has already been remarked that RIF-Core is closely related to datalog in this matter. Since the semantics of the latter has already been detailed in Section 6.2.2, it is sufficient to translate RIF rules into datalog in order to specify their semantics. Strictly speaking, this is not always possible, since our earlier presentation did not discuss the use of data literals within datalog. But for the logical expressivity of RIF-Core it is indeed enough to consider data literals as a special form of constants. In other words, their given datatype does not affect the conclusions that can be drawn in the part of RIF that we consider.

The case of frames is not quite so simple. Clearly, there is no direct counterpart in datalog for this special feature. But we have remarked above that frames essentially can be viewed as (RDF) triples. This statement bears the insight that frames can always be decomposed into one or more statements that have exactly three components. For example, we could rewrite the frame expression

$$a[b \rightarrow c \qquad b \rightarrow d \qquad e \rightarrow f]$$

into a conjunction of three frame formulae

$$a[b \rightarrow c] \qquad a[b \rightarrow d] \qquad a[e \rightarrow f].$$

Encoding such triples in datalog can be done by means of an auxiliary ternary predicate symbol that we shall simply call `triple`. We could now represent the above example as the formula

$$\texttt{triple}(a, b, c) \land \texttt{triple}(a, b, d) \land \texttt{triple}(a, e, f).$$

This simple syntactic transformation also agrees with our earlier statement that all URIs in frames are assumed to occur as individual names: logically speaking, they do exactly that.

After these preliminary considerations, we are now ready to give the complete transformation from RIF-Core to datalog in Fig. 6.8. The transformation function is called δ, and can be applied recursively to convert (fragments of) RIF-Core rules to datalog. For simplicity, it is assumed that RIF identifiers for objects (URIs) and variables are directly used as predicates, constant symbols, and variable names in datalog without any further transformation.

6.4.4 XML Syntax for RIF-Core

The presentation syntax that we used for introducing RIF-Core so far is convenient for explaining the structural and semantic features of RIF. For exchanging rules in information systems, however, the presentation syntax might not be the best choice. The syntactic form that RIF suggests for encoding rules therefore is based on XML (see Appendix A).

RIF-Core: *input*	datalog: $\delta(input)$
`Forall ?`$x_1 \ldots$`?`x_n (*content*)	$\forall x_1 \ldots . \forall x_n . \delta(content)$
head `:-` *body*	$\delta(body) \rightarrow \delta(head)$
`And(`*content$_1$* ... *content$_n$*`)`	$\delta(content_1) \wedge \ldots \wedge \delta(content_n)$
predicate`(`t_1 ... t_n`)`	$predicate(t_1, \ldots, t_n)$
o`[`a_1 `->` v_1 ... a_n `->` v_n`]`	`triple`$(o, a_1, v_1) \wedge \ldots \wedge$ `triple`(o, a_n, v_n)

FIGURE 6.8:   Transformation of RIF-Core rules to datalog

The XML syntax can easily be given by providing another translation function that maps presentation syntax to XML syntax. This function, denoted by χ, is defined in Fig. 6.9. Note that the translation does not provide any special handling of abbreviated URIs of the form `prefix:name`. Instead, it is assumed that those abbreviations have first been expanded to literals of the form `"`*value*`"^^<`*datatype*`>`, where even *datatype* is a complete URI and not an abbreviation such as `xsd:string`. The RIF XML syntax thus is not aware of namespaces.

The definition in Fig. 6.9 covers only single rules in presentation syntax. To obtain complete RIF XML documents, it is also needed to translate the `Document` and `Group` parts that enclose collections of RIF rules in presentation syntax. Given an input document of the form `Document(Group(`*rule$_1$* `...` *rule$_n$*`))`, the transformation yields the following XML document:

```
<Document>
  <payload>
    <Group>
      <sentence>χ(rule₁)</sentence>
        ...
      <sentence>χ(ruleₙ)</sentence>
    </Group>
  </payload>
</Document>
```

For now, `payload` is the only kind of XML element that we consider as content of a RIF `Document`. We will encounter another kind of possible child element in Section 6.4.5 below. The direct child element of `payload` is `Group`, which in turn contains `sentence` elements that contain the encodings of the actual rules.

RIF presentation syntax: *input*	RIF XML syntax: $\chi(input)$
| Forall $?x_1 \ldots ?x_n$ (*content*) | ```
<Forall>
  <declare>χ(?x₁)</declare>
  ...
  <declare>χ(?xₙ)</declare>
  <formula>χ(content)</formula>
</Forall>
``` |
| *head* :- *body* | ```
<Implies>
  <if>χ(body)</if>
  <then>χ(head)</then>
</Implies>
``` |
| And(*content₁* ... *contentₙ*) | ```
<And>
  <formula>χ(content₁)</formula>
  ...
  <formula>χ(contentₙ)</formula>
</And>
``` |
| *predicate*($t_1$ ... $t_n$) | ```
<Atom>
  <op>χ(predicate)</op>
  <args ordered="yes">
    χ(t₁)
    ...
    χ(tₙ)
  </args>
</Atom>
``` |
| $o[a_1 \rightarrow v_1 \ldots a_n \rightarrow v_n]$ | ```
<Frame>
  <object>χ(o)</object>
  <slot ordered="yes">
    χ(a₁)
    χ(v₁)
  </slot>
  ...
  <slot ordered="yes">
    χ(aₙ)
    χ(vₙ)
  </slot>
</Frame>
``` |
| "*literal*"^^*datatype* | `<Const type="datatype">literal</Const>` |
| ?*variablename* | `<Var>variablename</Var>` |

FIGURE 6.9: Transformation of RIF presentation syntax to XML syntax
```

This completes the translation of RIF-Core into XML syntax. We immediately see that this syntactic form is much more verbose than the functional presentation syntax. But even for an XML serialization, RIF XML syntax appears to be rather verbose. The reason for this is that the syntax follows a strict translation pattern using two kinds of XML tags: tags starting with upper case letters represent so-called *type tags*, and tags written lower case represent *role tags*. The two kinds of tags always alternate, so that each function symbol of the BLD presentation syntax introduces two levels of XML. This way of designing an XML syntax is called *alternating* or *fully striped*. It necessarily leads to XML that is rather lengthy, but it also is a very regular encoding that allows for simple implementations. Also note that, in contrast to RDF, RIF never uses identifiers of semantic objects as names of XML tags. This avoids some of the unpleasant encoding problems that RDF/XML has to cope with (cf. Section 2.2.4).

6.4.5 Combining RIF with OWL DL

Since we have identified RIF-Core to be a semantic extension of datalog, we can readily apply the results of Section 6.3 to combine RIF rule bases with OWL DL. RIF, however, also provides specific support for doing this. In particular, RIF provides a mechanism for indicating that a certain OWL ontology is to be *imported* into a rule base, and it provides an official specification of the semantics of this import. As we will see, RIF's syntactic approach of integrating OWL is slightly different from our datalog OWL integration: instead of considering OWL class and property names as unary and binary predicates, respectively, RIF uses frame formulae to represent OWL axioms.

Importing OWL DL ontologies into RIF documents is achieved by extending the Document declaration with Import statements as follows:

```
Document(
    Import(
        <location>
        <http://www.w3.org/2007/rif-import-profile#OWL-DL>
    )
    ...
)
```

In this declaration, *location* is a URL that specifies where the imported OWL ontology can be found. The second URI in the import clause states that the imported knowledge base is to be interpreted as an OWL DL ontology. This suffices to indicate that the given ontology is to be taken into account when computing consequences of the RIF-Core rule base. Extending the transformation function χ from Fig. 6.9, the above RIF fragment in presentation syntax is converted to the following XML expression:

```
<Document>
    <directive>
```

```
    <Import>
        <location>χ("location"^^<rif:iri>)</location>
        <profile>χ("http://...#OWL-DL"^^<rif:iri>)</profile>
    </Import>
  </directive>
  ...
</Document>
```

Note that, strictly speaking, the QNames `rif:iri` must be replaced by full URIs before the transformation χ is applied.

RIF and OWL use different ways of encoding axioms, and even slightly different ways of referring to predicates and individual names. Hence, RIF must also specify how exactly the OWL and RIF parts of a combined knowledge base interact. Recall that, in Section 6.3, we have achieved such an interaction by assuming that OWL class and property names can be used as unary and binary predicates in datalog. Our semantic integration thus was built upon the observation that OWL and datalog, in essence, are both fragments of first-order logic that have a natural common semantic interpretation.

The approach taken in RIF is slightly different, even though it is still based on the same idea. The main difference is that a description logic property statement of the form

$$predicate(subject, object)$$

is now considered to correspond to a frame formula

$$subject\,[predicate\,\,\text{->}\,\,object]\,.$$

This approach emphasizes the relationship of OWL DL and RDF, and indeed it was chosen in order to obtain a more uniform way of integrating both RDF and OWL with RIF. This also dictates our treatment of class inclusions, which are represented in RDF as triples with predicate `rdf:type`. Thus, class membership assertions such as

$$Class(member)$$

are now represented by statements of the form

$$member\,[\texttt{rdf:type}\,\,\text{->}\,\,Class]\,.$$

In practice, these differences from our earlier integration method do not impose major difficulties, since we may simply replace datalog atoms of the former shape by the corresponding frame formulae. As an example, Fig. 6.10 shows RIF-Core rules that correspond to the first three rules in Fig. 6.1, reformatted to interpret all former datalog predicates as OWL elements based on the frame notation.

From a logical perspective, this integration of OWL and RIF may appear slightly odd. Property and class names that play the role of logical predicates

```
Forall ?x ?y (
  ?x[ex:dislikes -> ?y] :-
      And ( ?x[rdf:type ex:Vegetarian]   ?y[rdf:type ex:FishProduct] )
)


Forall ?x ?y (
  ?x[rdf:type ex:Unhappy] :-
      And ( ?x[ex:orderedDish ?y]   ?x[ex:dislikes ?y] )
)


Forall ?x ?y ( ?y[rdf:type ex:Dish] :- ?x[ex:orderedDish ?y] )
```

FIGURE 6.10:   Example RIF-Core rules, formatted for OWL-RIF integration

in OWL do now correspond to constant symbols in RIF-Core. Does this not violate the type separation in first-order logic that strictly separates constants from predicates? In a way it does, but the problem is easily fixed with the *punning* method that was first introduced in Section 4.3.1. This means that, given an OWL class or property name n, we simply consider the predicate n and the constant n to be two distinct entities. In first-order logic, it is always clear from the context whether n is used in one or the other sense. So, strictly speaking, the RIF-Core part always refers to n as constants, while the OWL part uses n in the sense of a first-order predicate.

This alone would leave us with a rather weak form of integration, where rules and ontologies hardly interact. The expected interchange between both worlds can be expressed by first-order logic axioms of the following forms:

- $\forall x.\forall y.\texttt{triple}(x, p, y) \leftrightarrow p(x, y)$ (for all OWL property names p)

- $\forall x.\forall y.\texttt{triple}(x, \texttt{rdf:type}, c) \leftrightarrow c(x)$ (for all OWL class names c)

Recall that `triple` is the auxiliary predicate symbol that we use to encode frame formulae as in Section 6.4.3. The above axioms make a semantic connection between constant names in RIF frame formulae and class or property names in OWL axioms. The two kinds of axioms provide us with a simple way to explain the semantics of combinations of RIF and OWL by means of a translation to first-order logic. While this approach provides us with a common semantic framework for many Semantic Web languages, optimized tools typically have this semantics built into their reasoning algorithms instead of considering the above first-order axioms explicitly.

Like our earlier discussions in this chapter, the above does not consider the use of data literals in OWL or RIF. Many datatypes cannot be faithfully modeled in first-order logic, and their interpretation thus would require a corresponding extension of this semantic framework. The result would be a first-order logic in which datatype literals are available, and behave in a similar way as in RDF and OWL. The translation then can mostly be achieved by treating literals as a new special kind of logical constants, with minor adjustments to ensure compatibility between the slightly different datatype systems of RIF and OWL. The technical details are omitted here, since they contribute little to the overall understanding of RIF and OWL.

6.4.6   Combining RIF with RDF(S)

The previous section also provides us with the basics for being able to combine RIF rules with RDF data bases: the frame syntax, which appeared slightly unwieldy when dealing with OWL DL, is a very natural choice for representing RDF triples in RIF-Core. Yet, specifying the semantics of combinations of RIF and RDF poses some difficulties. The primary reason is that the (various) RDF semantics given in Chapter 3 are not based on first-order logic, which so far has been our primary framework for semantic integration.

We thus need to find a way of combining the model theory of RDF, with all the semantic entailments it provides, with the first-order semantics of RIF-Core. One way of doing this is to define a combined semantics that introduces a new notion of model, such that each model is constituted by a first-order logic interpretation and an RDF interpretation that suitably interact. A similar approach is taken in the RIF documents. The downside of this solution is that it requires us to give extended definitions to establish a new model theory.

An alternative option is to try and define the semantics of RDF in terms of first-order logic. This approach can also be viewed as an attempt to simulate the RDF semantics in first-order logic. In other words, we wish to establish an (auxiliary) first-order logic theory that produces the same conclusions that we would obtain under the RDF semantics. We prefer this approach since it is close in spirit to the other semantic approaches discussed in this chapter. In addition, this perspective allows us to view RDF(S) as a formalism of first-order logic similar to OWL DL and RIF-Core. Thus, of all Semantic Web languages considered in this book, OWL Full remains the only one that does not fit into this common semantic framework.[9]

Recall that there are multiple semantics that can be used with RDF(S). The semantics that were discussed in Chapter 3 are simple semantics, RDF semantics, and RDFS semantics. When using the RDF semantics, more conclusions can be drawn from an RDF document than when using the simple semantics.

---

[9]This might seem surprising, given that OWL Full is sometimes, incorrectly, described as the "union" of RDF(S) and OWL DL. But the consequences of OWL Full cannot be described by the mere union of the consequences obtained individually from OWL DL and RDF(S). Indeed, it is an open question whether the OWL Full semantics can be simulated by a consistent first-order logic theory.

The RDFS semantics allows for yet more conclusions that reflect the intended meaning of RDFS vocabulary. Not surprisingly, this increasing strength of the semantics for RDF(S) is also mirrored in the first-order logic axioms that we shall employ to simulate them. Finally, additional entailments in RDF(S) are obtained when considering the meaning of datatypes. As before, we do not detail this aspect here.

6.4.6.1 Simple Semantics

Intuitively speaking, the simple semantics views RDF data merely as the specification of a graph structure, without special meanings for any parts of the RDF vocabulary. The only RDF statements that can be concluded from an RDF graph thus essentially are its own triples, possibly "weakened" by inserting blank nodes for URIs or literals.

This can readily be simulated in first-order logic. Indeed, the frame-based translation used for triples in Section 6.4.5 is almost enough to achieve this. Thus, an RDF triple

$$subject \; predicate \; object \; .$$

is again considered to correspond to a frame formula

$$subject \, [predicate \; \text{->} \; object]$$

which eventually is represented as a first-order formula

$$\texttt{triple}(subject, predicate, object).$$

Though we omit the detailed treatment of literals here, we still need to specify how blank nodes are to be treated in this case. As explained earlier, blank nodes behave like existentially quantified variables, and in first-order logic we can therefore simply represent them in this way.

For instance, given the triple (in Turtle notation)

```
ex:markus ex:orderedDish _:1 .
```

the corresponding first-order translation would be

$$\exists x.\texttt{triple}(\texttt{ex:markus}, \texttt{ex:orderedDish}, x).$$

RDF triples can now be translated into first-order logic, and the `triple`-formulae that are entailed by the resulting first-order theory are exactly the triples that would be entailed under simple semantics.

Moreover, the translation allows us to combine RDF data with RIF-Core rules based on this common semantics. To import an RDF graph under simple semantics, a RIF document needs to include an import declaration of the form

```
Import(
  <location>
  <http://www.w3.org/2007/rif-import-profile#Simple>
)
```

similar to the import declaration used for OWL DL. Imports need to indicate the intended import semantics since it cannot be determined from the imported document. An OWL DL document in RDF/XML encoding, e.g., could also be imported as an RDF data set under simple semantics, leading to rather different conclusions.

6.4.6.2 RDF Semantics

The RDF semantics extends the simple semantics by ensuring proper interpretations for basic RDF vocabulary. First and foremost, this is achieved through a number of *axiomatic triples*, i.e. triples that must be satisfied in any RDF interpretation. It is easy to account for such a triple in first-order logic, using the same translation as for simple semantics. For example, the triple

<code>rdf:subject rdf:type rdf:Property .</code>

yields the first-order formula

$$\mathsf{triple}(\mathtt{rdf\!:\!subject}, \mathtt{rdf\!:\!type}, \mathtt{rdf\!:\!Property}).$$

The required axiomatic triples are listed in Section 3.2.2. A closer look at this list reveals a problem: it is infinite. Indeed, RDF requires axiomatic triples of the form `rdf:_`n `rdf:type rdf:Property` . for all natural numbers $n \geq 1$ (recall that the predicates `rdf:_`n are used for encoding RDF containers of arbitrary size). However, we would like to prevent our semantics from depending on infinitely large first-order logic theories. The way to achieve this is to restrict to axiomatic triples that are really needed for logical derivations.

Given some RDF document, we *require* the following axiomatic triples:

- all axiomatic triples that do not contain a URI of the form `rdf:_`n for some $n \geq 1$,

- all axiomatic triples of the form `rdf:_`n `rdf:type rdf:Property` . for which `rdf:_`n occurs in the document.

The first item covers all triples that are not problematic. The second one covers all axiomatic triples related to predicates `rdf:_`n that are really used. When embedding RDF into RIF, the required triples in the above definition must be extended to consider all URIs of the form `rdf:_`n that occur within the given RIF document, within any imported (RDF) document, or within any document for which entailment is to be checked.

The first-order logic axiomatization of RDF semantics now simply needs to translate all *required* axiomatic triples, which is always a finite set. Moreover, we require one additional axiom:

$$\forall x. \forall y. \forall z. \big(\texttt{triple}(x, y, z) \rightarrow \texttt{triple}(y, \texttt{rdf:type}, \texttt{rdf:Property}) \big).$$

This corresponds to the derivation rule *rdf1* in Section 3.3.2. This axiom completes our first-order translation of RDF semantics, so that we can now translate RDF documents triple-by-triple as in the case of simple semantics. This also allows us again to interpret RDF data that is imported into RIF under this semantics. The URI used in the import declaration for this semantics is `http://www.w3.org/2007/rif-import-profile#RDF`.

6.4.6.3 RDFS Semantics

The RDFS semantics further extends the RDF semantics by ensuring a proper interpretation of RDFS vocabulary. The first-order translation used in the previous section can thus still be used, but additional axioms are needed to account for the new entailments. RDFS again comes with a number of axiomatic triples that are discussed in Section 3.2.3. As before, this set of triples is infinite due to the infinite amount of container predicates `rdf:_n`. We can restrict to a finite set of required axiomatic triples just like in the previous section.

In addition, RDFS semantics includes a number of additional axioms that are closely related to the derivation rules given in Section 3.3.3. The required axioms are shown in Fig. 6.11, labeled to indicate the deduction rule(s) that correspond to each axiom. The purpose of each axiom is explained with the rules in Section 3.3.3.

Together with the required axiomatic triples and all axioms introduced for RDF semantics, the axioms of Fig. 6.11 suffice to obtain all RDFS entailments (without literals involved). In particular, the problem of incompleteness that was discussed on page 100 for the deduction rules in Section 3.3.3 does not occur in first-order logic, since we are not confined by the syntactic restrictions of RDF for finding entailments.

When importing RDF data under the RDFS semantics into RIF, the URI `http://www.w3.org/2007/rif-import-profile#RDFS` is used in the import declaration.

6.4.7 Further Features of RIF-Core and RIF-BLD

Even the rather small rule language RIF-Core includes various further features that have not been discussed in this chapter. The most important such features are listed below:

rdfs2:
$$\forall x.\forall y.\forall u.\forall v.\mathtt{triple}(x, \mathtt{rdfs:domain}, y) \land \mathtt{triple}(u, x, v)$$
$$\rightarrow \mathtt{triple}(u, \mathtt{rdf:type}, y)$$

rdfs3:
$$\forall x.\forall y.\forall u.\forall v.\mathtt{triple}(x, \mathtt{rdfs:range}, y) \land \mathtt{triple}(u, x, v)$$
$$\rightarrow \mathtt{triple}(v, \mathtt{rdf:type}, y)$$

rdfs4a, rdfs4b:
$$\forall x.\mathtt{triple}(x, \mathtt{rdf:type}, \mathtt{rdfs:Resource})$$

rdfs5:
$$\forall x.\forall y.\forall z.\mathtt{triple}(x, \mathtt{rdfs:subPropertyOf}, y)$$
$$\land \mathtt{triple}(y, \mathtt{rdfs:subPropertyOf}, z)$$
$$\rightarrow \mathtt{triple}(x, \mathtt{rdfs:subPropertyOf}, z)$$

rdfs6:
$$\forall x.\mathtt{triple}(x, \mathtt{rdf:type}, \mathtt{rdf:Property})$$
$$\rightarrow \mathtt{triple}(x, \mathtt{rdfs:subPropertyOf}, x)$$

rdfs7:
$$\forall x.\forall y.\forall u.\forall v.\mathtt{triple}(x, \mathtt{rdfs:subPropertyOf}, y) \land \mathtt{triple}(u, x, v)$$
$$\rightarrow \mathtt{triple}(u, y, v)$$

rdfs8:
$$\forall x.\mathtt{triple}(x, \mathtt{rdf:type}, \mathtt{rdf:Class})$$
$$\rightarrow \mathtt{triple}(x, \mathtt{rdfs:subClassOf}, \mathtt{rdfs:Resource})$$

rdfs9:
$$\forall x.\forall y.\forall z.\mathtt{triple}(x, \mathtt{rdfs:subClassOf}, y) \land \mathtt{triple}(z, \mathtt{rdf:type}, x)$$
$$\rightarrow \mathtt{triple}(z, \mathtt{rdf:type}, y)$$

rdfs10:
$$\forall x.\mathtt{triple}(x, \mathtt{rdf:type}, \mathtt{rdf:Class})$$
$$\rightarrow \mathtt{triple}(x, \mathtt{rdfs:subClassOf}, x)$$

rdfs11:
$$\forall x.\forall y.\forall z.\mathtt{triple}(x, \mathtt{rdfs:subClassOf}, y)$$
$$\land \mathtt{triple}(y, \mathtt{rdfs:subClassOf}, z)$$
$$\rightarrow \mathtt{triple}(x, \mathtt{rdfs:subClassOf}, z)$$

rdfs12:
$$\forall x.\mathtt{triple}(x, \mathtt{rdf:type}, \mathtt{rdfs:ContainerMembershipProperty})$$
$$\rightarrow \mathtt{triple}(x, \mathtt{rdfs:subPropertyOf}, \mathtt{rdfs:member})$$

rdfs13:
$$\forall x.\mathtt{triple}(x, \mathtt{rdf:type}, \mathtt{rdfs:Datatype})$$
$$\rightarrow \mathtt{triple}(x, \mathtt{rdfs:subClassOf}, \mathtt{rdfs:Literal})$$

FIGURE 6.11: Additional first-order axioms for simulating RDFS semantics; initial labels refer to the corresponding deduction rule in Section 3.3.3

- Further logical operators: Even RIF-Core supports some further logical operators that were not introduced here. An example is the existential quantifier `Exists`. The use of those operators is restricted to ensure that they can be expressed by the basic operators we have introduced.

- Equality: RIF supports the symbol = as a predefined predicate for expressing equality. In RIF-Core, the use of equality is not allowed in rule conclusions, however.

- Subclass and instance operators for frame formulae: RIF offers binary operators # and ## that can be used to express relations between constants similar to `rdf:type` and `rdfs:subclassOf`. At the time of the writing of this book, these features are considered to be "at risk" for RIF-Core; they will most certainly be available in RIF-BLD, however.

- Externally defined symbols: RIF enables the use of symbols that are defined "externally", i.e. which have a semantics that is not (completely) determined by the RIF rule base at hand. Typical examples of this are the "built-ins" of some logic programming languages, e.g., predicates that express arithmetic operations on their arguments.

- Local symbols: RIF allows the use of symbols that are "local" to the current document, i.e. which do not have the universal meaning that URIs have. Such local symbols can be compared to blank nodes in RDF, but they are semantically treated as simple constants, not as existentially quantified variables.

- RIF Imports: Import declarations have been introduced for the purpose of using OWL ontologies and RDF data, respectively, in combination with RIF. In addition, RIF also allows the import of other RIF documents.

- OWL Full compatibility: RIF-Core can be combined with OWL Full. Since there is no (known) mapping of OWL Full to first-order logic, the semantics for this combination needs to be specified by providing a new model theory for this combination. As in the case of OWL Full, it is not known whether this combined model theory is free of logical contradictions.

Moreover, RIF-BLD adds further features:

- Equality: RIF-BLD allows for the use of equality in rule conclusions.

- Predicates with named arguments: The atomic RIF formulae in this chapter have always used a list of arguments with a fixed length (arity). In this case, the order of arguments determines their meaning. RIF supports an alternative syntax where predicate arguments are referred to by names: Each predicate receives a set of name-value pairs that denote a parameter "slot" and its value. The order is not relevant in this case, since the slot name determines the meaning of the filler.

- Function symbols: As mentioned before, RIF-BLD supports function symbols that can be used to form complex terms instead of plain constant and variable symbols. As in the case of predicates, parameters can be given to a function symbol either as an ordered list, or as a set of name-value pairs.

Of those additions, the introduction of function symbols is the main semantic extension. Due to this addition, reasoning becomes undecidable for RIF-BLD, while it is decidable for RIF-Core. Note that the latter result may also be lost if OWL DL ontologies are imported into a RIF document. The discussion in Section 6.3 shows ways of avoiding this by means of Description Logic Rules and DL-safe rules. Both concepts can readily be adopted for RIF.

6.5 Summary

In this chapter, we have discussed *rules* as an alternative way of specifying knowledge. After a brief introduction to the rather diverse notions of "rule" that are considered in knowledge representation, we have specifically focused on first-order logic rules which are relevant as a basic formalism in a number of approaches. We then focused on the basic first-order rule language *datalog* and its possible combination with description logics, leading us to a highly expressive (and undecidable) knowledge representation language. Two decidable fragments of this language were presented. *Description Logic Rules* are based on the idea of exploiting "hidden" expressivity of the description logic $\mathcal{SROIQ}$ – the basic logic used in OWL 2 DL – for encoding rules. The second decidable fragment, *DL-safe rules*, approaches the problem by restricting the applicability of datalog rules to the comparatively small set of named individuals.

These discussions have clarified the semantics of a combination of datalog rules and description logic axioms. To actually use such combinations in practical applications, a machine-processable syntax with a clearly defined meaning is required. For this purpose, we have introduced the *Rule Interchange Format* (RIF), and in particular its most simple fragment *RIF-Core* that is closely related to datalog. We have seen that RIF offers specific import mechanisms to combine rules with ontologies in OWL (2) DL format. Since the latter semantically correspond to description logic knowledge bases, this enabled us to encode (fragments of) the presented datalog/description logic combination within RIF. Besides such highly expressive mergers of ontologies and rules, it can also be useful to apply RIF rules to RDF database. To this end, we have introduced a first-order formulation of the RDF(S) semantics that is compatible with the semantics of datalog. The meaning of importing RDF(S) into RIF-Core could thus be defined using the same framework of first-order logic that has enabled us to combine RIF with OWL DL.

6.6 Exercises

Exercise 6.1 Decide for each of the following predicate logic formulae if it can be syntactically translated into a datalog rule. Note that `father` and `mother` are function symbols.

1. $\text{Intelligent}(x) \rightarrow \text{Proud}(\text{father}(x)) \vee \text{Proud}(\text{mother}(x))$

2. $\text{Intelligent}(x) \vee (\text{knows}(x, y) \wedge \text{Intelligent}(y)) \rightarrow \text{Clever}(x)$

3. $\text{Sailor}(x) \wedge \text{Spinach}(y) \wedge \text{loves}(x, y) \wedge \text{loves}(x, \text{olive\_oyl})$
   $\rightarrow \text{Little}(x) \wedge \text{Strong}(x)$

4. $(\text{Intelligent}(x) \vee \text{Old}(x)) \wedge \exists y.(\text{marriedWith}(x, y))$
   $\rightarrow (\text{Wise}(x) \wedge \text{Bald}(x)) \vee \neg\text{Male}(x)$

Exercise 6.2 Express the following in $\mathcal{SROIQ}$.

1. $D(y) \wedge C(x) \wedge r(x, y) \rightarrow E(x)$

2. $r(x, x) \rightarrow s(x, y)$

3. $C(x) \wedge D(y) \wedge E(z) \wedge r(z, x) \rightarrow s(x, y)$

Exercise 6.3 Translate the rules from Exercise 6.1 into $\mathcal{SROIQ}$ whenever possible.

Exercise 6.4 Translate the knowledge bases from Exercises 5.4, 5.7, and 5.11 into DL rules. Use as few class constructors as possible. Identify which of the resulting rules are datalog rules.

Exercise 6.5 Translate the datalog rules you identified in Exercise 6.4 into RIF presentation syntax.

Exercise 6.6 Translate the first rule from Exercise 6.5 into RIF XML syntax.

Exercise 6.7 We have seen that the datalog rule

$$\text{orderedDish}(x, y) \wedge \text{dislikes}(x, y) \rightarrow \text{Unhappy}(x)$$

from Fig. 6.1 is not a Description Logic Rule. Consider the following set of description logic axioms, where R_{Unhappy} is a new role name:

$$\text{Unhappy} \equiv \exists R_{\text{Unhappy}}.\text{Self}$$

$$\text{orderedDish} \circ \text{dislikes}^- \sqsubseteq R_{\text{Unhappy}}$$

1. Explain why this set of axioms can be used to simulate the above rule under the usual description logic semantics.

2. Why is it not possible to use this translation in $\mathcal{SROIQ}$? (Hint: Review the syntactic restrictions explained in Section 5.1.4.)

6.7 Further Reading

A comprehensive textbook reference for datalog is [AHV94]. The combination of OWL DL and datalog was originally proposed in [HPS04]. This subsequently led to the W3C Member Submission on the *Semantic Web Rule Language* [HPSB+04], which is also known as SWRL (pronounced as *swirl*). Conceptually, this language is essentially the same as the combination of datalog and OWL that we discussed in Section 6.3, and indeed it is common to use the term "SWRL" in the literature to refer to first-order combinations of datalog and description logics in general. However, the original proposal of SWRL also includes a number of built-in functions for handling datatype values, and it uses an XML-based syntax that is rather different from the RIF syntax that we have introduced. The undecidability of SWRL is shown in [HPSBT05], but can in fact be obtained in many ways: a variety of well-known undecidable extensions of OWL DL can easily be encoded using SWRL. An early example is found in [SS89] where undecidability of KL-ONE [BS85] – a predecessor of today's description logics – was shown.

A first approach for reconciling OWL and rules in a decidable fashion was dubbed *Description Logic Programming* (DLP) and is discussed in [GHVD03]. In contrast to the approaches considered in this chapter, DLP is a common subset of both OWL DL and datalog, and thus it is strictly weaker than either formalism. Description Logic Rules were first introduced in [KRH08a], and a related extension toward computationally tractable ontology languages is studied in [KRH08b]. DL-safe rules were presented in [MSS05], where they were introduced as part of the KAON2 system.

The essential documents of the RIF specification are

- "RIF Core" [BHK⁺08], where the core language discussed above is defined,

- "RIF Basic Logic Dialect" [BK08a], which defines syntax and semantics of RIF-BLD upon which the definition of RIF-Core is based,

- "RIF RDF and OWL Compatibility" [dB08], where the semantics for importing OWL and RDF into RIF-BLD are described,

- "RIF Datatypes and Built-Ins 1.0" [PBK08], which defines RIF's basic datatype system and the *symbols spaces* that are used for constant symbols,

- "RIF Framework for Logic Dialects" [BK08b], which specifies a framework for guiding the definition of future logic-based RIF dialects,

- "RIF Production Rule Dialect" [dSMPH08], which defines the basic production rule language of RIF.

Besides the close integration of rules and ontologies presented in this chapter, there are further approaches of combining some forms of rule languages with OWL or with description logics in general. Many of those approaches consider rules in the sense of logic programming (see [Llo88] for a textbook introduction), focusing specifically on the non-monotonic inferencing features of the latter. Some noteworthy approaches are discussed in [MR07, MHRS06, Ros06, ELST04, DLNS98, MKH08]. This field of research also closely relates to the study of non-monotonic operators in description logics (independently of particular rule languages); further literature on this topic can be found in the references given in the above works.

Finally, various rather different approaches to rule-based modeling have been mentioned in Section 6.1. The most well-known logic programming language, Prolog, has been officially standardized by the International Organization for Standardization (ISO) in the standard ISO/IEC 13211. This document is not freely accessible online; a guide to the standard is given in the reference manual [DEDC96]. More application-oriented introductions to Prolog are given in [Clo03] and [CM03], while Prolog's theoretical foundations are elaborated in [Llo88]. Various other logic programming semantics have been proposed as alternatives or extensions to pure Prolog. An overview is given in [DEGV01], where many different logic programming formalisms are compared with respect to their expressivity and computational complexity. In particular, this article also discusses the computational complexity of datalog. Another logic programming based approach to knowledge representation is *F-Logic* [KLW95], which can be viewed as a predecessor of various rule dialects that are now developed in RIF. In particular, the frame notation is closely related to the syntactic features of F-Logic.

Logic programming has many commonalities with first-order logic, such as the use of a declarative semantics based on model theory. The area of production rules, in contrast, takes a rather different approach where semantics emerges from the (often partial and informal) specification of evaluation algorithms. This operational view closely connects semantics to implementation, and different production rule engines typically implement different rule languages. A popular system and rule language is *CLIPS* [GR04], an extended version of which is supported by *Jess* [Hil03]. Various kinds of production rules are used in a variety of other systems such as *JBoss Rules*[10] (formerly *Drools*), Soar,[11] *Jeops*,[12] or even the business rule engine in *Microsoft BizTalk Server*.[13] While the rule languages supported by those systems may be very different, many of them are based on an evaluation strategy known as the *Rete Algorithm*, which was introduced in [For82].

---

[10]http://www.jboss.org/drools/

[11]http://sitemaker.umich.edu/soar

[12]http://www.di.ufpe.br/~jeops/

[13]http://www.microsoft.com/biztalk/

Chapter 7

Query Languages

In previous chapters, we learned about a number of possibilities for specifying information in a machine-readable way. RDF allows us to structure and relate pieces of information, and RDFS and OWL introduced further expressive means for describing more complex logical relations. The latter was further extended by means of logical rules that could be combined with OWL. For each of those description languages, we also introduced a notion of logical entailment: RDF(S) documents may entail other documents (Chapter 3), and OWL knowledge bases – possibly augmented with rules – can imply new axioms (Chapters 4, 5, 6).

But how exactly are we going to access in practice information which is thus specified? In principle, logical conclusions can be used for this purpose as well. As an example, one can query whether a knowledge base logically entails that the book "Foundations of Semantic Web Technologies" was published by CRC Press. To this end, one could cast the question into a triple like the following:

```
<http://semantic-web-book.org/uri>
  <http://example.org/publishedBy>   <http://crc-press.com/uri> .
```

An RDF processing tool now could check whether the RDF graph constituted by this single triple is actually entailed by a given RDF document. This approach can be used to formulate a number of queries, using RDF or OWL as the basic query language the semantics of which is clearly specified by the established semantics of these languages.

In practice, however, much more is often required. On the one hand, only a rather restricted set of questions can be asked, especially in simple formalisms such as RDF. We will see in this chapter that there are a number of interesting questions that cannot be expressed in either RDF or OWL. On the other hand, retrieving information from a knowledge base is not just a question of query expressivity, but must also address practical requirements such as post-processing and formatting of results. Typically a large knowledge base is not queried for *all* instances of a given class, but only for a limited number. Moreover, it is sometimes desirable to filter results using criteria that are not represented in the logical semantics of the underlying language. For instance, one might look for all English language literals specified in an RDF document

– but language information in RDF is an internal feature of single literals, and has no separate representation that could be queried in RDF.

In this chapter, we have a closer look at some important query languages for RDF and OWL. For RDF, this query language is SPARQL, while for OWL DL we have to be content with so-called *conjunctive queries* as a basic formalism that is not part of a standardized query language yet. We will see that the latter is also closely related to the kind of rules introduced in Chapter 6.

7.1 SPARQL: Query Language for RDF

SPARQL (pronounced as *sparkle*) denotes the *SPARQL Protocol and RDF Query Language*,[1] a rather young standard for querying RDF-based information and for representing the results. The core of SPARQL are simple queries in the form of simple graph patterns, similar to the initial query example in this chapter. On top of that, SPARQL provides a number of advanced functions for constructing advanced query patterns, for stating additional filtering conditions, and for formatting the final output. In this chapter, we only consider the *SPARQL query language* as the core of the formalism – the *SPARQL protocol* for communicating queries, and the *SPARQL result format* for representing query results in XML are not detailed. Readers familiar with SQL will notice many similarities in SPARQL's syntax and usage. It should not be overlooked that both languages are still fundamentally different since they operate on very different data structures.

7.1.1 Simple SPARQL Queries

SPARQL is conceived as a query language for (RDF) graphs, and accordingly simple RDF graphs are used as fundamental query patterns. Such query graphs, in essence, are represented using the Turtle syntax. SPARQL additionally introduces query variables to specify parts of a query pattern that should be retrieved as a result. Furthermore, each query specifies how results should be formatted. Let us now consider the following example:

```
PREFIX ex:  <http://example.org/>
SELECT ?title ?author
WHERE  { ?book    ex:publishedBy  <http://crc-press.com/uri> .
         ?book    ex:title        ?title .
         ?book    ex:author       ?author }
```

---

[1] A "recursive acronym."

This query consists of three major parts, denoted by the upper-case key words PREFIX, SELECT, and WHERE. The key word PREFIX declares a namespace prefix, similar to @prefix in Turtle notation. In SPARQL, however, no full stop is required to finish the declaration.

The key word SELECT determines the general result format – we will encounter further possible formats later on. The statements after SELECT refer to the remainder of the query: the listed names are identifiers of variables for which return values are to be retrieved. Consequently, the above query returns all values for the variables ?title and ?author.

The actual query is initiated by the key word WHERE. It is followed by a *simple graph pattern*, enclosed in curly braces. In our case, it consists of three triples in Turtle notation. A particular difference from Turtle is the fact that the triples may contain not only URIs and QNames, but also *variable identifiers* such as ?book. Intuitively speaking, these identifiers represent possible concrete values that are to be obtained in the process of answering the query. As our example shows, variables can be used in multiple places to express that the same value must be used in those positions. Another minor difference from Turtle is that not all triples need to be finished with a full stop – this symbol is rather used as a separator between triples. Yet a final full stop could well be added to the query pattern without changing the query's meaning.

Summing up, we can thus say that the above query retrieves all things that have been published by CRC Press, and for which both title and author are known. For building the final result, (pairs of) title and author are selected in each case. A concrete RDF document is required to see the practical effects of this query, so let us consider the following:

```
@prefix  ex:    <http://example.org/> .
@prefix  book:  <http://semantic-web-book.org/uri/> .
ex:SemanticWeb ex:publishedBy  <http://crc-press.com/uri> ;
               ex:title "Foundations of Semantic Web Technologies" ;
               ex:author book:Hitzler, book:Krötzsch, book:Rudolph .
```

For this document, the example query would retrieve the following result where we abbreviate the title for reasons of space:

title	author
"Foundations of ..."	http://semantic-web-book.org/uri/Hitzler
"Foundations of ..."	http://semantic-web-book.org/uri/Krötzsch
"Foundations of ..."	http://semantic-web-book.org/uri/Rudolph

As we can see, the use of SELECT creates a query output that is a table. To preserve the tabular structure it is required to include certain result values (the title in our case) multiple times. Moreover, we find that the result contains

values only for those variables that have been mentioned explicitly in the
SELECT line. The variable ?book, in contrast, is part of the query but has not
been selected for the result. We will discuss the available result formats in
SPARQL in greater detail later on, including some alternatives to SELECT.

7.1.2 Simple Graph Patterns: Triples and Variables

A simple graph pattern has been used in the above example to describe
the sought information. In general, simple graph patterns may represent arbitrary RDF graphs that should be searched in the given data set. SPARQL's
assumptions on the semantics of the underlying knowledge base are rather
weak, and only simple RDF entailment is taken into account. In particular,
neither RDFS nor OWL is directly supported. Simple graph patterns without
a specific semantics thus play a major role in SPARQL.

We are already quite familiar with the basic syntax of simple graph patterns,
since it is largely similar to the Turtle syntax for RDF. This also includes Turtle's abbreviations with semicolon and comma, as well as the specific ways of
encoding blank nodes and RDF collections. Thus we can already formulate a
number of interesting queries without learning any new syntax. Yet, SPARQL
also extends Turtle in various ways which will be detailed in this section.

First of all, variables are clearly an important ingredient of most queries.
Those specific identifiers are distinguished by the initial symbol ? or $, fol-
lowed by a sequence of numbers, letters, and various admissible special symbols such as the underscore. The special symbol ? or $ at the beginning of
variable identifiers is not part of the actual variable name, such that, e.g.,
the identifiers ?author and $author refer to the same variable. The choice
of variable names is of course arbitrary and has no impact on the meaning of
the query – yet it is advisable to pick a suggestive name like ?title instead
of the (formally equivalent) name ?_02ft.

Variables may appear as the subject and object in a triple, but also as
a predicate. The next query, e.g., retrieves all known relations between the
given URIs. Here we use a base namespace for abbreviating the query, similar
to the way we have used xml:base in RDF/XML. Identifiers that lack a
protocol part, such as <uri> below, are interpreted by appending them to the
base URI:

```
BASE    <http://semantic-web-book.org/>
SELECT ?relation
WHERE   { <uri>    ?relation    <http://crc-press.com/uri> }
```

Based on our earlier example document, this query would result in a table
with the URI http://example.org/publishedBy as its only entry. As in

Turtle, we may use line breaks and spaces rather freely in order to improve query readability.

Besides the use of variables, another peculiarity of SPARQL is the fact that literals are allowed to appear as the subjects of triples. This possibility was included to account for possible future extensions of RDF. For current documents, simple RDF entailment can never lead to such a triple being deduced, and hence queries with literal subjects would simply fail.

7.1.3   Blank Nodes in SPARQL

Blank nodes in SPARQL again deserve special consideration. On the one hand, it must be clarified what exactly a blank node means within a graph pattern. On the other hand, we may ask whether a blank node may appear in a query result, and how it should be understood in this case.

As in Turtle, blank nodes are of course allowed to occur as the subjects or objects of triples. When processing a query, they are treated like variables, i.e., they can be replaced by arbitrary elements of the given RDF graph. However, those replacements do not belong to the result of the query, and blank nodes cannot be chosen with SELECT. Using bnode IDs as in RDF, it is possible to ensure that multiple bnodes (of the same ID) refer to the same element. In contrast, a bnode ID that was once used in a simple graph pattern may not be used again in another graph pattern of the same query – this restriction will only become relevant later on when dealing with queries that comprise more than one simple graph pattern.

Besides the use of bnodes in queries, it may also happen that SPARQL returns blank nodes as part of a result. In other words, query variables might be instantiated by blank nodes. This situation is simply a consequence of the graph-oriented semantics of SPARQL. As we shall see below, SPARQL retrieves results essentially by looking for sub-graphs in the given RDF document. These graphs of course may contain blank nodes, which can be represented in the result only by means of blank nodes.

But how exactly are bnodes in SPARQL results to be interpreted? Most importantly, they only assert the existence of a corresponding element in the input graph, but they do not provide any information about the identity of this element. This does not preclude bnodes in results from having IDs – we will explain below why those may indeed be required to preserve some information in the result – but those IDs are not determined by the IDs occurring in the input graph. In other words, it is purely coincidental if a returned blank node uses an ID that is also occurring within the given RDF document or query.

If, however, multiple blank nodes in a query result are using the same ID, then it is certain that they do indeed refer to the same element. This might occur, e.g., if an auxiliary node that was introduced for an RDF container is connected to multiple elements. The individual table rows of a query result are thus not independent with respect to the bnode IDs they are using. These considerations also have some interesting ramifications for comparing results. Consider, e.g., the following three result tables:

subj	value
_:a	"for"
_:b	"example"

subj	value
_:y	"for"
_:g	"example"

subj	value
_:z	"for"
_:z	"example"

The first two result tables are completely equivalent, since renaming blank nodes is not significant. The last result, in contrast, is different from both other results, since it specifies that the same blank node occurs in both rows.

7.1.4 Complex Graph Patterns: Groups, Options, and Alternatives

SPARQL allows us to build complex graph patterns from multiple simple ones. Such a compound pattern is generally referred to as a *group graph pattern*. Group patterns can be used to restrict the scope of query conditions to certain parts of the pattern. Moreover, it is possible to define sub-patterns as being optional, or to provide multiple alternative patterns.

The main prerequisite for those applications is the possibility of separating multiple simple patterns from each other. Curly braces are used for this purpose in SPARQL. Indeed, we have already used this syntax in all of our earlier query examples, where single simple graph patterns have been enclosed in curly braces. We have thus produced a very basic group pattern containing a single simple pattern. It is also possible to represent such simple queries as a group of multiple simple patterns, though this will not affect the meaning of the query. The following query, e.g., corresponds to the previous example that featured only the outermost braces:

```
PREFIX ex:  <http://example.org/>
SELECT ?title ?author
WHERE  { { ?book    ex:publishedBy  <http://crc-press.com/uri> .
           ?book    ex:title        ?title }
         { }
           ?book    ex:author       ?author
         }
```

This example contains a group pattern with three elements: first another group pattern containing a simple pattern of two triples, second an *empty* group pattern, and third a simple graph pattern with a single triple. Empty group patterns are allowed but of little use – their only effect is in separating multiple simple patterns.

Dividing patterns in separate groups becomes interesting when additional expressive features are added. A first option for doing this is the specification of *optional patterns*. Such patterns are indicated by the key word OPTIONAL. Optional patterns are not required to occur in all retrieved results, but if they are found, may produce bindings of variables and thus extend the query result. The next pattern, e.g., matches all books of CRC Press for which a title is provided. The authors of each book are retrieved if given, but not all results need to have specified authors.

```
{ ?book      ex:publishedBy  <http://crc-press.com/uri> .
  ?book      ex:title        ?title .
  OPTIONAL { ?book    ex:author     ?author }
}
```

As this example suggests, OPTIONAL refers to the subsequent group pattern. In general, every occurrence of OPTIONAL must be followed by a group pattern, which is exactly that pattern that the key word refers to. A new aspect of optional patterns is the fact that variables in query results might possibly be unbound. In our example this applies to the variable ?author to which a value is assigned only in cases where the optional pattern is found. If a variable is not bound for a particular result, the corresponding cell in the result table is simply left empty. Note that this is clearly not the same as if a blank node occurs in the result: a blank node indicates the existence of an element that was not specified further, while an unbound variable expresses the lack of any matching element. Even if the input data provides only a blank node to refer to some author in the above example, the variable ?author would still be bound to a value. The query therefore does not just retrieve authors that are identified by some URI. Below, we will consider filters that can be used to impose further constraints on result values to realize even such queries.

A query may easily contain multiple optional patterns that are checked independently. The following example shows such a pattern together with a possible result table that shows some of the situations that might be encountered in a real data set.

```
{ ?book      ex:publishedBy  <http://crc-press.com/uri> .
  OPTIONAL { ?book    ex:title     ?title  }
  OPTIONAL { ?book    ex:author    ?author }
}
```

book	title	author
http://example.org/book1	"Title1"	http://example.org/author1
http://example.org/book2	"Title2"	
http://example.org/book3	"Title3"	_:a
http://example.org/book4		_:a
http://example.org/book5		

Group graph patterns are not only used for representing optional patterns, but also for specifying multiple *alternative patterns*. This is accomplished by means of the key word UNION that can be used to join patterns. This expression is closely related to logical disjunction: every result must match at least one of the provided alternative patterns, but it might well match more than one (i.e. UNION is not an exclusive or). The following example shows a pattern with two alternatives:

```
{ ?book      ex:publishedBy   <http://crc-press.com/uri> .
  { ?book      ex:author        ?author . } UNION
  { ?book      ex:writer        ?author . }
}
```

Here we have used two alternatives to account for multiple URIs that might possibly be used to refer to the author of a book. An important aspect of alternative patterns is that the individual parts are processed independently of each other. This means that the fact that both alternative patterns refer to the same variable ?author does not impose any additional restrictions. The results of the query are obtained by taking the union of the results of two separate queries of the form

```
{ ?book      ex:publishedBy   <http://crc-press.com/uri> .
  { ?book      ex:author        ?author . }
}
```

and

```
{ ?book      ex:publishedBy   <http://crc-press.com/uri> .
  { ?book      ex:writer        ?author . }
}
```

As in the case of OPTIONAL, the key word UNION can be used more than once to combine the results of multiple alternative patterns. When combining OPTIONAL and UNION, it is important to know exactly how individual patterns are grouped. This is illustrated by the following example:

```
{ ?book      ex:publishedBy   <http://crc-press.com/uri> .
  { ?book      ex:author        ?author . } UNION
  { ?book      ex:writer        ?author . } OPTIONAL
  { ?author    ex:lastName       ?name . }
}
```

This query could allow for two possible interpretations. One possibility is that OPTIONAL refers to the entire preceding pattern, such that an optional name is sought for all results that match the first part of the query. Alternatively, it might be that UNION refers to the entire following pattern, such that the OPTIONAL pattern is merely a part of the second alternative pattern; then the optional name would only be sought for authors that were found to be the object of ex:writer. SPARQL specifies the first of these two options as the correct interpretation, so the above example could also be formulated as follows:

```
{ ?book     ex:publishedBy  <http://crc-press.com/uri> .
  { { ?book     ex:author    ?author . } UNION
    { ?book     ex:writer    ?author . }
  } OPTIONAL { ?author   ex:lastName   ?name . }
}
```

A few simple rules can be used to determine the correct interpretation in arbitrary cases. First we may observe that both UNION and OPTIONAL refer to *two* patterns: a preceding and a succeeding one. For OPTIONAL this may at first be a little surprising, but the previous example should have illustrated why it is relevant to know the preceding pattern in this case as well. Both key words thus are binary operators. The following rules unambiguously describe how to correctly interpret their combination:

1. OPTIONAL always refers to exactly one group graph pattern immediately to its right.

2. OPTIONAL and UNION are left-associative, and none of the operators has precedence over the other.

Being left-associative means that each operator refers to all of the expressions that are found to its left within the same group pattern. The fact that there is no further precedence merely states that the order of the operators is indeed all that has to be considered. A well-known example where this is not the case iw multiplication and addition, where the former has precedence over the latter. Thus, we can put braces in query patterns by starting from the rightmost operator and grouping all patterns found to its left (within the same group, of course). The next example illustrates this:

```
{ {s1 p1 o1} OPTIONAL {s2 p2 o2} UNION {s3 p3 o3}
            OPTIONAL {s4 p4 o4} OPTIONAL {s5 p5 o5}
}
```

Grouping these patterns explicitly thus results in the following:

```
{ { { { {s1 p1 o1} OPTIONAL {s2 p2 o2}
      } UNION {s3 p3 o3}
    } OPTIONAL {s4 p4 o4}
  } OPTIONAL {s5 p5 o5}
}
```

By left-associativity, each operator indeed refers to all preceding patterns. It is not hard to see that an alternative, right-associative way of grouping patterns would be far less natural, since it would lead to nested optional patterns.

7.1.5   Queries with Data Values

A number of different datatypes can be used in RDF, and especially many datatypes of XML Schema are available. Naturally, querying for typed and untyped RDF literals is particularly important in SPARQL as well. It is, however, necessary to distinguish between the various possible forms of literals and datatypes, such that a number of specific situations can occur. The following RDF document recalls the various kinds of literals that were discussed in Section 2.3.1:

```
@prefix xsd: <http://www.w3.org/2001/XMLSchema#> .
@prefix ex:  <http://example.org/> .
ex:s1  ex:p  "test" .
ex:s2  ex:p  "test"^^xsd:string .
ex:s3  ex:p  "test"@en .
ex:s4  ex:p  "42"^^xsd:integer .
ex:s5  ex:p  "test"^^<http://example.org/datatype1>" .
```

The example shows an untyped literal, a literal of type xsd:string, an untyped literal with language setting en, a literal of type xsd:integer, and finally a literal with a custom datatype – as mentioned earlier, RDF does not require datatypes to stem from XML Schema only, and arbitrary URIs may be used to denote further types.

We will look at various example queries based on this input document. Let us first consider the following query pattern:

```
{ ?subject  <http://example.org/p>  "test" . }
```

What results could be expected from a query based on this pattern? The input data for ex:s1, ex:s2, and ex:s3 all seem to match the pattern to some extent, at least from a user perspective. As explained in Section 2.3.2, however, RDF strictly distinguishes typed and untyped literals, and literals with and without language setting. Hence, the property values for the three resources are different with respect to the simple RDF semantics, and the above query would indeed return ex:s1 as its only result. This behavior can of course be confusing, since the various literals do still appear rather similar. In addition, language settings in RDF/XML can be inherited, such that certain untyped literals might receive some language setting that was specified on a higher level, even if they have not been assigned such a setting explicitly. Language settings are not merely additional pieces of information, but rather lead to a completely different semantic interpretation that must also be taken into account when querying. To obtain ex:s2 or ex:s3 in query results, one would thus need to formulate different queries, using the exact representation of the literal values used in the input.

Yet there are cases when deviations from a given syntactic form in the RDF document may still lead to query results. This is shown by the next query:

```
{ ?subject  <http://example.org/p>  "042"^^xsd:integer . }
```

This query will usually return ex:s4, even though the number in the query includes a leading zero that is not given in the input document. Every SPARQL implementation that supports the datatype xsd:integer will recognize that both of these lexical descriptions refer to the same data value. This is of course only possible for known datatypes. Moreover, applications may take overlappings between value spaces into account, e.g., since certain decimal numbers (xsd:decimal) may describe values that can also be represented as integer numbers (xsd:integer). For unknown datatypes as in ex:s5, in contrast, the input string and datatype URI is compared with the one in the query, and a match will be found only if both agree exactly.

SPARQL also provides syntactic abbreviations for some particularly common datatypes. Plain numerical inputs are interpreted based on their syntactic form to refer to literals of type xsd:integer, xsd:decimal (if decimal digits are given), or as xsd:double (floating point number, used with exponential notations). The following pattern thus could also be used to retrieve ex:s4:

```
{ ?subject  <http://example.org/p>  42 . }
```

Besides numerical values, SPARQL allows only for the abbreviations **true** and **false** for the corresponding values of type xsd:boolean (truth values).

7.1.6   Filters

Our present knowledge about SPARQL allows us to query for basic patterns in RDF documents, including optional and alternative conditions and data literals. Yet, even this is still not enough for many practical applications. As an example, one often needs to query not just for a single exact data value, but for all values within a certain range. Likewise, we have no means yet to search for literals within which a certain word is contained. Another problem is the language settings that have been discussed in the previous section: how can we query for a value without being sure of its specified language? Those examples and many further queries are enabled in SPARQL by so-called *filters*.

Filters are additional conditions in a query that further restrict the set of matching results. As opposed to graph patterns, filters are not strictly based on the RDF data model, but may contain any requirement that can be checked computationally. Accordingly, filters occur in a variety of different forms that we will consider in greater detail below. Let us first have a look at a simple example:

```
PREFIX ex: <http://example.org/>
SELECT ?book WHERE
  { ?book      ex:publishedBy  <http://crc-press.com/uri> .
    ?book      ex:price        ?price
    FILTER (?price < 100)
  }
```

This query retrieves all books that were published by CRC Press, and for which the property ex:price has been assigned a value that is smaller than 100 (note that we use the abbreviated syntax for numerical literals that was introduced in Section 7.1.5). As the example shows, filter conditions are initiated by the key word FILTER. This is followed by the filter expression, typically with parameters, that evaluates to a concrete value (often "true" or "false") or that returns an error. The query results will comprise only those matches for which the given filter expressions effectively[2] evaluate to true. In our example, a filter function is given by the comparison operator < and the enclosing parentheses, and the parameters to this function are a constant value and a SPARQL variable.

Filter conditions always refer to the whole group graph pattern within which they appear. It is thus not relevant whether a filter is given at the beginning, at the end, or somewhere in the middle of a graph pattern. However, it usually does matter which group graph pattern a filter belongs to. As a basic

---

[2]SPARQL also defines which strings or numbers are considered to be "effectively true," to cover cases where filter functions are not Boolean.

principle, filters can be used in all group graph patterns, including those that belong to some optional or alternative condition.

SPARQL supports a multitude of filter functions. These functions can usually not be expressed in RDF, such that the RDF specification is not a suitable source for definitions of filters. However, suitable functions have already been defined in the context of the XML query languages *XQuery* and *XPath*, and SPARQL makes use of this specification as a basis for many filters. It can also be sensible to nest some of the available filter functions, e.g., to form a complex Boolean expression, or to compose numerical values with arithmetic operations before applying further filters. In the following sections, we introduce the most important filtering conditions.

7.1.6.1 Comparison Operators

Our first example above employed the comparison operator <. Similarly, SPARQL also supports the operators = ("equal"), > ("greater than"), <= ("less than or equal"), >= ("greater than or equal"), and != ("not equal"). Each of those operators is defined for all datatypes that SPARQL specifically supports, so that, e.g., specifications of time (xsd:dateTime,) too, can be compared in a meaningful way. The supported datatypes are xsd:boolean, xsd:string, xsd:dateTime,[3] as well as various numerical datatypes and untyped RDF literals without language settings. In each of those cases, the "natural" order is used for comparing literals, e.g., literals of type xsd:string are ordered alphabetically while xsd:decimal comes with the usual numerical order.

All other elements in RDF and all literals that have different (incompatible) datatypes are not comparable with the above operators. The only exceptions are = and !=, which can be used for all RDF elements. Those operators, however, create an error if two lexically different values with unknown datatype are given, since it is impossible in this case to determine whether both literals describe the same value or not. Thus, the equality operator behaves differently from the use of literal values in graph patterns, where literals of unknown types are compared syntactically; i.e. patterns with literals of unknown datatypes match exactly if they are syntactically equal.

7.1.6.2 Special Operators

SPARQL also defines a number of operators for accessing RDF-specific information. First of all, these are various unary operators for accessing specific parts of RDF literals. Figure 7.1 provides an overview. Using these functions, one can query, e.g., for all books for which the property "author," if specified, has a value of type xsd:string:

---

[3]Only if time zone information was given; the comparison always returns "false" otherwise.

BOUND(A)	true if A is a bound variable
isURI(A)	true if A is a URI
isBLANK(A)	true if A is a blank node
isLITERAL(A)	true if A is an RDF literal
STR(A)	maps RDF literals or URIs to the corresponding lexical representation of type xsd:string
LANG(A)	returns the language code of an RDF literal as xsd:string, or an empty string if no such setting is specified
DATATYPE(A)	returns the URI of an RDF literal's datatype or the value "xsd:string" for untyped literals without language setting; not applicable to literals with language settings

FIGURE 7.1:   Unary operators for accessing specific parts of RDF literals

```
PREFIX ex: <http://example.org/>
SELECT ?book WHERE
  { ?book     ex:publishedBy  <http://crc-press.com/uri> .
    OPTIONAL { ?book  ex:author  ?author . }
    FILTER ( DATATYPE(?author) =
                    <http://www.w3.org/2001/XMLSchema#string> )
  }
```

The following binary operators are also worth mentioning:

sameTERM(A,B)	true if A and B are the same RDF terms
langMATCHES(A,B)	true if the literal A is a language tag that matches the pattern B
REGEX(A,B)	true if the regular expression B can be matched to the string A

These functions deserve some further explanation. For example, one might ask what the difference might be between sameTERM and the equality symbol introduced above. The answer is that sameTERM performs a direct term comparison on RDF level, for which the specific semantics of certain datatypes is not taken into account. This also allows for the comparison of different literals of unknown datatypes.

The operator langMATCHES, too, has its justification, even though some language checks could be achieved by comparing the output of the above operator LANG with a given language constant. However, language settings may have hierarchical forms, such as in the case of en-GB. The condition

(LANG("Test"@en-GB) = "en" is not satisfied, but the alternative condition
langMATCHES(LANG("Test"@en-GB), "en") is. The pattern in langMATCHES
thus is interpreted in a more general way. Moreover, the special pattern "*"
can be used to filter for literals that have arbitrary language settings.

The function REGEX serves to match general patterns within strings. Regular
expressions are used for this purpose, and the special syntax of those is part
of the function and operator definitions for XPath 1.0 and XQuery 2.0. We
will not go into the details of this feature, but it should be noted that regular
expressions enable a rather powerful search for string patterns.[4] The following
query realizes a search for all things whose titles begin with "Foundations of"
(the special character ^ denotes the start of the string):

```
PREFIX ex: <http://example.org/>
SELECT ?book WHERE
  { ?book     ex:Title  ?title .
    FILTER ( REGEX(?title, "^Foundations of") )
  }
```

7.1.6.3 Boolean Operators

It can be useful to combine multiple filter conditions or to invert a condition to its opposite. For this purpose, SPARQL offers the operators &&
(logical conjunction, *and*), || (logical disjunction, *or*), and ! (logical nega-
tion, *not*). It is easy to see that conjunction and disjunction can be expressed
with the SPARQL features we encountered above, without using additional
filter operators. Conjunction can be expressed by simply using multiple filters
within one graph pattern, while for disjunction a graph pattern could be split
into multiple alternative patterns that use equal conditions but only one of
the disjunctive filter parts each. Negations, in contrast, provide additional
expressivity.

7.1.6.4 Arithmetic Operations

In addition, SPARQL offers various fundamental arithmetic operations that
can be used to combine numerical values. These are + (addition), - (subtrac-
tion), * (multiplication), and / (division).

---

[4]In general, searching strings by regular expressions is not easily implemented in an efficient
way, since common indexing methods for databases are not available for optimization – there
are good reasons why major Web search engines do not offer regular expressions in their
search.

7.1.6.5   Errors

Most filter functions can only be meaningfully applied to certain kinds of input data. The function +, e.g., can be used to compute the sum of two numbers, but it does not have a natural definition for the case where URIs are given as inputs. Unfortunately, it is not possible to prevent such situations by careful query construction: even if a particular RDF property is intended to have only numerical literals as values, it is always possible that a given RDF database includes triples where this is not the case. RDF is not powerful enough to enforce the use of intended datatypes. Moreover, variables that are used in an optional graph pattern may happen to be unbound, which is again not a suitable input for most filter functions.

It is therefore necessary to deal with the case that a filter function is invoked on inputs that it is not able to process in a meaningful way. For this reason, every filter function may also produce an error. If the expression used in FILTER returns an error, the effect is the same as if the filter expression had returned false. Yet the return value "error" is not the same as the return value "false" in all cases. For example, if an error occurs in the input to the logical negation function !, then the function will also produce an error. In general, most filter functions preserve any errors that occur in their inputs, so that errors within nested filter expressions are propagated. A notable exception is logical disjunction (||), which never returns an error if either input is true, no matter what the other input consists of. Details about the error handling of all filter functions are found in the SPARQL specifications; see Section 7.5 for pointers.

7.1.7   Result Formats

All of the above queries have used the key word SELECT to create a result table with the assignments of the selected variables. In this section, we encounter the further possible result formats CONSTRUCT, DESCRIBE, and ASK.

We have already seen a sufficient number of example queries using SELECT. The tabular representation of results that SELECT produces is well-suited for processing results one by one. In practical applications, such results are accessed either via some programming interface or returned in the form of XML-based result serializations. The key word SELECT is always followed by a list of variable names, or by the symbol *. The latter simply selects all variables that appear in the query for the result.

The tabular representation is particularly useful for processing results sequentially. If, in contrast, the structure and mutual relations of objects in the result are more important, an RDF document might actually be a more appropriate representation. Another problem is the undesirable duplication of (parts of) table rows that is often required to encode results into the strict tabular format. The next example shows this effect:

```
@prefix ex: <http://example.org/> .
ex:Alice    ex:email    "alice@example.org" .
ex:Alice    ex:email    "a_miller@example.org" .
ex:Alice    ex:phone    "123456789" .
ex:Alice    ex:phone    "987654321" .
```

The following SPARQL query retrieves the email addresses and telephone numbers of all persons within an RDF document:

```
PREFIX ex: <http://example.org/>
SELECT *
WHERE { ?person  ex:email  ?email .
        ?person  ex:phone  ?phone . }
```

Using this on the above RDF, we obtain the following table:

person	email	phone
`http://example.org/Alice`	`"alice@example.org"`	`"123456789"`
`http://example.org/Alice`	`"alice@example.org"`	`"987654321"`
`http://example.org/Alice`	`"a_miller@example.org"`	`"123456789"`
`http://example.org/Alice`	`"a_miller@example.org"`	`"987654321"`

Clearly, there is considerable redundancy in this result set. This is the case since the value for `?email` and the value for `?phone` are determined independently, such that all possible combinations of the matching values are valid solutions. In practice, such situations may easily occur with many more independent variables and it is not always possible to prevent this in simple ways. Obviously, the above result table is hardly suitable for presenting Alice's contact data to a user.

SPARQL thus can return results that are formatted as an RDF document presenting results in a possibly more adequate structure. The construction of such result graphs is requested by the key word `CONSTRUCT`. Where `SELECT` expects a list of variables, `CONSTRUCT` requires a *template* for the RDF document that is to be created. This might look as follows in the case of the previous example:

```
PREFIX ex: <http://example.org/>
CONSTRUCT { ?person  ex:mailbox     ?email .
            ?person  ex:telephone   ?phone . }
WHERE { ?person  ex:email  ?email .
        ?person  ex:phone  ?phone . }
```

The rather unspectacular result of this query would consist of an RDF document that is essentially the same as the input document, though the given template has changed the names of the predicates. However, CONSTRUCT can of course achieve a variety of more complex formattings. The exact result of a CONSTRUCT query can easily be derived from a similar query that uses the format SELECT *, simply by instantiating the CONSTRUCT template with the variable binding from each result row, and returning all of the resulting triples in a single RDF document. If URIs or literals appear more than once within those triples, they do of course refer to the same resource, so that result rows may be interrelated in the constructed RDF graph. A collection of variable assignments thus leads to a single, integrated result. On the other hand, the sequential processing of results is hardly possible with such a representation.

Blank nodes in templates play a special role when constructing RDF results. They do not represent single blank nodes in the final result, but are replaced by new blank nodes for each of the result's variable assignments – i.e. for each table row in SELECT format. This can be illustrated by the next query:

```
PREFIX ex: <http://example.org/>
CONSTRUCT { _id1  ex:email   ?email .
            _id1  ex:phone   ?phone .
            _id1  ex:person  ?person . }
WHERE { ?person  ex:email   ?email .
        ?person  ex:phone   ?phone . }
```

The resulting graph resembles the table that we have created with SELECT above. Each table row is represented by a blank node that has relations to the single entries of that row. The result therefore would contain the following triples:

```
_a ex:email "alice@example.org" ;
   ex:phone "123456789" ;            ex:person ex:Alice .
_b ex:email "alice@example.org" ;
   ex:phone "987654321" ;            ex:person ex:Alice .
_c ex:email "a_miller@example.org" ;
   ex:phone "123456789" ;            ex:person ex:Alice .
_d ex:email "a_miller@example.org" ;
   ex:phone "987654321" ;            ex:person ex:Alice .
```

Another interesting feature of CONSTRUCT is the possibility of inserting constant values into the result graph. It is even possible to create queries of the following form:

```
PREFIX ex: <http://example.org/>
CONSTRUCT { ex:Query   ex:hasResults  "Yes" . }
WHERE { ?person  ex:email   ?email .
        ?person  ex:phone   ?phone . }
```

This query returns a predefined RDF graph with a single triple whenever the query has any solutions, and an empty document otherwise. To simply find out whether a query has any results, however, SPARQL offers a simpler solution. Namely, queries with the key word ASK only return "true" or "false," depending on whether or not some result matches the query conditions. The key word WHERE is omitted in this case:

```
PREFIX ex: <http://example.org/>
ASK { ?person  ex:email   ?email .
      ?person  ex:phone   ?phone . }
```

Besides SELECT, CONSTRUCT, and ASK, SPARQL offers a fourth output format DESCRIBE. This is motivated by the observation that it is often not obvious in a distributed Web environment which data is relevant in a given context. Deciding which information is "relevant" for describing a particular object is of course strongly application dependent, and SPARQL thus does not provide a normative specification of the required output. A SPARQL query pattern can be used, however, to select a collection of resources to be described – which further properties of the selected objects are delivered then is left to the concrete implementation. An example query might look as follows:

```
PREFIX ex: <http://example.org/>
DESCRIBE <http://www.example.org/Alice> ?person
WHERE { ?person  ex:email   _a . }
```

This query requests a description for all URIs that match the query pattern for ?person, as well as for the fixed URI http://www.example.org/Alice. In a similar fashion, descriptions can be obtained for a list of variables, or simply for a list of fixed URIs (in which case the WHERE part can be omitted completely). If the above query were presented to an application for managing data about people, then one might expect the result to contain relevant contact information and possibly references to other people. A user could visualize these data by means of some generic RDF browsing tool, possibly selecting further resources for which more information could again be retrieved using DESCRIBE. Thus it is possible to search and browse an RDF database without knowing the details of its structure or the URIs of the referenced properties.

7.1.8   Modifiers

Various forms of query patterns and filters can be used to narrow down
the overall result set of a query. Nonetheless, queries in typical applications
may return large amounts of results that cannot be processed completely.
This is specifically problematic in decentralized Web environments, where
one often has no way of knowing how large a result set a query to a remote
Web Service might return. SPARQL therefore includes so-called *(solution
sequence) modifiers* for controlling details regarding the form and size of result
lists.

When limiting the amount of returned results, it is useful to specify the
order of results as well. When only part of the results is to be processed,
one can thus ensure beginning with the "topmost" results according to some
meaningful order.

```
SELECT ?book, ?price
WHERE { ?book  <http://example.org/price>  ?price . }
ORDER BY ?price
```

This query is expected to sort books in ascending order based on their
price, i.e. with cheapest items on top. The order of sorting can be specified explicitly by replacing ?price with DESC(?price) (descending order), or
with ASC(?price) (ascending order, default). ORDER BY of course affects only
results obtained with SELECT, since CONSTRUCT, ASK, and DESCRIBE do not
return results in a format that is sensitive to the order of results.

In the above example, one would assume all possible values for ?price
to be numerical, such that the order corresponds to the natural ordering of
these values. For numerical values and a number of other kinds of literal,
a suitable ordering has already been given for the operator <, as introduced
in Section 7.1.6. URIs are sorted in SPARQL by considering their syntactic
form as strings that are treated like values of type xsd:string using <. But
which behavior is to be expected when values of different types are bound
to a particular variable? For instance, one of the bindings for ?price in the
above example could actually be a URI, even though this case would probably
constitute an error within the data set. To still be able to return a well-
defined result in such cases, SPARQL specifies an order among different types
of RDF elements. Whenever two elements of different kinds are compared,
the following order is applied (smallest elements first):

1. no value (the variable by which results are ordered is not bound)

2. blank nodes

3. URIs

4. RDF literals

In general, SPARQL does not specify how literals of different datatypes are to be compared. Only for the case where a literal of type `xsd:string` is compared to an untyped literal that has the same lexical value, the untyped literal is defined to be smaller. The order among two unbound variables, two blank nodes, or two literals of unknown datatype is also not defined, and can be different in individual implementations, which might possibly support additional datatypes for which SPARQL does not prescribe any order. Moreover, it is possible to sort results by more than one variable. In this case, the order of statements determines its relevance: only if the first selected variable contains the same value for two different result bindings, the second variable is used for sorting, and so on. The order can then be defined separately for each variable, as, e.g., in `ORDER BY DESC(?price) ?title` which realizes a descending order by price and an (ascending) alphabetic order by title for items with the same price.

A crucial feature for essentially any query language is the possibility of selecting a slice of a result sequence. In SPARQL, this is achieved with the parameters `LIMIT` and `OFFSET`. Those key words allow us to select a result segment containing at most as many results as specified by `LIMIT`, and starting with the result at the position given in `OFFSET`.

```
SELECT * WHERE { ?s ?p ?o . }  ORDER BY ?s  LIMIT 5  OFFSET 25
```

This query, e.g., shows the five triples starting with triple number 25, according to the order of subject elements (presumably URIs). The slicing parameters thus allow for a piecewise retrieval of results, as is common for the output of many search engines. Which result is the 25th in a concrete case of course depends on the chosen result order. If no such order is specified in the query, the result of using `LIMIT` and `OFFSET` is thus not predictable in general. The order might even change from query to query (based on implementation details), such that no reliable retrieval is possible at all. Queries that select a certain segment of the result set therefore should always define a concrete order using `ORDER BY`. For this reason, `ORDER BY` is still useful for `CONSTRUCT`, `ASK`, and `DESCRIBE`.

A final option for making large result sets more manageable is to remove unnecessary repetition from the result list. In particular, it is often useful if no two result rows are exactly identical. The latter is achieved with the key word `DISTINCT`, which is only allowed to occur immediately after `SELECT`. Indeed, this feature would clearly be of little use for all other result formats (though, arguably, it could still have some effect; see Exercise 7.6). Results in which all variables are bound to the same RDF terms are combined into a single row. It should be noted that this does not necessarily eliminate all redundancy from the result. For example, it could happen that two rows differ only in the ID of an occurring blank node. As discussed in Section 7.1.3, the ID of a blank node in a result can in fact be relevant, but only in cases where the same ID is used in other triples. It would be too complicated (and computationally costly) to try to eliminate all forms of redundancy, so DISTINCT treats only the most obvious cases.

If all parameters discussed in this section are to be combined, then it is essential to define the order of their application. SPARQL defines the following sequence of processing steps:

1. Sort results based on ORDER BY.

2. Remove non-selected variables from the result set (*projection*).

3. Remove duplicate results, if requested.

4. Remove the number of initial results as specified by OFFSET.

5. Remove all results after the number specified by LIMIT.

Based on this processing sequence, one can, e.g., tell that results might also be sorted by variables that are not selected for the result, whereas DISTINCT is based on the selected set of variables only. OFFSET and LIMIT in turn refer to the possibly reduced result set that remains after DISTINCT was taken into account.

7.1.9　Semantics and Algebra of SPARQL

Up to now, we have always described the meaning of SPARQL queries rather informally. While this is useful for a general understanding, it is hardly satisfactory for defining the correct behavior of a SPARQL implementation in an objective way. Naturally, any standard must provide clear criteria for determining whether or not a given tool conforms to that standard. For this reason, the SPARQL specification, too, encompasses a formal semantics, which strives to clarify the admissible result for any conceivable SPARQL query and queried data set. In this section, we have a closer look at this semantics. Though our treatment includes a concrete algorithmic evaluation for SPARQL, it is by no means necessary that SPARQL tools implement the algorithms described below – as long as they produce the same results, they may choose any implementation technique and optimization.

The core of the SPARQL semantics is the so-called *SPARQL algebra*, a system of clearly defined computational operations which can be used to calculate the result of a query. In this sense, SPARQL resembles SQL – the most relevant query language for relational databases – which is based on the *relational algebra*. Some of the computational operations that are used by

SPARQL are indeed very similar to those employed for defining SQL. On the other hand, the formal semantics of SPARQL thus is less closely related to the model theoretic semantics of RDF and OWL.[5] Besides the SPARQL algebra as such, it is of course also necessary to define how to transform SPARQL queries into expressions of this algebra in the first place. This section is concerned only with the direct computation of query results. These can then be formatted in various ways using the formats introduced in Section 7.1.7; yet all formats base their output upon the same underlying collection of query results that is determined by the SPARQL algebra.

7.1.9.1 Translating Queries to SPARQL Algebra

The SPARQL algebra is constituted by a number of computational operations representing the various expressive features of a SPARQL query. One distinguishes operators that describe graph patterns from those that express solution sequence modifiers. The graph pattern operators that we consider are *BGP* (basic graph pattern), *Join* (conjunctions), *LeftJoin* (optional conditions), *Filter*, and *Union*. In principle, each of these operators returns the result of the sub-query it describes, which is essentially a representation of the corresponding result table. By computing the result of a nested expression formed from these operators, the overall result of a corresponding query can be determined.

To arrive at such a computable expression, the graph pattern of a SPARQL query is successively replaced by an expression using these operators. Let us consider the following example pattern:

```
{ ?book    ex:price    ?price .   FILTER (?price < 15)
  OPTIONAL { ?book    ex:title    ?title .  }
  { ?book    ex:author    ex:Shakespeare .  } UNION
  { ?book    ex:author    ex:Marlowe .  }
}
```

As a first step, all abbreviations of triples and URIs within the query graph are expanded. Thereafter, all simple graph patterns (lists of triples) are expressed using the operator *BGP*, using the list of triples as its only argument.

---

[5]This apparent gap can be bridged by alternative formulations of the SPARQL semantics; pointers to related literature are given in Section 7.5.

```
{ BGP(?book <http://example.org/price> ?price.)
  FILTER (?price < 15)
  OPTIONAL {BGP(?book <http://example.org/title> ?title.)}
  {BGP(?book <http://example.org/author>
                      <http://example.org/Shakespeare>.)} UNION
  {BGP(?book <http://example.org/author>
                      <http://example.org/Marlowe>.)}
}
```

Next, all occurrences of UNION are expressed using the binary operator *Union*. In case of a longer chain of alternatives, the patterns are processed two at a time in accordance with the association rules for UNION (recall that UNION is left-associative). In any case, UNION refers only to the directly adjacent expressions. Disjunctions in SPARQL therefore are binding stronger than conjunctions (encoded as mere juxtaposition of patterns).

```
{ BGP(?book <http://example.org/price> ?price.)
  FILTER (?price < 15)
  OPTIONAL {BGP(?book <http://example.org/title> ?title.)}
  Union({BGP(?book <http://example.org/author>
                      <http://example.org/Shakespeare>.)},
        {BGP(?book <http://example.org/author>
                      <http://example.org/Marlowe>.)})
}
```

Group graph patterns are now resolved from inside to outside, i.e. starting with the innermost pattern. The operators used for this purpose have the following intuitive meaning:

$Join(P_1, P_2)$	The results P_1 and P_2 are combined conjunctively.
$Filter(F, P)$	The filter expression F is applied to the result P.
$LeftJoin(P_1, P_2, F)$	The results of P_1 are conjunctively combined with the results of P_2 and the filter condition F is applied; the results of P_1 that are eliminated by this operation are directly added to the output.

In each step, we consider one of the innermost graph patterns P, i.e., all possibly existing sub-patterns have already been processed. At first, all filter conditions are removed from P. For later reference, these removed filter expressions are combined into a single expression using && (conjunction); we call the resulting aggregated filter condition AF. Later, AF is re-introduced as a parameter to the operator *Filter*. Note that the following transformation rules take the possible occurrence of *Filter* into account, since the algorithm is working from inside to outside, such that this operator may have been introduced in earlier steps of the transformation.

After removing all filter conditions, P consists simply of a list of various SPARQL expressions containing parts in SPARQL algebra that have already been processed, and this list will be processed successively. In the process we construct a new algebra expression R that will be the result of the algorithm. Initially, this expression is *empty*; this state is represented by the empty SPARQL expression Z that simply encodes no condition or variable binding. Now the following steps are executed for each sub-expression SE that occurs in P:

- If SE is of the form OPTIONAL *Filter(F,A)* then set R := *LeftJoin(R, A, F)*.

- Otherwise, if SE is of the form OPTIONAL *A* then set R := *LeftJoin(R, A, true)*.

- Otherwise set R := *Join(R, SE)*.

In this way, a nested algebraic expression R is constructed. If the filter expression AF computed initially is not empty, then it is now added to R: set R:=*Filter(AF, R)*. Finally, the processed pattern P is replaced by the computed expression R. In this way, all sub-patterns of the query graph can be transformed.

In our running example, there are multiple innermost patterns that contain only a single expression with the operator BGP and that have no filter conditions. These parts are replaced by single *Join* expressions, within which the empty expression Z appears.

```
{ BGP(?book <http://example.org/price> ?price.)
  FILTER (?price < 15)
  OPTIONAL
      Join(Z, BGP(?book <http://example.org/title> ?title.))
  Union( Join(Z, BGP(?book <http://example.org/author>
                        <http://example.org/Shakespeare>.)),
        Join(Z, BGP(?book <http://example.org/author>
                        <http://example.org/Marlowe>.)))
}
```

Now it only remains to replace the outer pattern, containing a filter condition, an optional expression, and two further expressions (*BGP* and *Union*). This finishes the transformation and we arrive at the following overall expression:

```
Filter((?price < 15),
 Join(
  LeftJoin(
   Join(Z, BGP(?book <http://example.org/price> ?price.)),
   Join(Z, BGP(?book <http://example.org/title> ?title.)),
   true
  ), Union( Join(Z, BGP(?book <http://example.org/author>
                        <http://example.org/Shakespeare>.)),
         Join(Z, BGP(?book <http://example.org/author>
                        <http://example.org/Marlowe>.) ))
 )
)
```

One can simplify *Join* expressions that contain the empty expression Z as one of their parameters by replacing them with their other parameters. This is allowed since Z is the *neutral element* of the *Join* operation – similar to the way in which 0 is the neutral element of addition. With a little exercise, it is not too difficult to transform arbitrary SPARQL queries directly into SPARQL query expressions, without necessarily documenting each intermediate step. To answer the query, we now simply need to calculate the result of this expression, not entirely unlike the way in which we would calculate the numerical result of an arithmetic expression.

7.1.9.2 Calculations in SPARQL Algebra

It has been mentioned above that every operator of the SPARQL algebra essentially returns a query result which might be further processed by other operators in case of nestings. To explain how to calculate the result of algebra expressions, we therefore must first define what exactly we mean when speaking of a "query result" in this context. We can well imagine results in the form of tables, consisting of individual table rows. Each table row in turn represents a variable binding, where some of the variables might be unbound (and thus are not assigned any value). Therefore, each table row can formally be encoded as a *partial function* that maps variables to RDF terms. An RDF term might be a blank node, a URI, or an RDF literal. To avoid confusion with other short names and identifiers, we will usually denote such partial functions by the Greek letter μ. Such a "result row" μ is often called a *solution* for a given query, and the set of variables that is mapped by μ to an RDF term is referred to as the *domain* of μ. The function μ is partial since it does not need to assign a value to every variable.

Every result table contains an arbitrary number of such variable assignments (or "solutions") in a certain order. We can thus consider a result to be simply a sequence of solutions, and this is what we will always have in mind when speaking of a "result" within this section.[6] To imagine and display such results, it is still most convenient to use the same tables as before. Every operator of the SPARQL algebra thus is a function that returns a result of this form. The input parameters of each of these functions usually are again results or filter conditions, with the exception of *BGP*. The previously introduced expression Z represents the empty result, which contains exactly one solution that does not assign a value to any variable, i.e. a function that is as "partial" as possible. It will become apparent from the following definitions why this is more appropriate than using the empty sequence as a way of interpreting Z. Now we can proceed by giving a proper definition to each of the SPARQL algebra operations. This definition of course must refer to a given input RDF document, to which the query was directed. For further reference, we will call the corresponding RDF graph G.

A partial function μ is a solution for an expression of the form "*BGP(list of triples)*" exactly if the following two conditions are satisfied:

1. The domain of μ consists exactly of the variables that occur in the given list of triples.

2. It is possible to replace the blank nodes in the given triples by RDF terms in such a way that the RDF graph that is obtained by applying μ to those triples occurs in the input graph G.

In other words: a solution μ for a simple graph pattern must assign RDF terms to variables in such a way that the given pattern can be found in the queried document. In this process, blank nodes are interpreted as place holders which might represent other RDF terms; hence the initial replacement in the second condition. The sequence (in arbitrary order) consisting of all such solutions is the result returned by *BGP*. In the special case that no triples have been specified at all, the above definition allows only for a single solution, which does not assign a value to any variable. The result of *BGP* in this case thus corresponds to the interpretation of the empty pattern Z.

Strictly speaking, the above definition contains two replacement steps: one for blank nodes, and one for variables. The order of these replacements is important to ensure that blank nodes introduced by μ are not further replaced by other RDF terms. Otherwise one would obtain arbitrarily many solutions by simply assigning all variables to blank nodes.

Now we can also define results for all other operators. In some cases, this will require us to form a *union of two solutions*. A pair of solutions μ_1 and μ_2 is said to be *compatible* if every variable that is mapped by both μ_1 and μ_2 is also mapped to the same RDF term by both solutions. If μ_1 and μ_2 are

---

[6]The SPARQL specification actually encodes results by so-called *multi-sets*, i.e. "unordered sequences," as long as their order is not defined. We simplify our presentation by using sequences right from the start, even if the initial order of solutions is not further specified.

```
@prefix ex:  <http://example.org/> .
@prefix xsd: <http://www.w3.org/2001/XMLSchema#> .
ex:Hamlet            ex:author  ex:Shakespeare ;
                     ex:price   "10.50"^^xsd:decimal .
ex:Macbeth           ex:author  ex:Shakespeare .
ex:Tamburlaine       ex:author  ex:Marlowe ;
                     ex:price   "17"^^xsd:integer .
ex:DoctorFaustus     ex:author  ex:Marlowe ;
                     ex:price   "12"^^xsd:integer ;
                     ex:title   "The Tragical History of Doctor Faustus" .
ex:RomeoJuliet       ex:author  ex:Brooke ;
                     ex:price   "9"^^xsd:integer .
```

FIGURE 7.2:   Example RDF document for illustrating query evaluation in SPARQL

compatible, their union $\mu_1 \cup \mu_2$ can be defined as follows:

$$(\mu_1 \cup \mu_2)(x) = \begin{cases} \mu_1(x) & \text{if } x \text{ occurs in the domain of } \mu_1 \\ \mu_2(x) & \text{if } x \text{ occurs in the domain of } \mu_2 \\ \text{undefined} & \text{in all other cases} \end{cases}$$

Whenever x is in the domain of both μ_1 and μ_2 in this definition, compatibility ensures that both functions yield the same result. Intuitively speaking, we thus combine two compatible rows of a result table into one longer row. In the following definitions, we use the parameters Ψ, Ψ_1, and Ψ_2 to denote results that have already been computed, and we use F for filter expressions.

- $Filter(F, \Psi) = \{\mu \mid \mu \in \Psi$ and the expression $\mu(F)$ evaluates to $\texttt{true}\}$

- $Join(\Psi_1, \Psi_2) = \{\mu_1 \cup \mu_2 \mid \mu_1 \in \Psi_1, \mu_2 \in \Psi_2,$ and μ_1 compatible with $\mu_2\}$

- $Union(\Psi_1, \Psi_2) = \{\mu \mid \mu \in \Psi_1$ or $\mu \in \Psi_2\}$

- $LeftJoin(\Psi_1, \Psi_2, F) =$
  $\{\mu_1 \cup \mu_2 \mid \mu_1 \in \Psi_1, \mu_2 \in \Psi_2,$ and μ_1 is compatible to $\mu_2,$ and
  the expression $(\mu_1 \cup \mu_2)(F)$ evaluates to $\texttt{true}\} \ \cup$
  $\{\mu_1 \mid \mu_1 \in \Psi_1$ and for all $\mu_2 \in \Psi_2$ we find that:
  either μ_1 is not compatible with μ_2 or $(\mu_1 \cup \mu_2)(F)$ is not $\texttt{true}\}$

Note that in the above items, solutions μ are applied to filter expressions F even though we have defined them as partial functions on *variables*. We use this notation as a shortcut for the filter expressions that is obtained from F by applying μ to all variables in F.

We thus have defined all SPARQL operators for graph patterns discussed herein, and we can now evaluate SPARQL algebra expressions accordingly.

Now it can also be seen that the result defined for Z is indeed neutral with respect to the *Join* operation. If, instead of Z, a result without any solutions would be used with *Join*, then the result of *Join* would also be empty.

To illustrate the evaluation of SPARQL expressions, we consider an extended example for the query introduced above. As the underlying data set to answer this query, we take the RDF document given in Fig. 7.2.

We can remove *Join* operations with Z from our example query to arrive at the following expression in SPARQL algebra, where we enumerate lines for future reference.

```
(01)  Filter((?price < 15),
(02)    Join(
(03)    LeftJoin(
(04)     BGP(?book <http://example.org/price> ?price.),
(05)     BGP(?book <http://example.org/title> ?title.),
(06)     true
(07)    ), Union(BGP(?book <http://example.org/author>
(08)                      <http://example.org/Shakespeare>.),
(09)            BGP(?book <http://example.org/author>
(10)                      <http://example.org/Marlowe>.) )))
```

This expression can now easily be evaluated inside to outside. The results are displayed in Fig. 7.3, using tables where each row represents a solution. Each table describes the result of a sub-expression that is identified by a line number and operator name, and thus the last table *"Filter* (01)*"* provides the final result. For reasons of space, we use QNames to abbreviate URIs; internally, SPARQL of course deals with full URIs without such syntactic shortcuts. The evaluation also demonstrates how different kinds of numeric XML datatypes can be combined in a query.

7.1.9.3 Operators for Modifiers

For completely describing the capabilities of SPARQL in algebraic terms, we still lack the formal semantics for modifiers such as ORDER BY or LIMIT. The translation to SPARQL algebra in these cases is conceivably simple: modifiers cannot occur in any complex nesting, and merely need to be applied to the final query result in proper order. We thus further extend the SPARQL expression R obtained from a query by the following operators:

- $R := OrderBy(R, \text{list of sorting conditions})$, if the query uses the modifier ORDER BY with the corresponding sorting conditions.

- $R := Project(R, \text{list of variables})$, if the query uses the output format SELECT with the given list of selected variables.

BGP (04)	
book	price
ex:Hamlet	"10.50"^^xsd:decimal
ex:Tamburlaine	"17"^^xsd:integer
ex:DoctorFaustus	"12"^^xsd:integer
ex:RomeoJuliet	"9"^^xsd:integer

BGP (09)
book
ex:Tamburlaine
ex:DoctorFaustus

BGP (05)	
book	title
ex:DoctorFaustus	"The Tragical History of Doctor Faustus"

BGP (07)
book
ex:Macbeth
ex:Hamlet

LeftJoin (03)		
book	price	title
ex:Hamlet	"10.50"^^xsd:decimal	
ex:Tamburlaine	"17"^^xsd:integer	
ex:DoctorFaustus	"12"^^xsd:integer	"The Tragical History of Doctor Faustus"
ex:RomeoJuliet	"9"^^xsd:integer	

Union (07)
book
ex:Hamlet
ex:Macbeth
ex:Tamburlaine
ex:DoctorFaustus

Join (02)		
book	price	title
ex:Hamlet	"10.50"^^xsd:decimal	
ex:Tamburlaine	"17"^^xsd:integer	
ex:DoctorFaustus	"12"^^xsd:integer	"The Tragical History of Doctor Faustus"

Filter (01)		
book	price	title
ex:Hamlet	"10.50"^^xsd:decimal	
ex:DoctorFaustus	"12"^^xsd:integer	"The Tragical History of Doctor Faustus"

FIGURE 7.3: Intermediate results in computing the result of a SPARQL query

- $R := Distinct(R)$, if the query contains `DISTINCT`.

- $R := Slice(R, o, l)$, if the query contains the directives "`OFFSET` o" and "`LIMIT` l." If o is not given, o is assumed to be 0. If l is not given, it is replaced by the number of solutions of R less o.

These translations are relatively simple, and the function of each operator is mostly obvious: *OrderBy* orders the solution sequence according to the given sorting conditions, *Distinct* eliminates multiple occurrences of any solution in the result, and *Slice* combines `OFFSET` and `LIMIT` to cut down the solution sequence to the corresponding segment. The operator *Project* restricts the domains of all solutions in a result to the variables chosen in `SELECT`, i.e. each solution is replaced by one that does not define any value for non-selected variables. The above transformation steps also formalize the order of modifier applications that we have already discussed.

7.1.10 Further Expressive Features of SPARQL

The central expressive features of SPARQL have been discussed in detail in the previous sections. Here, we add a brief overview of some aspects of SPARQL that have been omitted in our treatment.

- *Named graphs*: SPARQL allows an input data set to be separated into multiple parts. These parts can be referred to by URIs, and are thus known as named graphs. SPARQL offers a number of options for working with named graphs, and to use the URIs of such graphs within queries.

- Result format `REDUCED`: SPARQL defines an additional output format `REDUCED` that can be used to produce partly reduced results. It can be viewed as an optional version of `DISTINCT` which leaves it to the implementation whether or not duplicates should be eliminated. This modifier thus is mostly useful for admitting application-specific optimizations in cases where one does not have a strong preference regarding the occurrence of duplicates.

- Results in XML: SPARQL defines a specific XML format for serializing results. Essentially, this can be viewed as an XML version of the tables that we have used to display results informally.

- Protocol: SPARQL also includes a transmission protocol for queries and results, which can be used for the (Web-based) communication with query services.

7.2   Conjunctive Queries for OWL DL

In this section, we turn to the task of querying knowledge bases that use advanced ontology languages like OWL DL. So far, SPARQL has been conceived only as a query language for RDF graphs with simple RDF semantics, and neither RDFS nor OWL are supported directly. For instance, while the matching of graph patterns is an important basis of SPARQL, complex ontology languages do not describe mere graphs but a multitude of possible interpretations (models). To a certain extent, graphs can still be found in OWL interpretations as well: properties in OWL DL are modeled by binary relations between elements of the interpretation domain, and such relations can surely be visualized as connections within a graph. An axiom $R(a, b)$ (using description logic syntax here), e.g., would express that the elements referred to by a and b are connected by an "arrow" labeled with R. Thus any OWL DL interpretation also can be viewed as a graph consisting of elements of the domain of interpretation that are connected by relations. OWL classes to which a certain element belongs can be considered as additional labels of each element node. In essence, this way of viewing OWL interpretations is closely related to the way in which the tableau algorithm represents them; cf. Section 5.3.

So can we simply extend SPARQL to OWL DL by considering interpretations as logically described graphs that can be the basis for queries? Unfortunately, there are two basic problems with this approach:

1. Each OWL DL ontology does not describe a single but many possible interpretations. While this could also be said of RDF, the situation in OWL is different in that there is generally no "most specific" interpretation that would suggest itself as the basis for a graph to which the query could refer.

2. Interpretations in OWL DL may comprise infinitely many elements, and hence the query graph could become infinitely large. It can even happen that an ontology admits only models with infinite domain.

Both aspects yield certain problems, and it is still not fully clear how an extension toward "SPARQL for OWL" should look. At the same time, there is already a well-established query formalism for OWL DL which is suitable as the foundation of such an approach. These so-called *conjunctive queries* will now be introduced. It is also useful to compare these queries not only to SPARQL, but also to the rule languages for OWL discussed in Chapter 6. As in that chapter, we again find it most convenient to employ (description) logical syntax in this presentation – indeed, there is no official XML or RDF syntax for conjunctive queries yet.

7.2.1 The Limits of OWL

As opposed to RDF, OWL DL offers extensive expressive features as part of the ontology language. Using class expressions it is possible to describe complex structures which can be composed using conjunctions, disjunctions, or negations. Most OWL DL reasoners are able to determine the set of all instances that are deduced to belong to such a class description. This yields a significant expressivity that can also be used for querying a knowledge base. Would a query language for OWL DL thus simply need to allow for a better specification of result formats and other technical properties – or is there indeed relevant information that cannot be determined using OWL DL?

In fact, the latter is the case, and there are essentially two reasons for this. First of all, a single OWL DL class can obviously query for values of only a single variable, corresponding to result tables with a single row. The second, more subtle, restriction is that relationships described in an OWL class in principle are always tree structures, where the queried variable describes objects at the root of the tree. This means that a query can describe the relations of various other objects to the query variable, while these objects may hardly have any direct relationships between each other. This might also be compared to the restrictions that were imposed on DL Rules in Section 6.3.3, which essentially also can be said to allow only for tree-shaped dependencies. In combination with the first restriction, this excludes a number of interesting queries.

In order to understand these restrictions better, it is helpful to consider some concrete examples. Thus assume we are given a knowledge base with properties `childOf` and `livesTogetherWith`, both of which are used to express relationships between people. The following questions cannot be answered by simple OWL classes:

1. Find all pairs of people with a common parent.

2. Find all people who live together with their parents.

3. Find all pairs of people where the first person is a (direct or indirect) ancestor of the second.

The first two queries could be answered relatively easily even in SPARQL, and we will also see a corresponding solution for OWL DL below. The third example essentially asks for the transitive extension of the relation `childOf`, which is possible neither in SPARQL nor in the kind of OWL DL queries discussed here. There are, however, extended query languages for description logics that address such use cases by allowing regular expressions for describing patterns of properties; see Section 7.5. Moreover, the query could be addressed in OWL DL by extending the knowledge base with a new transitive super-property of `childOf` that could then be queried. However, not all applications in which queries are used also allow modifications of the underlying knowledge base.

In spite of the lack of support for these examples, there are various rather similar queries that could be formulated in OWL DL. This is generally the case if variable or unspecified elements are replaced by concrete individuals. For instance, it would be possible to use multiple queries for finding out which people have a concrete person Bob as their parent, and which of those people live together with Bob. This is achieved by simply querying for individual property instances, or by using class expressions with nominal classes.

7.2.2 Introduction to Conjunctive Queries

As opposed to SPARQL, conjunctive queries are not an officially specified query language. Therefore, there is no normative syntax and many of the technical details that were elaborated for SPARQL are not spelled out. The semantics of conjunctive queries, too, can be presented in various ways, but there is still a general agreement regarding their correct formal interpretation. The definitions provided here are thus not the only ones to be found in the literature, yet they are essentially compatible with all common definitions.

Just as in SPARQL, variables play an important role in conjunctive queries. As on prior occasions, we denote logical variables with lowercase letters x, y, z, ... and we generally adhere to the syntactic conventions of first-order logic that were used in Chapters 5 and 6. The following is a simple example of a conjunctive query for all books that have been published by CRC Press together with their respective authors:

$$\text{Book}(x) \land \text{publishedBy}(x, \text{CRCPress}) \land \text{author}(x, y)$$

As the name suggests, a conjunctive query is primarily a conjunction of multiple query conditions. Individual conditions are simple description logic formulae without any logical operators, or the negations of such conditions. These basic types of formulae are known as *atoms* of the query, and they may occur in one of the following forms:

- $C(e)$ or $\neg C(e)$, where C is a class name and e is a variable or the name of an individual.

- $R(e, f)$, where R is a property name, and e and f are either variables or individual names.

Note that negated property atoms are not allowed in this definition. In contrast to negated class atoms, they would indeed have a significant effect on the expressive power of the language, rendering it undecidable if not restricted. In consequence, we can *not* directly use conjunctive queries to search for books that have not been published by CRC Press since the following is *not* allowed:

$$\texttt{Book}(x) \land \lnot\texttt{publishedBy}(x, \texttt{CRCPress}) \land \texttt{author}(x, y)$$

However, it is not a problem in principle to allow conjunctive queries to contain arbitrary class expressions instead of simple class names only. The reason is that we can always introduce a new name C for a complex class expression D by adding an axiom $C \equiv D$ to the knowledge base. With this extension, the above query could indeed be expressed as

$$\texttt{Book}(x) \land \lnot(\exists\texttt{publishedBy}\{\texttt{CRCPress}\})(x) \land \texttt{author}(x, y)$$

By submitting such a query, one is asking for a concrete value assignment for each query variable, i.e. for a solution which substitutes all variables with names of individuals – we do not consider datatype literals in this section. This constitutes an important restriction, since in OWL there are many possibilities to assert the existence of some object without providing a concrete identifier (individual name) for that object. The following description logic knowledge base illustrates what this means in a concrete case:

$\texttt{Book}(a)$	(a is a book)
$\texttt{Book} \sqsubseteq \exists\texttt{author}.\top$	(every book has an author)

Now this knowledge base does not entail any solution for the query $\texttt{Book}(x) \land \texttt{author}(x, y)$, as there is no *known* individual that could serve as a value for y. While we know that a corresponding author must exist for the book a, we do not know any name for that person which could be returned as a solution. Variables in conjunctive queries therefore do not have the same meaning as variables in first-order logic formulae, where all possible elements of the domain of interpretation are taken into account. To emphasize this special meaning, variables in conjunctive queries are also referred to as *distinguished variables*.

As in SPARQL, we can again represent variable assignments by functions. A variable assignment for a conjunctive query is a function μ that maps every variable in the query to the name of an individual. Such a variable assignment is a *solution* for a conjunctive query C with respect to a given OWL DL knowledge base B, if the formula obtained by applying μ to the query C is a (first-order) logical consequence of B. In symbols we could also write: $B \models \mu(C)$.

This definition of solutions also takes into account the fact that any given knowledge base might allow for a multitude of possible interpretations. After all, the query formula $\mu(C)$ is only entailed by B if it is true in all possible interpretations of B, i.e. if it is entailed by each admissible interpretation. Furthermore, the semantics of conjunctive queries also copes with the possibility of infinite models: since there is only a finite number of individual names in any knowledge base, query results will always be finite, too.

7.2.3　Non-Distinguished Variables

Distinguished variables are useful when querying for concrete instances, but there are also cases when a query should merely ask for the existence of a suitable element without determining its exact identity. This can be expressed in conjunctive queries by binding the respective variable with an existential quantifier, as in the following example:

$$\exists x. (\texttt{author}(x, y) \land \texttt{Book}(x))$$

This query asks for all authors who have written any book. The name of the book, in contrast, is not queried for. For example, a knowledge base might contain the axiom $\texttt{Bookauthor} \equiv \exists\texttt{author}^-.\texttt{Book}$ which defines the class of book authors by means of an inverse role. Each individual in this class would thus lead to a solution of the previous query, even if the identity of the corresponding book is not specified further within the knowledge base.

For this reason, the variable x in the above example is also referred to as a *non-distinguished variable*. Thus, in general, a conjunctive query might contain two kinds of variables, only one of which is part of solutions for this query.

7.2.4　Conjunctive Queries and Rules

In Chapter 6, we introduced various rule languages that can be combined with OWL DL in a semantically direct way. In particular, we focused on two paradigms – DL-safe rules and DL Rules – both of which can be viewed as fragments of the generic first-order rule language *datalog*. It turns out that these approaches are closely related to conjunctive queries, and we can obtain new insights by highlighting these relationships within this section. Readers who did not study the necessary parts of Chapter 6 may safely skip this section.

Rule languages and query languages in general are very closely related. This is so, since a query (of whatever kind) always extracts information from a data set or a knowledge base, which can then be used as a basis for extending the given data with new conclusions – the query thus describes the antecedent of a rule. This is a very general observation that is applicable well beyond the formalisms considered in this book. In our concrete scenario, this boils down to the observation that conjunctive queries are highly similar to the bodies of datalog rules.

As an example, the query from Section 7.2.3 could equivalently be expressed in a datalog rule that might look as follows:

$$\texttt{author}(x, y) \wedge \texttt{Book}(x) \rightarrow \texttt{Answer}(y)$$

By augmenting the knowledge base with this rule, and querying for the entailed instances of Answer, we would obtain the same results as when asking the above query directly. Note that the query contains an existential quantifier for y which we have now omitted. This is semantically correct since the antecedent of a rule is implicitly negated – $p \rightarrow q$ is equivalent to $\neg p \vee q$ – and the negated existential can be turned into a universal quantifier that we may omit when writing rules. In a similar way, arbitrary queries can be cast into rules, where the variables that occur in the rule head mirror the distinguished variables in the query. Note that this may require us to use predicates with more than two variables in cases where more distinguished variables occur, but this is no problem in datalog.

A closer look shows that the characteristics of distinguished variables appear quite naturally in this encoding of queries into datalog rules. Indeed, the actual rule only contains common first-order logic variables that are neither distinguished nor non-distinguished as such. But when querying for concrete instances of the answer predicate, we are only interested in individual names as variable fillers. Thus the variable y in the above rule in fact only ever needs to take values that are represented by concrete individual names. In Chapter 6, we encountered a very similar restriction in DL-safe rules, and we learned that this constraint can be imposed on any datalog rule by simply adding an auxiliary predicate O to the knowledge base. Using the same encoding, we can thus also write the above rule as follows:

$$\texttt{author}(x, y) \wedge \texttt{Book}(x) \wedge O(y) \rightarrow \texttt{Answer}(y)$$

This does not make this rule DL-safe yet – it still contains the "unsafe" variable x – but it shows how distinguished and non-distinguished variables relate to DL-safety in rules.

Recognizing these intimate relationships between rules and queries can help to improve our understanding of both topics. First of all, the above translation gives us the spelled-out formal semantics for conjunctive queries without further effort: the semantics of datalog has been discussed in detail in Section 6.2.2, and the semantics of conjunctive queries turns out to be a mere special case of it. Secondly, the correspondences between both areas yield insights on the difficulty of both approaches. For example, it is now clear that any implementation of a datalog extension for (some fragment of) OWL DL would also support arbitrary conjunctive queries on this fragment. Conversely, we found that certain sublanguages of datalog are much easier to handle than full datalog, and it is promising to try out the same restrictions on conjunctive queries.

In general, reasoning with the combination of OWL DL and datalog is not even decidable. This does not need to be the case for conjunctive queries: even if all conjunctive queries can be answered by some program, there are still many datalog programs that cannot be expressed by any conjunctive query, so the program would not be an (impossible) tool for reasoning with datalog and OWL. What makes datalog harder is, intuitively speaking, the possibility of encoding recursive rules that can be applied indefinitely to obtain more and more results without ever terminating. It is known that conjunctive querying is decidable for the description logics $\mathcal{SHIQ}$ and $\mathcal{SHOQ}$, for which the combination with datalog is no longer decidable. On the other hand, it is an open question whether conjunctive querying for OWL DL ($\mathcal{SHOIQ}$) is decidable at all.

Since conjunctive querying is very difficult even in the decidable cases, it makes sense to seek restrictions that simplify the task. The two sub-languages of datalog that we considered in Chapter 6 highlight different ways of doing so. DL Rules have been defined by restricting to datalog rules that have a certain restricted shape, ensuring that the dependencies expressed in rule bodies are not cyclic. It turned out that rules of this form can always be rewritten to a set of axioms in the (decidable) description logic $\mathcal{SROIQ}$. Analogously, any conjunctive query that, when viewed as a rule, meets the restrictions of DL Rules can also be re-cast into plain description logic axioms, so that no special conjunctive query support is required to obtain its solutions. Referring to their cycle-free structure, those conjunctive queries are also known as *tree-shaped queries*, and it is known that they are often much easier to answer than arbitrary conjunctive queries. Note that all example queries in this section are tree-shaped.

The second restriction of datalog that we have discussed was DL-safe rules, which obtain their favorable computational features by constraining rule applications to named individuals – elements of the interpretation domain that are identified by an individual name. It has been mentioned above how this relates to conjunctive queries: all distinguished variables in a query can be encoded to be DL-safe without losing any results. Hence, whenever a query contains only distinguished variables, the corresponding datalog rule is essentially DL-safe. Again, this restriction often yields substantial computational advantages in practice, and we can immediately see that any tool which handles DL-safe rules can also handle queries with only distinguished variables. On the other hand, this observation also hints at the fact that the treatment of non-distinguished variables really adds an additional level of difficulty when it comes to implementation.

7.2.5 Conjunctive Queries and SPARQL

At first glance, conjunctive queries seem to be rather different from SPARQL queries. While SPARQL uses graph patterns, conjunctive queries consist of logical conjunctions. At second glance, however, those two formulations are not really so different: a query atom of the form $R(e, f)$ can be considered as a triple "e R f" and a conjunction of such atoms again describes a graph structure. Alternative and optional patterns, in contrast, are not available in conjunctive queries, and only the former has an immediate counterpart in first-order logic in the form of logical disjunction.

Another basic incompatibility lies in SPARQL's capability of querying for property names. While SPARQL allows us to use variables in place of property names, conjunctive queries are subject to the syntactic restrictions of first-order logic, where variables are a special kind of term and thus may never occur in a predicate position. SPARQL does not provide this distinction and in this sense follows RDF and OWL Full. On the other hand, this restriction of conjunctive queries in comparison to SPARQL can also be viewed as a natural consequence of the prior restriction of OWL Full to OWL DL, which has been our starting point for introducing conjunctive queries.

Another compatibility problem is the different usage of variables in both formalisms. SPARQL represents place holders in queries by variables or blank nodes, while conjunctive queries allow for distinguished and non-distinguished variables. Furthermore, not all variables in SPARQL need to be part of a query result: it is possible to select only certain variables by means of SELECT. These different characteristics of variables can be summarized by two features:

- Anonymous values: Can the variable take values for which no concrete identifier (URI or literal) is known?

- Output: Will the variable appear in the result of the query?

We thus arrive at the following classification:

	Anonymous values	Output
Distinguished variable	—	Yes
Non-distinguished variable	Yes	—
Blank node	Yes	—
SPARQL variable	Yes	Yes
Non-selected SPARQL variable	Yes	—

Accordingly, non-distinguished variables, blank nodes in SPARQL, and non-selected SPARQL variables behave very similarly. The major difference is between SPARQL variables and distinguished variables. While SPARQL variables may return anonymous individuals by using blank nodes, distinguished variables are restricted to elements with concrete names. Semantically, OWL DL does not distinguish "blank nodes" from any other element for which no identifier is given. Thus, if the semantic approach of SPARQL would be extended to OWL DL, it would be necessary to return all entailed elements as a result – and these could easily be infinitely many (truly different) individuals!

This may be the strongest technical reason why there is no official extension of SPARQL to OWL DL yet. One possible solution to this problem would be to treat blank nodes in a knowledge base like individual names. Queries then would return only those blank nodes, and no additional blank nodes used to represent newly entailed elements. This does not strictly correspond to the semantics of blank nodes in OWL, but it largely preserves compatibility with SPARQL and RDF. On the other hand, blank nodes in query patterns might still be treated as non-distinguished variables, such that blank nodes in queries would have a different semantics than blank nodes in a knowledge base. The alternative to this solution would be to simply assume all variables to be distinguished, and thus never to return blank nodes as part of a result. In this case, SPARQL for OWL would no longer return all results that are now returned by SPARQL on RDF, which may or may not be a significant problem in practical applications.

Beyond said incompatibilities, the extension of SPARQL to OWL based on conjunctive queries would not be too difficult. Problematic features, such as UNION or OPTIONAL, can be disallowed, which would also make the extension with FILTER a mere post-processing step that would not interfere with reasoning.[7] Likewise, support for datatype literals can be achieved along the lines of the existing datatype semantics of OWL DL, and solution sequence modifiers such as LIMIT would not impose major problems either. Indeed, various OWL DL systems today support a restricted amount of queries in SPARQL syntax, e.g., by treating variables as being distinguished.

7.3 Summary

In the first part of this chapter, we have discussed the SPARQL query language for RDF in great detail. We have encountered different query conditions in the form of graph patterns and filters, as well as result formats and modifiers. The exact formal semantics of those expressive features has been described by using the SPARQL algebra.

---

[7]Support for some such advanced features may also be possible. There are, e.g., various research results on unions of conjunctive queries.

In the second part, we have taken a closer look at conjunctive queries for OWL DL, and we have compared this formalism to SPARQL and to OWL-compatible rule languages that were introduced in Chapter 6.

7.4   Exercises

Exercise 7.1 Consider the following RDF document with information about celestial bodies.

```
@prefix  ex: <http://example.org/> .
ex:Sun    ex:radius "1.392e6"^^xsd:double ;
          ex:satellite ex:Mercury, ex:Venus, ex:Earth, ex:Mars .
ex:Mercury ex:radius    "2439.7"^^xsd:double .
ex:Venus   ex:radius    "6051.9"^^xsd:double .
ex:Earth   ex:radius    "6372.8"^^xsd:double ;
           ex:satellite  ex:Moon .
ex:Mars    ex:radius    "3402.5"^^xsd:double ;
           ex:satellite  ex:Phobos, ex:Deimos .
ex:Moon    ex:name      "Mond@de", "Moon@en" ;
           ex:radius    "1737.1"^^xsd:double .
ex:Phobos  ex:name      "Phobos" .
ex:Deimos  ex:name      "Deimos" .
```

Specify SPARQL queries which yield the following results in the form of a table.

- Objects which orbit around the sun or around a satellite of the sun.

- Objects with a volume greater than $2 \cdot 10^{10}$ (km^3) together with the object – if it exists – of which they are a satellite. Assume for this that all celestial bodies are spherical.

- Objects with a satellite for which an English name is given, and which furthermore are satellites of an object with diameter greater than 3000 (km).

- Objects with two or more satellites. Assume for this that different URIs denote different objects.

Exercise 7.2 Translate the queries from Exercise 7.1 into expressions in SPARQL algebra. You can simplify Join expressions with the empty graph Z as parameter.

Exercise 7.3 Compute the solutions to the expressions from Exercise 7.2 with respect to the knowledge base from Exercise 7.1 step by step as in Figure 7.3 on page 290.

Exercise 7.4 It is possible to use SPARQL for searching for elements for which certain information is *not* given. This is done by combining filters with optional graph patterns.

Formulate a query which asks for all celestial bodies which do not have a satellite. Assume for this that the knowledge base from Exercise 7.1 has been completed with triples which assign to every celestial body the `rdf:type` `CelestialBody`.

Exercise 7.5 The game *Sudoku* is about completing incomplete tables with numbers while respecting certain rules. We consider the following simple 4×4 Sudoku:

			3
			4
2			
3			

You have to fill in numbers with values 1 to 4 in the empty slots in the table so that no number occurs twice in any row or any column, and so that no number is duplicated within any of the marked 2×2 squares.

We now want to use SPARQL for solving this Sudoku, i.e. we want to obtain all possible solutions by means of answers to a SPARQL query. In order to do this, set up a suitable RDF document and SPARQL query.

Exercise 7.6 This exercise focuses on the use of modifiers in SPARQL. Consider the following RDF document:

```
@prefix  ex: <http://example.org/> .
ex:a    ex:value  "1"^^xsd:integer ;
        ex:value  "3"^^xsd:integer .
ex:b    ex:value  "2"^^xsd:integer .
```

Which result would each of the following SPARQL queries return for this RDF input?

1. `SELECT ?s ?v WHERE { ?s <http://example.org/value> ?v }`
   `ORDER BY ?v`

2. `SELECT ?s WHERE { ?s <http://example.org/value> ?v }`
   `ORDER BY ?v`

3. `SELECT ?s WHERE { ?s <http://example.org/value> ?v }`
   `ORDER BY DESC(?v) LIMIT 2`

4. `SELECT DISTINCT ?s WHERE { ?s <http://example.org/value> ?v }`
   `ORDER BY ?v`

Which result would you expect the last query to return when `LIMIT 1` is added?

Exercise 7.7 State the following as conjunctive queries. Use the class names `Male`, `Female`, `Catholic`, and `Priest` and the role names `killed`, `childOf`, and `marriedWith`.

1. all married couples which have a child together

2. all married female Catholic priests

3. all persons whose parents are married

4. all women who killed their husband

5. all married couples both of whom committed suicide

7.5   Further Reading

The essential documents of the SPARQL specification are

- "SPARQL Query Language for RDF" [PS08], where query syntax and semantics are defined,

- "SPARQL Query Results XML Format" [BB08], which specifies the encoding of result for (`SELECT`) queries in XML, and

- "SPARQL Protocol for RDF" [CFT08], where the communication with SPARQL query services is described.

The filter operators that were borrowed from *XQuery* and *XPath* have been defined in [MMW07]. An in-depth discussion of the semantics and complexity of SPARQL is given in [APG06], and connections between SPARQL and the relational algebra known from relational databases are fleshed out in [Cyg05]. As in the case of relational algebra, it is also possible to formulate the SPARQL semantics in a model theoretic fashion based on a translation of SPARQL to datalog (discussed in Chapter 6). This approach, which is discussed in [Sch07], locates SPARQL in the general framework of first-order logic that has already been identified as the semantic basis of most formalisms considered in this book. This also provides an alternative viewpoint for studying the compatibility of SPARQL and conjunctive queries.

The general idea of conjunctive queries was already considered in 1977 for relational databases [CM77], and generally plays an important role in this area. For description logics (and thus for OWL) these queries have been studied since the end of the 1990s [CGL98]. Many current systems support conjunctive queries only partially, mostly due to the very high computational complexity of query answering. KAON2,[8] e.g., allows only queries all variables of which are distinguished, and which satisfy certain additional restrictions on role (property) atoms [Mot06]. *Pellet*,[9] in contrast, offers the most extensive support for conjunctive querying among today's OWL reasoners, though this might require substantial amounts of computational resources, also when compared to more restricted systems like KAON2. Relevant tools are discussed in greater depth in Section 8.5.

Decidability and complexity of conjunctive queries in general is still subject to ongoing research, especially for very expressive description logics. Transitive roles and their generalization to role chains (available in OWL 2) constitute a particular difficulty [GHLS07], and the processing of conjunctive queries can be quite challenging even for rather restricted description logics [Lut07, KRH07, CEO07]. The paper [CEO07] also discusses an extended form of conjunctive queries that allow for property patterns based on regular expression. As mentioned earlier, it is still unknown at the time of the writing of this book whether or not conjunctive queries are decidable for OWL DL.

---

[8] http://kaon2.semanticweb.org/
[9] http://pellet.owldl.com/

Part IV

Beyond Foundations

Chapter 8

Ontology Engineering

In the previous chapters, we have investigated various formalisms for specifying and querying semantic data – or phrased even more boldly: knowledge – be it on the Web, in some company's intranet, or elsewhere. We have seen that those formalisms come with standardized, precisely defined syntax and formal semantics.

So, knowledgeable about those knowledge representation formalisms and their grounding in formal logic, we could argue that we are well-equipped and readily prepared to go about bringing semantics to everybody in need of it.

However, being able to come up with semantic descriptions of toy examples in some sandbox domain (such as a nut-allergic person consuming an inappropriate dish) does not guarantee that real-world modeling tasks (such as coming up with a comprehensive description of patients, allergies, allergens, and medical treatments) can be effortlessly tackled in the same way. As an analogy, imagine the situation of a programmer able to create a "Hello World!" program faced with the task of producing a desktop publishing system or the like. It is clear that the sheer size and complexity of real-world modeling tasks will easily exceed what can be done by an RDF(S) or OWL expert by just sitting down and creating an ontology document.

This directly brings us to the discipline of *ontology engineering* which – in analogy to software engineering – is concerned with the challenges of designing complex systems (in our case: ontologies) by providing methodologies and auxiliary tools for their development, evaluation, and maintenance. In the following sections, we briefly sketch the central topics in ontology engineering. However, note that, as opposed to the formalisms introduced in the previous chapters, this area is still very much in flux and subject to active research. Therefore, our review is necessarily preliminary and less detailed, as it aims at providing just an overview. Furthermore, our choice of which aspects of ontology engineering to present here is of course very influenced by our subjective view of the emerging field.

Software engineering has been around for many more years than ontology engineering and the process of creating software bears some similarities to designing an ontology (despite the foundational difference between the operational vs. declarative paradigm). Hence, it is worthwhile to investigate the central ideas of this neighboring field and see whether they can be transferred.

One of the basic principles in software engineering is the idea of a life cycle, meaning a process model of subsequent, partly intertwined steps for software development and maintenance. Clearly, the design of large-size and complex knowledge bases requires a similarly structured approach. In the following three sections, 8.1, 8.2, and 8.3, we focus on the subtasks of requirement analysis, ontology creation, and ontology quality assurance which will be further subdivided.

Thereafter, in Section 8.4, we address the somewhat orthogonal issue of ontology modularization which is particularly important for ontology reuse and collaborative ontology creation as well as for optimizing automated inference.

We finish the chapter by naming some of the most popular and mature software tools in the context of ontology engineering.

8.1   Requirement Analysis

As in software engineering, it is immediately clear that a thorough requirement analysis is crucial for the development of an ontology that is appropriate for a given purpose.

In the very first place, it should be decided whether a semantic representation is at all needed or whether an alternative approach (like using a classical database) would be a better choice. In some cases, this question may already be subject to heavy controversy, be it because a "non-semantic" solution already exists or the possibly expensive modeling effort is not accompanied by an obvious added value. There are essentially two major points in favor of an ontology-based system: First, the knowledge represented in a semantic format can be more easily exchanged as well as integrated with knowledge from other sources. Second, by employing deduction algorithms, the implicit knowledge following from a semantic specification becomes accessible.

Another related question which might be discussed is whether a representation based on formal logic is reasonable for the intended purpose. We do not want to discuss one of the early questions of artificial intelligence: whether every kind of knowledge can be represented in a symbolic, logical way. Still, experiments in cognitive science have shown that few people think strictly logically.[1] Therefore, if an application is focused on interhuman knowledge exchange (possibly using computers only as a communication device) it might even be better off using non-logical means of knowledge representation.

Another aspect to be considered at this stage is the available tool support for the different knowledge representation options. This in turn depends on

---

[1]See, e.g., the experiments carried out by P. Wason [Was68]. In a similar way in economics, the idea of the *homo oeconomicus*, a person optimizing its action toward the greatest financial benefit in an entirely rational way, has lately been shown to be a questionable model of human economical behavior.

the purpose of the system to be designed. When reviewing the available technologies the following criteria should be considered: Will the choice require the commitment to one specific tool? What specific licenses are associated with the available software? How mature is it? What kind (if any) of support does the tool vendor offer? Is the tool sufficiently interoperable with other tools one might use or want to use?

If the decision to use a semantic, formal-logic-based formalism is made, the subsequent question is: which one? This again depends on the requirements of the specific scenario. If large amounts of data have to be handled and a less expressive formalism is sufficient, RDF(S) might be the right choice. If the size of the represented information is moderate and more expressive means of knowledge representation (as well as elaborate support for inferring implicit knowledge) are desired, OWL DL would be a better recommendation. In the case of OWL 2, some profiles might also be adequate for scenarios situated in the middle of this spectrum. Again, tool support might be another decision criterion, likewise the availability of skills in handling those formalisms and prior experiences.

Once the modeling formalism has been agreed upon, the requirements of the ontology have to be specified more precisely by answering the following questions:

- What domain has to be modeled? What aspects of this domain have to be captured?

- What is the needed granularity, i.e. the level of detail, of the specification?

- What are the tasks to be accomplished with the help of the ontology: browsing a body of knowledge, search for information, querying or checking inferences? What kind of inferences are expected or desired?

Depending on the answers to those questions, the domain-specific primitives (typically individuals, classes, and roles) and the degree of axiomatization have to be chosen.

8.2   Ontology Creation – Where Is Your Knowledge?

As ontologies are meant to specify knowledge about some domain, the process of creating an ontology can be seen as transferring knowledge into a computer-accessible form. Clearly, there are several possible sources of the knowledge to be formalized. These might be categorized with respect to the extent to which they are already accessible to computer systems, and, more precisely, to what extent the structure of the current representation of the provided knowledge can be exploited to facilitate the formalization process (i.e. the process of making the inherent semantics formally explicit). Based on that criterion, we distinguish human, unstructured, semi-structured, and structured sources of knowledge which will be treated in the following sections.

But first, one more remark: we might have given the impression that formalizing a piece of knowledge is more or less straightforward, provided the underlying formalism is expressive enough. However, there may be several ways to model a situation correctly (or better: appropriately for a certain use); in some cases, it might be not at all clear how to do it. Usually, this problem becomes especially apparent if comparably abstract terms or situations are to be modeled. For example, try to come up with a formal definition of "game" or "democracy." Now, one might argue that a formal definition of such terms is rather a philosophical than an engineering task. But even terms that are much more down-to-earth may require serious thought when they are to be modeled. Consider the term "school" for instance. It may represent a building, an institution, a body of people. Still all those meanings are not completely independent but somewhat related, which – linguistically speaking – qualifies the word "school" as a *polyseme*. Obviously the decision which of those aspects one should model also depends on the purpose of the ontology. In our case, an ontology characterizing buildings and their functions would model the concept "school" very differently from an ontology describing a country's educational system.

In general, akin to software engineering, there is no unique correct way to build a system satisfying the requirements; sometimes there are some design decisions to be made. However, certain ways of dealing with certain modeling tasks have proven useful and viable which makes them a reasonable recommendation in future similar cases. Therefore, in analogy to software engineering, certain best practices and *modeling patterns* have been and are being established. In this spirit, we provide some methodological guidelines on ontology creation in Section 8.3.2.

8.2.1   It's in Your Heads: Human Sources

A rather immediate source of knowledge about a domain of interest is a person knowledgeable about that domain, a so-called *domain expert*. Ideally, the domain expert is acquainted with the used ontology language and capable of formalizing his knowledge. However, not in all cases the domain expert is able to formulate his knowledge in such a way that it can directly be written down in some knowledge representation formalism. There may be several reasons for that.

One the one hand, though being a luminary in his field of expertise, the domain expert might be anything but an expert in logic. In particular, he might be unable to express his knowledge (which might nevertheless be very clear and formal) by means of one of the representation languages discussed in this book. In that case, some kind of mediation is needed. A person knowledgeable in the representation formalism, often called the *knowledge engineer*, will conduct interviews with one or more domain experts in order to get hold of their knowledge. She will interpret the answers (naturally making extensive use of his background knowledge) and cast them into logical specifications. Of course this communication process might lead to information loss or – even worse – introduce errors, just as misunderstandings frequently arise in human communication. To reduce the danger of misunderstanding on the communication level, it is essential to introduce redundancy, feedback, and double checks in the interview process. For instance the knowledge engineer should rephrase the knowledge she just formalized in her own words and ask the domain experts for their confirmation. Therefore besides being an expert in the used knowledge representation formalisms, a knowledge engineer must have excellent communication skills.

On the other hand, the expert's knowledge might not (or not consciously) be based on clear definitions or rules. For example, an experienced physician might be able to identify carcinogenic cells under the microscope without being capable of giving a clear definition distinguishing pathological from normal cells.[2] In such cases, one might employ indirect methods: based on a comprehensive set of examples that has been classified by an expert, automated techniques can be applied to generate logical expressions that characterize the commonalities of the positive as opposed to the negative examples. Techniques from machine learning, most notably decision tree learning or inductive logic programming, can be used to this end (essentially, the generated classifier must be expressible in the used formalism). Also interactive techniques that actively ask the expert to classify interesting examples or to confirm or deny hypothetical axioms exist, for example, techniques from the field of formal concept analysis.

In general, carefully designed tools for knowledge authoring might alleviate the task of specifying knowledge. With appropriate interaction paradigms, it is possible to "hide" a lot of the formal machinery from the person in charge of entering the knowledge. One option is to allow for natural language input. The next section will elaborate on the potential and limits of this approach.

8.2.2 It's in Your Books: Unstructured sources

Clearly, asking somebody who knows the field is the best choice when looking for a certain piece of knowledge. However, another option that comes to mind immediately when asked for a source of knowledge is just books or – more generally – all kinds of textual resources including also magazines,

---

[2]It is well known that humans, just like other animals, can learn from a set of examples, without ever being given or producing explicit rules. The famous 1964 quotation "I know it when I see it" from Potter Stewart, Associate Justice of the United States Supreme Court, is an anecdotal example of this phenomenon. He was asked to give an explicit definition of hardcore pornography.

Web pages, and the like. While (spoken) language was a "solution" to conveying knowledge directly from one person to another, writing was a solution to externally storing information for the purpose of later retrieval. So when looking for large amounts of directly accessible knowledge, it seems to be a straightforward idea to collect written texts – at least those that are available digitally.

Still, texts in natural language are easily accessible to human information processing only. Extracting formal specifications from arbitrary written texts is still considered a hard problem, although intense research has been carried out in the fields of artificial intelligence and in particular computational linguistics.

Approaches to knowledge acquisition from textual resources can be categorized based on the degree to which they attempt to analyze the grammatical structure of the sentences under consideration – in linguistics, this analysis is usually referred to as *parsing*.

Methods that do not apply any parsing can still be useful in certain scenarios, depending on the level of detail (also called *granularity*) that is required from the resulting knowledge base. If the information to be extracted is just what a certain text roughly is about, a statistical analysis of the words occurring in a document will most likely give sufficient hints. Techniques, in which the pure occurrence and frequency of certain words are measured without taking the word order into account are called *bag-of-word* approaches.

It is quite obvious that bag-of-word techniques cannot extract all the knowledge in a text: the two sentences "Pascal supervises Markus" and "Markus supervises Pascal" cannot be distinguished by an algorithm just counting words while they certainly carry different meanings.[3]

In the following, we make an attempt to sketch the necessary bits and pieces to come up with a system that employs extensive parsing to extract as much knowledge from a written text as possible. En route we will see the difficulties that arise when trying to construct such a system. We choose the following sentence to illustrate our explanations:

Markus does not like animal food. But he ordered a Thai dish that contains fish.

Parsing and Pronoun resolution   In this step, each sentence of the text under consideration is grammatically analyzed. Usually, this step is composed of several subtasks such as part-of-speech tagging, named entity recognition, chunking, word-sense disambiguation. We will not go into further details here. The result of this procedure is a structural representation of the grammatical

---

[3]A somewhat more subtle example would be: "Clearly, not all of Sebastian's jokes are witty" vs. "Clearly, all of Sebastian's jokes are not witty."

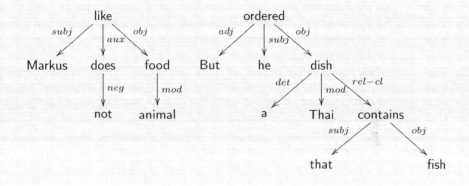

FIGURE 8.1:   Parse trees for the two example sentences

interdependencies. A dependency structure generated for our example might look like the one depicted in Fig. 8.1.

Designing reliable and robust parsing algorithms is not trivial and heavily depends on the considered language; moreover, there are sentences that have several admissible parse trees. Usually humans resolve such parsing problems by context information or background knowledge. Still, at least for English, off-the-shelf parsers are available which work well in most cases.

Next, note that the considered text contains words that actually substitute other words, so-called pronouns. For each of those pronouns (he, that) the referent has to be determined. In our case he refers to Markus and that to dish.

Clearly both parsing and pronoun resolution cannot always be correct: often, sentences are ambiguous and therefore, no unique correct syntactic analysis is possible.[4] This constitutes just one of the many severe obstacles to the acquisition of knowledge from text.

Formalization   The next step that we have to tackle is to transform the linguistic structure into a logical description. This step is certainly the most intricate one. Clearly a thorough description of all technical details would be beyond the scope of this book so we will just very informally sketch the general strategy and possible problems.

Well, taking a step back, why should the grammatical structure of a sentence in natural language be of any use when trying to grasp its semantics? The basic idea behind this is the assumption of the *compositionality* of natural language semantics: the meaning of a (part of a) sentence can be derived from the meaning of its components. So, in the end, the meaning of the

---

[4]Remember just the frequently cited example: "The man saw the girl with a telescope."

sentence relies on the meaning of the words contained in it. However, the grammatical structure of a sentence is assumed to provide the information on how to combine the partial meanings to a composite meaning. Mark that this principle is strictly applied in artificial formalisms: clearly the meaning (i.e. the interpretation) of a description logic class expression can be derived from the meaning of its atomic constituents, the class names, by combining them as indicated by the constructors.

Thus, it is plausible to interpret grammatical interdependencies of sentence parts as logical interdependencies. Therefore the parse trees of a text are usually converted into logical statements by recursively applying a set of transformation rules. What those look like exactly depends on the target formalism and on some more encoding decisions. In the case of OWL, named entities (like Markus) are usually translated into individuals, adjectives (like Thai) and intransitive verbs (like sleep) into classes, and transitive verbs (like like) into roles.[5] Nouns (like dish) are normally translated into classes unless they express some relation (like brother).

The description logic counterpart of the noun phrase "dish that contains fish" would be constructed from the class names Dish and Fish and the role name contains, yielding the class expression Dish ⊓ ∃contains.Fish.

Finally, the above text might be translated into the following DL axioms:

$$\neg\exists \texttt{likes}.(\texttt{Animal} \sqcap \texttt{Food})(\texttt{markus})$$
$$\exists \texttt{ordered}(\texttt{Dish} \sqcap \exists \texttt{contains}.\texttt{Fish})(\texttt{markus})$$

Some problems or peculiarities become apparent from this small example. Some words from the original sentence have disappeared. While this is okay for pronouns that have been linked to their referents and for articles like a or the that do not carry a separate meaning, the disappearance of the word but indicates that our transformation has not been entirely lossless. Although certainly carrying a meaning, this word is hard to convert into a logic formalism like RDF(S) or OWL, unlike other words or phrases like and, or, or not that have a straightforward logical counterpart.[6] Generally, we can note that it is next to impossible to formalize natural language in a way that preserves all its subtleties.

The attentive reader might have already spotted another sloppiness that we were committing. By our translation, different tense forms of the same verb would be assigned to completely unrelated classes (like sleeps and slept) or roles (like orders and ordered). One remedy to this problem would be to

---

[5] In linguistics, a verb is referred to as *transitive* if it requires an object, whereas *intransitive* verbs don't.

[6] Essentially, "but" is used to object to an intuitive consequence of previously expressed information.

use only normalized words, e.g., nouns in nominative singular form and verbs in infinitive form. But then, the temporal information carried by the original sentence is lost. In fact it is non-trivial to accommodate temporal information in the standard ontology languages and there is no well-established best practice how to do this.

Integration with Lexical Background Knowledge Another step that has to be taken when converting language into a formal representation is to account for semantic relationships between the involved words. The usage of language in human communication relies on the presence of a shared body of knowledge, usually referred to as *common sense* or *background knowledge*. This knowledge contains facts such as "fishes are animals" and "a dish consists of food" that can be expected to be clear to all humans (whence those facts are excluded from the communication for efficiency reasons). However, such interdependencies between the lexical atoms – the words – are not accessible to an automated system. Hence, in order to extract the meaning of a given text to a larger extent, the relevant lexical background knowledge has to be explicitly provided. There are well-known free resources of this kind of knowledge, also called *thesauri*. WordNet[7] is certainly the most popular one for the English language.

As we have seen, the imprecisions and ambiguities that natural languages exhibit make the creation of reliable tools that convert arbitrary written texts into ontological descriptions a very challenging task which will arguably never be fully accomplished. Nevertheless, a natural language "format" for entering new knowledge into a system would be a very user friendly and thus desirable feature, in line with the discussion at the end of Section 8.2.1. A way to overcome at least some of the above problems while keeping the benefits of having a rather intuitive "knowledge interface" is to use natural language but restrict it by allowing only certain (unambiguous) grammatical constructions. This way, one can make sure that the text entered into the system is interpreted correctly. A natural language constrained in this way is usually referred to as a *controlled language*.

8.2.3 It's on the Web: Semistructured Sources

Sometimes, the source to be "ontologized" comes with some structure that already reflects part of the semantic interdependencies. Link structures of any kind are one example: hyperlinks between Web pages or, say, wiki articles referencing each other provide crisp relatedness structures between information elements. Though being rather unspecific on the concrete type of related-

---

[7]http://wordnet.princeton.edu/; see also [Fel98]

ness,[8] those structures can be directly transformed into an RDF or OWL representation, allowing at least a shallow capturing of the semantics of the used resource. Also, more sophisticated statistical graph analysis techniques might be performed to extract information on a metalevel like the relevance of specific information items.[9]

Another ubiquitous example of a semistructured source of information is file systems. While a large fraction of the knowledge stored on a computer is not directly automatically accessible (e.g., what objects a certain digital photo shows), certain facts can be effortlessly retrieved such as a file's type and size, the date when a photo was taken, or the name of the creator of a piece of music. Likewise, the folder structure and the respective location of the stored files are explicitly available. Naturally, all this data can be cast into RDF or OWL and consequently used for querying and reasoning.

On top of the more or less directly accessible information in semistructured sources, additional information might be drawn from their unstructured parts (like the written information on the Web pages or in wiki articles) by using techniques described in the previous chapter.

8.2.4   It's in the Databases: Structured Sources

Some sources of knowledge contain only directly accessible information. At this end of the unstructured vs. structured spectrum we have databases but also existing ontologies that we might want to reuse in another setting.

Clearly, the content of relational databases can be translated into RDF or OWL (possibly, *n*-ary relationships have to be reified as described in Section 2.3.3). The necessary additional information that is required for such a translation is how exactly to transform a row of a table into a set of RDF or OWL statements. Such "import" of databases into an ontology is mostly used for *ontology population*, meaning that assertional knowledge (i.e. knowledge about single individuals) is added to an ontology.

On top of their actual content, databases might also contain schema information that, e.g., specifies cardinality constraints on certain relations (such as "every person has at least one nationality"). Partially, this schema information can also be translated into terminological axioms. There are even applications using description logic reasoners for checking the consistency of database schemata.

Besides databases, another structured source of knowledge is other ontologies. Before starting to construct a new ontology from scratch, it might make sense to look for other ontologies that can be (maybe partially) reused. Possibly, there is already an ontology available which thoroughly covers some

---

[8]Note, however, that there are wiki-based content management systems that allow users to specify the type of a link explicitly. We elaborate on them in Section 9.2.

[9]Google's PageRank algorithm is one prominent example of this.

aspects of the domain or maybe an upper-level ontology (an ontology covering the most general concepts of a domain or even of everything) can be used and extended by more specific information.

While extending one given ontology by more information (or pruning it) is arguably more or less straightforward, problems usually arise as soon as two or more formerly independent ontologies are involved and have to be reconciled. They might rely on different ways of modeling, on different naming schemes, or even on different modeling languages.

No matter whether several source ontologies are to be integrated into one (*ontology merging*) or to be more loosely coupled (*ontology alignment*), the usual way of overcoming the mentioned differences is to come up with *ontology mappings* that clarify how the (individual, class, or role) names of one ontology correspond to those of the other. Those mapping correspondences might be equivalences (e.g., `ukonto:Lorry` and `usonto:Truck`), subclass relationships (e.g., `bioonto:Loxodonta_africana` and `circusonto:Elephant`), or others.

Mappings can be either manually specified, automatically determined, e.g., from the names and labels used in the ontologies, or extracted from other sources like texts – with a corresponding error rate. Of course, combinations of those approaches are also possible.

Clearly, the task of using existing ontologies as knowledge source does also touch on aspects of modularity that we will briefly discuss in Section 8.4.

8.3 Quality Assurance of Ontologies

After having discussed various ways of creating ontologies, we now address the question how the quality of a created ontology can be assessed. Moreover, we will see how an existing ontology can be improved in order to rank better in terms of the presented evaluation criteria.

8.3.1 Ontology Evaluation: What Makes an Ontology Good

So, how to tell if an ontology is good or not? The most straightforward criterion is just: does it fulfill the intended purpose? Is it possible to infer the knowledge that one wants to capture with the ontology? Do its logical consequences interpreted by the user coincide with the reality as conceived by the user? And finally: does the information provided by the ontology together with a reasoning framework help the user in accomplishing his task?

It becomes clear that many of those questions can be answered only in the context of the concrete application scenario that an ontology is being developed for. Notwithstanding, we can identify several basic criteria that an ontology has to satisfy irrespective of the specific intended usage.

Logical Criteria   The first group of criteria comprises ontology characteristics that can be checked on a purely logical level, based on the notion of
logical consequence as discussed in Section 5.2.1.3.

We remember that an ontology is called *inconsistent* or *unsatisfiable*, if it
has no model, i.e. if there is no possible world in which all the statements
of the ontology hold. Yet, as the purpose of an ontology is to characterize a
world (namely, the domain it is supposed to describe), ontology inconsistency
does in almost every case indicate a modeling error. Moreover, an inconsistent ontology entails any statement as a logical consequence, whence it cannot
be reasonably used for tasks involving automated deduction. Therefore, logical consistency is one of the essential necessary criteria for an ontology to
be useful. In the previous chapters, algorithms for automatically checking
an ontology's consistency were introduced. By means of these, continuous
consistency checks during the design phase of an ontology can be performed
and the ontology engineer can be alerted as soon as his way of modeling the
domain leads to an inconsistency.

In addition to this "severe" form of global inconsistency, there exists the
weaker version of *inconsistent* (or *unsatisfiable*) *classes*. A class is called
unsatisfiable if it is interpreted as the empty set in any model. Let's have a
look at the following example:

$$\text{Horse} \sqsubseteq \neg \text{Flies}$$
$$\text{FlyingHorse} \equiv \text{Horse} \sqcap \text{Flies}$$

The first statement claims that every horse does not fly while the second
defines a new class exactly as those horses that fly. This forces the class of
flying horses to be empty in every model. Note that this ontology is still
globally consistent. However, it turns inconsistent if we add an instance of
the inconsistent class, like FlyingHorse(pegasus). Normally, an ontology
engineer defines a new class only if it (at least possibly) has instances – defining
a class of male sisters would be just pointless. Thus, a class that is necessarily
empty due to logical constraints often indicates some modeling flaw. An
ontology that does not contain unsatisfiable classes is called *coherent*. As
indicated by the example above, a consistent ontology can be incoherent, but
a coherent ontology cannot be inconsistent. Today's standard ontology editors
(see Section 8.5.1) provide tools for diagnosing incoherency and inconsistency.

Inconsistency and incoherency often arise when too restrictive statements
are made about the domain of interest, thereby constraining the possible
models too much. By weakening or abolishing the statements, an ontology can
be made consistent or coherent again, thereby fulfilling the criteria mentioned
above.

However, weakening an ontology does certainly not always improve its quality. On the contrary: clearly, we want an ontology to contain as much infor-

mation about the domain as possible. *Logical completeness* is a criterion that captures this desire by formal means.

To illustrate this notion, consider the following ontology snippet. Its terminological part tells us that no bird is a mammal, that birds lay eggs, and that every egg-laying species does not give live birth. The assertional part states that ostriches are a bird species while lions are a mammal species that give live birth.

$$
\begin{array}{ll}
\text{Bird} \sqsubseteq \neg\text{Mammal} & \text{Bird(ostrich)} \\
\text{Bird} \sqsubseteq \text{Oviparous} & \text{Mammal} \sqcap \text{Viviparous(lion)} \\
\text{Oviparous} \sqsubseteq \neg\text{Viviparous} &
\end{array}
$$

From this specification, we are able to derive that ostriches are oviparous animals and that lions are not birds. However, the knowledge base does not inform us whether the axiom

$$\text{Mammal} \sqsubseteq \text{Viviparous}$$

is true in the described domain, as we can neither infer it from the above axioms nor can we be sure that it does not hold, since due to the open world assumption, there might be additional information not recorded in the knowledge base. This means that our ontology is incomplete with respect to subclass statements on atomic classes. In this case, we could resolve this incompleteness by adding the fact

$$\text{Mammal} \sqcap \text{Oviparous(platypus)}$$

giving account of an oviparous mammal species and thereby refuting the above axiom.

Note that, besides subclass statements, the logical completeness with respect to other types of axioms – such as class disjointness, property restrictions, or even more complex statements – might be worthwhile aspiring to.

Structural and Formal Criteria In addition to the aforementioned logical criteria, there are further situations that can be more or less automatically diagnosed and that are indicative of possible modeling problems. For some of them, no sophisticated reasoning is necessary. For example, explicit taxonomic cycles can be read directly from an ontology. Consider the following specification.

Architecture ⊑ Faculty   Faculty ⊑ University
University ⊑ Building   Building ⊑ Architecture

Through the circular chain of subclass statements, this taxonomy collapses semantically, i.e. logically, all the involved classes `Architecture`, `Faculty`, `University`, and `Building` are equivalent. However, it is rather unlikely that an ontology deliberately contains many semantically equivalent classes, so this might be hinting at a flaw in the ontology.

Further evaluation criteria based on the subclass hierarchy of an ontology examine the nature of the used classes. As an example of the general qualities a class may have, we consider *rigidity*. A class is considered rigid if every member of it cannot cease to be a member without losing existence. As an example, a person cannot just stop being a person, whereas a student can stop being a student while retaining his existence and most of his other attributes. In the latter case, one can even state that every (not just some) instance of the class of students has the potential of not being a student. In that case, a class will be called anti-rigid.

This way, every class can be marked as being rigid, anti-rigid, or none of both, where the decision might not always be that clear and people might disagree on certain cases; the choice might even depend on the specific modeling task. However, it isn't too hard to see that, for instance, a rigid class cannot be a subclass of an anti-rigid one. Rather, every subclass of an anti-rigid class must itself be anti-rigid. Hence, this criterion can be used to check whether a class hierarchy is correctly modeled. *Identity, unity,* and *dependence* are examples of more qualities a class might have and which give rise to further constraints and evaluation criteria for class hierarchies. An elaborate methodology based on those called OntoClean.[10]

Accuracy Criteria   Obviously, a central requirement (and hence evaluation criterion) is whether the ontology accurately captures those aspects of the modeled domain that it has been designed for. In particular, the logical statements that it contains or allows us to infer should faithfully correspond to the state of affairs in the real world.

The aforementioned evaluation criteria can provide useful hints with respect to this question in that they are necessary preconditions for accuracy. Yet, even if everything seems to be all right from that perspective, conceptual modeling errors (as opposed to logical ones) might have been overlooked.

Clearly, real-world-conformance of an ontology cannot be checked entirely automatically as this would require that the outer world state of affairs has

---

[10]http://www.ontoclean.org/

to be accessed by the agent performing this check.[11] Therefore, the question whether an ontology adequately represents certain aspects of reality relies on the judgment of humans and is therefore subjective. However, as humans usually agree on a number of domain-related statements, it is at least possible to check whether the ontology in question entails those statements – provided the humans also agree on how the common statement is to be translated into a formal representation.

On the more practical side, it is at least possible to identify common modeling flaws, i.e. frequent cases in which the way a domain is modeled most likely does not coincide with the modeler's intention. Some of such "bad practices" are listed in the following section.

8.3.2 How to (Not) Model Correctly

This section aims at being a checklist for people modeling an ontology in RDF(S) or OWL. It does not claim to be exhaustive nor objective. It just enumerates some suggestions that the authors consider relevant when modeling an ontology. As there is no unique way of modeling a situation and it is often a matter of taste which option is the best one, most of our suggestions will refer to "*don'ts*" instead of "*dos*," indicating misconceptions and imprecisions that should be avoided.

8.3.2.1 Don't forget disjointness

Consider the following simple knowledge base:

Man ⊑ Human	Human ⊑ Man ⊔ Woman	Woman ⊑ Human
Man(pascal)		Woman(anne)

At first glance, it might seem that all the dependencies between the classes Human, Woman, and Man are completely specified. But when asking a reasoner whether $\neg Woman(pascal)$ is entailed by the above axioms, it turns out that this is not the case. The point is that no logical reasons prevent pascal from being both Man and Woman. To logically fix this shortcoming one has to state that Man and Woman are disjoint, i.e. there is no individual contained in both classes.

In practice, disjointness statements are often forgotten or neglected. The arguable reason for this could be that intuitively classes are considered disjoint unless there is other evidence. By omitting disjointness statements, many potentially useful consequences can get lost. The following is a good strategy to counter the problem in case of a class hierarchy that is already formalized:

---

[11]Philosophically, this issue is closely related to the widely discussed so-called *symbol grounding problem*.

> *Explicitly consider all siblings, i.e. classes having a common su-*
> *perclass, whether it is possible that an individual is an instance of*
> *both classes. If not, declare them as disjoint.*

8.3.2.2   Don't forget role characteristics

Just like class disjointness, characteristics that can be assigned to roles (or properties, respectively) can enable a lot of useful deductions.

> *Consider for every role occurring in an ontology whether it rep-*
> *resents a transitive, symmetric, functional, and/or inverse func-*
> *tional relation.*

Note that in OWL 2, even more information about roles can (and should) be expressed: reflexivity and irreflexivity, antisymmetry and role disjointness, as well as interdependencies involving role chains. As a caveat, note that declaring a role transitive might turn an OWL DL ontology into an OWL Full ontology, for which less tool support is available. In that case, expressivity has to be weighed against what is computationally manageable.

8.3.2.3   Don't choose too specific domains or ranges

The problem of too narrow domain or range restrictions has been already addressed twice in previous chapters: in Section 2.4.5 as well as in Section 4.1.9. We will not elaborate on them in detail.

> *It is worthwhile to check all occurrences of a property (or role, re-*
> *spectively) in an ontology and make sure that the declared domains*
> *and ranges apply to every single one of those usages.*

8.3.2.4   Be careful with quantifiers

The usage of quantifiers on roles or – speaking in terms of OWL – the `owl:someValuesFrom` and `owl:allValuesFrom` restrictions may cause some conceptual confusion to "modeling beginners." As a rule of thumb, when translating a natural language statement into a logical axiom, existential quantification occurs far more frequently; e.g., a proposition like "birds have wings" should be translated as $Bird \sqsubseteq \exists has.Wing$. The erroneous translation $Bird \sqsubseteq \forall has.Wing$ would convey the information that birds have *only* wings (if they have anything at all) and nothing else. Natural language indicators for the usage of universal quantification are words like "only," "exclusively," or "nothing but."

There is one particular misconception concerning the universal role restriction. As an example, consider the statement

$$Happy \equiv \forall hasChild.Happy$$

that could be translated to "somebody is happy exactly if all his/her children are happy." However, the intuitive reading suggests that in order to be happy, a person must have at least one happy child. Yet, this is not the case: any individual that is not the starting point of any role R is a class member of any class $\forall R.C$ irrespective of the class C.[12] Hence, by our above statement, every childless person would be qualified as happy. In order to formalize the aforementioned intended reading, the statement would have to read as follows:

$$\text{Happy} \equiv \forall\text{hasChild.Happy} \sqcap \exists\text{hasChild.Happy}$$

Make sure that the intended meaning is correctly cast into role quantifications. Use existential quantification as default. Be aware that universal quantification alone does not enforce the existence of a respective role.

8.3.2.5 Don't mistake parts for subclasses

Have a look at the following small TBox of a knowledge base:

Finger $\sqsubseteq$ Hand	Hand $\sqsubseteq$ Arm	Arm $\sqsubseteq$ Body
Toe $\sqsubseteq$ Foot	Foot $\sqsubseteq$ Leg	Leg $\sqsubseteq$ Body
	Arm $\sqcap$ Leg $\sqsubseteq \bot$	

Seems all right, doesn't it? We can even employ a reasoner to deduce Hand $\sqsubseteq$ Body or that Finger and Toe are disjoint.

However, some problems occur as soon as we have a closer look at individuals. Suppose that the ABox of the knowledge base ABox contains the fact Finger(sebastiansRightThumb). But this obviously allows us to deduce Arm(sebastiansRightThumb), hence Sebastian's right thumb is not only a finger but an arm as well. What's wrong here? Well, we have mistaken the part-of relation for the subclass relation or in linguistic terms *meronymy* for *hyponymy*.

Admittedly, it is tempting to do so, as those two relations share both the intuition of "belonging to something" as well as some formal properties such as being transitive.[13] However, as we have just seen, this can lead to considerable

---

[12] In particular, note that the class description $\forall R.\bot$ characterizes exactly those individuals without an outgoing R role.

[13] The general question whether a part-whole relationship should be transitive is a more difficult discussion we do not want to take up here. If it is understood in a physical sense, then it should be transitive, but there are other usages where transitivity would not be appropriate. See, e.g., [WCH87] for a detailed discussion.

confusion and unintuitive logical consequences. Therefore, a better practice to model meronymy is by using a dedicated role, say `partOf`, which may be declared transitive. The corrected above example would then read like this:

$$\text{Finger} \sqsubseteq \exists \text{partOf.Hand} \qquad \text{Hand} \sqsubseteq \exists \text{partOf.Arm} \qquad \text{Arm} \sqsubseteq \exists \text{partOf.Body}$$
$$\text{Toe} \sqsubseteq \exists \text{partOf.Foot} \qquad \text{Foot} \sqsubseteq \exists \text{partOf.Leg} \qquad \text{Leg} \sqsubseteq \exists \text{partOf.Body}$$
$$\text{Arm} \sqcap \text{Leg} \sqsubseteq \bot$$

Actually there is a rather reliable way to diagnose whether one class should be declared as a subclass of another one.

> *A class A should be modeled as a subclass of B only if the statement "every A is a B" makes sense and is correct.*

8.3.2.6 Watch the direction of roles

The following RDFS snippet illustrates another typical modeling error:

```
ex:author    rdfs:range    ex:Publication .
ex:author    rdfs:domain   ex:Person .
ex:macbeth   ex:author     ex:shakespeare .
```

A closer look reveals that something is wrong with the "direction" of the authorship property. In fact, RDFS consequences of the above triples would be that Macbeth is a person (which might be somewhat acceptable) and that Shakespeare is a publication (which is certainly wrong). In fact those modeling errors are surprisingly frequent and not always as obvious as in our case, in particular in cases where one ontology is edited by several people. Essentially, there are two ways to avoid these problems.

> *When introducing a new property or role name, add a comment that clarifies what its source and target are. Moreover, use names which allow only one unique intuitive reading.*

In the case of nouns (like "author"), such unambiguous names might be constructions with "of" or with "has" (`authorOf` or `hasAuthor`). For verbs (like "to write") an inflected form (`wrote` or `writes`) or a passive version with "by" (`writtenBy`) would prevent unintended readings.

8.3.2.7 Don't confuse class subsumption and class equivalence

When modeling correspondences between classes, some uncertainty might arise whether to use subsumption or equivalence (i.e. `rdfs:subClassOf` or `owl:equivalentClass`).

Usually, class subsumption is used to provide some information about members of a certain class, e.g., to express that all fish live in water. In this sense, living in water is a *necessary* condition for being a fish (as not living in the water excludes a being from that class). However (as witnessed by plankton, dolphins, etc.), not every being that lives in water is a fish or, in other words, living in water is no *sufficient* criterion for the class-membership as it does not fully characterize fishes.

> *Only if a class description is both necessary and sufficient, an equivalence statement should be used.*

This is normally the case if a new class is introduced and defined in terms of known classes, as for instance an orphan is defined as a person all of whose parents are dead:

$$\text{Orphan} \equiv \text{Person} \sqcap \forall\text{hasParent.Dead}$$

8.3.2.8 Don't translate too verbally

Although there are many useful heuristics for translating natural language into ontological specifications, one has to be careful when using them. As a basic example, the word "and" is not always meant to be an intersection of classes. Clearly, the "and" in the sentence "university staff members and students will get a login" will be translated into a union ($\text{UniStaffMember} \sqcup \text{Student} \sqsubseteq \exists\text{gets.Login}$) and not into an intersection ($\text{UniStaffMember} \sqcap \text{Student} \sqsubseteq \exists\text{gets.Login}$). The latter would express the weaker statement that an individual gets a login if it is both a university staff member and a student.

> *If in doubt about the correct formalization, two strategies that might help are paraphrasing and testing.*

On the one hand, one might paraphrase the proposition in order to get a clearer view. In our case, the reformulated sentence might be "somebody will get a login, if he is a university staff member or a student." On the other hand, having reasoning tools at hand, one might do some kind of testing. Knowing that the above statement, e.g., allows us to deduce $\exists\text{gets.Login(paul)}$ if we assert Student(paul), we might simply try either of the above options and employ a reasoner to check whether the desired consequence is entailed.

8.3.3 Ontology Refinement: How to Make Ontologies Better

After having identified basic characteristics for the quality of ontologies, we now investigate ways of improving an existing ontology in the light of some criteria introduced in the previous section. Thereby, we will put special emphasis on automated techniques.

We start by considering the situation where an ontology is inconsistent or incoherent. As explained earlier, this indicates that something is wrong with the ontology, in other words: some part of the specification does not correspond with the actual state of affairs. There are several ways to deal with this. One way is to "manually" examine the ontology and look for incorrect statements. The ontology might be too large to check every single statement or the modeling error could result from an intricate interplay of several axioms and therefore be hard to detect. However, reasoning methods can be used to identify the set of axioms responsible for the inconsistency or incoherency. In general, so-called *explanation* tools are capable of coming up with justifications for derived consequences of a knowledge base. This enables the knowledge engineer to focus on the relevant parts of the ontology when looking for errors. Another way of handling a flawed inconsistent or incoherent ontology is to employ automated methods that try to reestablish consistency resp. coherency by committing as few changes as possible to the ontology. Most of the employed techniques originate from the area of *belief revision* having a long tradition in AI research.

In the case of an ontology not containing enough information to allow for the retrieval of the wanted information, one can again distinguish between human-driven and machine-driven approaches. A human user might experience that a consequence he would expect cannot be inferred from the current specification and try to "debug" the knowledge base with respect to this shortcoming. Thereby certain non-standard reasoning methods called *abductive reasoning* might be helpful.[14]

On the more automated side, there are algorithms that step by step enumerate those statements (of a certain form) which can neither be deduced from the given ontology nor refuted on its grounds. The knowledge engineer can then decide for each of those statements whether to add it or its negated counterpart to the ontology. This way the ontology can be successively completed.

8.4   Modular Ontologies: Divide and Conquer

Another engineering aspect that is gaining more and more attention is the modularization of ontologies. Essentially, the field of ontology modularization

---

[14]Together with deduction and induction, abduction constitutes the three modes of human reasoning due to C.S. Peirce [Ket92]. Essentially, abduction answers the question what premise would entail a desired conclusion, given a body of knowledge.

investigates how large ontologies can be composed of smaller parts, called *modules*.

This is a desirable strategy for several reasons. Just as in software engineering, the increasing size and complexity of the artifacts necessitates strategies for collaborative and sustainable ontology design. Now, if ontologies are designed as loosely coupled, essentially self-contained systems, this facilitates diverse typical engineering activities. First, many maintenance tasks can be done locally by changing just the specific module in question. Next, the single components resp. modules can be reused in other contexts more easily. Further, from a more technical perspective, under certain circumstances reasoning tasks can be done more efficiently, as only a small part of the modules might be relevant for specific deductions or the reasoning itself can be distributed to several machines separately handling the modules. The latter point is also relevant if privacy and security issues come into play: an ontology owner might not be willing to disclose the entire ontology but only to offer some reasoning services. Then for the integrated querying of this and other ontologies, distributed reasoning approaches are necessary.

As there are already large ontologies that do not or not sufficiently abide by this modularity rationale, there is also ongoing research on automatically or semi-automatically subdividing monolithic ontologies into modules in order to exploit the above mentioned advantages modular ontologies bring about.

OWL and OWL 2 provide basic support for the distribution resp. module aspects through `owl:imports` allowing for the inclusion of other ontologies that might be situated elsewhere on the Web (see Section 4.1.1).

8.5   Software Tools

There is a considerable number of tools available for different aspects of ontology engineering. Many of them are research prototypes, however, and do not keep up to the standards of commercial solutions. Rather than giving a complete listing, we provide in this section pointers to the most popular and mature tools with recent releases,[15] including commercial systems, and mention only a few additional ones because we deem them important for some reason. Our selection is necessarily subjective.

Comprehensive lists of Semantic Web tools – including research prototypes – can be found under `http://semanticweb.org/wiki/Tools/` and under `http://esw.w3.org/topic/SemanticWebTools/`.

---

[15]We are always referring to the most recent version at the time of this writing, i.e. March 2009.

8.5.1　Ontology Editors

8.5.1.1　Protégé

Protégé is currently the most well-known ontology editor, is freely available, open source, and based on Java. Protégé is extensible and supported by a large community of users and of developers providing a considerable number of plug-in extensions. It also provides a plug-and-play environment to aid rapid prototyping and application development.

Protégé was developed by the Stanford Center for Biomedical Informatics Research in collaboration with The University of Manchester. It is available from `http://protege.stanford.edu/`. Besides RDF support, it comprises an OWL editor, called Protégé-OWL, which is actually an extension of the core system.

Protégé comes with two built-in reasoners, FaCT++ and Pellet (see below), and provides reasoning support during the editing process, e.g., by allowing one to compute all subclass relationships, called classification of the ontology. It also provides SWRL support and is tightly integrated with Jena (see below).

8.5.1.2　TopBraid Composer

The commercial TopBraid Composer, by the company TopQuadrant, is available from `http://www.topquadrant.com/topbraid/composer/`. It has built-in support for Pellet, Jena, and OWLIM (see below) and supports RDFS and OWL. SWRL is supported via Jena, and SPARQL can be used. The TopBraid Composer sports a considerable number of built-in features for ontology engineering tasks.

8.5.1.3　NeOn Toolkit

The NeOn Toolkit is an extensible ontology engineering environment available from `http://www.neon-toolkit.org` and developed as open source software by a consortium of European research facilities and companies. It is built on the code-base of OntoStudio (see below). The NeOn Toolkit sports various extensions and modules, some of which are commercial. It supports RDF and OWL DL and has native reasoning support through the KAON2 reasoner (see below). At the same time, the NeOn Toolkit also supports rule languages around RIF.

8.5.1.4　OntoStudio

OntoStudio, by ontoprise GmbH, is a commercial modeling environment for the creation and maintenance of ontologies. It supports RDF and rules in F-Logic, and can be used for collaborative ontology development. For further information see `http://www.ontoprise.de/en/home/products/ontostudio/`.

8.5.1.5 SWOOP

SWOOP is an open source tool for creating, editing, and debugging OWL ontologies available from `http://code.google.com/p/swoop/` under the MIT free software license. It was originally developed by the mindswap group at the University of Maryland. It takes the standard Web browser as user interface paradigm, and provides native support of Pellet (see below).

8.5.2 RDF Stores

8.5.2.1 Virtuoso

Virtuoso is a cross-platform integrated database engine with (among many other protocols) RDF and SPARQL support developed by OpenLink Software. It can be employed as the RDF store/query processor for the frameworks of Jena and Sesame (see below). It is available as Pay Licensed Closed Source or as a GPL Open Source version under the name OpenLink Virtuoso. See `http://virtuoso.openlinksw.com/` for more information and downloads.

8.5.2.2 Redland

Redland is a collection of free software libraries that enable RDF support. It was developed by Dave Beckett while he was at the University of Bristol, UK. It provides APIs for RDF data manipulation and querying via SPARQL, allows for in-memory and persistent graph storage, and comes with command line utility programs. It is available under GPL, LGPL, and Apache License. For downloads and more information see `http://librdf.org/`.

8.5.2.3 Sesame

Sesame is an RDF framework with inferencing and SPARQL querying support originally developed by Aduna. It comes with a native store but can also be used with other storage systems. It includes various developer tools and is available from `http://www.openrdf.org/` under a BSD-style Open Source license.

8.5.2.4 AllegroGraph

AllegroGraph RDFStore, by Franz Inc., is a Pay Licensed Closed Source RDF database. It supports RDFS reasoning and querying via SPARQL. For further details, see `http://agraph.franz.com/allegrograph/`.

8.5.2.5 OWLIM

OWLIM supports RDFS by means of Sesame and a rather small fragment of OWL DL – as well as a combination of these – but does so rather efficiently. It is freely available from `http://ontotext.com/owlim/` under the GNU LGPL and commercially supported by ontotext.

8.5.3   OWL DL Reasoning Engines

The strongest and most mature reasoners available for OWL DL are based
on tableaux algorithms presented in Section 5.3, and foremost to mention are
Pellet, FaCT++, and RacerPro as the most well-known systems.

8.5.3.1   Pellet

Pellet is an open source OWL reasoner written in Java and available from
http://pellet.owldl.com/. It supports OWL DL (more precisely $\mathcal{SHOIQ}$),
and is commercially supported by Clark & Parsia LLC. It also supports the
$\mathcal{SROIQ}$ description logic which underlies OWL 2 DL, and conjunctive querying using SPARQL syntax. It furthermore sports a number of features to
support ontology engineering, including the lightweight ontology browser Owl-
Sight, some analysis and repair functionalities, and support of DL-safe rules.

8.5.3.2   RacerPro

RacerPro is a commercial OWL reasoner by Racer Systems, and available
from http://www.racer-systems.com/. It supports OWL DL, although reasoning with nominals is only done in an approximate manner. Various pro-
priety extensions, e.g., for datatype reasoning, are available.

8.5.3.3   FaCT++

FaCT++ is an open source reasoner under the GNU public license, written
in C++ and developed at The University of Manchester. It is available from
http://owl.man.ac.uk/factplusplus/ and supports OWL DL as well as
OWL 2 DL.

8.5.3.4   KAON2

KAON2 is a commercial system, by ontoprise GmbH under the name OntoBroker OWL, with binaries freely available and free for use for universities
for noncommercial academic usage. In contrast to the aforementioned reasoners, KAON2 is not based on tableaux algorithms, but on the resolution
calculus. KAON2 supports $\mathcal{SHIQ}$ and DL-safe rules. Conjunctive queries
can be expressed using SPARQL syntax. KAON2 binaries are available from
http://kaon2.semanticweb.org/.

8.5.3.5   SHER

SHER is a reasoner for $\mathcal{SHIN}$ based on Pellet which uses some enhance-
ments of database indexing to obtain higher reasoning speed. It was developed
by IBM and is available from http://www.alphaworks.ibm.com/tech/sher/.

8.5.4 Reasoning Engines for OWL 2 Profiles

8.5.4.1 CEL

CEL was the first dedicated reasoner for $\mathcal{EL}^{++}$, though without support for nominals and ABoxes. $\mathcal{EL}^{++}$ will be part of the forthcoming OWL 2 standard as OWL 2 EL. It is restricted to classifying such ontologies, i.e. to computing all subclass relationships. It is free for evaluation and research purposes and can be obtained from `http://lat.inf.tu-dresden.de/systems/cel/`. It was developed by the Technical University of Dresden.

8.5.4.2 Owlgres

Owlgres is a reasoner for the DL-Lite fragment of the forthcoming OWL 2 standard, i.e. OWL 2 QL. It is available under the GNU AGPL 3 open source license from `http://pellet.owldl.com/owlgres`, while commercial support is provided by Clark & Parsia LLC. Owlgres allows one to formulate conjunctive queries in SPARQL syntax.

8.5.5 QuOnto

QuOnto, developed by "Sapienza" University of Rome is an OWL 2 QL reasoner. It is available from `http://www.dis.uniroma1.it/quonto/` as a demo version for testing purposes. It supports conjunctive queries and SPARQL.

8.5.5.1 Oracle 11g

Oracle 11g supports RDF(S) and the OWL 2 RL profile of OWL 2 for ontology management. It comes with an adaptor for Jena. For more information, see `http://www.oracle.com`.

8.5.6 Datalog and Rules Engines

We obviously restrict ourselves to rules engines which can handle rules as introduced in Chapter 6.

8.5.6.1 XSB

XSB is a well-known open source Prolog system developed by the Computer Science Department of Stony Brook University and others. It is available from `http://xsb.sourceforge.net/`. Among the systems building on it is FLORA-2 – available from `http://flora.sourceforge.net/` – which is an object-oriented knowledge base language and application development environment. Its underlying language is F-Logic.

8.5.6.2   SWI-Prolog

SWI-Prolog is another very popular open source Prolog system, developed by Jan Wielemaker at the University of Amsterdam. It is available from http://www.swi-prolog.org/.

8.5.6.3   Ontobroker

Ontobroker is a commercial logic programming system developed by ontoprise GmbH, with a long history of ontology-based application development. It supports reasoning with RIF, with F-Logic, but also with RDF and OWL, and querying with SPARQL and conjunctive queries. Information is available from http://www.ontoprise.de/en/home/products/ontobroker/.

8.5.6.4   DLV

DLV is a datalog system which is free for academic and non-commercial use developed by the University of Calabria. It sports some extensions which allow one to integrate OWL reasoning in a hybrid way, i.e. rules and OWL can be used together, but they interact in a less obvious way. It is available from http://www.dbai.tuwien.ac.at/proj/dlv/.

8.5.6.5   IRIS

IRIS is a system for reasoning with a restricted form of datalog programs developed by STI Innsbruck under the LGPL license and used for Semantic Web purposes. It is available from http://www.iris-reasoner.org/.

8.5.7   Further Systems

8.5.7.1   OWL API

The OWL API is a Java interface and implementation for OWL 2. It is open source and available from http://owlapi.sourceforge.net/ under the LGPL license. The OWL API includes an API for OWL 2 and an efficient in-memory reference implementation, parsers and writers for different syntaxes, support for integration with OWL reasoners, and support for black-box debugging. It is primarily maintained at The University of Manchester.

8.5.7.2   Jena

Jena is a mature Java framework for building Semantic Web applications developed by Hewlett-Packard, available from http://jena.sourceforge.net and open source. It provides a programmatic environment for RDF(S) and OWL, and sports a rule-based OWL inference engine which is incomplete with respect to the OWL semantics. Jena also supports SPARQL.

8.6   Summary

As ontologies are widely adopted also for large-scale applications, strategies for their creation, evaluation, and maintenance are needed. The related field of software engineering can provide some useful insights into how to create successful ontology engineering processes. For the creation of ontologies, sources of knowledge can be: human experts, unstructured sources such as texts, semistructured sources like wikis or hypertext documents and structured sources as databases or already existing ontologies. For quality assurance, ontologies can be evaluated based on several criteria, among them logical, structural, and formal criteria as well as accuracy. For improving an ontology's quality, semiautomatic methods are available. Modularization of ontologies provides benefits in terms of management and reuse. Several tools for assisting in diverse ontology management tasks are available.

8.7   Further Reading

As stated earlier, Ontology Engineering is a broad and diverse field still in its infancy. Therefore, the following set of literature recommendations is necessarily both subjective and tentative.

Edited volumes containing comprehensive overviews on topics related to ontology engineering are [SS09] and [GPCFL04]. As a shorter first read, [PM04] outlines the parallels of ontology and software engineering.

The question how to make experts' implicit knowledge explicit is a central issue in the scientific field of knowledge management. [NT95] is one of the standard references addressing this question in the context of companies. Automated techniques for knowledge acquisition from sets of training examples provided by experts clearly fall into the realm of machine learning. [Mit97] gives an excellent introduction on machine learning in general. For the particular field of inductive logic programming, [LD94] provides an in-depth treatment.

As stated before, techniques for extracting knowledge from natural language documents can be roughly divided into statistical vs. structural approaches. Statistically oriented methods are focused on by the discipline of information retrieval; [MRS07] gives a profound introduction. In particular, latent semantic analysis, a prominent word-bag method, is described in [LD97]. The term ontology learning refers to the extraction of ontological knowledge from textual sources; see [MS01]. Diverse approaches to ontology learning are presented in [BC08], wherein [VHH08] is an example for a structural rather than statistical approach to that problem. An overview of ontology learning tools can be found in [GPMM04]. On a more abstract level, problems of transferring natural language texts via structural analysis into logical specifications have been intensely dealt with by discourse representation theory [KR93].

References and ongoing work on constrained natural language ("controlled English") related to ontologies for the Semantic Web can be found under http://wiki.webont.org/page/OwlCnl.

Network or link analysis [The04] deals with the extraction of information from graph structures and can be used for coming up with "shallow" semantic information about interlinked Web pages or wiki articles.

Ontology matching and its subfields ontology alignment, ontology mapping, and ontology merging have become an increasingly hot topic in ontology management as evidenced by numerous workshops and publications. [ES07] gives a good overview of this vibrant field.

Techniques for explaining automated inferences to the user are well-established and implemented in most related tools. A nicely written explanation on explanations can be found in [HPS08]. Foundations of the technique of belief revision and also some hints on its employment for ontology repair are described in [Gär92].

OntoClean [GW04] is an elaborate, philosophically inspired methodology for ontology evaluation based on formal criteria that rely on class qualities such as rigidity.

When modeling his very first ontology, the reader may find the seminal guideline [NM] helpful. For avoiding common modeling errors, [RDH+04] gives valuable hints.

Formal Concept Analysis [GW97] can be used as a basis for methods to complete insufficiently axiomatized ontologies as described in [Rud06] and [Ser07].

The topic of modular ontologies is another example of an emerging field and is currently gaining much interest from the research community. For a substantial contribution to that field, see [CHKS08]; for a thorough and comprehensive overview of the state of the art, we refer the interested reader to [SPS09].

Many Semantic Web tools, including research prototypes, are listed with references and pointers under http://semanticweb.org/wiki/Tools/ and http://esw.w3.org/topic/SemanticWebTools/.

Chapter 9

Applications

There is no shortage of potential future use case scenarios for Semantic Web technologies, ranging from information integration over ambient intelligence to expert systems. Such scenarios are reported in the proceedings of various research and industrial conferences, edited research books, and project reports, and we give corresponding pointers in Section 9.10. These reports are a clear indication of the current state of the art, namely, that Semantic Web technologies are currently in a transition phase from research into applications. This is also witnessed by the industrial development of ontology editors and reasoners, as presented in Section 8.5.

Rather than providing yet another compilation of potential use cases, in this chapter we focus instead on a selected few real life applications, i.e. applications which are really being used. They show the uptake of Semantic Web technologies in practice, and witness the currently ongoing transition from research into applications. Our selection is necessarily subjective; however, we are confident that we have captured some of the most relevant applications to date.

But before we actually come to the applications, let us dwell for a moment on the question what – and what not – *applications of Semantic Web technologies* actually are. It turns out that it is not easy to give such a definition.

Naively speaking, something is an application of Semantic Web technologies if it actually uses Semantic Web technologies. But this leaves us with the question what Semantic Web technologies are. And in attempting to define this term, we have to realize that Semantic Web technologies, generally speaking, are rather a vaguely defined *class* of technologies than a concrete technology – vaguely defined as having something to do with metadata, data exchange and integration, knowledge representation, the Web, ontologies, and following the general visions explained in Chapter 1, but not defined in any crisp way. Perhaps Semantic Web technologies are still too young for such a crisp definition. But let's try anyway.

A workable and straightforward definition of *applications of Semantic Web technologies* is that they are applications which use any of the standardized ontology languages, i.e. RDF or OWL. This might probably be a safe definition considering the fact that we have these languages available. However, it leaves out applications using RIF (which at the time of this writing is in the last stages of becoming a W3C recommendation, but isn't one yet). Likewise, what about applications using other ontology languages which were around before OWL was there,[1] or ontology languages which are not standardized but appear to be viable alternatives?[2] The definition would miss these. And at the same time it would include uses of RDF which are, probably, not at all in the spirit of the Semantic Web.

So let us attempt a much more general definition and say that *applications of Semantic Web technologies* are defined by using metadata in a metadata-specific way. This sounds about right, but if you think about it for a while then you may start to wonder about the precise definition of *metadata* and of *metadata-specific*. In some sense, metadata is simply data describing other data – but again this definition is not entirely crisp.

None of the suggestions above is a satisfactory definition, and indeed, we think it is futile to dwell on this point longer at this stage. Future developments will clarify matters.[3]

As for this chapter, we mainly take the naive stance and discuss applications which use any of the ontology languages which we have introduced in this book. We even go a step further and almost exclusively include applications where we were able to verify the use of such languages by means of documentation or publications. We are aware that there are some prominent applications which are commonly said to use them as well, but it is not documented. We are also aware that there are prominent applications which have the look and feel of Semantic Web technologies but are not labeled or marketed or conceived as such, for whatever reason. Such applications are also not included.

9.1   Web Data Exchange and Syndication

There is already a considerable number of sources for knowledge expressed in RDF or OWL on the Web.[4] A recent effort, initiated by Tim Berners-Lee and commonly referred to as the *linked data* initiative,[5] is currently gathering and channeling interested parties in order to strengthen links between available semantic data on the Web. Some of this data comes from Semantic

---

[1] Like GRAIL; see page 346.

[2] Like F-Logic, for example.

[3] The interested reader may want to reread Chapter 1 at this stage.

[4] We're already easily talking about billions of RDF triples on the Web – although we have to say that it doesn't really make much sense to talk about exact numbers, for many reasons, including the fact that many triples are automatically generated when requested or crawled.

[5] See http://esw.w3.org/topic/SweoIG/TaskForces/CommunityProjects/LinkingOpenData and http://www.w3.org/DesignIssues/LinkedData.html.

Portals (which are discussed in Section 9.3) and other sources which we will encounter throughout this chapter.[6]

9.1.1 Endowing Web Data with Metadata

Many prominent websites and Web portals are now endowed with metadata or (partially) cast into RDF, and have become part of the linked data "cloud," which is the term used for describing the collection of data sets which have been interlinked by this initiative. This includes TV program information, music databases, census data, research literature datasets, prominent Web 2.0 portals like Flickr[7] and MySpace,[8] etc.[9] A rather prominent example is the DBPedia knowledge base[10] which is created from extracting structured information from Wikipedia.[11]

Freebase,[12] by Metaweb Technologies, Inc., is an open RDF-based database anybody can add to, and which also integrates data available on the Web, including data from Wikipedia. Freebase is also part of the linked data cloud.

9.1.2 Vocabularies

A vocabulary is a collection of identifiers with predefined meanings which are informally specified. In the Semantic Web context vocabularies may be accompanied by some (simple) ontological relationships. They are usually used for the transmission of data between software applications, but they also contribute significantly to the linked data effort.

Creative Commons,[13] for example, which is a non-profit organization dedicated to providing free licenses and legal tools, has defined a vocabulary which allows us to describe copyright licenses in RDF.[14] The Yahoo! Creative Commons Search,[15] for example, allows us to use these descriptions in order to search for Web content based on reuse licenses.

In the following, we briefly present two vocabularies which we deem to be of particular importance for the Semantic Web – although there are certainly many others.

---

[6]See the first link in Footnote 5 for further major sources of semantic data related to the linked data initiative.

[7]http://www.flickr.com/

[8]http://www.myspace.com/

[9]Please see the first link in footnote 5 for more information on these efforts.

[10]http://dbpedia.org/

[11]http://www.wikipedia.org/

[12]http://www.freebase.com/

[13]http://creativecommons.org/

[14]http://creativecommons.org/ns

[15]http://search.yahoo.com/cc/

RSS RDF Site Summary 1.0[16] (RSS) is probably the most commonly used Semantic Web vocabulary. It is used in Weblogs (Blogs), and is expressed in RDF. Weblog software, like WordPress,[17] is designed to simplify the creation and maintenance of such weblogs. The specified vocabulary defines authors, dates, titles, etc. Using an RSS feed reader, any user can access RSS feeds which usually contain news items and brief reports, and which are provided by many sites on the World Wide Web. The content is downloaded as RDF, and displayed to the user. Figure 9.1 shows an example of an RSS feed.

The benefit of using RSS feeds is the aggregation of information into the feed reader, which is controlled by the user. This contrasts, for example, with the use of email, where the sender determines which information is received by the recipient. RSS feeds can further be aggregated on the Web, resulting in websites which provide all the aggregated items from these feeds through one single feed. The structured format of RSS feeds furthermore allows for an elaborate further processing of the information.

In February 2009, the U.S. government issued a memorandum with the subject *Initial Implementing Guidance for the American Recovery and Reinvestment Act of 2009* which includes a statement that some reporting must be done using a feed – with RSS mentioned as one of the possible protocols.[18]

Note that the alternative format *Really Simple Syndication* (RSS 2.0), although related, is realized in XML, and not in RDF.

FOAF Friend of a Friend[19] (FOAF) is a vocabulary for data about persons and for social networking. FOAF files contain information about a person's name, age, gender, acquaintances, etc., and allow the browsing and analysis of social networks. To date, there are roughly one million FOAF files on the World Wide Web, most of them generated automatically on Web portals. There are also tools for generating FOAF files, like FOAF Creator[20] and FOAF-a-matic.[21]

FOAF uses RDF and OWL for describing the vocabulary, e.g., by means of owl:sameAs to identify resources belonging to the same person. Figure 9.2 shows an example of a FOAF file.

FOAF files can be browsed using applications like the FOAF Explorer.[22] FOAF is often used in conjunction with SIOC (Semantically Interlinked On-

---

[16]http://web.resource.org/rss/1.0/

[17]http://wordpress.org/

[18]http://www.recovery.gov/files/
                        Initial%20Recovery%20Act%20Implementing%20Guidance.pdf

[19]http://www.foaf-project.org/

[20]http://neverfriday.com/foaf/create.html

[21]http://www.ldodds.com/foaf/foaf-a-matic.html

[22]http://xml.mfd-consult.dk/foaf/explorer/

```
<rdf:RDF
    xmlns:rdf="http://www.w3.org/1999/02/22-rdf-syntax-ns#"
    xmlns="http://purl.org/rss/1.0/">
 <channel rdf:about="http://example.org/rss/examples.rss">
  <title>Example News Feed</title>
  <link>http://example.org</link>
  <description>
  Example News
  </description>
  <items>
   <rdf:Seq>
    <rdf:li resource="http://example.org/rss/example1.html" />
    <rdf:li resource="http://example.org/rss/example2.html" />
   </rdf:Seq>
  </items>
 </channel>
 <item rdf:about="http://example.org/rss/example1.html">
  <title>First Example</title>
  <link>http://example.org/rss/example1.html</link>
  <description>
  This is the text of the first example in this RSS feed.
  </description>
 </item>
 <item rdf:about="http://example.org/rss/example2.html">
  <title>Second Example</title>
  <link>http://example.org/rss/example2.html</link>
  <description>
  This is the text of the second example in this RSS feed.
  </description>
 </item>
</rdf:RDF>
```

FIGURE 9.1:   Example RSS file

```
<rdf:RDF>
 <foaf:PersonalProfileDocument rdf:about="">
  <foaf:maker rdf:resource="http://simia.net/foaf.rdf#denny" />
 </foaf:PersonalProfileDocument>
 <foaf:Person rdf:about="http://simia.net/foaf.rdf#denny">
 <foaf:name>Zdenko Vrandecic</foaf:name>
 <foaf:name>Denny Vrandecic</foaf:name>
 <foaf:openid rdf:resource="http://denny.vrandecic.de" />
 <owl:sameAs rdf:resource=
   "http://dblp.l3s.de/d2r/resource/authors/Denny_Vrandecic" />
 <foaf:givenname>Zdenko</foaf:givenname>
 <foaf:family_name>Vrandecic</foaf:family_name>
 <foaf:nick>denny</foaf:nick>
 <foaf:homepage rdf:resource="http://denny.vrandecic.de" />
 <foaf:knows>
  <foaf:Person rdf:about=
    "http://anupriya.ankolekar.name/foaf.rdf#anupriya">
   <foaf:name>Anupriya Ankolekar</foaf:name>
  </foaf:Person>
  </foaf:knows>
 <foaf:knows>
 <foaf:knows>
  <foaf:Person rdf:about="http://ontoworld.org/wiki/
                                Special:URIResolver/Rudi_Studer">
   <foaf:name>Rudi Studer</foaf:name>
   <rdfs:seeAlso rdf:resource="http://www.aifb.uni-karlsruhe.de/
                          Personen/viewPersonFOAF/foaf_57.rdf" />
  </foaf:Person>
 </foaf:knows>
</rdf:RDF>
```

FIGURE 9.2:   Example FOAF file

line Communities),[23] which is an ontology for integrating online community information. FOAF is also supported by Google's Social Graph API.[24]

9.2 Semantic Wikis

The wiki paradigm of collective knowledge management has been around for many years, almost as long as the Web itself. However, only the enormous success of Wikipedia truly started the interests in this quick and simple new way of sharing information. Today, wikis have become common in many applications, including Web-based information portals, but also non-public corporate intranet sites and write-restricted collaboration platforms. What sets wikis apart from traditional HTML content management systems is that they make authoring of Web content very easy even for non-experts, and that they invite user contributions. This observation soon led to the idea of pursuing a similar approach for semantic Web content, resulting in what is now known as *semantic wikis*.

Generally speaking, wikis are systems for managing hypertext and related data such as images or file uploads. The main characteristic of a wiki is that it allows users to add and modify content *quickly* and *easily*. This vague description is usually approached by allowing users to author content in a simple mark-up language that hides some of the complexities of HTML. This syntax, usually called *wiki text*, differs among implementations, and even is sometimes hidden beneath a graphical user interface. Typical wikis contain *pages*, or *articles*, that constitute the basic units of wiki text that users can edit. Editors of the wiki may then create, modify, delete, or rename articles in order to improve the content of the wiki.[25]

A basic concept of semantic wikis is to extend the features of a given wiki text to allow semantic information to be specified together with other content of wiki pages. A typical assumption of semantic wikis is that semantic content is related to the page on which it is specified, such that semantic information augments the hypertext that the wiki contains. As a result, semantic information in semantic wikis also follows a page-based structure, and pages are often assumed to represent ontological elements. In fact, there is another possible notion of "semantic wiki" as a system that applies wiki-like interaction paradigms to arbitrary ontological data, not necessarily connected to other wiki content. Such systems are more closely related to collaboratively used

---

[23]See http://sioc-project.org/ and http://www.w3.org/Submission/sioc-spec/.

[24]http://code.google.com/apis/socialgraph/

[25]Note that, in spite of the well-known case of Wikipedia, wiki editors are not necessarily the same as wiki users. Especially corporate wikis often regulate access rights and user privileges.

ontology editors, and should thus be compared with the systems mentioned in Section 8.5.1, some of which do also offer collaboration options. This said, it is still possible that semantic wikis support the authoring of ontological axioms, yet the underlying paradigm differs from generic ontology editors.

9.2.1   Semantic MediaWiki

As a concrete example implementation, we consider *Semantic MediaWiki* (SMW), which has been a forerunner for semantic wiki technology and which is in wide use today. SMW is an extension to the wiki engine *MediaWiki*[26] that is also used to run Wikipedia. Both systems are available as free software.

The basic structure of semantic data in SMW is inspired by RDF and OWL. Individuals are represented by wiki articles, and basic assertions are created by assigning property-value pairs to these pages. This corresponds to the triple structure that we encountered in RDF. Such assertions are typically entered in a special syntax that is derived from the wiki text of MediaWiki. For example, the text

```
This textbook was published by [[publisher::CRC Press]] in
[[publication date::2009]].
```

might be the content of the page "Foundations of Semantic Web Technologies." When viewed in a browser, the page then would display the sentence "This textbook was published by CRC Press in 2009" where "CRC Press" might be a link to another page of that name. In addition, SMW would extract two assertions (triples) that assign to the article about the textbook a property value CRC Press for the property publisher, and a property value 2009 for the property publication date. The example shows how semantic annotation and hypertext authoring can be combined into a single interface. Also note that we did not specify the datatype of any of the values here, so the above wiki text does not specify if 2009 refers to a date, to the name of another wiki page, or to something else.

Editors of the wiki are free to define properties that are to be used in asserting semantic data: a special subset of pages in the wiki-namespace Property represents existing properties. As opposed to RDF, properties in SMW have a specific datatype, and all values that are assigned for a property are considered to be of that datatype. This explains why we did not have to specify any typing information in the example above. Assigning datatypes to properties is done in the style of generic property assertions. For example, the input

---

[26]http://www.mediawiki.org/

```
This property is used to refer to the [[has type::date]] of
publications.
```

on the page entitled "Property:Publication date" defines a datatype `date` for this property. The available datatypes in SMW are different from XML Schema, since they are more tailored toward wiki use. For example, there is a type `page` that is used for properties that refer to other wiki pages. Properties for which no datatype was specified will be assumed to have this type by default. The datatype also defines to which property types of OWL, such as `owl:ObjectProperty` or `owl:DatatypeProperty`, an SMW property corresponds.

Besides basic property assertions, SMW allows us to specify semantic information in a number of further ways. For example, pages can be tagged with *categories*, a mechanism already available in MediaWiki, to denote a class membership assertion. Moreover, hierarchies of properties and classes can be encoded, as well as various other forms of ontological axioms. We do not provide the details of these mechanisms here.

The practical success of SMW relies on the fact that it provides immediate benefits of entering semantic data. Of course, semantic data can be more easily exchanged, and SMW indeed offers a number of export facilities to support this. This alone, however, is hardly enough to motivate users to contribute semantic data. The main application of semantics in SMW is *semantic search*, i.e. the retrieval of data based on entered queries. The query language of SMW is syntactically based on the wiki text used for creating annotations, and we will not provide further details here. We note, however, that queries in SMW can be answered in polynomial time, and thus are less expressive than conjunctive queries or SPARQL (see Chapter 7). An important innovation introduced in SMW is *inline queries*. These queries are entered during wiki editing as part of the wiki text, and the resulting HTML page displays the query results in their place. This enables readers to profit from SMW even without being aware of semantic queries. Due to extensive formatting options, inline queries can be fully integrated with hand-written page contents.

In spite of its success, SMW is neither the only nor the first semantic wiki. See Section 9.10 for pointers to further tools in this area.

9.2.2 Applications

Just like wikis, semantic wikis can be applied in essentially any application domain. As of today, more than 300 public sites are known to use SMW,[27] excluding an unknown number of non-public sites in corporate environments.

---

[27]http://semantic-mediawiki.org/wiki/Sites_using_Semantic_MediaWiki/

Various commercial wiki hosts, including the world's largest wiki provider, Wikia,[28] offer SMW to their customers. Mirroring the general structure on the Web, most public semantic wiki sites deal with recreational topics, but also scientific and technological applications are common. In general, SMW is particularly useful in applications that feature significant amounts of *semi-structured* data – textual information that involves a large number of concrete relations and data values.

9.3   Semantic Portals

Semantic portals are websites where the human-readable content is accompanied by machine-readable information using ontology languages. This can range from the provision of FOAF files to providing complex page content by means of OWL ontologies.

Through the use of ontologies, a semantic portal provides its content in a format which can easily be reused by Semantic Web applications which utilize data from the open Web. It can also easily be integrated into the linked data cloud. Another advantage is that internal content management can also be done using ontologies, which simplifies integration with other data and also allows us to realize better search and browsing facilities for the user of the portal.

A number of websites of research groups and projects sport such information.[29] Semantic MediaWiki, discussed in Section 9.2, also features RDF exports. Twine[30] by Radar Networks is a social networking portal which heavily uses RDF and OWL.

Yahoo! SearchMonkey[31] is an example of an application which leverages semantic data provided by semantic portals. SearchMonkey internally uses a format based on RDF and allows us to create small applications for enhancing Yahoo! search results with additional data and structure, like giving direct links to related pictures. It allows us to incorporate RDF data gathered by the Yahoo! Search Crawler into the displayed results.

On some Web portals, internal data management is done using RDF, although RDF exports are not provided. Examples include Yahoo! Food,[32]

---

[28]http://wikia.com/

[29]See, e.g., the KMI portal http://semanticweb.kmi.open.ac.uk at the Open University, or the AIFB website http://www.aifb.uni-karlsruhe.de/about.html at the University of Karlsruhe.

[30]http://www.twine.com/

[31]http://developer.yahoo.com/searchmonkey/

[32]http://food.yahoo.com/

which is a site for recipes, cooking, restaurants, etc., and Vodafone life!,[33] which provides downloads for mobile phones.

9.4   Semantic Metadata in Data Formats

Some data formats for documents allow us to include metadata about the document. This allows us to convey information like authorship, creation date, and the like, in a machine-readable form, and to do so even if the visual appearance of the document, e.g., a picture, would not state this information. To aid portability and reuse of this metadata, some data formats use RDF for expressing it.

Probably the most prominent example is Adobe XMP,[34] which allows us to include RDF-based metadata, for example, in PDF files.[35] It is supported by Adobe applications like Photoshop 7.0, Acrobat 5.0, and Illustrator 10.

The World Wide Web Consortium (W3C) has established a recommended standard for graphics, called Scalable Vector Graphics (SVG).[36] It is based on XML and editable in text editors. It allows us to directly embed metadata in RDF and is supported, for example, by Inkscape[37] and popular Web browsers like Mozilla Firefox or Microsoft Internet Explorer.

9.5   Semantic Web in Life Sciences

Life Sciences is a candidate for applications of Semantic Web technologies with high impact. Indeed there are substantial research activities in adopting Semantic Web technologies for Life Sciences, as witnessed, e.g., by the W3C Semantic Web Health Care and Life Sciences Interest Group.[38] This comes as no surprise considering the discussion in Chapter 1, where we pointed out that Life Sciences have prompted historical modeling efforts like the Linnaean taxonomy.

---

[33]http://www.vodafone.de/vodafonelive.html

[34]http://www.adobe.com/products/xmp/

[35]http://www.adobe.com/products/xmp/pdfs/whitepaper.pdf

[36]http://www.w3.org/Graphics/SVG/

[37]http://www.inkscape.org/ – we actually used this for producing some of the figures in this book.

[38]See http://www.w3.org/2001/sw/hcls/ and also the proceedings of a corresponding workshop at the 17th International World Wide Web Conference 2008, which can be found under http://esw.w3.org/topic/HCLS/WWW2008.

The rationale behind these activities is to leverage Semantic Web technologies in order to make the best use of the rapidly accumulating knowledge in Life Sciences, e.g., by establishing ways to integrate data repositories and to make them available in a structured form.

In the course of these actions, a number of highly visible ontologies have been developed, and we mention some of them below. They are often also used as unofficial benchmarks for OWL reasoners.

The **Gene Ontology**[39] is maintained by the Gene Ontology Consortium, which includes several of the world's most important genome repositories. The Gene Ontology serves the need to have consistent descriptions of gene products over different databases, and thus allows, for example, uniform queries across participating databases. The Gene Ontology has become a standard tool in the bioinformatics arsenal. It is available in different formats, including RDF and OWL.

SNOMED CT, the Systematized Nomenclature of Medicine – Clinical Terms, developed by the International Health Terminology Standards Development Organisation,[40] is an ontology for clinical terminology designed to support the exchange and aggregation of health data. It is now further maintained and developed by SNOMED Terminology Solutions,[41] which is a division of the College of American Pathologists. Among its applications are electronic medical records, clinical decision support, medical research studies, image indexing, and consumer health information services.

SNOMED CT can be expressed in $\mathcal{EL}^{++}$, i.e. in OWL 2 EL, and its classification by the reasoner CEL (see Section 8.5.4.1) was the landmark result in pushing the development of tractable languages and reasoners around OWL.

GALEN is an ontology developed by the non-profit organization Open-GALEN.[42] It is designed for building clinical applications, to support clinicians in everyday work. It thus represents medical information which such applications require. It is multilingual and commercial products based on it are available on the market. Its origin dates back to the early 1990s, and it is coded in an ontology language developed for this purpose, called GRAIL. GALEN is also available in OWL.

---

[39]http://www.geneontology.org/

[40]http://www.ihtsdo.org/

[41]http://www.cap.org/apps/cap.portal?_nfpb=true&_pageLabel=snomed_page

[42]http://www.opengalen.org/

9.6 Ontologies for Standardizations

Ontology languages are made for expressing complex relationships. As such, they can be used in application areas for expressing technical standards. Due to the fixed semantics coming with the ontology languages, ambiguities in the expressed standards are reduced.

A particularly prominent example of such an application is the **IEC 61970** standard, known as Common Information Model (CIM), maintained and developed by the International Electrotechnical Commission,[43] which is the world's leading organization for international standards related to electrical, electronic, and related technologies. The standard is used for describing power networks and addresses interdisciplinary challenges over a variety of fields related to the realization of electrotechnical solutions. It provides, for example, for the modeling of power net topologies including transformers, wires, circuit breakers, and transformer stations, but also some artifacts from business administration like contracts and clients.

CIM has recently been ported into RDF and OWL, specifically due to the required expressivity for formulating the standard.

At the time of this writing, there is also a proposal to use an OWL ontology as a part of the forthcoming IEEE 802.21 standard.[44]

9.7 RIF Applications

We discuss RIF applications separately, simply because RIF is closely related to logic programming, which in turn has been around for more than 40 years and thus has already been applied within a multitude of contexts. It would be out of the scope of this book to go into details on this. However, we would like to point out that some of the more recent applications are clearly applications of semantic technologies.

A particular example of this is an expert system realized by ontoprise GmbH for the KUKA Roboter GmbH, a prominent vendor of industrial robots.[45] It is essentially an ontology-based error diagnosis system which aids service engineers with robot maintenance.

For a selection of possible further use cases of RIF we refer the reader to the current version of the *RIF Use Cases and Requirements* document[46] by

---

[43]http://www.iec.ch/

[44]http://tools.ietf.org/html/draft-ohba-802dot21-basic-schema-05/

[45]http://www.ontoprise.de/en/home/references/kuka-roboter-gmbh/

[46]http://www.w3.org/2005/rules/wiki/UCR/

the W3C RIF working group.

9.8   Toward Future Applications

The applications presented in this chapter substantiate the claim that Semantic Web technologies are currently in a transition from research to real-life applications. Most of the applications to date make only very shallow use of ontology languages; in particular, the reasoning capabilities over ontological knowledge are not yet being exploited to their full potential. So there is a lot of scope for future developments, and we want to mention a number of promising use case scenarios and emerging applications. Further pointers will be given below in Section 9.10.

A much-cited article from 2001, co-authored by Tim Berners-Lee, describes a long-term vision for the development of semantic technologies. Projecting a world where online services (such as information portals), offline services with online interfaces (like online shops), and electronic household items (like PDAs and TV sets) can freely interact due to commonly shared ontology-based representation languages, the scenario exemplifies how Semantic Web technologies have the potential to enhance our everyday lives through support of shopping, timetable scheduling, and the like. While such a vision is still rather futuristic, it projects some of the grand goals behind the Semantic Web efforts related to ubiquitous computing and ambient intelligence.

Central in the development of such powerful applications is the flexible use of Web Services, enhanced with semantic descriptions. The central idea is to use semantic descriptions of Web Service functionalities to facilitate the finding of relevant services, their composition for solving complex tasks, and their automatic invocation for providing the desired functionalities. On a more mundane level, Semantic Web Services are projected to be important for the next generation of software engineering based on Service Oriented Architectures, again because of the flexibility and automation in finding and composing Web Services. Considerable efforts are under way in academic and industrial research for realizing such goals.

Another application area with high potential is Semantic Search, which refers to the use of metadata and background knowledge in the form of ontologies to enhance search for information on the World Wide Web and in corporate intranets. This will lead away from a search paradigm based on keyword matching to a more conceptual scenario, where it is possible to search for content even if specific keywords in the desired documents are unknown. Semantic Search can make use of reasoning functionalities and provide hits which are more relevant.

Information integration is one of the major challenges of our information age. The amount of knowledge on the Web and in databases and applications is breathtaking, and even within companies the access to and finding of relevant information and data remain difficult. Ontologies provide means to describe information items conceptually, which aids integration and search. The development of corresponding frameworks and tools for information integration is currently being pursued in academia and in the industry.

One of the many example use case scenarios for information integration is being explored by the Food and Agriculture Organisation (FAO) of the United Nations in the context of the project NeOn,[47] funded by the European Union. Semantic technologies will be used for the integration of fishery data which is collected from all over the world. The concrete goal of the study is the development of an overfishing alert system based on semantic technologies.

Ontologies are also increasingly used as general knowledge representation formalisms for intelligent systems. The rationale behind this is that they provide a favorable trade-off between expressivity of the representation language and scalability of reasoning support. An example application is the use of ontologies in computer vision, e.g., for the automatic recognition of topology and driving lanes in traffic intersections [HTL07]. Standard technology from image recognition is supplemented by background knowledge, represented in OWL, on possible intersection topologies. OWL reasoning support then allows us to severely cut down on the possible interpretations of the sensor data, thus allowing us to correctly identify driving lanes.

9.9 Summary

We have provided a number of real-life examples of applications of Semantic Web technologies to illustrate the current transfer from research into practice. We have also discussed some potential future use cases. Application areas range over many topics in Computer Science to uses in other fields, and considerable impact of these technologies can be forecast.

9.10 Further Reading

The examples in this chapter are only a fraction of the available and possible applications of semantic technologies. We have not mentioned the use of RDF

---

[47]http://www.neon-project.org/

for Web page child safety labels[48] and many others.

For further reading about applications and use case scenarios, we refer to the considerable number of edited books on ontologies and the Semantic Web, including [DSW06, SS09, HS09] and others. Recommended also is the article [FHH+07]. Good resources are also the proceedings of the workshop series OWL – Experiences and Directions,[49] and of major Semantic Web conferences such as the International Semantic Web Conference,[50] the Semantic Technology Conference,[51], the International Conference on Semantic Systems,[52] and the European Semantic Technologies Conference.[53]

Semantic MediaWiki was discussed in some detail in [KVV+07], though the most relevant source for applications is clearly the online documentation [SMW09]. In addition, a number of projects build upon Semantic MediaWiki, for instance, by offering advanced input interfaces. Examples include the Halo Extension[54] and Semantic Forms.[55] Information on other semantic wiki implementations can be found e.g. in [Sch06, Kie06, NS06, ADR06, Kuh06].

References for the role of RDF and OWL in the IEC 61970 standard are [UG07, UD07].

The landmark article from 2001 by Tim Berners-Lee et al. was mentioned in Chapter 1. The reference is [BLHL01].

For further information on Semantic Web Services, see, e.g., [SGA07] or the Web pages of the Semantic Web Services Initiative.[56]

---

[48]http://www.fosi.org/icra/

[49]http://www.webont.org/owled/

[50]http://iswc.semanticweb.org/

[51]http://www.semantic-conference.com/

[52]http://triple-i.tugraz.at/i_semantics/

[53]http://www.estc2008.com/

[54]http://halowiki.ontoprise.de/

[55]http://www.mediawiki.org/wiki/Extension:Semantic_Forms/

[56]http://www.swsi.org/

Part V

Appendices

Appendix A

Extensible Markup Language XML

The Extensible Markup Language XML is a fundamental data format for the World Wide Web which is widely in use. It is recommended by the World Wide Web Consortium (W3C) for data exchange and electronic publishing. In this appendix we briefly review those parts of the XML specification which we need in this book, and a little bit more in order to convey an intuition about XML. It is not a complete introduction: For an in-depth study, see the documents provided by the W3C,[1] or any of the numerous books on XML and XML Schema which you can find in your bookshop or your library.

A.1 XML in a Nutshell

XML is a *markup* language. The most well-known example of a markup language is probably the Hypertext Markup Language HTML,[2] which is also a recommendation by the W3C and is used for describing elements of Web pages, and Web browsers use them for the visual display of Web pages. For example, the HTML code `<h2>About XML</h2>` states that `About XML` should be typeset as a level 2 heading. The HTML code

```
<a href="http://semantic-web-grundlagen.de">German SW book</a>
```

indicates that a hyperlink should be set.

In HTML, the meaning of the so-called *tags* like `<h2>` and `</a>` is predefined. In contrast to this, tags in XML can be chosen freely. Their meaning is not predefined, and their sole purpose is to structure the document. The following is an example which expresses that `Foundations of Semantic Web Technologies` is a `title`.

---

[1] http://www.w3.org/XML/Core/
[2] http://www.w3.org/HTML/

```
<title>
  Foundations of Semantic Web Technologies
</title>
```

Tags can be nested, for example, as follows.

```
<book>
  <title>
    Foundations of Semantic Web Technologies
  </title>
  <author>
    Pascal Hitzler
  </author>
  <author>
    Markus Kroetzsch
    <homepage>
      http://korrekt.org
    </homepage>
  </author>
  <author>
    Sebastian Rudolph
  </author>
  <publisher>
    CRC Press
  </publisher>
</book>
```

Note that each opening tag (i.e. a tag not starting with </) must be accompanied by a matching closing tag (i.e. one starting with </). Furthermore, the tags must be nested correctly. Essentially, this yields a tree structure on the nested tags. For the example above, this could be depicted as in Fig. A.1.

XML also allows us to attach so-called attributes to tags. They are written inside the < and > brackets, for example, as follows.

```
<author name="Markus Kroetzsch">
  <homepage>
    http://korrekt.org
  </homepage>
</author>
```

A tag can also bear several attributes.

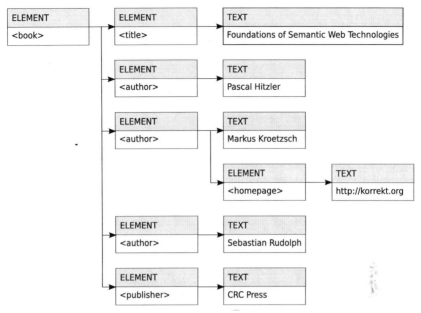

FIGURE A.1: The tree structure of XML

```
<author name="Markus Kroetzsch" homepage="http://korrekt.org">
</author>
```

We see that information can be contained in attributes to tags or in subtrees of the tags. The XML standard does not tell us where to put specific information. But we will come back to this point later when talking about XML Schema in Section A.3.

A.2   Syntax of XML

An XML document is a text document. It always starts with a declaration which contains as attribute the version number of the W3C standard used, and may also contain as attribute information about the character encoding used.

```
<?xml version="1.1" encoding="utf-16">
```

An *XML element* is an object which starts with an opening tag and ends with a matching closing tag. Every XML element may contain free text and other XML elements between its matching tags. Elements can also be empty, i.e. such as `<email></email>`, and such elements can be abbreviated as `<email />`.

In every XML document there must be exactly one outermost XML element. It is referred to as the *root* of the document.

Opening tags (and also tags indicating empty XML elements) may contain attributes. They are written as `attribute-name="attribute-value"`. Every opening tag may contain several attributes, but each attribute name must appear only once. Not all characters can be used for attribute names and values.

We explain these notions by means of another example. The following is an example of a complete XML document.

```
<?xml version="1.1" encoding="utf-16">
<book>
  <title>
    Foundations of Semantic Web Technologies
  </title>
  <author name="Pascal Hitzler" />
  <author name="Markus Kroetzsch">
    <homepage>
      http://korrekt.org
    </homepage>
  </author>
  <author name="Sebastian Rudolph" />
  <publisher>
    CRC Press
  </publisher>
</book>
```

In this example, the root element starts with `<book>` and ends with `</book>`. `<author name="Pascal Hitzler" />` is an empty XML element, where the tag has an attribute with attribute name `name` and attribute value `Pascal Hitzler`.

XML documents which are syntactically correct are said to be *well-formed*.

A.3　XML Schema

We have seen that XML allows a lot of freedom in encoding information. For example, the information contained in the element

```
<author>Sebastian Rudolph</author>
```

could also be written as

```
<author name="Sebastian Rudolph" />
```

or even as

```
<author>
  <fullname>Sebastian Rudolph</fullname>
</author>
```

or as

```
<author>
  <firstname>Sebastian</firstname>
  <secondname>Rudolph</secondname>
</author>
```

or

```
<author givenname="Sebastian" surname="Rudolph" />.
```

When exchanging XML documents between applications, these degrees of freedom get in the way: The application does not know whether firstname and givenname express the same thing, or how to combine givenname and surname to fullname.

In order to aid information exchange, then, it is necessary to come up with agreements about the structure of the information, including the names of tags and attributes, but also information whether certain subelements are required or not. XML Schema[3] is a language developed by the W3C which allows us to describe such structures. XML schemas are themselves written in XML. And an XML document is said to be *valid* if it adheres to a corresponding XML schema.

Before we go into specifics, let us remark that there are other languages for defining XML document schemas. The most popular is probably DTD, which

---

[3] http://www.w3.org/XML/Schema

stands for Document Type Definition. DTDs are less expressive than XML Schema, and in fact DTDs can be translated to XML Schema. Specifics are contained in the W3C document on XML.[4]

A.3.1   Elements, Attributes, and Datatypes

An XML Schema document is a well-formed XML document which contains XML schema definitions. An XML schema definition is an XML element with an opening tag like

```
<xsd:schema xmlns:xsd="http://www.w3.org/2001/XMLSchema">
```

The attribute `xmlns:xsd="http://www.w3.org/2001/XMLSchema"` is a so-called *namespace* declaration, and we say more about them in Section 2.2. For now, let us simply note that it makes `xsd` point to the XML Schema document on the W3C website, and that tag names starting with `xsd` obtain their meaning from the specification given there.

An XML schema further contains so-called *element types* and *attribute types*. They define schematically what the elements and attributes of an XML document under this XML schema contain. Element and attribute types can themselves refer to predefined datatypes or user-defined datatypes.

Let us start with predefined datatypes. They include `xsd:integer`, `xsd:ID`, `xsd:string`, `xsd:time`, and `xsd:date`. Some further datatypes are listed in Fig. 4.3 on page 117. Most of these datatypes are self-explanatory, and the XML Schema datatypes specification[5] explains them in detail. `xsd:ID` is a specific kind of `xsd:string` which is used as an identifier of XML elements.

Element types are XML elements with opening tags which are of the form `<xsd:element name="..." ...>`. The `name` attribute identifies the name of an XML element which may occur in an XML document adhering to the schema. Further attributes can specify, for example, cardinalities, i.e. how often an element with this name must at least (or may at most) occur in the XML document. They can also specify the schema type of the XML element.

The following is an example of an element type.

```
<xsd:element name="author" type="xsd:string"
  minOccurs="1" maxOccurs="unbounded" />
```

This element type specifies that an XML document must contain at least one element with name `author`, the contents of which are of type `xsd:string`.

---

[4]http://www.w3.org/TR/REC-xml/#dt-doctype

[5]http://www.w3.org/TR/2004/REC-xmlschema-2-20041028/datatypes.html

Furthermore, it may contain multiple such elements, and there is no bound on the number of occurrences. The attribute `minOccurs` can have any positive integer (including zero) as value. The attribute `maxOccurs` can have any positive integer (excluding zero) as value, and can also have the predefined value `unbounded`.

Attribute types are defined very similarly, with opening tags starting with `<xsd:attribute name="...".` They are used to declare which attributes an XML element may or must have.

The following are two examples of attribute types.

```
<xsd:attribute name="email" type="xsd:string" use="required">
<xsd:attribute name="homepage" type="xsd:anyURI" use="optional">
```

This would specify that an `email` attribute is required, while the occurrence of the `homepage` attribute is optional. `xsd:anyURI` allows as value any URI, such as a homepage location. We say more about URIs in Section 2.1.2.

Let us put these things together now. The following XML schema document expresses that there must be at least one `author` element, the contents are of type `xsd:string`, and which has an `email` attribute, and optionally a `homepage` attribute.

```
<?xml version="1.1" encoding="utf-16">
<xsd:schema xmlns:xsd="http://www.w3.org/2001/XMLSchema">
  <xsd:element name="author" type="xsd:string"
      minOccurs="1" maxOccurs="unbounded">
    <xsd:attribute name="email" type="xsd:string" use="required">
    <xsd:attribute name="homepage" type="xsd:anyURI" use="optional">
  </xsd:element>
</xsd:schema>
```

The following would be an XML document which adheres to this schema.

```
<?xml version="1.1" encoding="utf-16">
<authors
    xmlns:xsi="http://www.w3.org/2001/XMLSchema-instance"
    xsi:schemaLocation="http://example.org/authors.xsd">
  <author email="email1@example.org" homepage="http://korrekt.org">
    Markus Kroetzsch
  </author>
  <author email="email2@example.org">
    Sebastian Rudolph
  </author>
</authors>
```

Note how the XML document uses `xsi:schemaLocation` to refer to the schema, assuming that the XML schema document is located at the indicated address.

A.3.2 User-Defined Types

There are two kinds of user-defined types, and we introduce them here by examples.

The first kind of user-defined type is indicated by the `xsd:simpleType` identifier. These datatypes are obtained by restrictions on other types, e.g., by tightening the numerical constraints which are allowed in `minOccurs` or `maxOccurs`, or by restricting the range of `xsd:integer`. It is not allowed to make use of embedded element or attribute types in simple type definitions.

The following example defines a type `humanAge` derived from integer, which has 0 as minimum and 200 as maximum value. A corresponding attribute definition could be `<xsd:attribute name="age" type="humanAge" />`.

```
<xsd:simpleType name="humanAge">
  <xsd:restriction base="xsd:integer">
    <xsd:minInclusive value="0" />
    <xsd:maxInclusive value="200" />
  </xsd:restriction>
</xsd:simpleType>
```

Modifiers such as `xsd:minInclusive` and `xsd:maxInclusive` are called datatype *facets*.

The second kind of user-defined datatype is indicated by the identifier `xsd:complexType`. They may contain embedded element or attribute definitions. We first give an example.

```
<xsd:complexType name="bookType">
  <xsd:sequence>
    <xsd:element name="author" type="&xsd;string"
        minOccurs="1" maxOccurs="unbounded" />
    <xsd:element name="title" type="&xsd;string"
        minOccurs="1" maxOccurs="1" />
    <xsd:element name="publisher" type="&xsd;string"
        minOccurs="1" maxOccurs="1" />
    <xsd:element name="year" type="&xsd;gYear"
        minOccurs="1" maxOccurs="1" />
  </xsd:sequence>
  <xsd:attribute name="ISBNnumber" type="xsd:nonNegativeInteger"
      use="optional" />
</xsd:complexType>
```

The example declares that a book must have at least one author, and exactly one title, publisher, and publication year. Optionally, an ISBN number can be given as an attribute value.

The identifier xsd:sequence indicates a number of elements which have to appear in the given order. The identifiers xsd:all and xsd:choice can also be used. The first indicates that all the elements must occur but their order is not important. The second states that exactly one of the subsequent elements must be chosen.

Complex datatypes can also be constructed by extending existing ones. The following is an example, which uses the definition of the complex type book just given.

```
<xsd:complexType name="researchBookType">
  <xsd:extension base="bookType">
    <xsd:sequence>
      <xsd:element name="field" type="&xsd,string" />
    </xsd:sequence>
    <xsd:attribute name="price" type="&xsd,nonNegativeInteger"
      use="optional" />
</xsd:complexType>
```

Appendix B

Set Theory

This appendix briefly introduces basic notations and notions of set theory used in this book.

B.1 Basic Notions

The notion of a *set* as a mathematical term was introduced by Georg Cantor in 1877 who defined a set as "a collection of certain well-distinguished objects of cognition or thinking, which will be called elements, to a whole."

Conventionally sets are represented by capital letters whereas lowercase letters are used to denote their elements. In order to express that an entity e is an *element* of a set S, we write $e \in S$ (the contrary would be displayed as $e \notin S$).

Note that a set cannot contain an element twice or many times, rather, the element is either contained or not.

There are essentially two ways of specifying a set: by enumerating its elements or by characterizing their properties. In both cases, curly brackets are used for the representation.

For example, the set of natural numbers from 1 to 10 can be written as

$$\{1, 2, 3, 4, 5, 6, 7, 8, 9, 10\}$$

or equivalently as

$$\{n \mid n \in \mathbb{N}, 1 \leq n \leq 10\},$$

where, for the second case, we assume that the set $\mathbb{N}$ of natural numbers is known.

A set A is a *subset* of a set B (write $A \subseteq B$), if every element of A is also an element of B. If additionally, there is even an element of B which is not contained in A, we call A a *proper subset* of B (write $A \subset B$).

Two sets A and B are equal (write $A = B$), if they contain the same elements. Obviously, this holds exactly if both $A \subseteq B$ and $B \subseteq A$ are the case.

A and B are called *disjoint* if there is no element which is contained in both sets.

The *empty set* (denoted by $\emptyset$ or $\{\}$) does not contain any elements. Furthermore, it is easy to see that the empty set is a subset of any arbitrary set.

The *cardinality* of a set M (written as $\#M$ or $\text{card}(M)$) describes—roughly speaking—the number of its elements. More precisely, this only holds for finite sets. Contrarily, no such size can be assigned to, say, the set of all natural numbers. Notwithstanding, the cardinality of the latter can be characterized precisely (and turns out to be equal to the cardinality of the set of all rational numbers, yet smaller than the cardinality of the reals); however, this would go beyond the scope of this brief overview.

B.2   Set Operations

There are several operations which can be applied to given sets, yielding sets as a result:

- The *union* of two sets A and B (write $A \cup B$) contains exactly those elements that are contained in A or in B (or in both of them).

- The *intersection* of A and B (write $A \cap B$) comprises all elements which are contained in both A and B. Consequently, two sets are disjoint if and only if their intersection is empty (explaining the common notation $A \cap B = \emptyset$ for disjointness).

- The *difference* of A and B (written as $A \setminus B$ or $A - B$) contains those elements contained in A, but not contained in B.

These three set operations return sets, whose elements are, so to speak, "of the same type" as the elements from the original sets. This is not the case for the operations presented in the following.

- The *Cartesian product* or *product set* of two sets A and B (write $A \times B$) contains all pairs, the first component of which is an element of A and the second component of which is an element of B; therefore we can write

$$A \times B = \{(a,b) \mid a \in A, b \in B\}.$$

The symbol used for the Cartesian product bears some correct intuition as the cardinality of the resulting set can be calculated by multiplying the initial sets' cardinalities (given their finiteness).

- The *power set* of a set A (write 2^A or $\mathcal{P}(A)$) contains all subsets of A as elements, hence:

$$2^A = \{B \mid B \subseteq A\}.$$

Thus, we have, for example,

$$2^{\{a,b\}} = \{\emptyset, \{a\}, \{b\}, \{a, b\}\}.$$

Also in this case the notation as a power of 2 is straightforward, due to the correspondence $\#(2^A) = 2^{\#A}$ for arbitrary finite sets A.

B.3   Relations and Functions

A *(binary) relation* between two sets A and B is a subset of their Cartesian product: $R \subseteq A \times B$. For $a \in A$ and $b \in B$ often the notation aRb is used instead of the longer $(a, b) \in R$.

If A and B are equal, R will be called a Relation on A.

Relations on a set A may have several interesting properties. $R \subseteq A \times A$ will be called:

- *reflexive*, if aRa holds for all $a \in A$,

- *symmetric*, if aRb implies bRa for all $a, b \in A$,

- *transitive*, if for all $a, b, c \in A$ from aRb and bRc follows aRc.

A relation between A and B is called *left-total*, if for every $a \in A$, (at least) one $b \in B$ with aRb can be found. It is called *right-unique* (also: *functional*), if for every $a \in A$ at most one $b \in B$ with aRb exists. In case of both a left-total and right-unique relation, exactly one $b \in B$ is assigned to every $a \in A$, enabling (due to the uniqueness) us to write $R(a)$ for b. Such a relation f (which then is mostly denoted with a lowercase letter) is called *function* or *mapping* from the *domain* A to the *range* B. In this case it is common to write $f : A \rightarrow B$ instead of $f \subseteq A \times B$ and, moreover, $f : a \mapsto b$ is an alternative notation for $f(a) = b$.

Finally, applying the information given in this section, you should be able to check whether the following proposition is true or false:

For arbitrary sets A and B the relation $\subset \cap((2^A \times 2^A) \cup (2^{B \cup \emptyset} \times 2^B))$ is transitive.

Appendix C

Logic

In this appendix, we very briefly recall some logical foundations which are needed for our discussions of formal semantics. We will completely introduce syntax and semantics of first-order predicate logic, but will refrain from doing formal proofs or extended examples.

For acquiring a more comprehensive background on logic, we suggest [Sch08] or [EFT96].

C.1 Syntax

An *signature* (V, C, F, P) of a *first-order language* consists of

- a set V of *variables*, which is countably infinite,

- a set C of *constant symbols*,

- a set F of *function symbols*, each of which comes with an *arity*, which is a positive integer, and

- a set P of *predicate* or *relation symbols*, each of which also comes with a nonnegative integer as its *arity*.

Terms are inductively defined as follows.

- Each variable is a term.

- If f is a function symbol with arity k and $t_1, \ldots, t_k$ are terms, then $f(t_1, \ldots, t_k)$ is a term.

- Nothing else is a term.

(*First-order predicate logical*) *formulae* are inductively defined as follows.

- If p is a predicate symbol of arity k and $t_1, \ldots, t_k$ are terms, then $p(t_1, \ldots, t_k)$ is a formula. These formulae are called *atomic*.

- If F is a formula, then $\neg F$ is also a formula, called the *negation* of F.

- If F and G are formulae, then $F \wedge G$ and $F \vee G$ are also formulae, called the *conjunction* and the *disjunction*, respectively, of F and G.

- If F is a formula and x is a variable, then $(\exists x)F$ and $(\forall x)F$ are also formulae. The symbol $\exists$ is called *existential quantifier*, and the symbol $\forall$ is called *universal quantifier*. In either case, the occurrences of x in F are said to be *bound* by the quantifier.

- Nothing else is a formula.

We use the following abbreviations:

- $F \rightarrow G$ abbreviates $\neg F \vee G$.

- $F \leftrightarrow G$ abbreviates $(F \rightarrow G) \wedge (G \rightarrow F)$.

The symbols $\neg, \wedge, \vee, \rightarrow, \leftrightarrow$ are called *(logical) connectives*. When writing down formulae, we consider $\neg$ to be of higher precedence than the other connectives, i.e. it binds more strongly. Variable occurrences which are not bound are called *free*.

The set of all first-order predicate logical formulae over (V, C, F, P) is called the *first-order language* over (V, C, F, P).

A *propositional* formula is a predicate logical formula which does not contain any quantifiers, and where all predicates have arity zero.

A *sentence* is a first-order predicate logical formula in which all variable occurrences are bound.

A *theory* (or *knowledge base*) is a set of sentences.

An example of a first-order formula is

$$(\forall x)(\text{exam}(x) \rightarrow (\forall y)(\text{hasExaminer}(x, y) \rightarrow \text{professor}(y))).$$

The intuition behind it is that all examiners of an exam must be professors.

C.2   Semantics

An *interpretation* (or *structure*) $I = (D, \cdot^I)$ for a first-order language over (V, C, F, P) consists of a set $D \neq \emptyset$, called the *domain* of I, and a partial *interpretation function* $\cdot^I$, commonly written as an exponent, which

- maps every constant symbol for which it is defined to an element of D,

- maps every function symbol f with arity k for which it is defined to a function $f^I : D^k \rightarrow D$, and

- maps every predicate symbol p with arity k for which it is defined to a relation $p^I \subseteq D^k$, i.e. a set of k-tuples, which is sometimes called the *extension* of p.[1]

The interpretation mapping may be partial because it is only important how it maps those constant symbols, function symbols, and predicate symbols which actually occur in the considered theory. In the following, we will always assume that the partial interpretation mappings have all these relevant symbols in their domain.

Interpretations may be quite unintuitive: Consider again the example

$$(\forall x)(\texttt{exam}(x) \rightarrow (\forall y)(\texttt{hasExaminer}(x, y) \rightarrow \texttt{professor}(y)))$$

from above. Then the following is an interpretation.

- The domain D are the non-negative integers.

- Every constant symbol gets assigned $0 \in D$.

- Every function symbol gets assigned the function which is constantly $0 \in D$.

- $\texttt{exam}^I = D$

- $\texttt{hasExaminer}^I = \{(n, m) \mid n \leq m\}$

- $\texttt{professor}^I = \{n + n \mid n \in D\}$

Under this interpretation, the formula states that for every non-negative integer n we have that every $m \geq n$ is an even number. This statement is obviously wrong, but the given interpretation is still a valid interpretation. *Correct* interpretations are called *models*, which are defined further below.

A *variable assignment* for an interpretation I is a function from the set V of variables to the interpretation domain D of I.

Every interpretation $I = (D, \cdot^I)$ together with a corresponding variable assignment Z can now be lifted recursively to the set of all terms and the set of all formulae of the underlying language: If t is a term, then we define

- $t^{I,Z} = x^Z$ if $t = x$ for some variable x,

- $t^{I,Z} = a^I$ if $t = a$ for some constant symbol a, and

---

[1] Considering $k = 0$, note that D^0 is the set containing the (only) 0-tuple (); hence for p with arity 0 there are only two choices for p^I, namely, $\emptyset$ and $\{()\}$.

- $t^{I,Z} = f^I(t_1^{I,Z}, \ldots, t_k^{I,Z})$ if t is of the form $t = f(t_1, \ldots, t_k)$ for a function symbol f with arity k.

This way, every term t gets assigned some element $t^{I,Z} \in D$.

If F is a formula, then we can define very similarly the *truth value* $F^I \in \{\text{false}, \text{true}\}$ of F under I as follows. If Z is a variable assignment, x is a variable, and $d \in D$, then $Z[x \mapsto d]$ denotes the variable assignment which assigns x to d and otherwise coincides with Z on V.

- If F is an atomic formula of the form $F = p(t_1, \ldots, t_k)$, then $F^{I,Z} = \text{true}$ if and only if $(t_1^{I,Z}, \ldots, t_k^{I,Z}) \in p^I$. Otherwise $F^{I,Z} = \text{false}$.

- If F is of the form $F = \neg G$, then $F^{I,Z} = \text{true}$ if and only if $G^{I,Z} = \text{false}$. Otherwise $F^{I,Z} = \text{false}$.

- If F is of the form $F = G \wedge H$, then $F^{I,Z} = \text{true}$ if and only if $G^{I,Z} = \text{true}$ and $H^{I,Z} = \text{true}$. Otherwise $F^{I,Z} = \text{false}$.

- If F is of the form $F = G \vee H$, then $F^{I,Z} = \text{false}$ if and only if $G^{I,Z} = \text{false}$ and $H^{I,Z} = \text{false}$. Otherwise $F^{I,Z} = \text{true}$.

- If F is of the form $F = (\forall x)G$, then $F^{I,Z} = \text{true}$ if and only if $G^{I,Z[x \mapsto d]} = \text{true}$ for all $d \in D$. Otherwise $F^{I,Z} = \text{false}$.

- If F is of the form $F = (\exists x)G$, then $F^{I,Z} = \text{true}$ if and only if $G^{I,Z[x \mapsto d]} = \text{true}$ for at least one $d \in D$. Otherwise $F^{I,Z} = \text{false}$.

If F is a formula, then an interpretation I is called a *model* of F if $F^{I,Z} = \text{true}$ for all variable assignments Z. We write $I, Z \models F$ in this case. Note that if F is a sentence then the truth value of $F^{I,Z}$ does not depend on Z and we can write F^I in this case.

Two formulae F and G are called *equivalent* if they have exactly the same models. We write $F \equiv G$ in this case. A formula F is called a *tautology* if every interpretation is a model for F. It is called *satisfiable* or *consistent* if it has at least one model. It is called *contradictory* (or *unsatisfiable* or *inconsistent*) if it has no model. It is called *falsifiable* if it is not a tautology.

THEOREM C.1

The equivalences in Fig. C.1 hold for arbitrary formulae F and G. The following equivalences hold if x is not free in G.

$$(\forall x)F \wedge G \equiv (\forall x)(F \wedge G)$$
$$(\forall x)F \vee G \equiv (\forall x)(F \vee G)$$
$$(\exists x)F \wedge G \equiv (\exists x)(F \wedge G)$$
$$(\exists x)F \vee G \equiv (\exists x)(F \vee G)$$

$$\neg\neg F \equiv F$$
$$\neg(F \vee G) \equiv \neg F \wedge \neg G$$
$$\neg(F \wedge G) \equiv \neg F \vee \neg G$$
$$(F \wedge G) \vee H \equiv (F \vee H) \wedge (G \vee H)$$
$$(F \vee G) \wedge H \equiv (F \wedge H) \vee (G \wedge H)$$
$$\neg(\forall x)F \equiv (\exists x)\neg F$$
$$\neg(\exists x)F \equiv (\forall x)\neg F$$
$$(\forall x)(\forall y)F \equiv (\forall y)(\forall x)F$$
$$(\exists x)(\exists y)F \equiv (\exists y)(\exists x)F$$
$$(\forall x)F \wedge (\forall x)G \equiv (\forall x)(F \wedge G)$$
$$(\exists x)F \vee (\exists x)G \equiv (\exists x)(F \vee G)$$

FIGURE C.1:   Logical equivalences from Theorem C.1.

An interpretation I is called a *model* for a theory T if $F^I = \texttt{true}$ for all $F \in T$. We write $I \models T$ in this case. A theory is *satisfiable* if it has a model. It is *contradictory* (or *unsatisfiable* or *inconsistent*) if it has no model.

If T is a theory and F a formula, then we call F a *logical consequence* of T if every model of T is also a model of F. We write $T \models F$ in this case.

To give an example, $p(a)$ is a logical consequence of the theory

$$\{q(a), (\forall x)(p(x) \rightarrow q(x))\}.$$

The following *deduction theorem* is one of the most important properties of predicate logic.

THEOREM C.2
If $T = \{F_1, \ldots, F_n\}$ is a theory and F a formula, then $T \models F$ if and only if $(F_1 \wedge \cdots \wedge F_n) \rightarrow F$ is a tautology.

Theorem C.2 is important because it allows us to express the notion of logical consequence in terms of tautology of a formula. Automated reasoning can thus be reduced to tautology checking. Likewise, reduction to checking unsatisfiability of a formula can be used. The following is a reformulation of Theorem C.2.

THEOREM C.3

If $T = \{F_1, \ldots, F_n\}$ is a theory and F a formula, then $T \models F$ if and only if $(F_1 \wedge \cdots \wedge F_n) \wedge \neg F$ is unsatisfiable.

First-order predicate logic is *monotonic* in the following formal sense.

THEOREM C.4

Let T and S be two theories over the same first-order language and let $T \subseteq S$. Then $\{F \mid T \models F\} \subseteq \{F \mid S \models F\}$.

There exist alternative logics, i.e. logics stemming from logic programming, or logics stemming from attempts to model "common sense" in artificial intelligence, which are *non-monotonic* in the sense that statements like that from Theorem C.4 do not hold for them.

Closely related to monotonicity is the notion of *Open World Assumption* (OWA). However, the OWA is an informal notion and can thus not be as precisely defined as monotonicity. In order to explain the OWA, it is best to start with the *Closed World Assumption* (CWA), which states that everything which is not explicitly true is considered to be false. Typically, conventional databases are interpreted under the CWA: If something is not stated in the database, then it is assumed to be *not* the case. The OWA, however, generally leaves such things *undefined*, i.e. something which is not explicitly stated to be the case – or not the case – is considered to be unknown. The OWA seems to be more suitable for the open and always incomplete Semantic Web, and RDF(S) and OWL adhere to the OWA. However, logics with a semantics under the CWA have their uses.

The relation between OWA and monotonicity is not a formal one, simply because the OWA is not a formal notion. But generally speaking, monotonic logics adhere to the open world assumption. Historically speaking, non-monotonic logics usually adhere to the CWA – or to be more precise, logics under the CWA are usually non-monotonic. Recently, in particular driven by Semantic Web research, logics related to OWL and description logics have been established which combine open and closed world features, and are often said to have *local closed world* features.

We will not go into any further details on these matters – we have chosen to include this brief discussion only because the distinction between OWA and CWA is something which is often encountered in the Semantic Web literature.

C.3   Proof Theory and Decidability

A *proof theory* for first-order predicate logic is a deduction calculus[2] which, given a theory T and a sentence F, can be applied to determine whether F is a logical consequence of T. If the calculus (correctly or incorrectly) determines that this is the case, i.e. if one can apply the calculus to derive this result within finitely many steps, then we use the notation $T \vdash F$ for this.

A deduction calculus is *sound* if $T \vdash F$ implies $T \models F$. It is *complete* if $T \models F$ implies $T \vdash F$.

First-order logic is said to be *semi-decidable*, which formally means the following.

THEOREM C.5
There exists a sound and complete proof theory for first-order predicate logic.

Note that semi-decidability implies that whenever $T \models F$, then it is possible to apply the deduction calculus so that $T \vdash F$ is derived after finitely many steps. This means that it is possible to implement the calculus in a concrete algorithm that terminates and returns the correct result on all inputs T and F for which $T \models F$ holds. However, if $T \not\models F$, then it is possible that the deduction calculus does not allow us to derive this within a finite number of steps – an algorithm that implements the calculus would not terminate. A sound and complete algorithm that is guaranteed to terminate on all inputs is called a *decision procedure*.

The above notions are easily applied to other logical formalisms, and in particular to fragments of first-order logic like the ones considered within this book. A logic is *decidable* if there is a decision procedure for this logic. The following basic results are well-known.

THEOREM C.6
Propositional logic is decidable.

THEOREM C.7
First-order predicate logic is not decidable.

---

[2]A calculus is usually given as a set of deduction rules that can be the basis of a concrete algorithm. But in contrast to an algorithm, a calculus does usually not specify which rule is to be applied next, or how exactly the rule applications should be implemented.

Appendix D

Solutions to the Exercises

D.1 Solutions for Chapter 2

Solution to Exercise 2.1
There are many ways to describe the contents of this document in natural language. Below is one possibility.

germany is a country.
capital_of is a property which relates cities to countries.
country is a class which is called *Land* in German.
berlin is a city which is the capital of germany. It is called *Berlin* in German.
city is a class which is called *Stadt* in German.

The graph representation of the document looks as follows.

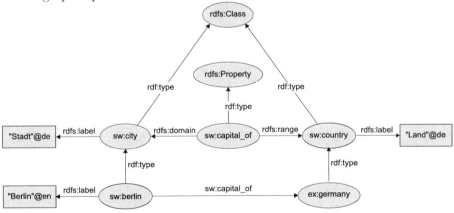

Solution to Exercise 2.2

```
@prefix swb: <http://www.semantic-web-book.org/> .
@prefix rdf: <http://www.w3.org/1999/02/22-rdf-syntax-ns#> .
@prefix ex:  <http://example.org/> .
```

```
swb:uri      ex:authors      _:id1 .
_:id1        rdf:type        rdf:Seq .
_:id1        rdf:_1          swb:uri/Hitzler .
_:id1        rdf:_2          swb:uri/Krötzsch .
_:id1        rdf:_3          swb:uri/Rudolph .
```

Solution to Exercise 2.3

```
<rdf:RDF
  xmlns:rdf="http://www.w3.org/1999/02/22-rdf-syntax-ns#"
  xmlns:rdfs="http://www.w3.org/2000/01/rdf-schema#"
  xmlns:ex="http://www.example.org/"
>

<rdf:Description
    rdf:about="http://www.example.org/vegetableThaiCurry">
  <ex:thaiDishBasedOn
      rdf:resource="http://www.example.org/coconutMilk" />
</rdf:Description>

<rdf:Description rdf:about="http://www.example.org/sebastian">
  <rdf:type rdf:resource="http://www.example.org/AllergicToNuts" />
  <ex:eats rdf:resource="http://www.example.org/vegetableThaiCurry" />
</rdf:Description>

<rdf:Description rdf:about="http://www.example.org/AllergicToNuts">
  <rdfs:subClassOf rdf:about="http://www.example.org/Pitiable" />
</rdf:Description>

<rdf:Description rdf:about="http://www.example.org/thaiDishBasedOn">
  <rdfs:domain rdf:resource="http://www.example.org/Thai" />
  <rdfs:range rdf:resource="http://www.example.org/Nutty" />
  <rdfs:subPropertyOf
      rdf:resource="http://www.example.org/hasIngredient" />
</rdf:Description>

<rdf:Description rdf:about="http://www.example.org/hasIngredient">
  <rdf:type rdf:resource="http://www.w3.org/2000/01/rdf-schema#
                                    ContainerMembershipProperty" />
</rdf:Description>

</rdf:RDF>
```

Solution to Exercise 2.4

The first example is a straightforward reification. Note that in most cases,
statements including forms of "to be" are best translated into a `rdf:type`
statement.

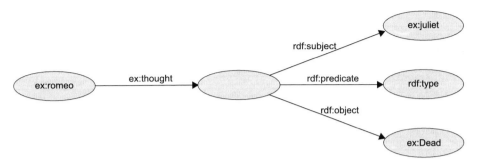

The second example requires some more thought, as both John and Mary occur in several nested propositions. To see this, it is best to dismantle the sentence in the following way:

- John believes X.

- X: Mary wants Y.

- Y: Marry marries John.

After that, subject, predicate and object of each part can be determined and one comes easily up with an RDF graph like the following:

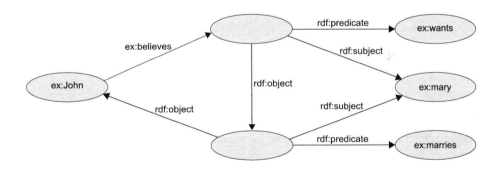

The third example is rather easy with respect to reification; however, it is useful to discuss how to model certain language constructs: the "his" in the sentence indicates that the referred plate belongs to the initially mentioned dwarf which could be modeled by a property like ex:owns. The "somebody" is an existential statement which, however, restricts the possible instantiations to persons (otherwise one would use "something") which can be modeled by an rdf:type triple. So a possible triplification of the sentence would look like this:

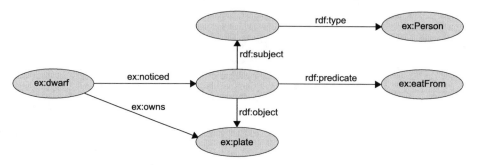

Solution to Exercise 2.5

The following sentences cannot be modeled satisfactorily in RDFS:

- Pizzas always have at least two toppings.

- Everything having a topping is a pizza.

- No pizza from the class `PizzaMargarita` has a topping from the class `Meat`.

The other sentences can be modeled as follows.

```
@prefix rdf:  <http://www.w3.org/1999/02/22-rdf-syntax-ns#> .
@prefix rdfs: <http://www.w3.org/2000/01/rdf-schema#> .
@prefix ex:   <http://example.org/> .

ex:Pizza            rdf:type          ex:Meal .
ex:PizzaMargarita   ex:hasTopping     ex:Tomato .
ex:hasTopping       rdf:type          rdfs:ContainerMembershipProperty .
```

D.2   Solutions for Chapter 3

Solution to Exercise 3.1

To make the solution really simple, set $IR = IP = \{a\}$ and $I_{\text{EXT}}(a) = \{\langle a, a \rangle\}$. Furthermore, I_S maps everything to a and $LV = I_L = \emptyset$.

Solution to Exercise 3.2

To solve this exercise, it is easiest to use the deduction rules from Section 3.3.
    An example of a simple entailment is
`ex:vegetableThaiCurry ex:thaiDishBasedOn _:id1 .`
    An example of an RDF-entailed triple which is not simply entailed is
`ex:thaiDishBasedOn rdf:type rdf:Property .`

An example of an RDFS-entailed triple which is not RDF-entailed is
`ex:vegetableThaiCurry rdf:type ex:Thai` .

Solution to Exercise 3.3
It is really not possible to specify this in RDFS.

Solution to Exercise 3.4
Using rdfsax, all the axiomatic triples listed for the RDF and RDFS semantics
are derivable. We can now use the deduction rules for RDFS entailment to
obtain further triples.

From `rdfs:domain rdfs:range rdfs:Class` .
and `rdf:type rdfs:domain rdfs:Resource` .
we can deduce using rdfs3 that
    `rdfs:Resource rdf:type rdfs:Class` .

From `rdfs:range rdfs:range rdfs:Class` .
and `rdfs:range rdfs:range rdfs:Class` .
we can deduce using rdfs3 that
    `rdfs:Class rdf:type rdfs:Class` .

From `rdfs:range rdfs:range rdfs:Class` .
and `rdfs:comment rdfs:range rdfs:Literal` .
we can deduce using rdfs3 that
    `rdfs:Literal rdf:type rdfs:Class` .

From `rdfs:subClassOf rdfs:domain rdfs:Class` .
and `rdf:XMLLiteral rdfs:subClassOf rdfs:Literal` .
we can deduce using rdfs2 that
    `rdfs:XMLLiteral rdf:type rdfs:Class` .

From `rdf:type rdfs:range rdfs:Class` .
and `rdf:XMLLiteral rdf:type rdfs:Datatype` .
we can deduce using rdfs3 that
    `rdfs:Datatype rdf:type rdfs:Class` .

From `rdfs:subClassOf rdfs:domain rdfs:Class` .
and `rdf:Seq rdfs:subClassOf rdfs:Container` .
we can deduce using rdfs2 that
    `rdfs:Seq rdf:type rdfs:Class` .

From `rdfs:subClassOf rdfs:domain rdfs:Class` .
and `rdf:Bag rdfs:subClassOf rdfs:Container` .
we can deduce using rdfs2 that
    `rdfs:Seq rdf:type rdfs:Class` .

From `rdfs:subClassOf rdfs:domain rdfs:Class .`
and `rdf:Alt rdfs:subClassOf rdfs:Container .`
we can deduce using rdfs2 that
       `rdfs:Seq rdf:type rdfs:Class .`

From `rdfs:subClassOf rdfs:range rdfs:Class .`
and `rdf:Alt rdfs:subClassOf rdfs:Container .`
we can deduce using rdfs3 that
       `rdfs:Container rdf:type rdfs:Class .`

From `rdfs:domain rdfs:range rdfs:Class .`
and `rdf:first rdfs:domain rdfs:List .`
we can deduce using rdfs3 that
       `rdfs:List rdf:type rdfs:Class .`

From `rdfs:subClassOf rdfs:domain rdfs:Class .`
and `rdf:ContainerMembershipProperty`
                     `rdfs:subClassOf rdfs:Property .`
we can deduce using rdfs2 that
       `rdf:ContainerMembershipProperty rdf:type rdfs:Class .`

From `rdfs:range rdfs:range rdfs:Class .`
and `rdfs:subPropertyOf rdfs:range rdf:Property .`
we can deduce using rdfs3 that
       `rdf:Property rdf:type rdfs:Class .`

From `rdfs:domain rdfs:range rdfs:Class .`
and `rdf:subject rdfs:domain rdf:Statement .`
we can deduce using rdfs3 that
       `rdf:Statement rdf:type rdfs:Class .`

From `rdfs:range rdfs:domain rdf:Property .`
we can deduce using rdf1 that
       `rdfs:domain rdf:type rdf:Property .`

From `rdfs:subPropertyOf rdfs:range rdf:Property .`
we can deduce using rdf1 that
       `rdfs:range rdf:type rdf:Property .`

From `rdfs:isDefinedBy rdfs:subPropertyOf rdfs:seeAlso .`
we can deduce using rdf1 that
       `rdfs:subPropertyOf rdf:type rdf:Property .`

From `rdf:Alt rdfs:subClassOf rdfs:Container .`
we can deduce using rdf1 that
       `rdfs:subClassOf rdf:type rdf:Property .`

From `rdf:Alt rdfs:subClassOf rdfs:Container .`
we can deduce using rdf1 that
    `rdfs:subClassOf rdf:type rdf:Property .`

From `rdfs:range rdfs:domain rdf:Property .`
and `rdfs:member rdfs:range rdfs:Resource .`
we can deduce using rdfs2 that
    `rdfs:member rdf:type rdfs:Property .`

From `rdfs:range rdfs:domain rdf:Property .`
and `rdfs:seeAlso rdfs:range rdfs:Resource .`
we can deduce using rdfs2 that
    `rdfs:seeAlso rdf:type rdfs:Property .`

From `rdfs:range rdfs:domain rdf:Property .`
and `rdfs:isDefinedBy rdfs:range rdfs:Resource .`
we can deduce using rdfs2 that
    `rdfs:isDefinedBy rdf:type rdfs:Property .`

From `rdfs:range rdfs:domain rdf:Property .`
and `rdfs:comment rdfs:range rdfs:Literal .`
we can deduce using rdfs2 that
    `rdfs:comment rdf:type rdfs:Property .`

From `rdfs:range rdfs:domain rdf:Property .`
and `rdfs:label rdfs:range rdfs:Literal .`
we can deduce using rdfs2 that
    `rdfs:label rdf:type rdfs:Property .`

D.3 Solutions for Chapter 4

Solution to Exercise 4.1

```
<owl:Class rdf:about="Vegetable">
  <rdfs:subClassOf rdf:resource="PizzaTopping" />
</owl:Class>
<owl:Class rdf:about="PizzaTopping">
  <rdfs:disjointWith rdf:resource="Pizza" />
<Vegetable rdf:about="aubergine" />
<owl:ObjectProperty rdf:about="hasTopping">
  <rdfs:domain rdf:resource="Pizza" />
```

```
      <rdfs:range rdf:resource="PizzaTopping" />
    </owl:ObjectProperty>
    <owl:Class rdf:about="VegPizza">
      <owl:intersectionOf rdf:parseType="Collection">
        <owl:Class rdf:about="NoMeatPizza" />
        <owl:Class rdf:about="NoFishPizza" />
      </owl:intersectionOf>
    </owl:Class>
    <owl:ObjectProperty rdf:about="hasIngredient">
      <rdfs:subPropertyOf rdf:resource="hasTopping" />
    </owl:ObjectProperty>
    </owl:Class>
```

Solution to Exercise 4.2

hasIngredient should be transitive. To give an example: If milk is an ingredient of cheese, and cheese is an ingredient of a pizza (as a topping), then milk is an ingredient of the pizza.

hasTopping should not be functional: A pizza may have several toppings.

hasTopping should probably be inverse functional: A particular aubergine cannot be a topping on more than one pizza (unless the aubergine is chopped up – in which case the aubergine pieces would be the toppings, and not the aubergine itself.

Solution to Exercise 4.3

```
<owl:Class rdf:about="Pizza">
  <rdfs:subClassOf>
    <owl:Restriction>
      <owl:onProperty rdf:resource="hasTopping" />
      <owl:minCardinality rdf:datatype="&xsd;nonNegativeInteger">
        2
      </owl:minCardinality>
    </owl:Restriction>
  </rdfs:subClassOf>
</owl:Class>
<owl:Class rdf:about="Pizza">
  <rdfs:subClassOf>
    <owl:Restriction>
      <owl:onProperty rdf:resource="hasTopping" />
      <owl:hasValue rdf:resource="tomato" />
    </owl:Restriction>
  </rdfs:subClassOf>
</owl:Class>
<owl:Class rdf:about="PizzaMargarita">
  <rdfs:subClassOf>
    <owl:Restriction>
      <owl:onProperty rdf:resource="hasTopping" />
```

```
        <owl:allValuesFrom>
          <owl:oneOf rdf:parseType="Collection">
            <Topping rdf:about="tomato" />
            <Topping rdf:about="cheese" />
          </owl:oneOf>
        </owl:allValuesFrom>
      </owl:Restriction>
    </rdfs:subClassOf>
</owl:Class>
<owl:Class rdf:about="PizzaMargarita">
  <rdfs:subClassOf>
    <owl:Class>
      <owl:intersectionOf rdf:parseType="Collection">
        <owl:Restriction>
          <owl:onProperty rdf:resource="hasTopping" />
          <owl:hasValue rdf:resource="tomato" />
        </owl:Restriction>
        <owl:Restriction>
          <owl:onProperty rdf:resource="hasTopping" />
          <owl:hasValue rdf:resource="cheese" />
        </owl:Restriction>
      </owl:intersectionOf>
    </owl:Class>
  </rdfs:subClassOf>
</owl:Class>
```

Note that we have to use two statements for modeling the information about `PizzaMargarita`.

Solution to Exercise 4.4
We obtain the following two triples from Fig. 4.7:

```
foundationsOfSemanticWebTechnologies rdf:type Book
Book rdfs:subClassOf Publication
```

There is more information, namely, about authors, but we won't need those triples. In the section on syntactic rules for RDFS inference, rule (rdfs9) on page 98 states that from the two triples above we can infer

```
foundationsOfSemanticWebTechnologies rdf:type Publication
```

as required.

Solution to Exercise 4.5
This is a hands-on exercise. Try it yourself.

D.4   Solutions for Chapter 5

Solution to Exercise 5.1

$$\text{Vegetable} \sqsubseteq \text{PizzaTopping}$$
$$\text{PizzaTopping} \sqcap \text{Pizza} \sqsubseteq \bot$$
$$\text{Vegetable(aubergine)}$$
$$\exists\text{hasTopping}.\top \sqsubseteq \text{Pizza}$$
$$\top \sqsubseteq \forall\text{hasTopping}.\text{PizzaTopping}$$
$$\text{VegPizza} \equiv \text{NoMeatPizza} \sqcap \text{NoFishPizza}$$
$$\text{hasIngredient} \sqsubseteq \text{hasTopping}$$

Solution to Exercise 5.2

$$(\forall x)(\text{Vegetable}(x) \rightarrow \text{PizzaTopping}(x))$$
$$\neg(\exists x)(\text{PizzaTopping}(x) \wedge \text{Pizza}(x))$$
$$\text{Vegetable(aubergine)}$$
$$(\forall x)(((\exists y)\text{hasTopping}(x,y)) \rightarrow \text{Pizza}(x))$$
$$(\forall x)(\forall y)(\text{hasTopping}(x,y) \rightarrow \text{PizzaTopping}(y))$$
$$(\forall x)(\text{VegPizza}(x) \leftrightarrow \text{NoMeatPizza}(x) \wedge \text{NoFishPizza}(x))$$
$$(\forall x)(\forall y)(\text{hasIngredient}(x,y) \rightarrow \text{hasTopping}(x,y))$$

Solution to Exercise 5.3

1. $\text{Honest} \sqcap \exists\text{commits}.\text{Crime} \sqsubseteq \exists\text{reports}.\text{Self}$

2. $\neg\text{reports}(\text{bonnie}, \text{clyde})$

3. $(\geq 10\,\text{commits}.\text{Crime})(\text{clyde})$

4. $(\exists\text{commits}.(\text{Crime} \sqcap \exists\text{commits}^-.\{\text{clyde}\}))(\text{bonnie})$

5. $\text{suspects} \circ \text{knows}^- \sqsubseteq \text{suspects}$

```
<owl:Class rdf:about="Human">
  <rdfs:subClassOf>
    <owl:Restriction>
      <owl:onProperty rdf:resource="hasMother" />
      <owl:someValuesFrom rdf:resource="Human" />
    </owl:Restriction>
  </rdfs:subClassOf>
</owl:Class>
<owl:Class rdf:about="hasMotherMother">
  <owl:equivalentClass>
    <owl:Restriction>
      <owl:onProperty rdf:resource="hasMother" />
      <owl:someValuesFrom>
        <owl:Restriction>
          <owl:onProperty rdf:resource="hasMother" />
          <owl:someValuesFrom rdf:resource="Human" />
        </owl:Restriction>
      </owl:someValuesFrom>
    </owl:Restriction>
  </owl:equivalentClass>
</owl:Class>
<owl:Class rdf:about="hasMotherMother">
  <rdfs:subClassOf rdf:resource="GrandChild" />
</owl:Class>
<Human rdf:about="anupriyaAnkolekar" />
```

FIGURE D.1:   Solution to Exercise 5.4

Solution to Exercise 5.4
See Fig. D.1. Note that we introduced the additional class `hasMotherMother`
to avoid having to deal with complex class descriptions in the subject of RDF
triples.

Solution to Exercise 5.5
In DL syntax, the statement from Fig. 4.11 is

$$\text{Professor} \sqsubseteq (\text{Person} \sqcap \text{FacultyMember}) \sqcup (\text{Person} \sqcap \neg\text{PhDStudent}).$$

We have to show that every `Professor` is a `Person`, i.e. for every model and
for every x in the corresponding extension of `Professor`, we must have that
x is in the extension of `Person`. So consider an arbitrarily chosen model, and
x in the respective extension of `Professor`. Then x must also either be in
the extension of `Person` ⊓ `FacultyMember` or x must be in the extension of
`Person` ⊓ ¬`PhDStudent`. In the first case, we have that x must in particular
be in the extension of `Person`. Likewise, in the second case, x must also
be in the extension of `Person`. So in either case we have that x is in the
extension of `Person`. Since this argument holds for every model, we have that
in every model x is in the extension of `Person`, provided it is in the extension
of `Professor`, which was to be shown.

Solution to Exercise 5.6
The triple `rdf:type rdfs:range rdfs:Class .` is an axiomatic triple of
RDFS and can thus be derived using the RDFS semantics. However, OWL
DL does not allow us to use `rdfs:Class`; hence this statement cannot be
derived using the OWL DL semantics.

The triple `r rdfs:domain A .` cannot be derived from the RDFS semantics. There is no easy way to check this, but you can exhaustively apply all
deduction rules and then this triple will not be included. In DL syntax the
triple becomes $A \sqsubseteq \forall r.\top$, which is a logical consequence of the two given
statements. To see this, let I be an arbitrarily chosen model for the two
given statements. Then, using the definition of model and the two given
statements, we obtain $A^I \subseteq B^I \subseteq (\forall r.\top)^I$ which shows that $A^I \subseteq (\forall r.\top)^I$.
Hence, $A \sqsubseteq \forall r.\top$ holds in I, and since I was an arbitrarily chosen model,
$A \sqsubseteq \forall r.\top$ holds in all models for the two given statements, and thus is a
logical consequence from these two statements.

Solution to Exercise 5.7
To simplify the presentation, we do some renamings, as follows.

$$S \sqsubseteq \exists a.L$$
$$L \sqsubseteq \exists b.(S \sqcap E)$$
$$S(s)$$
$$\neg E(s)$$

We can construct a complete tableau as follows, where z is blocked by x.

s $\qquad\quad \mathcal{L}(S) = \{S, \neg E, \neg S \sqcup \exists a.L, \exists a.L, \neg L \sqcup \exists b.(S \sqcap E), \neg L\}$

$\quad\big\downarrow a$

x $\qquad\quad \mathcal{L}(x) = \{L, \neg L \sqcup \exists b.(S \sqcap L), \exists b.(S \sqcap L), \neg S \sqcup \exists a.L, \neg S\}$

$\quad\big\downarrow b$

y $\qquad\quad \mathcal{L}(y) = \{S \sqcap E, S, E, \neg S \sqcup \exists a.L, \exists a.L, \neg L \sqcup \exists b.(S \sqcap E), \neg L\}$

$\quad\big\downarrow a$

z $\qquad\qquad\qquad\qquad \mathcal{L}(z) = \{L\}$

Solution to Exercise 5.8
We can construct the following tableau, where we have omitted some intermediate steps for simplicity.

a $\qquad\quad \mathcal{L}(a) = \{\forall r.\neg E, C, \exists r.D\}$

$\quad\big\downarrow r$

x $\qquad\quad \mathcal{L}(x) = \{D, E \sqcup F, \neg E, F, E\}$

Solution to Exercise 5.9
We can obtain a complete tableau with single node t and label

$$\mathcal{L}(t) = \{B, \neg H, \neg H \sqcup \exists p.H\}.$$

Solution to Exercise 5.10
We add the statement (Professor $\sqcap$ ¬Person)(x). We then construct a tableau with single node x and the label $\mathcal{L}(x)$ containing Professor$\sqcap$¬Person, Professor, ¬Person, and ¬Professor$\sqcup$(Person$\sqcap$FacultyMember$\sqcup$(Person$\sqcap$ ¬PhDStudent)). When further resolving the disjunction $\sqcup$, we are left with a contradiction no matter which side of the disjunction we choose: Professor is an immediate contradiction. Person$\sqcap$FacultyMember yields Person, which is a contradiction to ¬Person which is already in the label. From Person $\sqcap$ ¬PhDStudent we also obtain Person, which again is a contradiction because ¬Person is already in the label. So in any case we arrive at a contradiction as required.

Solution to Exercise 5.11
The tableau contains a single node tweety, with the following label, where we omit some intermediate calculations due to other choices of resolving disjunction: $\mathcal{L}$(tweety) = {Penguin, ¬Penguin$\sqcup$¬Flies, ¬Penguin$\sqcup$¬Bird, ¬Bird$\sqcup$ ¬Flies, ¬Flies, Bird, Flies}.

Solution to Exercise 5.12

We use the following abbreviations:

$$h(j, p)$$
$$h(j, a)$$
$$M(p)$$
$$M(a)$$
$$\leq 2h.M(j)$$
$$p \neq a$$

We can now start constructing the tableau. We first obtain the following.

$\mathcal{L}(j) = \{\exists h.\neg M, \leq 2h.M\}$

$\mathcal{L}(p) = \{M\}$

$\mathcal{L}(a) = \{M\}$

$\mathcal{L}(x) = \{\neg M\}$

We can now apply the $\leq$-rule, which yields the following, and thus a contradiction.

$\mathcal{L}(j) = \{\exists h.\neg M, \leq 2h.M\}$

$\mathcal{L}(p) = \{M\}$

$\mathcal{L}(a) = \{M, \neg M\}$

$\mathcal{L}(x) = \{\neg M\}$

Identifying x with p would yield a contradiction in the same way.

Solution to Exercise 5.13

We use the following abbreviations:

$$\geq 2s.\top(j)$$
$$s \sqsubseteq c$$

We can now construct the following tableau.

$\mathcal{L}(x) = \emptyset$

$\mathcal{L}(j) = \{\leq 1c.\top, \geq 2s.\top\}$

$\mathcal{L}(y) = \emptyset$

By definition, x and y are c-neighbors of j. Hence, the algorithm terminates with a contradiction due to the termination condition given on page 200.

D.5   Solutions for Chapter 6

Solution to Exercise 6.1

This exercise shows that even rules that are not syntactically datalog can sometimes be expressed by using multiple datalog rules. Simple syntactic transformations of this kind are generally known as *Lloyd-Topor transformations*.

1. This cannot be translated into datalog due to the presence of function symbols.

2. This can be translated into the following two datalog rules.

$$\texttt{Intelligent}(x) \rightarrow \texttt{Clever}(x)$$
$$\texttt{knows}(x, y) \wedge \texttt{Intelligent}(y) \rightarrow \texttt{Clever}(x)$$

3. This can be translated into the following datalog rules.

$$\texttt{Sailor}(x) \wedge \texttt{Spinach}(y) \wedge \texttt{loves}(x, y) \wedge \texttt{loves}(x, \texttt{olive\_oyl})$$
$$\rightarrow \texttt{Little}(x)$$
$$\texttt{Sailor}(x) \wedge \texttt{Spinach}(y) \wedge \texttt{loves}(x, y) \wedge \texttt{loves}(x, \texttt{olive\_oyl})$$
$$\rightarrow \texttt{Strong}(x)$$

4. This can be translated into the following four datalog rules.

$$\texttt{Male}(x) \wedge \texttt{Intelligent}(x) \wedge \texttt{marriedWith}(x, y) \rightarrow \texttt{Wise}(x)$$
$$\texttt{Male}(x) \wedge \texttt{Old}(x) \wedge \texttt{marriedWith}(x, y) \rightarrow \texttt{Wise}(x)$$
$$\texttt{Male}(x) \wedge \texttt{Intelligent}(x) \wedge \texttt{marriedWith}(x, y) \rightarrow \texttt{Bald}(x)$$
$$\texttt{Male}(x) \wedge \texttt{Old}(x) \wedge \texttt{marriedWith}(x, y) \rightarrow \texttt{Bald}(x)$$

These examples used two basic kinds of Lloyd-Topor transformations to show that, in general, it is always possible to allow for additional conjunctions in rule heads (item 2) and disjunctions in rule bodies (item 3). The correctness of these translation is a basic law of Boolean logic: $p \rightarrow q_1 \wedge q_2$ is equivalent to $(p \rightarrow q_1) \wedge (p \rightarrow q_2)$, and likewise for $\vee$. Item 4 further uses the equivalence of $p \rightarrow q \vee \neg r$ and $p \wedge r \rightarrow q$, and of $(\exists x.P(x)) \rightarrow Q(x)$ and $\forall x.(P(x) \rightarrow Q(x))$.

If certain translations are applied in a naive way to a nested expression like the one in item 4, then an exponential number of rules can be created. This can be avoided by adding additional rules to define the cases when a certain subexpression of the body is true, as in the following example:

$$\text{Intelligent}(x) \vee \text{Old}(x) \rightarrow \text{IntelligentOrOld}(x)$$
$$(\text{IntelligentOrOld}(x)) \wedge \exists y.(\text{marriedWith}(x,y)) \rightarrow (\text{Wise}(x) \wedge \text{Bald}(x))$$
$$\vee \neg \text{Male}(x)$$

This will not reduce the number of datalog rules in this example (since 2×2 happens to be the same as $2 + 2$), but it is generally sufficient to ensure that Lloyd-Topor transformations lead to only a linear increase in the size of a rule set. In other words, they are harmless for the performance of reasoning.

Solution to Exercise 6.2

1. $C \sqcap \exists r.D \sqsubseteq E$

2. $\exists r.\text{Self} \sqsubseteq \forall s.\top$

3. $\exists t.\text{Self} \equiv C \wedge \exists r^-.E$
   $\exists d.\text{Self} \equiv D$
   $t \circ U \circ d \sqsubseteq s$

Solution to Exercise 6.3
All the rules can be translated into $\mathcal{SROIQ}$, as follows.

$$\text{Intelligent} \sqsubseteq \text{Clever}$$
$$\exists.\text{knows}.\text{Intelligent} \sqsubseteq \text{Clever}$$
$$\text{Sailor} \sqcap \exists\text{loves}.\text{Spinach} \sqcap \exists\text{loves}.\{\text{olive\_oyl}\} \sqsubseteq \text{Little}$$
$$\text{Sailor} \sqcap \exists\text{loves}.\text{Spinach} \sqcap \exists\text{loves}.\{\text{olive\_oyl}\} \sqsubseteq \text{Strong}$$
$$\text{Male} \sqcap \text{Intelligent} \sqcap \exists\text{marriedWith}.\top \sqsubseteq \text{Wise}$$
$$\text{Male} \sqcap \text{Old} \sqcap \exists\text{marriedWith}.\top \sqsubseteq \text{Wise}$$
$$\text{Male} \sqcap \text{Intelligent} \sqcap \exists\text{marriedWith}.\top \sqsubseteq \text{Bald}$$
$$\text{Male} \sqcap \text{Old} \sqcap \exists\text{marriedWith}.\top \sqsubseteq \text{Bald}$$

Solution to Exercise 6.4
Exercise 5.4: The second and third expressions become datalog. The result is as follows.

$$\text{Human}(x) \rightarrow \exists\text{hasMother}.\text{Human}(x)$$
$$\text{hasMother}(x,y) \wedge \text{hasMother}(y,z) \wedge \text{Human}(z) \rightarrow \text{Grandchild}(x)$$
$$\rightarrow \text{Human}(\text{anupriyaAnkolekar})$$

Exercise 5.7: Only the third expression becomes datalog. The result is as follows.

$$\text{Student}(x) \rightarrow \exists \text{attends.Lecture}(x)$$
$$\text{Lecture}(x) \rightarrow \exists \text{attendedBy.}(\text{Student} \sqcap \text{Eager})(x)$$
$$\rightarrow \text{Student(aStudent)}$$
$$\rightarrow \neg\text{Eager(aStudent)}$$

Exercise 5.11: This is completely expressible in datalog, as follows.

$$\text{Bird}(x) \rightarrow \text{Flies}(x)$$
$$\text{Penguin}(x) \rightarrow \text{Bird}(x)$$
$$\text{Penguin}(x) \wedge \text{Flies}(x) \rightarrow$$
$$\rightarrow \text{Penguin(tweety)}$$

Solution to Exercise 6.5

```
Document(
 Prefix(ex http://example.com/)
 Group(
   Forall ?x ?y ?z(
    ex:Grandchild(?x) :- And( ex:hasMother(?x,?y)
                              ex:hasMother(?y,?z)
                              ex:Human(?z)        )
                  )
   Human(anupriyaAnkolekar)
   Student(aStudent)
   Forall ?x ( Flies(?x) :- Bird(?x) )
   Forall ?x ( Bird (?x) :- Penguin(?x) )
   Forall ?x ( :- And( Penguin(x) Flies(x)) )
   Penguin(tweety)
      )
)
```

Solution to Exercise 6.6
The result of the translation can be found in Fig. D.2.

Solution to Exercise 6.7

1. The role inclusion axiom ensures that the extension of R_{Unhappy} includes all pairs of individuals x and x' for which there is an individual y such that x is related to y with orderedDish, and x' is related to y with

```
<Document><payload><Group><sentence>
        <Forall><declare><Var>x</Var></declare>
                <declare><Var>y</Var></declare>
                <declare><Var>z</Var></declare>
            <formula>
             <And>
               <formula>
                 <Atom><op><Const
                         type="http://www.w3.org/2001/XMLSchema#string"
                         >http://example.org/hasMother</Const>
                         </op>
                         <args ordered="yes"><Var>x</Var>
                                             <Var>y</Var>
                         </args>
                 </Atom>
               </formula>
               <formula>
                 <Atom><op><Const
                         type="http://www.w3.org/2001/XMLSchema#string"
                         >http://example.org/hasMother</Const>
                         </op>
                         <args ordered="yes"><Var>y</Var>
                                             <Var>z</Var>
                         </args>
                 </Atom>
               </formula>
               <formula>
                 <Atom>
                         <op><Const
                         type="http://www.w3.org/2001/XMLSchema#string"
                         >http://example.org/Human</Const>
                         </op>
                         <args ordered="yes"><Var>z</Var>
                         </args>
                 </Atom>
               </formula>
             </And>
            </formula>
        </Forall>
</sentence></Group></payload></Document>
```

FIGURE D.2:   Solution to Exercise 6.6

dislikes. Note that x and x' need not be the same. However, R_{Unhappy} is only used in the first axiom in combination with a local reflexivity constructor. This states that, whenever x is related to itself via R_{Unhappy}, we find that x is part of the extension of Unhappy. Since the new role does not occur anywhere else, these are indeed the only additional instances of Unhappy that can generally be concluded from the knowledge base.

In other words, whenever there are individuals x and y in a model $\mathcal{I}$ such that $(x, y) \in \text{orderedDish}^{\mathcal{I}}$ and $(x, y) \in \text{dislikes}^{\mathcal{I}}$, then we also have $x \in \text{Unhappy}^{\mathcal{I}}$. This is exactly the content of the datalog rule that we are simulating, and it is not hard to see that all additional entailments of the given axioms affect the extension of R_{Unhappy} only.

2. As discussed in Section 5.1.4, concept expressions of the form $\exists S.\text{Self}$ are only allowed if S is a *simple* role. In our example, however, the role R_{Unhappy} is not simple, since it occurs on the right hand side of a complex role inclusion axiom. Thus, the given set of axioms is not an admissible $\mathcal{SROIQ}$ ontology.

D.6 Solutions for Chapter 7

Solution to Exercise 7.1

```
PREFIX ex: <http://example.org/>
SELECT ?object
WHERE
  {{ ex:Sun       ex:satellite  ?object . } UNION
   { ex:Sun       ex:satellite  ?satellite .
     ?satellite  ex:satellite  ?object .}}
```

```
PREFIX ex: <http://example.org/>
SELECT ?object ?center
WHERE
  {{ ?object    ex:radius    ?radius }
   OPTIONAL { ?center    ex:satellite    ?object . }
   FILTER (4 / 3 * 3.1416 * ?radius * ?radius * ?radius > 20000000000)
  }
```

```
PREFIX ex: <http://example.org/>
SELECT ?object
WHERE
  {  ?object     ex:satellite  ?satellite .
     ?satellite ex:name        ?name      .
```

```
      ?center      ex:satellite  ?object   .
      ?center      ex:radius     ?radius   .
   FILTER ( langMATCHES( LANG(?name), "en") )
   FILTER ( 2 * ?radius > 3000 )
 }
```

```
PREFIX ex: <http://example.org/>
SELECT DISTINCT ?object
WHERE
  { ?object       ex:satellite  ?satellite1 .
    ?object       ex:satellite  ?satellite2 .
    FILTER ( !sameTERM(?satellite1,?satellite2) )
  }
```

Solution to Exercise 7.2

```
Union(BGP(<http://example.org/Sun>
                        <http://example.org/satellite> ?object.),
      Join(BGP(<http://example.org/Sun>
                        <http://example.org/satellite> ?satellite.),
          BGP(?satellite <http://example.org/satellite> ?object.)
          )
     )
```

```
Filter((4/3 * 3.1416 * ?radius * ?radius * ?radius > 20000000000),
      LeftJoin(BGP(?object <http://example.org/radius> ?radius.),
              BGP(?center <http://example.org/satellite> ?object.),
              true
              )
      )
```

```
Filter(((langMATCHES( LANG(?name), "en")) && (2 * ?radius > 3000)),
      Join(Join(Join(BGP(?object
                        <http://example.org/satellite> ?satellite.),
                    BGP(?satellite
                        <http://example.org/name> ?name.)
                    ),
              BGP(?center <http://example.org/satellite> ?object.)
              ),
          BGP(?center <http://example.org/radius ?radius>)
          )
      )
```

```
Filter((!sameTERM(?satellite1,?satellite2)),
      Join(BGP(?object <http://example.org/satellite> ?satellite1.),
          BGP(?object <http://example.org/satellite> ?satellite2.),
          )
      )
```

Solution to Exercise 7.3

First query:

```
BGP(<http://example.org/Sun>
                <http://example.org/satellite> ?satellite.)
```

satellite
ex:Mercury
ex:Venus
ex:Earth
ex:Mars

```
BGP(?satellite <http://example.org/satellite> ?object.)
```

satellite	object
ex:Sun	ex:Mercury
ex:Sun	ex:Venus
ex:Sun	ex:Earth
ex:Sun	ex:Mars
ex:Earth	ex:Moon
ex:Mars	ex:Phobos
ex:Mars	ex:Deimos

```
Join(BGP(<http://example.org/Sun>
                <http://example.org/satellite> ?satellite.),
    BGP(?satellite <http://example.org/satellite> ?object.)
    )
```

satellite	object
ex:Earth	ex:Moon
ex:Mars	ex:Phobos
ex:Mars	ex:Deimos

```
BGP(<http://example.org/Sun>
                <http://example.org/satellite> ?object.)
```

object
ex:Mercury
ex:Venus
ex:Earth
ex:Mars

```
Union(BGP(<http://example.org/Sun>
                <http://example.org/satellite> ?object.),
    Join(BGP(<http://example.org/Sun>
                <http://example.org/satellite> ?satellite.),
        BGP(?satellite <http://example.org/satellite> ?object.)
        )
    )
```

object
ex:Mercury
ex:Venus
ex:Earth
ex:Mars

satellite	object
ex:Earth	ex:Moon
ex:Mars	ex:Phobos
ex:Mars	ex:Deimos

Second query:

```
BGP(?object <http://example.org/radius> ?radius.)
```

object	radius
ex:Sun	"1.392e6"^^xsd:double
ex:Mercury	"2439.7"^^xsd:double
ex:Venus	"6051.9"^^xsd:double
ex:Earth	"6372.8"^^xsd:double
ex:Mars	"3402.5"^^xsd:double
ex:Moon	"1737.1"^^xsd:double

```
BGP(?center <http://example.org/satellite> ?object.)
```

center	object
ex:Sun	ex:Mercury
ex:Sun	ex:Venus
ex:Sun	ex:Earth
ex:Sun	ex:Mars
ex:Earth	ex:Moon
ex:Mars	ex:Phobos
ex:Mars	ex:Deimos

```
LeftJoin(BGP(?object <http://example.org/radius> ?radius.),
         BGP(?center <http://example.org/satellite> ?object.),
         true
       )
```

object	radius	center
ex:Sun	"1.392e6"^^xsd:double	
ex:Mercury	"2439.7"^^xsd:double	ex:Sun
ex:Venus	"6051.9"^^xsd:double	ex:Sun
ex:Earth	"6372.8"^^xsd:double	ex:Sun
ex:Mars	"3402.5"^^xsd:double	ex:Sun
ex:Moon	"1737.1"^^xsd:double	ex:Earth

```
Filter((4/3 * 3.1416 * ?radius * ?radius * ?radius > 20000000000),
       LeftJoin(BGP(?object <http://example.org/radius> ?radius.),
                BGP(?center <http://example.org/satellite> ?object.),
                true
              )
     )
```

object	radius	center
ex:Sun	"1.392e6"^^xsd:double	
ex:Mercury	"2439.7"^^xsd:double	ex:Sun
ex:Venus	"6051.9"^^xsd:double	ex:Sun
ex:Earth	"6372.8"^^xsd:double	ex:Sun
ex:Mars	"3402.5"^^xsd:double	ex:Sun
ex:Moon	"1737.1"^^xsd:double	ex:Earth

Third query – we omit the tables for the BGP expressions:

```
Join(BGP(?object <http://example.org/satellite> ?satellite.),
    BGP(?satellite <http://example.org/name> ?name.)
  )
```

object	satellite	name
ex:Earth	ex:Moon	"Moon@en"
ex:Mars	ex:Phobos	"Phobos"
ex:Mars	ex:Deimos	"Deimos"

```
Join(Join(BGP(?object <http://example.org/satellite> ?satellite.),
        BGP(?satellite <http://example.org/name> ?name.)
      ),
    BGP(?center <http://example.org/satellite> ?object.)
  )
```

center	object	satellite	name
ex:Sun	ex:Earth	ex:Moon	"Moon@en"
ex:Sun	ex:Mars	ex:Phobos	"Phobos"
ex:Sun	ex:Mars	ex:Deimos	"Deimos"

```
Join(Join(Join(BGP(?object <http://example.org/satellite> ?satellite.),
            BGP(?satellite <http://example.org/name> ?name.)
          ),
        BGP(?center <http://example.org/satellite> ?object.)
      ),
    BGP(?center <http://example.org/radius ?radius>)
  )
```

center	radius	object	satellite	name
ex:Sun	"1.392e6"^^xsd:double	ex:Earth	ex:Moon	"Moon@en"
ex:Sun	"1.392e6"^^xsd:double	ex:Mars	ex:Phobos	"Phobos"
ex:Sun	"1.392e6"^^xsd:double	ex:Mars	ex:Deimos	"Deimos"

```
Filter(((langMATCHES( LANG(?name), "en")) && (2 * ?radius > 3000)),
     Join(Join(Join(BGP(?object
                    <http://example.org/satellite> ?satellite.),
                BGP(?satellite
                    <http://example.org/name> ?name.)
```

object	satellite1	satellite2
ex:Sun	ex:Mercury	ex:Mercury
ex:Sun	ex:Mercury	ex:Venus
ex:Sun	ex:Mercury	ex:Earth
ex:Sun	ex:Mercury	ex:Mars
ex:Sun	ex:Venus	ex:Mercury
ex:Sun	ex:Venus	ex:Venus
ex:Sun	ex:Venus	ex:Earth
ex:Sun	ex:Venus	ex:Mars
ex:Sun	ex:Earth	ex:Mercury
ex:Sun	ex:Earth	ex:Venus
ex:Sun	ex:Earth	ex:Earth
ex:Sun	ex:Earth	ex:Mars
ex:Sun	ex:Mars	ex:Mercury
ex:Sun	ex:Mars	ex:Venus
ex:Sun	ex:Mars	ex:Earth
ex:Sun	ex:Mars	ex:Mars
ex:Earth	ex:Moon	ex:Moon
ex:Mars	ex:Phobos	ex:Phobos
ex:Mars	ex:Phobos	ex:Deimos
ex:Mars	ex:Deimos	ex:Phobos
ex:Mars	ex:Deimos	ex:Deimos

FIGURE D.3: Exercise 7.3 fourth query: Table for `Join(BGP(`
`?object <http://example.org/satellite> ?satellite1.),`
`BGP(?object <http://example.org/satellite> ?satellite2.))`

```
                ),
        BGP(?center <http://example.org/satellite> ?object.)
            ),
        BGP(?center <http://example.org/radius ?radius>)
          )
    )
```

center	radius	object	satellite	name
ex:Sun	"1.392e6"^^xsd:double	ex:Earth	ex:Moon	"Moon@en"

Fourth query – we omit the tables for the BGP expressions:

```
Join(BGP(?object <http://example.org/satellite> ?satellite1.),
    BGP(?object <http://example.org/satellite> ?satellite2.)
    )
```

See Fig. D.3.

object	satellite1	satellite2
ex:Sun	ex:Mercury	ex:Venus
ex:Sun	ex:Mercury	ex:Earth
ex:Sun	ex:Mercury	ex:Mars
ex:Sun	ex:Venus	ex:Mercury
ex:Sun	ex:Venus	ex:Earth
ex:Sun	ex:Venus	ex:Mars
ex:Sun	ex:Earth	ex:Mercury
ex:Sun	ex:Earth	ex:Venus
ex:Sun	ex:Earth	ex:Mars
ex:Sun	ex:Mars	ex:Mercury
ex:Sun	ex:Mars	ex:Venus
ex:Sun	ex:Mars	ex:Earth
ex:Mars	ex:Phobos	ex:Deimos
ex:Mars	ex:Deimos	ex:Phobos

FIGURE D.4: Exercise 7.3 fourth query: Table for
Filter((!sameTERM(?satellite1,?satellite2)), Join(BGP(?object
<http://example.org/satellite> ?satellite1.), BGP(?object
<http://example.org/satellite> ?satellite2.)))

```
Filter((!sameTERM(?satellite1,?satellite2)),
      Join(BGP(?object <http://example.org/satellite> ?satellite1.),
          BGP(?object <http://example.org/satellite> ?satellite2.)
          )
      )
```

See Fig. D.4.

Solution to Exercise 7.4

```
PREFIX  ex:  <http://example.org/>
SELECT ?object
WHERE
   {        { ?object  rdf:type      ex:CelestialBody }
    OPTIONAL { ?object  ex:satellite  ?satellite       }
    FILTER ( !BOUND(?satellite) )
   }
```

Solution to Exercise 7.5
We need an RDF document because SPARQL variables can only obtain values
which occur in the queried RDF document. So let's simply use the following.

```
<http://example.org/square>   <http://example.org/allowed>
        "1"^^xsd:int, "2"^^xsd:int, "3"^^xsd:int, "4"^^xsd:int .
```

We now assign to each of the squares a variable name, say from ?F11 to ?F44. Finally, we need to formulate all conditions which constrain possible solutions:

- Every variable gets assigned one of the allowed numbers.

- Variables standing for table slots which are already filled in must get the corresponding value assigned.

- No two variables within the same row get assigned the same value.

- No two variables within the same column get assigned the same value.

- No two variables within the same marked 2×2 square get assigned the same value.

A possible solution now looks as follows.

```
PREFIX  ex:  <http://example.org/>
SELECT  ?F11 ?F12 ?F13 ?F14
        ?F21 ?F22 ?F23 ?F24
        ?F31 ?F32 ?F33 ?F34
        ?F41 ?F42 ?F43 ?F44
WHERE
{  ex:square ex:allowed ?F11, ?F12, ?F13, ?F14,
                        ?F21, ?F22, ?F23, ?F24,
                        ?F31, ?F32, ?F33, ?F34,
                        ?F41, ?F42, ?F43, ?F44.

  FILTER ( ?F14 = "3"^^xsd:int )
  FILTER ( ?F24 = "4"^^xsd:int )
  FILTER ( ?F31 = "2"^^xsd:int )
  FILTER ( ?F41 = "3"^^xsd:int )


  FILTER ( ?F11 != ?F12 )   FILTER ( ?F11 != ?F13 )
  FILTER ( ?F11 != ?F14 )   FILTER ( ?F12 != ?F13 )
  FILTER ( ?F12 != ?F14 )   FILTER ( ?F13 != ?F14 )

  FILTER ( ?F21 != ?F22 )   FILTER ( ?F21 != ?F23 )
  FILTER ( ?F21 != ?F24 )   FILTER ( ?F22 != ?F23 )
  FILTER ( ?F22 != ?F24 )   FILTER ( ?F23 != ?F24 )

  FILTER ( ?F31 != ?F32 )   FILTER ( ?F31 != ?F33 )
  FILTER ( ?F31 != ?F34 )   FILTER ( ?F32 != ?F33 )
  FILTER ( ?F32 != ?F34 )   FILTER ( ?F33 != ?F34 )

  FILTER ( ?F41 != ?F42 )   FILTER ( ?F41 != ?F43 )
  FILTER ( ?F41 != ?F44 )   FILTER ( ?F42 != ?F43 )
```

```
FILTER ( ?F42 != ?F44 )   FILTER ( ?F43 != ?F44 )


FILTER ( ?F11 != ?F21 )   FILTER ( ?F11 != ?F31 )
FILTER ( ?F11 != ?F41 )   FILTER ( ?F21 != ?F31 )
FILTER ( ?F21 != ?F41 )   FILTER ( ?F31 != ?F41 )

FILTER ( ?F12 != ?F22 )   FILTER ( ?F12 != ?F32 )
FILTER ( ?F12 != ?F42 )   FILTER ( ?F22 != ?F32 )
FILTER ( ?F22 != ?F42 )   FILTER ( ?F32 != ?F42 )

FILTER ( ?F13 != ?F23 )   FILTER ( ?F13 != ?F33 )
FILTER ( ?F13 != ?F43 )   FILTER ( ?F23 != ?F33 )
FILTER ( ?F23 != ?F43 )   FILTER ( ?F33 != ?F43 )

FILTER ( ?F14 != ?F24 )   FILTER ( ?F14 != ?F34 )
FILTER ( ?F14 != ?F44 )   FILTER ( ?F24 != ?F34 )
FILTER ( ?F24 != ?F44 )   FILTER ( ?F34 != ?F44 )


FILTER ( ?F11 != ?F22 )   FILTER ( ?F12 != ?F21 )
FILTER ( ?F13 != ?F24 )   FILTER ( ?F14 != ?F23 )
FILTER ( ?F31 != ?F42 )   FILTER ( ?F32 != ?F41 )
FILTER ( ?F33 != ?F44 )   FILTER ( ?F34 != ?F43 )
}
```

It is obviously possible to solve larger Sudokus along the same lines. This actually shows that SPARQL is at least as hard as Sudoku, which is known to be NP-complete.

Solution to Exercise 7.6

The result tables of the given queries are as follows:

1.

s	v
http://example.org/a	"1"^^xsd:integer
http://example.org/b	"2"^^xsd:integer
http://example.org/a	"3"^^xsd:integer

2.

s
http://example.org/a
http://example.org/b
http://example.org/a

3.

s
http://example.org/a
http://example.org/b

The result of the fourth query is not fully determined by the SPARQL specification, which states that "[t]he order of $Distinct(\Psi)$ must preserve any ordering given by $OrderBy$" but which also requires that each result row appears at most once in the result returned by $Distinct$. Hence, one occurrence of ex:a is to be deleted, but it is left to implementations to decide which one this is. Hence, the result might be the same as in the third query, or it might be in reversed order.

This also affects the final question of the exercise: the solution appearing with LIMIT 1 is the first of the computed sequence, and thus depends on the decision taken when applying $Distinct$. Note that this also exposes one of the rare cases where $Distinct$ could even influence the result of queries in CONSTRUCT format. Clearly, it is not recommended to formulate queries with such an unpredictable behavior, and CONSTRUCT does not admit the keyword DISTINCT to be used.

Solution to Exercise 7.7

1. $\exists z(\mathtt{marriedWith}(x, y) \wedge \mathtt{childOf}(z, x) \wedge \mathtt{childOf}(z, y))$

2. $\exists y(\mathtt{marriedWith}(x, y) \wedge \mathtt{Female}(x) \wedge \mathtt{Catholic}(x) \wedge \mathtt{Priest}(x))$

3. For the third query there are two possible interpretations. The first identifies those persons whose parents are married with *each other*.

$$\exists x, y(\mathtt{marriedWith}(x, y) \wedge \mathtt{childOf}(z, x) \wedge \mathtt{childOf}(z, y))$$

The second interpretation identifies those persons whose parents are married with *somebody* (but not necessarily with the other parent).

$$\exists x, y, v, w(\mathtt{marriedWith}(x, v) \wedge \mathtt{marriedWith}(y, w) \wedge \mathtt{childOf}(z, x)$$
$$\wedge \mathtt{childOf}(z, y))$$

4. $\exists y(\mathtt{Female}(x) \wedge \mathtt{marriedWith}(x, y) \wedge \mathtt{killed}(x, y))$

5. $\mathtt{marriedWith}(x, y) \wedge \mathtt{killed}(x, x) \wedge \mathtt{killed}(y, y)$

References

[ABMP08] B. Adida, M. Birbeck, S. McCarron, and S. Pemberton, editors. *RDFa in XHTML: Syntax and Processing*. W3C Recommendation, 14 October 2008. Available at http://www.w3.org/TR/rdfa-syntax/.

[ADR06] S. Auer, S. Dietzold, and T. Riechert. OntoWiki – A tool for social, semantic collaboration. In Y. Gil, E. Motta, R. V. Benjamins, and M. Musen, editors, *Proceedings of the 5th International Semantic Web Conference (ISWC 2006)*, volume 4273 of *Lecture Notes in Computer Science*, pages 736–749. Springer, 2006.

[AHV94] S. Abiteboul, R. Hull, and V. Vianu. *Foundations of Databases*. Addison Wesley, 1994.

[APG06] M. Arenas, J. Perez, and C. Gutierrez. Semantics and complexity of SPARQL. In I. Cruz, S. Decker, D. Allemang, C. Preist, D. Schwabe, P. Mika, M. Uschold, and L. Aroyo, editors, *The Semantic Web – ISWC 2006, 5th International Semantic Web Conference, ISWC 2006, Athens, GA, USA, November 5-9, 2006, Proceedings*, volume 4273 of *Lecture Notes in Computer Science*, pages 30–43. Springer, 2006.

[AvH08] G. Antoniou and F. van Harmelen, editors. *A Semantic Web Primer*. Cooperative Information Systems. MIT Press, Cambridge, Massachusetts, 2nd edition, 2008.

[BB08] D. Beckett and J. Broekstra, editors. *SPARQL Query Results XML Format*. W3C Recommendation, 15 January 2008. Available at http://www.w3.org/TR/rdf-sparql-XMLres/.

[BBL05] F. Baader, S. Brandt, and C. Lutz. Pushing the $\mathcal{EL}$ envelope. In L.P. Kaelbling and A. Saffiotti, editors, *Proceedings of the 19th International Joint Conference on Artificial Intelligence (IJCAI-05)*, pages 364–369. Morgan Kaufmann Publishers, 2005.

[BBL08] D. Beckett and T. Berners-Lee. *Turtle – Terse RDF Triple Language*. W3C Team Submission, 14 January 2008. Available at http://www.w3.org/TeamSubmission/turtle/.

[BC08]   P. Buitelaar and P. Cimiano, editors. *Ontology Learning and Population: Bridging the Gap between Text and Knowledge*, volume 167 of *Frontiers in Artificial Intelligence and Applications*. IOS Press, Amsterdam, 2008.

[BCM+07]   F. Baader, D. Calvanese, D. McGuinness, D. Nardi, and P. Patel-Schneider, editors. *The Description Logic Handbook: Theory, Implementation, and Applications*. Cambridge University Press, 2007.

[Bec04]   D. Beckett, editor. *RDF/XML Syntax Specification (Revised)*. W3C Recommendation, 10 February 2004. Available at http://www.w3.org/TR/rdf-syntax-grammar/.

[BG00]   D. Brickley and R.V. Guha, editors. *Resource Description Framework (RDF) Schema Specification 1.0*. W3C Candidate Recommendation, 27 March 2000. Available at http://www.w3.org/TR/2000/CR-rdf-schema-20000327/.

[BG04]   D. Brickley and R.V. Guha, editors. *RDF Vocabulary Description Language 1.0: RDF Schema*. W3C Recommendation, 10 February 2004. Available at http://www.w3.org/TR/rdf-schema/.

[BHK+08]   H. Boley, G. Hallmark, M. Kifer, A. Paschke, A. Polleres, and D. Reynolds, editors. *RIF Core*. W3C Working Draft, 18 December 2008. Available at http://www.w3.org/TR/rif-core/.

[BK08a]   H. Boley and M. Kifer, editors. *RIF Basic Logic Dialect*. W3C Working Draft, 30 July 2008. Available at http://www.w3.org/TR/rif-bld/.

[BK08b]   H. Boley and M. Kifer, editors. *RIF Framework for Logic Dialects*. W3C Working Draft, 30 July 2008. Available at http://www.w3.org/TR/rif-fld/.

[BLa]   T. Berners-Lee. Notation 3. http://www.w3.org/Design Issues/Notation3, retrieved on 11 January 2009.

[BLb]   T. Berners-Lee. Notation 3 Logic. http://www.w3.org/Design Issues/N3Logic, retrieved on 11 January 2009.

[BL00]   T. Berners-Lee. *Weaving the Web: The Original Design and Ultimate Destiny of the World Wide Web*. Collins Business, 2000.

[BLHL01]   T. Berners-Lee, J. Hendler, and O. Lassila. The Semantic Web. *Scientific American*, pages 96–101, May 2001.

[BS85]   R.J. Brachman and J.G. Schmolze. An overview of the KL-ONE knowledge representation system. *Cognitive Science*, 9(2), 1985.

[CEO07] D. Calvanese, T. Eiter, and M.M. Ortiz. Answering regular path queries in expressive description logics: An automata-theoretic approach. In *Proceedings of the 22nd AAAI Conference on Artificial Intelligence (AAAI-07)*, pages 391–396, 2007.

[CFT08] K.G. Clark, L. Feigenbaum, and E. Torres, editors. *SPARQL Protocol for RDF*. W3C Recommendation, 15 January 2008. Available at http://www.w3.org/TR/rdf-sparql-protocol/.

[CGL98] D. Calvanese, G. De Giacomo, and M. Lenzerini. On the decidability of query containment under constraints. In *Proceedings of the 17th ACM SIGACT-SIGMOD-SIGART Symposium on Principles of Database Systems*, pages 149–158. ACM Press, 1998.

[CGL+07] D. Calvanese, G. De Giacomo, D. Lembo, M. Lenzerini, and R. Rosati. Tractable reasoning and efficient query answering in description logics: The DL-Lite family. *Journal of Automated Reasoning*, 39(3):385–429, 2007.

[CHKS08] B. Cuenca Grau, I. Horrocks, Y. Kazakov, and U. Sattler. Modular reuse of ontologies: Theory and practice. *Journal of Artificial Intelligence Research*, 31:273–318, 2008.

[Clo03] W.F. Clocksin. *Clause and Effect: Prolog Programming for the Working Programmer*. Springer, 2003.

[CM77]   A.K. Chandra and P.M. Merlin. Optimal implementation of conjunctive queries in relational data bases. In J.E. Hopcroft, E.P. Friedman, and M.A. Harrison, editors, *Proceedings of the 9th Annual ACM Symposium on Theory of Computing (STOC-77), Boulder, Colorado, USA*, pages 77–90. ACM Press, 1977.

[CM03]   W.F. Clocksin and C.S. Mellish. *Programming in Prolog: Using the ISO Standard*. Springer, 5th edition, 2003.

[Con07] D. Connolly, editor. *Gleaning Resource Descriptions from Dialects of Languages*. W3C Recommendation, 11 September 2007. Available at http://www.w3.org/TR/grddl/.

[Cyg05] R. Cyganiak. A relational algebra for SPARQL. HP Labs Technical Report HPL-2005-170, 2005. Available at http://www.hpl.hp.com/techreports/2005/HPL-2005-170.html.

[dB08]   J. de Bruijn, editor. *RIF RDF and OWL Compatibility*. W3C Working Draft, 30 July 2008. Available at http://www.w3.org/TR/rif-rdf-owl/.

[DEDC96] P. Deransart, A. Ed-Dbali, and L. Cervoni. *Prolog: The Standard. Reference Manual.* Springer, 1996.

[DEGV01] E. Dantsin, T. Eiter, G. Gottlob, and A. Voronkov. Complexity and expressive power of logic programming. *ACM Computing Surveys*, 33(3):374–425, 2001.

[DLNS98] F.M. Donini, M. Lenzerini, D. Nardi, and A. Schaerf. AL-log: Integrating datalog and description logics. *Journal of Intelligent Information Systems*, 10(3), 1998.

[dSMPH08] C. de Sainte Marie, A. Paschke, and G. Hallmark, editors. *RIF Production Rule Dialect.* W3C Working Draft, 18 December 2008. Available at http://www.w3.org/TR/rif-prd/.

[DSW06] J. Davies, R. Studer, and P. Warren, editors. *Semantic Web Technologies: Trends and Research in Ontology-based Systems.* Wiley, 2006.

[EFT96] H.-D. Ebbinghaus, J. Flum, and W. Thomas. *Mathematical Logic.* Springer, 1996.

[ELST04] T. Eiter, T. Lukasiewicz, R. Schindlauer, and H. Tompits. Combining answer set programming with description logics for the semantic web. In D. Dubois, C.Welty, and M. Williams, editors, *Proceedings of the 9th International Conference on Principles of Knowledge Representation and Reasoning (KR-04)*, pages 141–151, 2004.

[ES07] J. Euzenat and P. Shvaiko. *Ontology Matching.* Springer, 2007.

[Fel98] C. Fellbaum. *WordNet: An Electronic Lexical Database.* MIT Press, 1998.

[FHH⁺07] L. Feigenbaum, I. Herman, T. Hongsermeier, E. Neumann, and S. Stephens. The Semantic Web in action. *Scientific American*, pages 90–97, November 2007.

[For82] C. Forgy. Rete: A fast algorithm for the many pattern/many object pattern match problem. *Artificial Intelligence*, 19:17–37, 1982.

[Gär92] P. Gärdenfors, editor. *Belief Revision.* Cambridge University Press, December 1992.

[GB04] J. Grant and D. Beckett, editors. *RDF Test Cases.* W3C Recommendation, 10 February 2004. Available at http://www.w3.org/TR/rdf-testcases/.

[GHLS07] B. Glimm, I. Horrocks, C. Lutz, and U. Sattler. Conjunctive query answering for the description logic $\mathcal{SHIQ}$. In M.M.

Veloso, editor, *Proceedings of the 20th International Joint Conference on Artificial Intelligence (IJCAI-07), Hyderabad, India*, pages 399–404. Morgan Kaufmann Publishers, 2007.

[GHVD03] B.N. Grosof, I. Horrocks, R. Volz, and S. Decker. Description logic programs: combining logic programs with description logic. In *Proceedings of the 12th International World Wide Web Conference (WWW-03), Budapest, Hungary*, pages 48–57. ACM, 2003.

[Göd31] K. Gödel. Über formal unentscheidbare Sätze der Principia Mathematica und verwandter Systeme. *Monatshefte für Mathematik und Physik*, 38:173–198, 1931.

[GPCFL04] A. Gomez-Perez, O. Corcho, and M. Fernandez-Lopez. *Ontological Engineering: With Examples from the Areas of Knowledge Management, e-Commerce and the Semantic Web*. Springer, July 2004.

[GPMM04] A. Gómez-Pérez and D. Manzano-Macho. An overview of methods and tools for ontology learning from texts. *Knowledge Engineering Review*, 19(3):187–212, 2004.

[GR04] J.C. Giarratano and G.D. Riley. *Expert Systems: Principles and Programming*. Course Technology, 4th edition, 2004.

[GW97] B. Ganter and R. Wille. *Formal Concept Analysis: Mathematical Foundations*. Springer-Verlag, 1997.

[GW04] N. Guarino and C.A. Welty. An overview of OntoClean. In S. Staab and R. Studer, editors, *Handbook on Ontologies*, International Handbooks on Information Systems, pages 151–172. Springer, 2004.

[Hay04] P. Hayes, editor. *RDF Semantics*. W3C Recommendation, 10 February 2004. Available at `http://www.w3.org/TR/rdf-mt/`.

[HHPS04] P. Hayes, I. Horrocks, and P.F. Patel-Schneider, editors. *OWL Web Ontology Language Semantics and Abstract Syntax*. W3C Recommendation, 10 February 2004. Available at `http://www.w3.org/TR/owl-semantics/`.

[Hil03] E.F. Hill. *Jess in Action: Java Rule-Based Systems*. Manning Publications, 2003.

[HKP+09] P. Hitzler, M. Krötzsch, B. Parsia, P.F. Patel-Schneider, and S. Rudolph, editors. *OWL 2 Web Ontology Language: Primer*. W3C Working Draft, 11 June 2009. Available at `http://www.w3.org/TR/2009/WD-owl2-primer-20090611/`.

[HKS06]   I. Horrocks, O. Kutz, and U. Sattler. The even more irresistible $\mathcal{SROIQ}$. In P. Doherty, J. Mylopoulos, and C. Welty, editors, *Proceedings of the 10th International Conference on Principles of Knowledge Representation and Reasoning (KR-06)*, pages 57–67. AAAI Press, 2006.

[HPS04]   I. Horrocks and P.F. Patel-Schneider. A proposal for an OWL rules language. In *Proceedings of the 13th International World Wide Web Conference (WWW-04)*, pages 723–731. ACM, 2004.

[HPS08]   M. Horridge, B. Parsia, and U. Sattler. Laconic and precise justifications in OWL. In A. P. Sheth, S. Staab, M. Dean, M. Paolucci, D. Maynard, T. W. Finin, and K. Thirunarayan, editors, *International Semantic Web Conference*, volume 5318 of *Lecture Notes in Computer Science*, pages 323–338. Springer, 2008.

[HPSB$^+$04]   I. Horrocks, P.F. Patel-Schneider, H. Boley, S. Tabet, B. Grosof, and M. Dean. *SWRL: A Semantic Web Rule Language*. W3C Member Submission, 21 May 2004. Available at http://www.w3.org/Submission/SWRL/.

[HPSBT05]   I. Horrocks, P.F. Patel-Schneider, S. Bechhofer, and D. Tsarkov. OWL Rules: A proposal and prototype implementation. *Journal of Web Semantics*, 3(1):23–40, 2005.

[HPSvH03]   I. Horrocks, P.F. Patel-Schneider, and F. van Harmelen. From $\mathcal{SHIQ}$ and RDF to OWL: The making of a web ontology language. *Journal of Web Semantics*, 1(1):7–26, 2003.

[HS99]   I. Horrocks and U. Sattler. A description logic with transitive and inverse roles and role hierarchies. *Journal of Logic and Computation*, 9(3):385–410, 1999.

[HS07]   I. Horrocks and U. Sattler. A tableau decision procedure for $\mathcal{SHOIQ}$. *Journal of Automated Reasoning*, 39(3):249–276, 2007.

[HS09]   P. Hitzler and H. Schärfe, editors. *Conceptual Structures in Practice*. Chapman & Hall/CRC, 2009.

[HST00]   I. Horrocks, U. Sattler, and S. Tobies. Reasoning with individuals for the description logic $\mathcal{SHIQ}$. In David McAllester, editor, *Proceedings of the 17th International Conference on Automated Deduction (CADE-00)*, volume 1831 of *Lecture Notes in Computer Science*, pages 482–496. Springer, 2000.

[HTL07]   B. Hummel, W. Thiemann, and I. Lulcheva. Description logic for vision-based intersection understanding. In *Proceedings of*

Cognitive Systems with Interactive Sensors, Stanford University, Palo Alto, CA, USA (COGIS'07), 2007.

[KC04] G. Klyne and J.J. Carroll, editors. *Resource Description Framework (RDF): Concepts and Abstract Syntax.* W3C Recommendation, 10 February 2004. Available at http://www.w3.org/TR/rdf-concepts/.

[Ket92] K.L. Ketner, editor. *Reasoning and the Logic of Things: The Cambridge Conferences Lectures of 1898.* Harvard University Press, Cambridge MA, 1992.

[Kie06] M. Kiesel. Kaukolu – Hub of the semantic corporate intranet. In M. Völkel and S. Schaffert, editors, *Proceedings of the 1st Workshop on Semantic Wikis – From Wiki to Semantics (SemWiki-06)*, 2006.

[KLW95] M. Kifer, G. Lausen, and J. Wu. Logical foundations of object-oriented and frame-based languages. *Journal of the ACM*, 42(4):741–843, 1995.

[KR93] H. Kamp and U. Reyle. *From Discourse to Logic.* Kluwer Academic Publishers, Dordrecht, 1993.

[KRH07] M. Krötzsch, S. Rudolph, and P. Hitzler. Conjunctive queries for a tractable fragment of OWL 1.1. In K. Aberer, K.-S. Choi, and N. Noy, editors, *Proceedings of the 6th International Semantic Web Conference (ISWC-07)*, volume 4825 of *Lecture Notes in Computer Science*, pages 310–323. Springer, 2007.

[KRH08a] M. Krötzsch, S. Rudolph, and P. Hitzler. Description logic rules. In M. Ghallab, C. D. Spyropoulos, N. Fakotakis, and N. Avouris, editors, *Proceedings of the 18th European Conference on Artificial Intelligence (ECAI-08)*, pages 80–84. IOS Press, 2008.

[KRH08b] M. Krötzsch, S. Rudolph, and P. Hitzler. ELP: Tractable rules for OWL 2. In A. Sheth, S. Staab, M. Dean, M. Paolucci, D. Maynard, T. Finin, and K. Thirunarayan, editors, *Proceedings of the 7th International Semantic Web Conference (ISWC-08)*, volume 5318 of *Lecture Notes in Computer Science*, pages 649–664. Springer, 2008.

[Kuh06] T. Kuhn. Combining semantic wikis and controlled natural language. In C. Bizer and A. Joshi, editors, *Proceedings of the Poster and Demonstration Session at the 7th International Semantic Web Conference (ISWC-08)*, 2006.

[KVV+07] M. Krötzsch, D. Vrandečić, M. Völkel, H. Haller, and R. Studer. Semantic Wikipedia. *Journal of Web Semantics*, 5:251–261, 2007.

[LD94] N. Lavrac and S. Dzeroski. *Inductive Logic Programming: Techniques and Applications*. Ellis Horwood, New York, 1994.

[LD97] Thomas K. Landauer and Susan T. Dumais. A solution to Plato's problem: The latent semantic analysis theory of acquisition, induction, and representation of knowledge. *Psychological Review*, 104(2):211–240, April 1997.

[Les05] L. Lessig. *Free Culture: The Nature and Future of Creativity*. Penguin, 2005.

[LG90] D. Lenat and R. V. Guha. *Building Large Knowledge-Based Systems: Representation and Inference in the Cyc Project*. Addison-Wesley, 1990.

[Llo88] J.W. Lloyd. *Foundations of Logic Programming*. Springer, 1988.

[LS99] O. Lassila and R. Swick, editors. *Resource Description Framework (RDF) Model and Syntax Specification*. W3C Recommendation, 22 February 1999. Available at http://www.w3.org/TR/1999/REC-rdf-syntax-19990222/.

[Lut07] C. Lutz. Inverse roles make conjunctive queries hard. In D. Calvanese, E. Franconi, V. Haarslev, D. Lembo, B. Motik, A.-Y. Turhan, and S. Tessaris, editors, *Proceedings of the 20th Description Logic Workshop (DL-07)*, volume 250 of *CEUR Workshop Proceedings*, 2007. Available at http://ceur-ws.org/Vol-250.

[MCGH+09] B. Motik, B. Cuenca Grau, I. Horrocks, Z. Wu, A. Fokoue, and C. Lutz, editors. *OWL 2 Web Ontology Language: Profiles*. W3C Candidate Recommendation, 11 June 2009. Available at http://www.w3.org/TR/2009/CR-owl2-profiles-20090611/.

[MHRS06] B. Motik, I. Horrocks, R. Rosati, and U. Sattler. Can OWL and logic programming live together happily ever after? In I.F. Cruz, S. Decker, D. Allemang, C. Preist, D. Schwabe, P. Mika, M. Uschold, and L. Aroyo, editors, *Proceedings of the 5th International Semantic Web Conference (ISWC 2006)*, volume 4273 of *Lecture Notes in Computer Science*, pages 501–514. Springer, 2006.

[Mit97] T. M. Mitchell. *Machine Learning*. McGraw-Hill, New York, 1997.

[MKH08] J. J. Alferes M. Knorr and P. Hitzler. A coherent well-founded model for hybrid MKNF knowledge bases. In M. Ghallab, C. D. Spyropoulos, N. Fakotakis, and N. Avouris, editors, *Proceedings of the 18th European Conference on Artificial Intelligence (ECAI-08)*, pages 99–103. IOS Press, 2008.

[MM04] F. Manola and E. Miller, editors. *Resource Description Framework (RDF). Primer.* W3C Recommendation, 10 February 2004. Available at http://www.w3.org/TR/rdf-primer/.

[MMW07] J. Melton, A. Malhotra, and N. Walsh, editors. *XQuery 1.0 and XPath 2.0 Functions and Operators.* W3C Recommendation, 23 January 2007. Available at http://www.w3.org/TR/xpath-functions/.

[Mot06] B. Motik. *Reasoning in Description Logics using Resolution and Deductive Databases.* PhD thesis, Universität Karlsruhe (TH), Germany, 2006.

[MPSCG09] B. Motik, P.F. Patel-Schneider, and B. Cuenca Grau, editors. *OWL 2 Web Ontology Language: Direct Semantics.* W3C Candidate Recommendation, 11 June 2009. Available at http://www.w3.org/TR/2009/CR-owl2-direct-semantics-20090611/.

[MPSP09] B. Motik, P.F. Patel-Schneider, and B. Parsia, editors. *OWL 2 Web Ontology Language: Structural Specification and Functional-Style Syntax.* W3C Candidate Recommendation, 11 June 2009. Available at http://www.w3.org/TR/2009/CR-owl2-syntax-20090611/.

[MR07] B. Motik and R. Rosati. A faithful integration of description logics with logic programming. In M.M. Veloso, editor, *Proceedings of the 20th International Joint Conference on Artificial Intelligence (IJCAI-07)*, pages 477–482. Morgan Kaufmann Publishers, 2007.

[MRS07] C. D. Manning, P. Raghavan, and H. Schütze. *Introduction to Information Retrieval.* Cambridge University Press, 2007.

[MS01] A. Maedche and S. Staab. Ontology learning for the semantic web. *IEEE Intelligent Systems and Their Applications*, 16(2):72–79, 2001.

[MSS05] B. Motik, U. Sattler, and R. Studer. Query answering for OWL DL with rules. *Journal of Web Semantics*, 3(1):41–60, 2005.

[MvH04] D.L. McGuinness and F. van Harmelen, editors. *OWL Web Ontology Language Overview.* W3C Recommendation, 10 February 2004. Available at http://www.w3.org/TR/owl-features/.

[NM] N. F. Noy and D. L. McGuinness. Ontology development 101: A guide to creating your first ontology. http://www.ksl.stanford.edu/people/dlm/papers/ontology101/ontology101-noy-mcguinness.html, retrieved on 15 February 2009.

[NS06] L. J. B. Nixon and E. Simperl. Makna and MultiMakna: towards semantic and multimedia capability in wikis for the emerging web. In S. Schaffert and Y. Sure, editors, *Proceedings of SEMANTICS 2006*. Österreichische Computer Gesellschaft, 2006.

[NT95] I. Nonaka and H. Takeuchi. *The Knowledge-Creating Company*. Oxford University Press, May 1995.

[OWL] W3C OWL website. http://www.w3.org/2004/OWL/.

[Pap94] C.H. Papadimitriou. *Computational Complexity*. Addison Wesley, 1994.

[PBK08] A. Polleres, H. Boley, and M. Kifer, editors. *RIF Datatypes and Built-Ins 1.0*. W3C Working Draft, 18 December 2008. Available at http://www.w3.org/TR/rif-dtb/.

[PM04] H. S. Pinto and J. P. Martins. Ontologies: How can they be built? *Knowledge and Information Systems*, 6(4):441–464, 2004.

[PS08] E. Prud'hommeaux and A. Seaborne, editors. *SPARQL Query Language for RDF*. W3C Recommendation, 15 January 2008. Available at http://www.w3.org/TR/rdf-sparql-query/.

[PSM09] P.F. Patel-Schneider and B. Motik, editors. *OWL 2 Web Ontology Language: Mapping to RDF Graphs*. W3C Candidate Recommendation, 11 June 2009. Available at http://www.w3.org/TR/2009/CR-owl2-mapping-to-rdf-20090611/.

[RDH+04] A.L. Rector, N. Drummond, M. Horridge, J. Rogers, H. Knublauch, R. Stevens, H. Wang, and C. Wroe. OWL Pizzas: Practical experience of teaching OWL-DL: Common errors & common patterns. In E. Motta, N. Shadbolt, A. Stutt, and N. Gibbins, editors, *Engineering Knowledge in the Age of the Semantic Web, 14th International Conference, EKAW 2004, Whittlebury Hall, UK, October 5-8, 2004, Proceedings*, volume 3257 of *Lecture Notes in Computer Science*, pages 63–81. Springer, 2004.

[RKH08] S. Rudolph, M. Krötzsch, and P. Hitzler. Cheap Boolean role constructors for description logics. In S. Hölldobler, C. Lutz, and H. Wansing, editors, *Proceedings of the 11th European Conference on Logics in Artificial Intelligence (JELIA-08)*, volume 5293 of *Lecture Notes in Artificial Intelligence*, pages 362–374. Springer, 2008.

[RN03] S. J. Russell and P. Norvig. *Artificial Intelligence: A Modern Approach (Second Edition)*. Prentice Hall, 2003.

[Ros06] R. Rosati. DL+log: A tight integration of description logics and disjunctive datalog. In *Proceedings of the 10th International Conference on Principles of Knowledge Representation and Reasoning (KR-06)*, pages 68–78, 2006.

[Rud06] S. Rudolph. *Relational Exploration – Combining Description Logics and Formal Concept Analysis for Knowledge Specification*. Universitätsverlag Karlsruhe, 2006. Dissertation.

[SBLH06] N. Shadbolt, T. Berners-Lee, and W. Hall. The Semantic Web revisited. *IEEE Intelligent Systems*, 21(3):96–101, 2006.

[Sch06] S. Schaffert. IkeWiki: A semantic wiki for collaborative knowledge management. In R. Tolksdorf, E. Simperl, and K. Schild, editors, *Proceedings of the 1st International Workshop on Semantic Technologies in Collaborative Applications (STICA-06)*, 2006.

[Sch07] S. Schenk. A SPARQL semantics based on datalog. In J.G. Carbonell and J. Siekmann, editors, *Proceedings of the 30th Annual German Conference on AI (KI-07)*, volume 4667 of *Lecture Notes in Artificial Intelligence*, pages 160–174. Springer, 2007.

[Sch08] U. Schöning. *Logic for Computer Scientists*. Birkhäuser, 2008.

[SD04] G. Schreiber and M. Dean, editors. *OWL Web Ontology Language Reference*. W3C Recommendation, 10 February 2004. Available at http://www.w3.org/TR/owl-ref/.

[Ser07] B. Sertkaya. *Formal Concept Analysis Methods for Description Logics*. Ph.D. dissertation, Institute of Theoretical Computer Science, TU Dresden, Germany, 2007.

[SGA07] R. Studer, S. Grimm, and A. Abecker, editors. *Semantic Web Services*. Springer, 2007.

[SHK09] M. Smith, I. Horrocks, and M. Krötzsch, editors. *OWL 2 Web Ontology Language: Conformance*. W3C Candidate Recommendation, 11 June 2009. Available at http://www.w3.org/TR/2009/CR-owl2-conformance-20090611/.

[SMW04] M.K. Smith, D.L. McGuinness, and C. Welty, editors. *OWL Web Ontology Language Guide*. W3C Recommendation, 10 February 2004. Available at http://www.w3.org/TR/owl-guide/.

[SMW09] SMW Project. Semantic MediaWiki online documentation, 2009. http://semantic-mediawiki.org.

[Sow84] J. F. Sowa. *Conceptual Structures: Information Processing in Mind and Machine*. Addison-Wesley, 1984.

[Sow00] J. F. Sowa. *Knowledge Representation: Logical, Philosophical, and Computational Foundations.* Brooks/Cole, 2000.

[SPS09] H. Stuckenschmidt, C. Parent, and S. Spaccapietra, editors. *Modular Ontologies.* Springer, 2009.

[SS89] M. Schmidt-Schauß. Subsumption in KL-ONE is undecidable. In H.J. Levesque and R. Reiter, editors, *Proceedings of the 1st International Conference on Principles of Knowledge Representation and Reasoning (KR-89)*, pages 421–431. Morgan Kaufmann Publishers, 1989.

[SS09] S. Staab and R. Studer, editors. *Handbook on Ontologies.* International Handbooks on Information Systems. Springer, 2nd edition, 2009.

[tH05] H.J. ter Horst. Completeness, decidability and complexity of entailment for RDF Schema and a semantic extension involving the OWL vocabulary. *Journal of Web Semantics*, 3(2-3):79–115, 2005.

[The04] M. Thelwall. *Link Analysis: An Information Science Approach.* Elsevier Academic Press, 2004.

[Tur37] A. M. Turing. On computable numbers, with an application to the Entscheidungsproblem. *Proceedings of the London Mathematical Society*, 42(2):230–265, 1937.

[UD07] M. Uslar and N. Dahlem. Semantic web technologies for power grid management. In R. Koschke, O. Herzog, K.-H. Rödiger, and M. Ronthaler, editors, *Informatik 2007: Informatik trifft Logistik, Beiträge der 37. Jahrestagung der Gesellschaft für Informatik, Bremen, Germany*, GI Proceedings 109 Vol. 1, pages 242–246, 2007.

[UG07] M. Uslar and F. Gruening. Zur semantischen Interoperabilität in der Energiebranche: CIM IEC 61970. *Wirtschaftsinformatik*, 49(4):295–303, 2007.

[VHH08] J. Völker, P. Haase, and P. Hitzler. Learning expressive ontologies. In Buitelaar and Cimiano [BC08], pages 45–69.

[Was68] P. C. Wason. Reasoning about a rule. *Quarterly Journal of Experimental Psychology*, 20:273–281, 1968.

[WCH87] M.E. Winston, R. Chaffin, and D. Herrmann. A taxonomy of part-whole relations. *Cognitive Science: A Multidisciplinary Journal*, 11(4):417–444, 1987.

[WR13] A. N. Whitehead and B. Russell. *Principia Mathematica.* Cambridge University Press, 1910, 1912 and 1913. 3 vols.

Index